Nonqualified Deferred Compensation Answer Book

Third Edition

Henry A. Smith, III, Esq.
Barry K. Downey, Esq.
Michael P. Connors, Esq.

THE PANEL ANSWER BOOK SERIES

A PANEL PUBLICATION
ASPEN PUBLISHERS, INC.

Copyright © 1996

by
PANEL PUBLISHERS
A division of Aspen Publishers, Inc.
A Wolters Kluwer Company

36 West 44th Street
New York, NY 10036
(212) 790-2000

ISBN 1-56706-098-6

Nonqualified Deferred Compensation, First Edition, and *Nonqualified Deferred Compensation—1993 Supplement* were written by Bruce J. McNeil, Esq. of Doherty, Rumble & Butler.

Printed in the United States of America

About Panel Publishers

Panel Publishers derives its name from a panel of business professionals who organized in 1964 to publish authoritative, timely books, information services, and journals written by specialists to assist business professionals and owners of small to medium-sized businesses and their legal and financial advisors in the areas of human resources, compensation and benefits management, and pension planning and compliance. Our mission is to provide practical, solution-based "how-to" information to business professionals.

Also available from Panel Publishers:

Executive Compensation Answer Book
Officer Compensation Report
The Pension Answer Book
Pension Distribution Answer Book
Estate and Retirement Planning Answer Book
Nonqualified Deferred Compensation: Forms & Worksheets
401(k) Answer Book
403(b) Answer Book
Individual Retirement Account Answer Book
Employment Law Answer Book
Journal of Deferred Compensation
Journal of Pension Benefits
Journal of Pension Planning & Compliance
Pension Benefits Newsletter

PANEL PUBLISHERS
A division of Aspen Publishers, Inc.
Practical Solutions for Business Professionals

SUBSCRIPTION NOTICE

This Panel product is updated on a periodic basis with supplements to reflect important changes in the subject matter. If you purchased this product directly from Panel Publishers, we have already recorded your subscription for this update service.

If, however, you purchased this product from a bookstore and wish to receive future updates and revised or related volumes billed separately with a 30-day examination review, please contact our Customer Service Department at 1-800-901-9074 or send your name, company name (if applicable), address, and the title of the product to:

PANEL PUBLISHERS
A division of Aspen Publishers, Inc.
7201 McKinney Circle
Frederick, MD 21701

Introduction

Regular developments in the law—both in terms of new legislation and regulation and in terms of case law—continue to have a major impact on the structure of deferred compensation plans in the United States. Panel Publishers' third edition of the *Nonqualified Deferred Compensation Answer Book* has been revised and expanded to address these changes. It explains how changes in the law affecting nonqualified plans and qualified plans are making nonqualified plans more attractive than ever. It reveals how to provide top management and highly compensated employees with adequate deferred compensation in spite of stringent new regulations affecting their qualified plans. Nonqualified plans have proven to be indispensable for attracting and retaining highly skilled employees in the past, and will be an even more important part of companies' deferred compensation planning in the future.

In straightforward, concise language, the *Nonqualified Deferred Compensation Answer Book, Third Edition* gives up-to-the-minute answers to the most pressing questions that confront pension compensation and benefits professionals and their clients. New topics that the third edition addresses in detail include:

- How to use mirror 401(k) plans to deal with the shrinking dollar limitations for tax-qualified plans
- The developing impact of two recent court cases on nonqualified deferred compensation arrangements: *Albertson's, Inc. v. Commissioner* and *Martin v. Commissioner*.

- The bankruptcy issues involved with nonqualified deferred compensation arrangements
- Why a heavenly trust can be a useful alternative to a rabbi trust or a secular trust
- The use of bona fide severance plans by tax-exempt and governmental sponsors of nonqualified deferred compensation arrangements
- Recent IRS guidance on the deduction rules applicable to nonqualified stock option plans
- The Financial Accounting Standards Board's recent pronouncements concerning accounting for equity-based deferred compensation

The questions and answers covering these—and many other—timely issues give the reader a practical overview of the intricacies of nonqualified deferred compensation planning. Although no single source can contain all of the specific rules for all conceivable scenarios, the pages that follow are filled with examples, practice pointers, and case studies illustrating hundreds of nonqualified plan concepts. We hope our readers will use these—and the detailed citations to hundreds of other sources—as a starting point for further research and inquiry into the fascinating area of nonqualified deferred compensation.

Henry A. Smith, III
Barry K. Downey
Michael P. Connors

How to Use This Book

The *Nonqualified Deferred Compensation Answer Book* is designed for business executives and professional advisors who need quick and authoritative answers to help them decide whether to institute or continue a nonqualified deferred compensation plan, how to choose the nonqualified deferred compensation plan that best suits their needs, and how to comply with the growing number of federal requirements and tax rules that apply to such plans.

This revised and expanded edition uses simple, straightforward language and avoids technical jargon whenever possible. Citations are provided as research aids for those who need to pursue a particular item in greater detail. For the reader's convenience they are placed within brackets immediately following the subject referenced.

Each chapter presents an overview of one kind of arrangement or issue, the specific IRS, ERISA, and securities laws that apply to that particular arrangement or issue, and the actual tax consequences to both the employer and the employee. Other relevant considerations that apply to a particular arrangement are discussed at the end of the chapter so that the user can easily compare and contrast a particular consideration—such as whether and when a plan will be considered "funded" for purposes of ERISA—when deciding on which nonqualified deferred compensation arrangement to establish.

Chapter Overview

This third edition contains two new chapters:

Chapter 12 examines Code Section 419 welfare benefit trusts and their implications for deferred compensation planning.

Chapter 13 provides an overview of the life cycle of a typical nonqualified plan, from its initial consideration through its design, implementation, operation, and potential termination.

In addition, chapters 1 through 11 have been thoroughly updated with new and revised questions that address the most recent developments in nonqualified deferred compensation.

Chapter 1 introduces the concept of nonqualified deferred compensation and explains how it differs from qualified deferred compensation.

Chapters 2 and 3 examine top-hat and excess benefit plans and discuss the various ERISA, IRS, and DOL requirements that apply to each as well as the tax effects of such plans on both the employer and the employee.

Chapters 4 and 5 examine two popular forms of trusts that can be established to fund nonqualified deferred compensation arrangements: rabbi trusts and secular trusts respectively. Each chapter explains the specific requirements for effectively establishing and administering these two popular kinds of funding arrangements.

Chapters 6 and 7 examine two additional methods of funding nonqualified deferred compensation plans: split-dollar life insurance and corporate-owned life insurance (COLI).

Chapter 8 examines stock-based plans and discusses specific kinds of these plans that can be used to give key employees and/or highly compensated executives deferred compensation. This chapter also explains the special securities law and accounting issues that apply to stock-based plans.

Chapter 9 examines parachute payments, which essentially provide key employees with deferred compensation in the event of a corporate sale, takeover, or other employment-terminating event.

Chapter 10 examines nonqualified deferred compensation arrangements that are established by governmental or tax-exempt entities and focuses on the special requirements and operating rules of Code Section 457.

Chapter 11 outlines the various types of income and employment taxes that apply to the various nonqualified deferred compensation arrangements discussed in this book.

Special Features

Numbering System. The question-and-answer format provides specific, concise responses to common concerns. The questions are numbered consecutively within each chapter (for example, 2:1, 2:2, etc.).

List of Questions. The detailed List of Questions following the Table of Contents is designed to help the reader locate specific areas of immediate interest. The list functions as a detailed table of contents and gives access to the exact question you are researching as well as the page number on which the answer appears.

Case Studies. Case studies at the end of each chapter apply the principles discussed in the chapters to a hypothetical company.

Practice Pointers. These paragraphs, located throughout the book, highlight practical steps to take in designing, implementing, and operating nonqualified deferred compensation arrangements.

Appendixes. For your convenience, supplementary reference material is reproduced in full in the appendixes following chapter 13. New to this edition is a selection of recent IRS notices and private letter rulings of significance to nonqualified deferred compensation.

Tables of Codes and Cases. Following the appendixes are tables that list the questions in which specific Code Sections, ERISA Sections, Treasury Regulations, etc., are cited.

Index. The index in the final section gives comprehensive locator information for all topics covered. References are to question numbers rather than to page numbers.

Abbreviations. Numerous statutes, rules, and agencies govern and regulate nonqualified deferred compensation arrangements. Many of these are abbreviated or commonly referred to by acronym. Following is a list of those used throughout this book:

- ACE—Adjusted Current Earnings
- AMT—Alternative Minimum Tax
- APB—Accounting Principles Board
- COBRA—The Consolidated Omnibus Budget Reconciliation Act of 1985
- Code—The Internal Revenue Code of 1986, as amended
- COLI—Corporate-Owned Life Insurance
- DCA—Deferred Compensation Agreement
- DOL—The U.S. Department of Labor
- DOT—The U.S. Department of Treasury
- DSO—Discounted Stock Options
- ERISA—The Employee Retirement Income Security Act of 1974, as amended
- Exchange Act—The Securities Act of 1934, as amended
- FASB—Financial Accounting Standards Board
- GCM—General Counsel's Memorandum
- ICF—Incentive Compensation Fund
- ICP—Incentive Compensation Plan
- IRA—Individual Retirement Arrangement
- IRC—Internal Revenue Code of 1986, as amended
- IRS—The Internal Revenue Service
- ISO—Incentive Stock Option
- Ltr Rul—Letter Ruling
- NSO—Nonstatutory Stock Option
- OBRA '86—The Omnibus Budget Reconciliation Act of 1986
- OBRA '89—The Omnibus Budget Reconciliation Act of 1989

- OBRA '93—The Omnibus Budget Reconciliation Act of 1993
- PPA '87—The Pension Protection Act of 1987
- Pub L No—Public Law Number
- PWBA—Pension and Welfare Benefits Administration
- Rev Proc—Revenue Procedure
- Rev Rul—Revenue Ruling
- Securities Act—The Securities Act of 1933, as amended
- SERP—Supplemental Executive Retirement Plan
- TAM—Technical Advice Memorandum
- TAMRA—The Technical and Miscellaneous Revenue Act of 1988
- TRA '86—The Tax Reform Act of 1986

Acknowledgments

We would like to thank Bob Dema, President of CPI Qualified Plan Consultants in Great Bend, Kansas, for recommending us to be the authors of the *Nonqualified Deferred Compensation Answer Book*. We also extend our thanks to Lou Rolla, Laura Kaiser, and Susan Holt of Panel Publishers for their astute guidance, their patience, and their encouragement on this project.

Finally, we deeply appreciate the unflagging support of our respective families—Donna Rae, Sonny, Sarah, Alex, Emily, and Ben; Rhonda, Kendyl, and Tyler; and Michelle, Emily, Jake, and Annie.

Henry A. Smith, III
Barry K. Downey
Michael P. Connors

About the Authors

Henry A. Smith, III is a founding partner of Smith & Downey, a law firm with offices in Baltimore and New York that concentrates in the areas of employee benefits, executive compensation, labor and employment, and estate planning. Mr. Smith formerly was a partner in the employee benefits department of Piper & Marbury, a law firm with offices in the United States and England. He received a BA degree from Frostburg State College, an MLA from The Johns Hopkins University, and a JD from the University of Maryland School of Law. He is a member of the Maryland and District of Columbia bars, is past Chair of the Maryland State Bar Association Employee Benefits Committee, is past Chair of the Maryland State Bar Association Section of Taxation, and is an Adjunct Professor in the University of Baltimore School of Law Graduate Tax Program. Mr. Smith is resident in Smith & Downey's Baltimore office.

Barry K. Downey is a founding partner of Smith & Downey. Mr. Downey formerly was an attorney in the employee benefits departments of Smith, Sommerville & Case, a Baltimore law firm with offices throughout Maryland, and of Piper & Marbury. Mr. Downey received a BS degree from the University of Maryland and a JD from the University of Maryland School of Law. He is a member of the Maryland and District of Columbia bars, and is past Chair of the Maryland State Bar Association Employee Benefits Committee. Mr. Downey is resident in Smith & Downey's Baltimore office.

Michael P. Connors is a partner of Smith & Downey. Mr. Connors formerly was an attorney in the employee benefits and corporate and securities departments of Piper & Marbury, serving in both the

Baltimore and New York offices of that firm. Mr. Connors received a BA degree from Villanova University and a JD from the Catholic University of America School of Law. He is a member of the New York and Maryland bars. Mr. Connors is resident in Smith & Downey's New York office.

Contents

Table of Contents

List of Questions

ERISA Considerations

Tax Consequences to the Employer

Tax Consequences to the Employee

Tax Consequences to the Employer

Tax Consequences to the Employee

Case Study 4-1

Chapter 5   Secular Trusts

Overview

Tax Consequences to the Employer

Tax Consequences to the Employee

Case Study 5-1

Chapter 6   Split-Dollar Life Insurance

Overview

ERISA Considerations

Case Study 6-1

Chapter 7 Corporate-Owned Life Insurance

Overview

Tax Considerations

Nonstatutory Stock Options

Discounted Stock Options

Restricted Stock

Stock Appreciation Rights

Phantom Stock

Employee Stock Purchase Plans

Securities Aspects of Stock Plans

Recent Developments

Case Study 8-1

Chapter 9   Parachute Payments

Overview

Eligible Plans

Case Study 10-1

Chapter 11 Withholding Rules for Nonqualified Plans

Case Study 11-1

Chapter 12 Multiple Employer Welfare Benefit Trusts

Comparison to Other Nonqualified Plans and Qualified Plans

Multiple Employer Death Benefit Trusts

Multiple Employer Severance Benefit Trusts

Implementing, Operating, and Terminating a Nonqualified Plan

Chapter 1

Nonqualified Deferred Compensation Plans

Nonqualified deferred compensation arrangements (nonqualified plans) are, in general, deferred compensation arrangements that have neither all of the tax-favored benefits nor all of the funding, vesting, distribution, and reporting liabilities that are associated with qualified deferred compensation plans. This chapter provides an overview of nonqualified plans that explains the characteristics of many of the various arrangements available, when and why nonqualified plans should be established, and the general ERISA, tax, and employer-employee considerations that should be addressed when determining whether and which type of nonqualified plan to establish.

Overview

Q 1:1   What is a nonqualified plan?

Generally, a nonqualified plan is an agreement or promise by an employer to certain of its employees to pay, at some future date, for services performed currently.

Q 1:2   How does a nonqualified plan differ from a qualified plan?

Nonqualified plans do not qualify for all of the special tax treatment afforded to deferred compensation plans that meet the qualification requirements contained in Section 401(a) of the Internal Revenue Code of 1986, as amended (Code; IRC). This favorable tax treatment for qualified plans includes a current deduction for the employer for its contributions, tax-deferred build-up of investment income of the trust maintained under the plan, rollover opportunities, income averaging of distributions, and so on. [IRC §§ 72, 401(a), 404; see Q 1:17]

Q 1:3   Why should a nonqualified plan be established?

Historically, nonqualified plans have been established to supplement the retirement benefits that are provided to a select group of management or highly compensated employees under their qualified deferred compensation plans. However, recently nonqualified plans have become more attractive and more important in retirement planning because qualified plans are subject to the following troublesome conditions which make them less appealing:

1. The shrinking dollar limitations on contributions to and benefits payable from qualified plans (e.g., the OBRA '93 reduction of the amount of compensation that may be considered for qualified plan purposes from $235,840 to $150,000, indexed) [IRC §§ 401(a)(17), 402(g), 415];

2. The ever more restrictive discrimination and participation rules imposed on qualified plans [IRC §§ 401(a)(4), 401(a)(26), 401(k), 401(m), 410(b)]; and

3. The complicated rules involved in maintaining and operating qualified plans.

Q 1:4   Who can benefit under a nonqualified plan?

Typically, nonqualified plans are designed to benefit the following individuals:

1. Key executives;
2. A select group of management or highly compensated employees; and/or
3. Employees whose benefits ordinarily would be limited under Code Section 415.

Code Section 415 generally limits contributions made with respect to a single participant in a *defined contribution* plan to the lesser of:

- $30,000 (or, if greater, one-quarter of the indexed dollar limitation applicable to defined benefit plans), or
- 25 percent of the participant's compensation.

Code Section 415 generally limits a participant's benefits from a *defined benefit* plan to the lesser of:

- $90,000 (indexed for cost of living increases), or
- 100 percent of the participant's average compensation for his or her highest paid three consecutive years of employment with the employer.

A nonqualified plan also may be designed to benefit individuals (e.g., outside directors) who do not satisfy the requirements for participating in a qualified plan.

Q 1:5   Are there different categories of nonqualified plans?

Yes, there are a number of basic categories of nonqualified plans. In addition, within many of the categories, both funded and unfunded versions of the nonqualified plans may be established. Generally, a nonqualified plan is funded if a source of cash or property is established for the sole purpose of paying benefits under the plan.

(See Qs 1:12, 1:13.) The categories of nonqualified plans are as follows:

Top-hat plan. Sometimes referred to as a Supplemental Executive Retirement Plan (SERP), a top-hat plan is, in general, an unfunded plan maintained by an employer primarily for the purpose of providing deferred compensation for a select group of management or highly compensated employees (see chapter 2). [ERISA §§ 201(2), 301(a)(3), 401(a)(1)]

Excess benefit plan. This is a funded or unfunded plan maintained by an employer solely for the purpose of providing benefits for certain employees in excess of the benefits which may be provided from qualified plans in light of the limitations on contributions and benefits imposed by Code Section 415 (see chapter 3). [ERISA § 3(36)]

Incentive stock options. These are rights granted by an employer to an employee to purchase shares of the employer's stock at a fixed price during a specified period of time. Incentive stock options must meet the requirements of Code Section 422 (see chapter 8).

Nonstatutory stock options. These are rights granted by an employer to participants (who need not be employees) to purchase shares of the employer's stock at a fixed price during a specified period of time. Nonstatutory stock options do not need to meet the requirements of Code Section 422. Nonstatutory stock options do not qualify for all of the favorable tax treatment afforded to incentive stock options (see chapter 8).

Discounted stock options. These are nonstatutory stock options which are granted at a below-market (discounted) exercise price (see chapter 8).

Restricted stock. This is stock of the employer issued to participants, usually at no cost or at a nominal cost, in connection with the performance of services for the employer. The stock is "restricted" because it is subject to forfeiture in the event certain conditions, such as continued employment or service, are not met. The participants will, however, have certain incidents of ownership of the stock beginning on the date of grant (see chapter 8).

Stock appreciation rights (SARs). These are rights to be paid an amount equal to the difference between the value of a specified number of shares of employer stock on the date the SARs are granted and the value of that stock on the date the SARs are exercised. This amount may be paid in cash, stock, or other consideration (see chapter 8).

Phantom stock. This is a right to a cash bonus based upon the performance of the employer's stock over a specified period of time. The right to receive the bonus typically is subject to certain conditions, such as continued employment or service (see chapter 8).

Code Section 457(b) plan. This is a plan for a governmental or tax-exempt employer under Code Section 457(b) that is an unfunded plan that provides for annual deferrals of the lesser of $7,500 or one third of includible compensation (unless a $15,000 catch-up provision applies) reduced by certain qualified plan deferrals (see chapter 10).

Code Section 457(f) plan. This is a plan for a governmental or tax-exempt employer under Code Section 457(f), which is an unfunded plan that provides for annual deferrals of any amount. To avoid taxation of the deferrals when made, they must be subject to a "substantial risk of forfeiture" (see chapter 10).

Q 1:6   Can an employer take steps to provide a source of funds or assets from which it can pay benefits under a nonqualified plan?

Yes. An employer may use one or more of several devices to provide a source of funds or assets from which it can pay benefits under a nonqualified plan. Each of these devices raises separate tax and ERISA issues and offers separate design challenges and opportunities. These devices may be grouped into the following categories:

1. Rabbi Trusts
2. Secular Trusts
3. Heavenly Trusts
4. Surety Bonds
5. Escrow Accounts

6. Agency Accounts
7. Letters of Credit
8. Corporate-Owned Life Insurance
9. Split-Dollar Life Insurance

Q 1:7   What types of trusts can an employer establish to fulfill its promise to pay deferred compensation to an employee?

There are two basic types of trusts that may be used by the employer to fulfill its promise of paying deferred compensation to the employee:

1. *Rabbi trust.* This is, in general, an irrevocable trust that is established for the benefit of the employee but that is subject to the claims of the employer's general bankruptcy and insolvency creditors (see chapter 4); and

2. *Secular trust.* This is, in general, an irrevocable trust that is established for the benefit of the employee who has a nonforfeitable right to the trust funds and that is protected from the employer and the employer's creditors (see chapter 5).

Q 1:8   How can an employer use life insurance as a source from which to pay deferred compensation to an employee?

A company may purchase insurance policies to provide a source from which to pay its deferred compensation promise. These policies are referred to as corporate-owned life insurance (COLI) and split-dollar life insurance.

COLI is similar to key person insurance except that a COLI contract generally covers the lives of several employees, and the financial interest that the employer seeks to "insure" bears little relation to the financial loss to the employer on the death of the covered employee.

An employer generally will purchase cash value life insurance policies on individual employees and borrow against the cash value contained in the policies. The cash value in a life insurance policy generates an investment income that grows tax-free (i.e., the inside buildup) and, subject to certain restrictions, the interest paid on the loan against the cash value is deductible. As a result, the purchase of a COLI contract makes it possible for an employer to generate tax deductions that can be used to shelter general income from tax.

Prior to TRA '86, employers often purchased COLI policies at high levels of coverage and borrowed large amounts from those policies. Under TRA '86, a $50,000 per-insured cap was placed on the amount of loans qualifying for an interest deduction.

The employer is the owner and beneficiary of the policies and pays the premiums. The employer will pay benefits to the employee with funds obtained from borrowing against the cash value of the policies or from withdrawals from the policies, and from the proceeds received on the death of the employee (see chapter 7).

Split-dollar life insurance plans of various types, where the ownership of the insurance policy rights is split between the employer and the employee, may also be used by an employer to provide deferred compensation benefits for an employee (see chapter 6).

Q 1:9 Can a termination agreement be used by an employer to provide deferred compensation benefits to an employee?

Yes, a termination agreement, such as a "golden parachute," may be used by an employer to provide a key employee with a benefit upon the employee's termination of employment. Typically, a "golden parachute" will provide a key employee who is terminated or who, under certain circumstances, resigns, as a result of a takeover or change in control, with either continued compensation for a specified period following the key employee's departure or with a lump-sum payment (see chapter 9).

Q 1:10 Can other techniques be used by an employer to provide a source from which to fulfill its promise to pay deferred compensation to an employee?

Yes, an employer may use an escrow account or an "agency" account to provide a source from which to fulfill its deferred compensation promise. These types of accounts may not provide the employee with all of the protections available under a trust account.

Q 1:11   Given the reality that, occasionally, employers are unable or unwilling to meet their financial obligations, can the employee take any steps to increase the likelihood that he or she will be paid the deferred compensation promised by the employer?

Yes, an employee may purchase a surety bond from a surety company or a letter of credit from a bank to provide a source for his or her deferred compensation payments in the event of an employer default on those payments. To be effective for tax purposes, care must be taken to ensure that the employer is not involved in the purchase of the surety bond or letter of credit, thereby creating a funded nonqualified plan that is currently taxable to the employee.

ERISA Considerations

Q 1:12   Is a nonqualified plan funded or unfunded for tax purposes and for purposes of ERISA Title I?

Nonqualified plans generally are unfunded plans. An unfunded plan is merely a promise by the employer to pay the employee compensation at some future date. However, a nonqualified plan also may be a funded plan. A funded plan generally is created when an amount is irrevocably set aside by an employer with a third party for the benefit of an employee. [GCM 39230, Jan 20, 1984; GCM 33373, Nov 21, 1966 as modified by GCM 35196, Jan 16, 1973, which was modified by GCM 35326, May 3, 1973]

Q 1:13   What is the difference between a funded plan and an unfunded plan?

Determining whether a plan is funded or unfunded generally requires an examination of the surrounding facts and circumstances.

Funded plans. A plan usually will be considered funded if an amount is irrevocably placed with a third party for the benefit of an employee and neither the employer nor any of its creditors has any interest in this amount. [DOL letter to Richard H. Manfreda, Chief, Individual Income Tax Branch, IRS, Dec 13, 1985; GCM 37256, Sept

15, 1977; GCM 33373, Nov 21, 1966 as modified by GCM 35196, Jan 16, 1973, which was modified by GCM 35326, May 3, 1973]

Unfunded plans. A plan usually will be considered unfunded if it is truly unaccompanied by any fund or if any fund established in connection with the plan is subject to some contingent or noncontingent claim of the employer or any of its creditors. An unfunded plan is treated for tax and ERISA Title I purposes as merely an unsecured promise by an employer to pay compensation to an employee at some future date. As noted, the employer may set aside assets in order to provide a source from which to fulfill its promise to the employee, but the assets which are set aside must at a minimum be subject to the claims of the employer's general bankruptcy and insolvency creditors. In other words, in such arrangements, the employee must rely on the solvency of the employer and, in the event of the employer's bankruptcy or insolvency, the employee must have no rights to the assets other than as a general unsecured creditor. [GCM 39230, Jan 20, 1984; Rev Rul 60-31, 1960-1 CB 174 as modified by Rev Rul 64-279, 1964-2 CB 121 and Rev Rul 70-435, 1970-2 CB 100]

Q 1:14 Are nonqualified plans affected by whether or not they are considered funded or unfunded for purposes of Title I of ERISA?

Yes. If a plan is funded, it generally will have to satisfy the requirements contained in Title I of ERISA, which pertain to participation and vesting, funding, and fiduciary requirements. For example, under ERISA's participation rules, even though the employer could limit participation to a select group of employees, the employer could not impose eligibility requirements on that group beyond the attainment of age 21 and one year of service. Under ERISA's vesting rules, benefits would have to vest over a period of seven years or less. Under ERISA's funding rules, the plan would have to be funded. And under ERISA's fiduciary rules, those persons who administer the plan need to meet strict and complex statutory requirements. If a plan is unfunded, it may be exempt from all of these requirements.

Q 1:15   Are top-hat and excess benefit plans affected differently when they are funded or unfunded for purposes of Title I of ERISA?

Under Title I of ERISA, whether a plan is funded or unfunded is significant with respect to top-hat plans and excess benefit plans.

Top-hat plans. A top-hat plan is, by definition, unfunded and maintained by an employer primarily for the purpose of providing deferred compensation for a select group of management or highly compensated employees (see chapter 2). This kind of plan is exempt from ERISA's participation, vesting, funding, and fiduciary requirements (see Q 1:14) pursuant to the exemptions contained in ERISA Sections 201(2), 301(a)(3), and 401(a)(1). If a plan maintained by an employer primarily for the purpose of providing deferred compensation for a select group of management or highly compensated employees is funded, the plan will not qualify for these top-hat plan exemptions, and the plan will be required to comply with all the provisions of Title I of ERISA. [DOL letter to Richard H. Manfreda, Chief, Individual Income Tax Branch, IRS, Dec 13, 1985]

Excess benefit plans. An excess benefit plan is defined in ERISA Section 3(36) as a funded or unfunded plan maintained by an employer solely for the purpose of providing benefits to certain employees in excess of the limitations on contributions and benefits imposed by Code Section 415. Under ERISA Section 4(b)(5), a plan that is only an unfunded excess benefit plan is exempt from all of ERISA Title I coverage. If, on the other hand, an excess benefit plan is funded, the plan will not qualify for the exemption from all of ERISA Title I. The funded excess benefit plan will be exempt from Parts 2 and 3 (the participation, vesting, and funding requirements) of Title I of ERISA pursuant to the exemptions contained in ERISA Sections 201(7) and 301(a)(9), but the reporting and disclosure requirements of Part 1 of ERISA Title I (for example, Summary Plan Descriptions, Summary Annual Reports, and annual Form 5500 filings) and the fiduciary requirements of Part 4 of that Title (for example, exclusive benefit, prudence, diversification, and prohibited transaction requirements) will apply to the plan. [DOL letter to Richard H. Manfreda, Chief, Individual Income Tax Branch, IRS, Dec 13, 1985; DOL Adv Op 89-22A, Sept 21, 1989]

Q 1:16   Who are the fiduciaries of a nonqualified plan?

Unlike ERISA-governed deferred compensation plans maintained for the benefit of rank-and-file and other employees, top-hat non-qualified plans need not be administered by named fiduciaries, and fiduciaries need not be named in nonqualified plan documents. In fact, top-hat plans are not subject to either the written plan document or the fiduciary rules of ERISA. The matter of who the fiduciaries of a nonqualified plans are turns on two questions: (1) what representations concerning plan fiduciaries, if any, have been made in connection with the plan—either in the plan documents, if any, or verbally; and (2) what impact state fiduciary law has on the non-qualified plan in question. For example, if the nonqualified plan expressly identifies a fiduciary or fiduciaries who serve in connection with the plan, these individuals or entities will be held to the standards imposed on fiduciaries by applicable state law. Even if no party is expressly identified as a plan fiduciary, the existence, for example, of a trust maintained in connection with the plan will cause at least the trustee of that trust to be determined a plan fiduciary subject to all provisions of applicable state fiduciary law.

In addition, it appears likely that the federal courts, which occasionally have held that a top-hat participant may bring claims for benefits under ERISA, will develop a federal common law of top-hat plans that will impose on those parties responsible for top-hat plan administration fiduciary or fiduciary-like duties and responsibilities.

In any event, certain parties (such as the employer, the trustee, and the recordkeeper) almost always have readily identifiable contractual—even if arguably not fiduciary—duties, under the top-hat plan, and they will be held to a reasonable standard of performance of these duties under standard contract, and possibly tort, theories, regardless of their status as "fiduciaries."

IRS Considerations

Q 1:17   How are nonqualified plans and qualified plans treated for tax purposes?

Contributions. As noted in Q 1:2, a nonqualified plan does not satisfy the requirements contained in Code Section 401(a) and, as a result, does not receive the favorable tax treatment afforded to plans that do satisfy those requirements. An employer contributing to a nonqualified plan will be entitled to a deduction in the year in which the amount attributable to the contribution is includible in the gross income of the participating employees, which may not be until some future date. [IRC § 404(a)(5)] Depending on the type and design of the nonqualified plan, an employee participating in a nonqualified plan is sometimes required to pay income taxes on benefits before he or she receives them, and any fund maintained in connection with the nonqualified plan may need to pay taxes on its earnings.

If a plan satisfies the requirements of Code Section 401(a), the employer will receive an immediate tax deduction, subject to certain limits, for the amount it contributes to the plan for a particular year. An employee participating in a qualified plan is not required to pay income tax on amounts contributed to the plan by the employer on the employee's behalf until he or she receives these amounts at some later date. Also, the trust maintained in connection with the qualified plan generally is tax-exempt, and the tax which the participant pays on the earnings on the contributions made pursuant to the qualified plan is deferred until the earnings are distributed. [IRC §§ 401, 402, 403, 404, 501]

Distributions. Participants in plans that satisfy the requirements of Code Section 401(a), unlike participants in nonqualified plans, are entitled to favorable tax treatment at the time amounts are distributed from those plans. When distributions are made from a qualified plan to a participating employee, the amounts distributed may be eligible to be rolled over to another qualified plan or to an individual retirement arrangement (IRA). These distributions also may be eligible for special tax treatment under the income averaging rules. [IRC § 402]

Q 1:18   Are contributions to a funded plan treated differently than contributions to an unfunded plan?

Yes. Generally, contributions to an unfunded plan are not deductible by an employer and are not includible in an employee's income until some future date when the benefits are distributed or made available to the employee (see Qs 1:21–1:26). Contributions to a funded plan generally are deductible by the employer and includible in the employee's income in the year the employee becomes vested in the contributions. [IRC §§ 83, 402(b), 404(a)(5), 451; Rev Rul 60-31, 1960-1 CB 174 as modified by Rev Rul 64-279, 1964-2 CB 121 and Rev Rul 70-435, 1970-2 CB 100]

Tax Consequences to the Employer

Q 1:19   When may an employer deduct its contribution to a nonqualified plan?

An employer generally may deduct its contribution to a nonqualified plan in the year in which an amount attributable to the contribution is includible in the participating employee's gross income. [IRC § 404(a)(5)]

Tax Consequences to the Employee

Q 1:20   When are contributions made to a nonqualified plan includible in the employee's gross income?

Amounts contributed to an unfunded nonqualified plan generally are includible in the employee's gross income at the time these amounts are paid or made available to the employee. Amounts contributed to a funded nonqualified plan generally are includible in the employee's gross income at the time these amounts become vested in the employee. [IRC §§ 83, 402(b), 451]

Q 1:21   Are contributions made to a nonqualified plan immediately includible in an employee's income under the doctrine of constructive receipt?

Generally, no. If the employee's control over the contributions is subject to substantial limitations, then contributions to a nonqualified plan should not be immediately includible in the employee's income under the constructive receipt doctrine. Generally, a taxpayer includes the amount of any item of income in his or her taxable income for the taxable year in which he or she receives it, unless, under the taxpayer's method of accounting, it is properly included in a different period. Generally, the employee, as a cash method taxpayer, includes amounts in gross income when they are actually or "constructively" received. [IRC § 451(a); Treas Reg § 1.451-1(a)]

Generally, under the tax doctrine of constructive receipt, income is taxable to the taxpayer in the tax year during which it is:

1. Credited to his or her account;

2. Set apart for him or her; or

3. Otherwise made available to him or her.

Under this doctrine, income can be taxable even if it is not actually in the taxpayer's possession. However, income is not treated as constructively received if the taxpayer's control of its receipt is subject to substantial limitations or restrictions. If, for example, an employer credits its employees with bonus stock but the stock is not available to the employees until some future date, the mere crediting on the books of the employer does not constitute constructive receipt by, or result in taxation to, the employees. [Treas Reg § 1.451-2(a)]

The leading IRS Revenue Ruling in this area is Revenue Ruling 60-31, which involved five different examples. In one of these examples, the taxpayer and the taxpayer's employer executed an employment contract under which the taxpayer agreed to be employed by the employer in an executive capacity for five years and, in return, the taxpayer was entitled to a stated annual salary and, in addition, compensation of $10x for each year. The additional compensation was not paid to the taxpayer when earned, but rather was credited by the employer to a bookkeeping reserve account for later payment to the taxpayer. The amount credited by the employer to this account was payable to the taxpayer when the taxpayer terminated service, became a part-time employee, or became partially or totally incapacitated. Under the terms of the agreement, the employer was under a contractual obligation to make the payments when due, and the parties did not intend that the amounts in the reserve account be held in trust for the taxpayer. There was no specific provision in the contract for forfeiture by the taxpayer of his right to a distribution from the reserve and, in the event of the taxpayer's death prior to his receipt in full of the balance in the account, the remaining balance was payable to his personal representative.

The IRS determined that the additional compensation credited to the reserve account was includible in the taxpayer's gross income only in the taxable years in which the taxpayer actually received the payments. The mere promise to pay, not represented by notes or secured in any way, was not regarded as a receipt of income within the meaning of the cash method of accounting. [Rev Rul 60-31, 1960-1 CB 174 as modified by Rev Rul 64-279, 1964-2 CB 121 and Rev Rul 70-435, 1970-2 CB 100]

In a subsequent ruling, Revenue Ruling 71-419, the IRS determined that an unfunded deferred compensation plan for corporate directors also would not result in constructive receipt by the directors of the contributions when made. The plan provided that a director could elect before the beginning of any year to defer receipt of all or a specified part of the director's annual fees for succeeding years. The amounts deferred under the plan, together with accumulated interest, would be distributed in annual installments over a ten-year period beginning the year after the year the director ceased to be a director. The IRS concluded that a director's right to receive the compensation was restricted because a director could receive the compensation only after the termination of his or her directorship. The plan was unfunded, and the corporation was under a mere contractual obligation to make payments when due. Thus, the directors were able to avoid constructive receipt by making an election before the income was earned to receive it at some later date. [Rev Rul 71-419, 1971-2 CB 220]

The determination made in Revenue Ruling 71-419 has been followed in rulings involving stock appreciation rights and phantom stock plans. In Revenue Ruling 80-300, a corporation granted 10 stock appreciation rights, or SARs, in 1975 to one of the key employees participating in the plan. On the date of the grant, the fair market value of the corporation's stock was $30x per share. In 1980, the key employee exercised the stock appreciation rights when the fair market value of a share of the corporation's stock was $80x, which meant that the key employee was entitled to a cash payment equal to the excess of the value of the stock on the exercise date over the value of the stock on the date the SARs were granted to the employee. The key employee in this case received $500x. The IRS ruled that there was no constructive receipt until the SARs were exercised, because the exercise of the SARs required the forfeiture of the right to future appreciation with respect to the stock. This was a substantial limitation which precluded constructive receipt. [Rev Rul 80-300, 1980-2 CB 165]

In a recent case, *Martin v. Commissioner,* the employer adopted an unfunded shadow stock plan for its key employees in order to improve an old plan. Under the old plan, a participant's benefits were payable only in ten equal annual installments. The new plan provided for payments in a lump sum unless participants elected to receive annual installments. In 1981, two participants elected annual installments and later that year terminated employment. The Tax Court considered the IRS's position that the addition or availability of the lump-sum option resulted in the participants' being in constructive receipt of a lump sum even though the installment option was elected. The IRS argued that the participants had an unqualified right to receive a lump-sum distribution under the plan and that, therefore, they were in constructive receipt of all of their plan benefits upon the termination of their employment. However, the court held that the participants did not constructively receive the entire amount of their plan benefits in 1981. The court noted that the benefits were not set apart for the participants and determined that the participants had to give up or forfeit certain rights and future benefits in exchange for current or installment benefits. [Martin v Comm'r, 96 TC No 39 (June 18, 1991)]

Q 1:22   In light of the decision in the *Martin* case, has the IRS indicated any willingness to revisit its ruling position on "downstream elections," as set forth in Revenue Procedure 71-19?

During 1995, the IRS has stated informally that it is planning to reconsider its ruling position as expressed in Revenue Procedure 71-19 on the issue of "downstream elections" made by participants in nonqualified plans. Specifically, the IRS has cited the decisions in *Veit v. Commissioner, Oates v. Commissioner,* and *Martin v. Commis-*

sioner as possibly suggesting that the IRS should revisit this issue and change its ruling position to permit downstream elections, at least where they are made prior to the first date on which nonqualified plan participants may receive any part of their nonqualified plan interests. However, this revisiting is not a particularly high priority for the IRS, whose resources are strained in this area in any event, and we do not expect any developments in this area in the near future. Nonetheless, the recent informal statements by the IRS concerning a possible change in its ruling position would seem to signal a softening of its position in this area, and we would not expect the IRS to litigate this issue or even make it a major point of contention in any particular audit or examination. [Veit v Comm'r, 8 TC 809 (1947), Oates v Comm'r, 18 TC 570 (1952), *aff'd* 207 F 2d 711 (7th Cir 1953); Martin v Comm'r, 96 TC 814 (1991)]

Q 1:23   What is the economic benefit doctrine?

Under the economic benefit doctrine, if any economic or financial benefit is conferred on an individual as compensation in a taxable year, it is taxable to the individual in that year. The doctrine was considered by the U.S. Supreme Court in *Commissioner v. Smith.* In that case, the employer gave the employee, as compensation for his services, an option to purchase from the employer certain shares of stock of another corporation at a price not less than the then value of the stock. In 1938 and 1939, when the market value of the stock was greater than the option price, the employee exercised the option, purchasing large amounts of the stock in each year. The Court determined that the excess of the market value of the shares over the option price in the years when the shares were received by the employee was compensation for his services, and taxable as income in those years. The Court concluded that the employee received an economic benefit at the time he received the shares and, as a result, the employee had taxable income in each year in which stock was acquired. [Comm'r v Smith, 324 US 177, 65 S Ct 591 (1945), *reh'g denied* 324 US 695, 65 S Ct 891 (1945)]

The economic benefit doctrine also was applied in *Sproull v. Commissioner.* In that case, a corporation created in 1945 a trust of $10,500 for an employee. The trustee was directed to invest the money and pay one-half of it to the employee in 1946 and pay the remainder to the employee in 1947. The court considered the doctrine of constructive receipt but determined that it did not apply because the employee was not able to reduce any part of the money to actual possession in 1945 as a result of the time limitation set on payments in the trust instrument.

The court determined, however, that the creation of the trust in 1945 had conferred an economic or financial benefit upon the employee in 1945 so that the sums paid into the trust were taxable to the employee in 1945. The court explained that, in 1945, the employer had completed its part of the transaction by irrevocably paying out the $10,500 for the employee's benefit, and the employee had to do nothing further to earn the benefit. The court said that this fact distinguished the case from those in which the exact amount of compensation is subject to a future contingency or subject to the possibility of return to the employer. The court also noted that the trustee's only duties were to hold, invest, accumulate, and distribute the funds to the employee; that no one else had any interest in or control over the funds held in the trust; and that the individual could have assigned or otherwise disposed of his beneficial interest in the trust. [Sproull v Comm'r, 16 TC 244 (1951), *aff'd per curiam,* 194 F 2d 541 (6th Cir 1952)]

The doctrine also was considered in *Cowden v. Commissioner,* which involved the issue of whether the promise of a lessee, under a mineral lease arrangement, to make future bonus payments was, when made, the equivalent of cash and, as such, taxable as current income. The court described the economic benefit doctrine as follows:

> We are convinced that if a promise to pay of a solvent obligor is unconditional and assignable, not subject to set-offs, and is of a kind that is frequently transferred to lenders or investors at a discount not substantially greater than the generally prevailing premium for the use of money, such promise is the equivalent of cash and taxable in like manner as cash would have been taxable had it been received by the taxpayer rather than the obligation.

The court determined that the Tax Court should reconsider the willingness of the lessee to pay and the unwillingness of the taxpayers to receive the full bonus upon the execution of the leases and remanded the case to the Tax Court for further consideration. [Cowden v Comm'r, 289 F 2d 20, 24 (5th Cir 1961)]

In a more recent case, *Minor v. United States,* the court held that a nonqualified plan adopted by Snohomish County Physicians Corporation for its participating physicians was unsecured from the corporation's creditors and therefore incapable of valuation; thus, contributions to the plan were not currently taxable. A physician's receipt of benefits under the plan was contingent upon his agreement to limit his practice after retirement to consulting services and to refrain from competing with Snohomish County Physicians Corporation if he left its practice. A trust was established to hold the assets of the plan. The Snohomish County Physicians Corporation was both the settlor and beneficiary of the trust, and the assets of the trust remained solely those of the corporation and subject to the claims of its general creditors.

The IRS conceded that the constructive receipt doctrine did not apply, but argued that the trust contributions were taxable under the economic benefit doctrine, arguing that an employer's promise to pay deferred compensation in the future may constitute a taxable economic benefit if the current value of the employer's promise can be given an appraised value. The court, in refusing to tax the physicians under the economic benefit doctrine, held that the physician's receipt of benefits was unsecured and thus incapable of valuation. In addition, the court concluded that the physician's benefits did not constitute property under Code Section 83. The court noted, however, that the plan "severely stretches the limits of a nonqualified deferred compensation plan." [Minor v US, 772 F 2d 1472 (9th Cir 1985)]

Q 1:24   Are contributions made pursuant to a nonqualified plan immediately includible in the employee's income under the economic benefit doctrine?

Generally, no. If contributions made or amounts set aside in accordance with a nonqualified plan are subject to the claims of the employer's general bankruptcy and insolvency creditors, then such contributions or amounts should not be immediately taxable under the economic benefit doctrine. If, on the other hand, contributions to the plan are protected from the employer's creditors and the rights of the participating employees to the benefits provided under the plan are nonforfeitable, the economic benefit doctrine will cause the contributions to be includible currently in the participating employee's income.

Q 1:25   Do the rules of Code Section 83, which govern the taxation of transfers of property as compensation for services rendered, control the taxation of nonqualified plans?

Generally, no. If contributions or amounts set aside under a nonqualified plan are subject to the claims of the employer's general bankruptcy and insolvency creditors, such contributions or amounts should not be considered a transfer of property under Code Section 83. In general, Code Section 83 provides rules for the taxation of property transferred to an employee in connection with the performance of services. This property generally is not taxable to the employee until it has been transferred to the employee or becomes substantially vested in the employee. The primary subsections of Code Section 83 Regulations provide as follows:

1. Section 1.83-3(a)(1) provides that a transfer of property occurs when a person acquires a beneficial ownership interest in the property.

2. Section 1.83-3(b) provides that a taxpayer's right to property is substantially vested for purposes of Section 83 when it is either transferable or not subject to a substantial risk of forfeiture.

3. Section 1.83-3(c) provides that a substantial risk of forfeiture exists where rights in property that are transferred are conditioned upon the future performance, or nonperformance, of substantial services by any person, or the occurrence of a condition related to a purpose of the transfer, and the possibility of forfeiture is substantial if the condition is not satisfied.

4. Section 1.83-3(d) provides that the rights of a person in property are transferable if the person can transfer any interest in the property to any person other than the transferor of the property, but only if the rights in the property of the transferee are not subject to a substantial risk of forfeiture.

5. Section 1.83-3(e) provides that, for purposes of Code Section 83, the term "property" includes real and personal property other than money or an unfunded and unsecured promise to pay money in the future. Property also includes a beneficial interest in assets, including money, transferred or set aside from the claims of creditors of the transferor.

If the contributions under a nonqualified plan are subject to the claims of the employer's general bankruptcy and insolvency creditors, then the contributions do not meet the definition of property. Therefore, such contributions do not result in a transfer of property within the meaning of Code Section 83. If, on the other hand, contributions under a nonqualified plan are not available either to the employer or the employer's general bankruptcy and insolvency creditors, and the participating employees are fully vested in the contributions, then there is a transfer of property within the meaning of Code Section 83, and the employee is subject to current tax on the transferred amount.

Q 1:26   Do contributions to a trust established in connection with a nonqualified plan result in a contribution of property to a "nonexempt trust" which triggers tax to the employee?

Generally, no. If there is no transfer of property under Code Section 83 because the contributions to a trust are subject to the claims of the employer's bankruptcy and insolvency creditors, then there can be no contribution of property to a nonexempt trust under Code Section 402(b). Code Section 402(b) provides that employer contributions to a nonexempt trust are included in the gross income of the employee in accordance with Code Section 83, except that the value of the employee's interest in the trust will be substituted for the fair market value of the property for the purposes of applying Section 402(b).

Section 1.402(b)-1(a)(1) of the Regulations provides that contributions made on behalf of an employee by an employer to a nonexempt trust will be included as compensation in the gross income of the employee for the year during which the contribution is made, but only to the extent that the employee's interest in the contribution is substantially vested at the time the contribution is made. The Regulation then refers to Section 1.83-3(b) of the Regulations for the definition of the term "substantially vested." Section 1.83-3(b) of the Regulations provides that property is substantially vested when it is either transferable or not subject to a substantial risk of forfeiture.

If contributions to a trust established in connection with a non-qualified plan are not considered property that is substantially vested within the meaning of Section 1.83-3 of the Regulations, then those contributions will not be considered property that is substantially vested within the meaning of Section 1.402(b)-1 of the Regulations. If, on the other hand, the contributions are considered property that is substantially vested under Section 1.83-3 of the Regulations and not subject to a substantial risk of forfeiture, then the contributions will be considered property that is substantially vested under Section 1.402(b)-1 of the Regulations, and the employee will be subject to current tax on such contributions.

Recent Developments

Q 1:27   How is the new $150,000 of compensation limit that is applicable to tax-qualified deferred compensation plans likely to affect nonqualified plans?

In 1993, the limit on an employee's compensation that could be taken into account by a tax-qualified deferred compensation plan was $235,840. OBRA '93 reduced this limit, beginning in 1994, to $150,000. OBRA '93 also slowed the cost of living increase adjustment applicable to this compensation limit.

Although the former $235,840 limit typically affected either no executives or only the most highly paid executives of a typical employer, the new $150,000 limit is likely to affect many more individuals. When the impact of the new, lower limit is combined with other recent changes making tax-qualified plans less attractive to highly paid individuals (see Q 1:3), nonqualified plans may well emerge as the primary deferred compensation alternative for highly paid executives.

A particular concern generated by the $150,000 limit and other recent changes is that the percentage of pre-retirement income that can be provided to an executive through a qualified plan typically is unacceptably low. Therefore, virtually all employers with executives compensated at more than $150,000 per year should review the effect of the $150,000 limit on those executives' qualified plan interests and should consider establishing or enhancing nonqualified plans.

Q 1:28 How will the recent elimination of the cap on the Medicare tax wage base affect nonqualified plans?

Prior to OBRA '93, only the first $135,000 (indexed) of an executive's wages were subject to the Medicare portion (1.45 percent for the employer and 1.45 percent for the employee) of FICA taxes, just as only the first $60,600 (indexed) of an executive's wages are subject to the Social Security portion of FICA taxes. However, beginning in 1994, OBRA '93 removed the cap on the amount of an executive's wages subject to the Medicare portion of FICA taxes.

Therefore, when an executive's interest under a nonqualified plan becomes "wages"—typically, at the later of the date the services creating the interest are performed or the date the interest vests—both the employer portion and the employee portion of the Medicare tax will be due on the full value of the interest (see chapter 11).

Before this OBRA '93 change, Medicare taxes were seldom paid on nonqualified plan interests because most executives participating in nonqualified plans had "maxed-out" against the former $135,000 (indexed) Medicare tax wage base.

Employers sponsoring nonqualified plans now will need to review the plans to determine whether any new Medicare taxes are due and to establish procedures for the withholding and remitting of those taxes.

Q 1:29 Will the other changes of OBRA '93 affecting executive compensation affect nonqualified plans?

In addition to lowering the compensation limit for tax-qualified plans to $150,000 (see Q 1:27) and un-capping the Medicare tax-wage base (see Q 1:28), OBRA '93 contains two changes that affect non-qualified plans.

First, effective January 1, 1993, the top marginal federal income tax bracket was increased from 31 percent to 39.6 percent. This change has resulted in increased interest in deferred compensation plans of all types, reflecting both a desire to avoid current taxes and enjoy tax-deferred build-up and an expectation that plan participants will be in a lower tax bracket when the deferred compensation is paid than when it is deferred. In addition, this change has resulted in some increased interest in ISOs and other compensation devices subject to the 28 percent capital gains tax rate rather than the new, increased ordinary income tax rates.

Second, beginning with 1994, remuneration in excess of $1 million paid to certain executives of publicly traded companies generally will not be deductible by their employers. Certain items of cash compensation are not included and certain items of noncash compensation are included in remuneration for purposes of this limitation. This potential loss of deductibility is likely to cause affected employers to think about reducing current compensation below this limit, perhaps by making careful use of nonqualified plans.

Q 1:30   What is the impact on nonqualified plans of the recent decisions in *Albertson's, Inc. v. Commissioner* concerning the deduction of interest credited to nonqualified plan accounts?

Confirming the expectations of many interested parties, the Ninth Circuit Court of Appeals held in December 1994 that its 1993 decision holding that interest credited by an employer to nonqualified plan accounts is deductible "interest" under Section 163 of the Code was erroneous. The court held that such interest was not deductible "interest" under Code Section 163 because, rather than being a time value of money charge imposed on a borrower by a lender in a lending situation, the interest credited to nonqualified plan accounts is merely additional deferred compensation credited to plan participants by their employer and, therefore, was deductible only under the rules of Code Section 404(a)(5) governing deductions for nonqualified plan costs. Those rules prevent an employer sponsoring a nonqualified plan from deducting nonqualified plan costs until the nonqualified plan interests are includible in the incomes of participating employees.

In its request for a rehearing before the Ninth Circuit, the IRS argued that upholding the taxpayer's position would have a revenue cost of approximately $7 billion over five years and would result in a substantial disincentive to employers' establishing tax-qualified retirement plans.

Nonqualified plan sponsors who relied upon the now-reversed Ninth Circuit decision and took deductions for nonqualified plan interest should consult with their tax advisors about how to proceed.

Note. The taxpayer in the *Albertson's* case has asked the U.S. Supreme Court to review the Ninth Circuit's decision in the case. In light of the fact that the Ninth Circuit noted in its opinion that "it may, indeed, ultimately turn out the United States Supreme Court will tell us that it is this second opinion which is in error," it is possible that the Supreme Court will grant the taxpayer's request for review. However, most commentators continue to expect the IRS's position to be upheld on this issue.

Q 1:31   What is a "mirror 401(k) plan" or a "nonqualified 401(k) plan"?

A mirror 401(k) plan (sometimes called a nonqualified 401(k) plan) is a nonqualified plan designed to supplement or "wrap around" an employer's existing tax-qualified 401(k) plan. Mirror 401(k) plans typically are designed to permit employee salary reduction contributions and employer basic and matching contributions that exceed the various limits on such contributions under 401(k) plans. These limits include the current $9,240 salary reduction limit of Code Section 402(g), the average deferral percentage (ADP) nondiscrimination limits on salary deferrals under Code Section 401(k), the average contribution percentage (ACP) nondiscrimination limits on matching contributions under Code Section 401(k), the Code Section 415 limits on aggregate employer and employee contributions, and the $150,000 limit on compensation that may be considered by a 401(k) plan under Code Section 401(a)(17).

Mirror 401(k) plans often include many features of the tax qualified 401(k) plans they supplement, but few if any of the limits on
contributions. However, designers of mirror 401(k) plans should
beware of three particularly difficult issues.

First, it often is not permissible to include in the mirror 401(k) plan
all of the employees who are affected by the 401(k) plan limits. This
is because the mirror 401(k) plans of ERISA-governed employers, as
nonqualified top-hat plans, may include as participants only employees who are members of a select group of management or highly
compensated employees, and, often, employees other than members
of this select group are affected negatively by the various 401(k) plan
limits. For example, for 1995, an employee earning more than
$66,000 and in the top 20 percent of the employer's payroll is a highly
compensated employee under the 401(k) plan but, absent some
meaningful management responsibilities, would not be considered a
member of the top-hat group by the DOL. (Some DOL personnel
would argue that no employee earning $66,000 could be a top-hat
group employee, regardless of management responsibility.) Similarly,
an employee earning $40,000 could theoretically run afoul of the
$9,240 limit of Code Section 402(g) but generally would not be a
top-hat employee eligible for participation in a mirror 401(k) plan
sponsored by an ERISA-governed employer.

Second, it would be inappropriate simply to replicate all of the
design features of a related 401(k) plan when designing a mirror
401(k) plan because many features found in 401(k) plans (plan loans,
ability to elect time and form of distributions after the first date on
which a distribution could be made, 401(k)-style hardship withdrawals, and so on) would cause immediate taxation to participants if
included in a mirror 401(k) plan, because of the lack of statutory
protection for nonqualified plans from the constructive receipt and
economic benefit doctrines. Also, in informal statements at professional meetings, the IRS has expressed concern that references in
mirror 401(k) plans to "accounts," "contributions," and "appeal
procedures" are "entirely foreign" to nonqualified plans and may
cause the plans to be determined to be funded under the Code and
ERISA. Most commentators disagree with this last comment.

Third, the IRS has suggested that some 401(k) plan/mirror 401(k)
plan designs will cause the 401(k) plan to lose its tax-qualified status

under the contingent benefits rule applicable to 401(k) plans. Under this rule, no components of an employee's benefit package may be "made contingent" on the employee's participation in a 401(k) plan. The IRS has stated that the following arrangements violate the contingent benefits rule: (1) making an employee ineligible for the mirror 401(k) plan if the employee participates in the 401(k) plan; or (2) imposing an overall dollar or percentage cap on aggregate deferrals to the mirror 401(k) plan and the 401(k) plan. However, the IRS has stated that the contingent benefits rule is not violated if: (1) mirror 401(k) plan participation is limited to individuals who have reached the various limits of the 401(k) plan; (2) mirror 401(k) plan participation occurs only after contributions by or on behalf of participants exceed the design limitations in the 401(k) plan, or (3) mirror 401(k) plan participation is limited to individuals (such as highly compensated employees as defined in Code Section 414) who are ineligible, by class, for participation in the 401(k) plan.

Q 1:32   Has the IRS issued any guidance on mirror 401(k) plans?

The IRS has issued at least three private letter rulings concerning mirror 401(k) plans. In Letter Ruling 9317037, the IRS commented on a rather complicated and atypical situation in which, during each January 1 to January 31 period, the employer conducts preliminary ADP and ACP tests under its 401(k) plan to determine the amount of additional salary reduction contributions that an executive could have made to the 401(k) plan during the prior year, given actual salary reduction contributions by HCEs and non-HCEs to the 401(k) plan for that year.

After the amount is determined, a distribution equal to that amount (or, if less, the executive's actual salary deferral amount under the employer's mirror 401(k) plan for the prior year) is distributed to the executive from the mirror 401(k) plan, unless the executive previously elects to have the amount contributed to the 401(k) plan as a salary reduction contribution. Any matching contribution due to the 401(k) plan because of such an election is made out of matching amounts previously credited to the executive's mirror 401(k) plan account.

Under this approach, the employer was able to emphasize that all salary reduction contributions to the 401(k) plan in year two are made from amounts otherwise payable, and taxable, to the executive in year two. The IRS held that the year-two salary reduction contributions to the 401(k) plan would qualify as pretax 401(k) plan contributions and would be recognized for 401(k) plan testing purposes in the year in which they are actually contributed to the 401(k) plan.

In Letter Ruling 9405009, the IRS commented on a more typical mirror 401(k) plan under which the employer credits the maximum permissible amount of an executive's elected salary reduction contributions to its 401(k) plan and any excess to its mirror 401(k) plan, and also credits to the executive's mirror 401(k) plan account any matching or other employer contribution amounts that may not be credited to its 401(k) plan under the various limits applicable to 401(k) plans.

The IRS held that this arrangement is effective to defer taxation on both the amounts credited to the 401(k) plan and the amounts credited to the mirror 401(k) plan.

In Letter Ruling 9530038, the IRS again addressed a situation in which the mirror 401(k) plan held participant salary reductions and employer matching contributions until the qualified 401(k) plan year had ended and preliminary discrimination testing had been completed. After the results of the testing are available, the lesser of (1) the maximum amount of salary reductions and employer matching contributions that may be made to the qualified 401(k) plan, or (2) the participant's actual salary reduction amount and associated employer matching contributions, are contributed from the mirror 401(k) plan to the qualified plan. No earnings credited under the mirror 401(k) plan during the period prior to the transfer to the qualified 401(k) plan are transferred to the mirror 401(k) plan.

The IRS concluded that the amounts transferred from the mirror 401(k) plan to the qualified 401(k) plan would not be included in participants' incomes but rather would be treated as salary reduction and matching contributions, as applicable, to the mirror 401(k) plan for the plan year of the deferral.

Q 1:33   May a mirror 401(k) plan be used to correct violations of the ADP test in the related 401(k) plan when they are discovered after the close of the plan year of the 401(k) plan?

The IRS has stated informally in professional meetings that the Code and the regulations thereunder provide the "exclusive means" for the correction of ADP violations, and the use of a nonqualified plan to effect these corrections is not mentioned in the Code or the regulations. The IRS position seems to be associated with its general position, which is not shared by all commentators, that nonqualified plan elections must be made in the calendar year before the year of the deferral and must be in a fixed amount or pursuant to a fixed formula. The IRS also has suggested that it has concerns about this issue under the exclusive benefit rule and the vesting/nonforfeitability rules applicable to 401(k) plans. Finally, the IRS has stated that, for the 401(k) plan to qualify as such, plan participants must have the choice between currently taxable cash and the 401(k) plan's deferral option, not simply the choice between a deferral to the 401(k) plan and a deferral to a nonqualified plan. Therefore, the IRS reasoned, nonqualified plan participants may not simply elect, even in advance, that any excess salary reduction contributions to their 401(k) accounts, when determined, will spill over to their nonqualified accounts. Under the IRS's position, the 401(k) plan must distribute any excess under the ADP test, in a taxable transaction, to the affected highly compensated employee, in a corrective transaction independent from the nonqualified plan. (The IRS actually issued a favorable private letter ruling on a transaction where ADP excess spilled over to a nonqualified plan. However, that ruling has been withdrawn.)

Q 1:34   Has the IRS announced any concerns with participant-directed investments in nonqualified plans?

The IRS has been somewhat inconsistent in its public, informal comments about permitting nonqualified plan participants to direct the investment of amounts held in their nonqualified plan accounts. Occasionally, IRS officials will suggest that permitting participants to make binding elections of investment media for their nonqualified plan accounts gives the participants too much "dominion and control" over their accounts, thereby resulting in the participants' constructively receiving—or, alternatively, receiving a taxable economic benefit from—their nonqualified plan interests.

It is fair to say that no Code section, regulation, or published IRS ruling provision supports this view, nor does any case law. In fact, the IRS officials who make these occasional statements often do so with less than persuasive conviction.

The authors believe that these comments may reflect instead the IRS's view that, in order for a rabbi trust maintained in connection with a nonqualified plan to be a "trust" subject to the Form 1041 annual filing requirements rather than an "agency account" not subject to those requirements, the rabbi trustee must have the ultimate authority to direct trust investments. (See Q 4:26.)

It is the view of the authors that, absent further authoritative guidance on this point, nonqualified plan sponsors should include binding participant investment election features in their nonqualified plans if they wish to do so.

Q 1:35   What rights do a nonqualified plan participant's bankruptcy and nonbankruptcy creditors have against the participant's nonqualified plan interest?

As discussed in further detail in Q 1:36 and in chapters 4 and 5, the rights of a sponsoring employer's bankruptcy and nonbankruptcy creditors against assets held in connection with a nonqualified plan are relatively clear.

Similarly, it now is clear that creditors of both the employer and participants may not make claims against assets held under an ERISA-governed retirement plan. [See, e.g., Patterson v Shumate, 112 SCt 2242 (1992)]

Unfortunately, two related questions concerning creditor claims against deferred compensation plan interests remain open. First, it remains unclear whether a participant's bankruptcy creditors may reach the participant's interest in a tax-qualified but non-ERISA-governed retirement plan. [See, e. g., In re Orkin, 170 Bankr 751, 753 (Bankr D Mass 1994)] Second, it remains unclear whether a participant's bankruptcy creditors (or, arguably, other creditors) may reach the participant's interest in a nonqualified plan. This second question is especially troublesome in light of the fact that, unlike ERISA-governed, tax-qualified retirement plans, nonqualified plans have no ERISA-based or Code-based anti-alienation rules, and, unlike non-ERISA-governed but tax-qualified retirement plans, nonqualified plans have no Code-based anti-alienation rules.

For a court to conclude that a participant's interest in a nonqualified plan is exempt from the participant's creditors, the court would need to conclude that the plan's contractual anti-alienation provisions were sufficient on their own to prevent creditor claims. In a bankruptcy situation, under 11 U.S. Code Section 541(c)(2), the court would need to conclude that the nonqualified plan assets were held in a trust (such as a rabbi trust or secular trust) subject to a restriction on transfer that is enforceable under applicable nonbankruptcy law. Because neither ERISA nor the Code imposes anti-alienation restrictions on nonqualified plan assets, a court could not look to these statutes for "applicable non-bankruptcy law" providing protective transfer restrictions on the nonqualified plan interest. Instead, the court would need to look to mere contract law and the plan's anti-alienation provision.

Although no case has yet dealt with this issue, some commentators fear that the bankruptcy bench's perceived bias in favor of creditors and against bankrupt business owners and executives might cause the courts to conclude that nonqualified plan interests may be reached by bankruptcy creditors, notwithstanding anti-alienation provisions contained in the plans and their related trusts, under the "self-settled trust" doctrine or some other theory. Nonbankruptcy courts might come to a similar conclusion concerning nonbankruptcy creditor claims. Until there is further litigation in this area, participants in nonqualified plans should be advised that, especially in the event of their bankruptcy, their nonqualified plan assets may be at risk. (For a discussion of plan sponsor creditor claims against nonqualified plan funds, see Q 1:36.)

Q 1:36   What rights do the bankruptcy and nonbankruptcy creditors of the sponsor of a nonqualified plan have against assets held in connection with the plan?

The rights of the sponsoring employer's bankruptcy and nonbankruptcy creditors against assets held in connection with a nonqualified plan are relatively clear.

First, if nonqualified plan benefits are paid out of an employer's general assets, those assets, naturally, are subject to the claims of all of the employer's bankruptcy and nonbankruptcy creditors. Second, if nonqualified benefits are payable from a rabbi trust, although the rabbi trust assets are not subject to the claims of the employer's nonbankruptcy creditors, the assets are subject to the claims of the employer's bankruptcy creditors because of the very nature of a rabbi trust. In the event of an employer bankruptcy, the nonqualified plan participants would claim against the rabbi trust assets along with all of the employer's other bankruptcy creditors.

Finally, in the case of secular trusts, the trust assets would not be subject to the claims of the employer's bankruptcy or nonbankruptcy creditors, because those assets are no longer assets of the employer for any purpose but, rather, are assets held and owned, for all purposes, by the trust itself for the benefit of trust beneficiaries. (For a discussion of participant creditor claims against nonqualified plan interests, see Q 1:35.)

Q 1:37   Is there any empirical evidence concerning the impact on nonqualified plans of the recent reduction to $150,000 of the compensation of a participant which may be taken into account by a tax-qualified retirement plan?

A number of studies have been made concerning the effect on nonqualified plans of the new, lower compensation limit of Code Section 401(a)(17). One such study reported by the Towers, Perrin, Foster, and Crosby consulting firm suggested that the reduction in the compensation limit has resulted in a fourfold increase in the number of participants in nonqualified plans and that approximately 10 percent of the total FAS 87 retirement benefit liability previously recognized in connection with tax-qualified plans has been shifted to nonqualified plans. If the results of this study are confirmed and this trend persists, the importance of nonqualified plans relative to tax-qualified retirement programs will have been radically altered. In light of these trends, employers should consider carefully the design and long-term implications of their nonqualified plans.

Q 1:38 Has the Securities and Exchange Commission made any recent statements concerning the status of nonqualified plan interests as securities under the federal securities laws?

Historically, the SEC has taken the position, discussed generally in a number of pre-1990 no-action letters, that participants' interests in nonqualified plans, at least in traditional, employer-funded plans, were not securities requiring registration with the SEC and were not subject to other issues of securities law.

However, beginning this year, SEC personnel have begun to suggest informally in professional meetings that, particularly in light of the considerable changes in the design of nonqualified plans and the considerable expansion in the number of employees covered by these plans, it may revise its historical position concerning the status of nonqualified plan interests as securities.

Of particular interest to the SEC are the effects of the $150,000 compensation limit and participant investment direction on nonqualified plans. Specifically, the SEC has indicated that, whereas nonqualified plans traditionally were maintained for a very select group of financially sophisticated top executives, because employers wish to make executives whole for losses in qualified plans resulting from the $150,000 compensation limit, more and more executives, many of them arguably not as well versed in investment issues, are now covered by nonqualified plans. The SEC also has stated its concerns about the transition of nonqualified plans from employer-funded, employer-directed retirement arrangements typically offering a predetermined fixed rate of return to employee-funded, employee-directed investment schemes.

Because of these concerns, SEC personnel have suggested that, at least with respect to voluntary, employee-funded nonqualified plans, and particularly with respect to such plans with participant contributions and participant investment direction, plan interests are securities that require either registration with the SEC as securities or qualification under one of the applicable exemptions from registration. Although the SEC has not stated its position in writing, it apparently believes that its position is clear from the statute and reflects only a change in typical nonqualified plan design and not a change in SEC position.

The following analysis lies behind the SEC's recent statements. The 1933 Securities Act generally requires that no security may be offered or sold unless it is subject to current registration with the SEC. Under the statute and applicable case law, a security is broadly defined to include any investment contact; that is, an investment of funds in a common enterprise, with the expectation of profits to be derived from the efforts of others. (This is the so-called "Howey test," derived from a Supreme Court case of the same name. [SEC v W.J. Howey Co, 328 US 293 (1946)])

The SEC apparently has concluded that certain nonqualified plan interests—at least those in voluntary, employee-funded, employee-directed arrangements—are investment contract securities under the Howey test and that the provision of these arrangements to employees is an offer and/or sale of those securities. Therefore, reasons the SEC, unless those securities qualify for one of the applicable exemptions from registration (e.g., for public companies, Regulation D or the private placement exemption, among others, and for private companies, Regulation D, Rule 701, or Regulation A, among others), registration is required.

In light of this evolving SEC position, sponsors of nonqualified plans are revisiting these issues and discussing with counsel whether they should register their plans or take steps to ensure that the plans satisfy one of the registration exemptions. One issue considered in this process is the consequence of failing to register a securities offering or sale that does not qualify for any exemption from registration. Generally, the only consequence of such a failure is the existence of the purchaser's right of rescission, a consequence that may not have much material impact in a nonqualified plan setting. However, a participant who suffered an investment loss arguably could restore that loss, at the employer's expense, by rescinding his or her deferral and receiving a distribution of the gross amount of the deferral, rather than the net amount after the loss.

One other important point that deferred compensation planners should remember is that the securities of tax-exempt entities generally are exempt from registration. Therefore, the Code Section 457 plans of tax-exempt employers generally are not affected under this new SEC position.

Investment Considerations

Q 1:39   What issues should an employer consider when choosing investments for assets maintained in connection with a nonqualified plan?

As discussed in further detail in chapters 4 through 8, the type of nonqualified plan selected by an employer often will dictate the type of investments maintained under or in connection with that plan. However, in the case of a typical nonqualified deferred compensation arrangement, two primary issues arise in connection with those investments.

First, unless the employer is a tax-exempt entity, the tax effect of the earnings on the investments maintained in connection with the plan must be considered. Unlike tax-qualified deferred compensation arrangements, the earnings on investments maintained in connection with nonqualified plans are not exempt from taxation. Therefore, employers should consider whether to place assets held in connection with their nonqualified plans in investments that do not generate taxable income (e.g., life insurance products, tax-free municipal bonds, etc.). However, before deciding, the plan participant should compare the net tax-free return on these investments to the net after-tax return on alternative taxable investments. For example, would the net tax-free return (or "inside buildup") on a variable universal life insurance contract with investment options similar to those of a mutual fund be larger than the net after-tax return on nearly identical mutual fund products maintained outside the insurance contract?

Many of these evaluations require the assistance of an investment professional because they involve "apples and oranges" comparisons (i.e., the insurance investment provides a death benefit, the economic value of which is not available with the pure mutual fund option) and because the financial condition of the insurance company offering the insurance option can be particularly important if insurance company general investment funds are used.

Second, the employer often will need to consider the investment wishes, and often the eccentricities, of the participating executives, especially where participant investment direction will be a feature of the plan. With respect to this issue, an important challenge for the employer is providing a sufficient number and variety of investment options to satisfy plan participants while not creating undue administrative burdens and/or making the plan overly complex for the participants.

Employers designing nonqualified plans should consider retaining qualified investment and insurance professionals with experience in the nonqualified plan area before selecting the investment options under their nonqualified plans.

Case Study 1-1

ABC Corporation is a for-profit operating company owned by five family members, A (the mother), B (the father), C (the eldest child), D (the middle child), and E (the youngest child). ABC's Board of Directors consists of A, B, C, D, E, and two outsiders. A owns 51 percent, B owns 19 percent, and C, D, and E each own 10 percent of the corporation. A is 55 years old, B is 60, C is 35, D is 33, and E is 30. A, B, C, and D are active in the business as CEO, Executive Vice President/Treasurer, Secretary/COO, and CFO, respectively. E, a physician, lives in a distant city and does not participate actively in the business.

ABC has 75 employees. A, B, C, D, and six other employees (F, G, H, I, J, and K) make up the corporation's management. The base compensation of each of ABC's management team members is as follows:

A: $250,000	G: $110,000
B: $175,000	H: $100,000
C: $155,000	I: $100,000
D: $135,000	J: $ 90,000
F: $120,000	K: $ 75,000

The remaining 65 employees of the corporation are blue collar, rank-and-file employees with an average age of 32.

The corporation has had gross revenues of $20 million for each of the last five years. The corporation has had no taxable income or losses over the five-year period. Its market share and position are relatively stable and are expected to remain so, and its credit-worthiness is high. Its attractiveness as an acquisition target also is high. The corporation has never paid a dividend over its 35-year history. The corporation maintains one deferred compensation plan, a tax-qualified 401(k) plan with a 10 percent of compensation salary deferral limit, a 50 percent employer match on the first 6 percent of compensation deferred by each participant, and a discretionary employer contribution feature permitting annual additional employer contributions of 0 percent to 3 percent of participant compensation. Rank-and-file participation in the 401(k) plan has been poor.

A, B, C, and D are becoming increasingly frustrated by the limits on annual contributions to their accounts under the 401(k) plan and the ever more complicated nondiscrimination, operational, and other rules which apply to the 401(k) plan. In addition, A, B, C, and D are viewing the contributions to the corporation of F, G, H, I, J, and K as increasingly important, and each of these individuals, with some regularity, is approached about employment opportunities by prospective employers. A, B, C, and D hope to retain these valued employees. Finally, A, B, C, and D would like to consider providing deferred compensation opportunities to the two outside directors of the corporation.

A, B, C, D, and E are avid readers of *The Wall Street Journal, Fortune,* and *Money,* and E also subscribes to *Medical Economics.* Each has a passing familiarity with deferred compensation as a concept and the general concepts of stock-based and non-stock-based compensation. *A* and *B* do not wish to give up control of the corporation to employees (except, ultimately, to *C*, *D*, and *E*).

The advisor begins a dialogue with *A*, *B*, *C*, and *D* about the various options open to them to enhance their deferred compensation and to "handcuff" *F*, *G*, *H*, *I*, *J*, and *K* to the corporation. *A*, *B*, *C*, and *D* are also interested in finding ways to collateralize the corporation's promise to pay any additional deferred compensation.

The first order of business is to determine whether the corporation has adequately reviewed the 401(k) plan and the other available qualified deferred compensation plan options to ensure that these techniques (which, at least in terms of overall tax treatment, are preferable to nonqualified plans) are being used to best advantage.

Discussion points include the possibility of integrating the employer contribution components of the 401(k) plan with Social Security in order to skew the allocation of employer contributions toward the higher paid participants and, in light of *A* and *B*'s advancing ages, converting the 401(k) plan's employer contribution formula to an age-weighted one. An actuary should be retained to run projections on these options and to advise the corporation about other possible qualified plan alternatives such as integrated defined benefit pension plans, target benefit plans, and cash balance plans. During this process, congressional proposals to repeal the family aggregation rules applicable to qualified plans and to prohibit age-weighted qualified plans should be monitored.

After the advisor concludes that the qualified plan side of ABC's deferred compensation plan picture is being fully utilized, given the goals of the owners of the corporation, a detailed discussion of the various nonqualified plan options should be initiated.

For an overview of these nonqualified plan options, see the Case Studies at the end of the following chapters.

Chapter 2

Top-Hat Plans

Top-hat plans, also known as Supplemental Executive Retirement Plans (SERPs), are used to provide unfunded deferred compensation benefits to a select group of management or highly compensated employees. This chapter examines top-hat plans—why an employer would establish a top-hat plan, the various arrangements that can be used in conjunction with a top-hat plan to help to secure the top-hat plan benefits, when a top-hat plan may be exempt from most ERISA requirements, the impact of whether an executive deferred compensation plan is funded or unfunded for ERISA and tax purposes, and some of the tax considerations that affect top-hat plans.

Overview

Q 2:1   What is a top-hat plan?

A top-hat plan, or Supplemental Executive Retirement Plan (SERP), is a nonqualified plan used to provide deferred compensation benefits to certain key employees. Under ERISA, a top-hat plan generally is defined as an unfunded nonqualified plan maintained "primarily for the purpose of providing deferred compensation for a select group of management or highly compensated employees." [ERISA §§ 201(2), 301(a)(3), 401(a)(1); see Healy v Rich Products Corp, DC WNY, No. CIV-89-1526E, Mar 29, 1991]

Q 2:2   Does a deferred compensation arrangement require an ongoing administrative program in order to be a plan subject to the top-hat rules?

In the recent case of *James v. Fleet/Norstar Financial Group, Inc.* [992 F 2d 463 (2nd Cir 1993)], the Second Circuit Court of Appeals held that an employer's severance pay arrangement was not a "plan" because it called only for a one-time payment and did not require an "ongoing administrative program."

Although the *James* case dealt with a welfare arrangement (i.e., severance payments) rather than a pension or deferred compensation arrangement, it does suggest that not all deferred compensation or supplemental retirement payments made by an employer to an executive or former executive are necessarily made pursuant to a plan within the meaning of ERISA.

Therefore, employers who sponsor ad hoc, one-time arrangements—rather than ongoing, nonqualified deferred compensation programs—may wish to discuss with ERISA counsel whether those arrangements implicate ERISA at all.

However, as will be shown later in this chapter, the requirements imposed by ERISA on top-hat plans are so minimal that employers often would be wise simply to concede top-hat plan status and satisfy the attendant compliance requirements. Doing so avoids the possibility of having to argue the issue with the DOL and also should preclude state law claims by participants relating to the arrangement.

Q 2:3   Why would an employer establish a top-hat plan?

Employers establish top-hat plans to provide deferred compensation to certain employees through a vehicle other than a tax qualified retirement plan. Prior to TRA '86, employers frequently established top-hat plans to provide employer-paid deferred compensation to key executives, or to allow key executives to defer their compensation voluntarily until retirement. Presumably, at retirement, their marginal tax rates would be substantially lower (because of lower total income) than their marginal tax rates when the deferred compensation was earned. Under TRA '86, the top marginal tax rate was reduced substantially and the various graduated tax brackets were essentially eliminated. This eliminated a significant benefit of deferring an executive's compensation. However, the economic benefit of deferring taxes on income currently earned, especially if deferred for a significant period of time, has caused top-hat plans to remain popular even after TRA '86.

Now that OBRA '93 has increased the top marginal tax rate from 31 percent to 39.6 percent, the benefit achieved by deferring compensation until the recipient is in a lower tax bracket once again is likely to become significant, and the value of the tax deferral, in and of itself, will increase.

In addition to tax rate and tax deferral incentives, employers may wish to establish top-hat plans because they are not subject to the significant limitations on contributions and benefits that affect tax qualified retirement plans. For example, in general, Code Section 415(c) limits the sum of employer contributions, employee contributions, and forfeitures that may be contributed annually to the account of a participant in a qualified defined contribution plan to the lesser of:

1. $30,000, or

2. 25 percent of the participant's compensation.

Likewise, Code Section 415(b) limits the benefits that may be paid annually to a participant in a qualified defined benefit plan to the lesser of:

1. $90,000 adjusted for cost of living increases (the benefit dollar limit for 1994 is $118,800), or

2. 100 percent of the participant's average compensation for the three consecutive calendar years during which the participant both was an active participant in the plan and had the greatest aggregate compensation from the employer.

Furthermore, as amended by OBRA '93, Code Section 401(a)(17) limits the amount of a participant's compensation that may be considered when making these calculations to $150,000 (indexed). Additionally, Code Section 402(g) generally limits any participant's annual pre-tax 401(k) plan deferrals to $7,000 (indexed to $9,240 for 1994) and Code Section 403(b) plan deferrals to $9,500 (to be indexed).

In contrast to these restrictions, a top-hat plan may be based on an executive's entire salary, and may provide contributions and benefits and permit deferrals without regard to the limits imposed by the Code on qualified plans.

Other reasons top-hat plans are established include:

1. Providing a pension supplement to attract an older executive in a case where the years-of-service factor in a qualified plan's benefit formula would limit the executive's benefits under that plan;

2. Providing funds to allow an executive to retire early with combined qualified plan/top-hat plan benefits equal to what would be his or her normal retirement age qualified plan benefit;

3. Providing an incentive for an executive to remain with the employer;

4. Providing a generous benefit package to attract desired executives;

5. Avoiding the 10-percent penalty tax under Code Section 72(t) on early distributions from qualified plans to executives; and

6. Avoiding the 15 percent penalty tax under Code Section 4980A on excess distributions from, and excess accumulation under, qualified plans.

Q 2:4   By providing deferred compensation benefits to one executive under an employment contract, does an employer create a pension plan that is subject to ERISA requirements?

Arguably, no. In two DOL advisory opinions, the DOL ruled that contractual deferred compensation arrangements with individual executives were merely employment contracts and were not "employee pension benefit plans" as defined by ERISA and, therefore, were not subject to the requirements of ERISA. [DOL Adv Op 76-79, May 25, 1976; DOL Adv Op 76-110, Sept 28, 1976; ERISA § 3(2); DOL Reg § 2510.3-2; see Healy v Rich Products Corp, DC WNY, No CIV-89-1526E, Mar 29, 1991]

However, in another ruling, the DOL stated that an agreement between an employer and an employee that provided specified monthly retirement income benefits to the employee upon retirement was an employee pension benefit plan subject to ERISA. [DOL Adv Op 79-75A, Sept 29, 1979] In addition, separate employment contracts that provide similar benefits to a number of executives may be considered to be an ERISA-governed plan in the aggregate. For example, an employer's identical severance agreements with key executives have been viewed, in substance, as an employee benefit plan subject to ERISA. [Pane v RCA Corp, 868 F 2d 631 (3rd Cir 1989) (relying on Fort Halifax Packing Co, Inc v Coyne, 482 US 1, 107 S Ct 2211 (1987), where the court noted that RCA's severance agreements were an ERISA-governed employee benefit plan because a potential class of participants was identified and the severance arrangements required an administrative scheme)]

Q 2:5   From what source does the employer pay the benefits provided under a top-hat plan?

An employer generally pays the benefits provided under a top-hat plan out of its general assets at the time the payments become due. Under these circumstances, the executive must rely solely on the employer's unfunded promise to pay these benefits and assumes the risk that these benefits may not be paid if there is an unfriendly change in the management of the employer or a change in the employer's financial situation. For example, if the employer becomes insolvent, the participating employees may not receive any benefits. In addition, where the employer is acquired in a hostile takeover or where there is a significant unfriendly change in the management of the employer, the employer may refuse to pay the benefits promised to the employees.

Q 2:6 Should employees attempt to obtain assurances that the benefits promised under a top-hat plan actually will be paid?

Yes, but employees should proceed with caution. If a nonqualified plan provides too much security that the promised benefits will be paid, the plan may be determined to be "funded" and the employee could be taxed currently on benefits that will not be paid until future years. In addition, if the plan is determined to be funded, it will lose the top-hat plan exemption from most ERISA requirements. The loss of this exemption means that the employer will be required to ensure that the plan complies with ERISA's fiduciary, reporting, disclosure, participation, vesting, and funding rules, limiting the design flexibility of the plan and adding to the expense of its operation. As a result, the designer of a top-hat plan is confronted with the issue of providing assurances to the employees that future benefits will be paid without causing the employees to incur current taxation or the plan to lose its exemption from most of ERISA. (See chapter 5 for a discussion of funded arrangements.)

Q 2:7 What arrangements can be used in connection with a top-hat plan to increase the likelihood that the promised benefits will be paid to participating employees without creating adverse tax consequences to the employees or causing the plan to lose its exemption from most of ERISA?

There are a number of arrangements that may be used to increase the likelihood of payment from a top-hat plan that will not create adverse tax consequences for the participating employees or cause the plan to lose its exemption from most of ERISA. These arrangements include the following:

1. *Corporate-Owned Life Insurance (COLI).* (See chapter 7.) A COLI policy on the life of a key executive is one method of providing a source of funds from which the employer may satisfy its obligations under a top-hat plan. If properly structured, the use of COLI avoids current taxation to the participants and will not cause the plan to be funded for ERISA purposes. The COLI's tax deferred cash value build-up and the tax-free receipt of death proceeds make the use of COLI an attractive funding vehicle because the policy will provide deferred compensation death benefits in the event the executive dies, or a cash value that the employer may borrow against in order to provide deferred compensation benefits to the executive. To be effective, the insurance policy used in connection with a top-hat plan must remain subject to the claims of the employer's creditors, and the existence of the policy must not guarantee that the promised benefits actually will be paid.

2. *Rabbi Trust.* (See chapter 4.) In general, a rabbi trust is a trust that may be used to hold assets of any type that the trustee is willing to hold and that are intended to be used to pay benefits due under a top-hat plan. A rabbi trust is an irrevocable trust; that is, it may not be revoked by the employer, and its assets may not be reached by the employer. Typically, a rabbi trust helps to protect the executive by providing a measure of security that the benefits promised under the top-hat plan will be paid because the assets held in the trust are not available to a corporate raider and are not subject to the discretion of management. However, in order to avoid current taxation and funded status for ERISA purposes, assets held in the rabbi trust must remain subject to the claims of the employer's creditors in the event of the employer's insolvency or bankruptcy.

3. *Third-Party Guarantee.* In this arrangement, a third party (such as the corporate parent or former corporate parent of the employer) guarantees payment of the benefits promised under the top-hat plan in the event the employer defaults. This arrangement will not cause the plan to be funded for ERISA purposes, and the IRS has ruled that there are no current tax consequences to the employee where the guarantor's promise to pay, like the employer's, is unsecured and unfunded. Of course, this arrangement will provide meaningful assurances

to the employee only where the guarantor is financially sound and disposed to honor its guarantee.

4. *Surety Bond.* Executives may be able to purchase surety bonds to ensure that the benefits promised under a top-hat plan will be paid. A surety bond is a type of performance bond issued by a surety insurance company. The executive pays a premium to the surety insurance company for the bond coverage. This arrangement will not cause the plan to be funded for ERISA purposes, and the IRS has indicated that the purchase of a surety bond by the executive to protect his or her future deferred compensation payments will not, by itself, cause the deferred amounts to be included in the executive's income, either at the time the executive purchases the bond or at the time the executive pays the premiums thereon. However, in order to ensure the effectiveness of this approach, the employer should play no part, directly or indirectly, in the executive's purchase of the surety bond. [Ltr Rul 8406012, Nov 3, 1983]

5. *Letter of Credit.* An executive may be able to purchase, from a bank, a letter of credit against which the executive may draw if the benefits promised under a top-hat plan are not paid. This arrangement is treated, for tax and ERISA purposes, like a surety bond.

Q 2:8   How is a defined contribution top-hat plan different from a defined benefit top-hat plan?

A defined contribution deferred compensation or retirement plan—whether an ERISA-governed, tax-qualified plan or a top-hat plan—is an arrangement under which the contributions to the arrangement (whether employer contributions, employee contributions, or both) are defined in the plan document. Although the participants can determine with some certainty the amounts that will be credited to their accounts as contributions, they cannot determine with certainty the amounts they ultimately will receive, because the investment performance of those amounts after they are credited to the accounts is uncertain (unless a fixed investment return is utilized and credited to accounts). In addition, if the defined contribution formula is fixed but based on variables such as age, service, and compensation, participants may not be able to determine reliably the contribution amounts that will be credited to their accounts in future years. Finally, some defined contribution arrangements contain contribution formulas that permit the employer and/or the employees to determine the amount of the "defined" contribution on a year-to-year basis, thereby eliminating any ability by participants even to estimate the benefits that ultimately will be paid to them.

Although participants in a defined contribution arrangement are unable to determine accurately the amounts that ultimately will be paid to them, these arrangements have the advantage of easing the fixed funding requirements for the sponsoring employer. This is especially significant where the contribution formula allows the employer the discretion to determine the contribution on a year-to-year basis and where no particular investment return is credited to participants' accounts, but instead, participants bear the investment risk (and enjoy the investment upside) with respect to amounts credited to their accounts.

In a defined benefit arrangement, the plan document specifies the ultimate benefit that will be paid to participants qualifying for benefits in a particular situation (at normal retirement, at early retirement, and so on). This type of arrangement permits participants to calculate with some certainty the benefits that they will receive, based on information available at the date of the calculation. For example, defined benefit formulas often calculate a participant's benefit based on factors such as the participant's compensation, age, and service up to the date of the calculation. Therefore, a participant can apply the plan's formula to these factors and arrive at an estimate of his or her ultimate benefit earned or likely to be earned to that date.

With a defined benefit arrangement, the investment return on any funds deposited is largely irrelevant to participants, because their ultimate benefits are determined by the applicable formula and are paid regardless of the investment return on those funds. In this type of plan, the sponsoring employer, rather than the participant, bears all of the investment risk and enjoys all of the investment upside.

Although there is no typical top-hat plan, the majority of top-hat arrangements are defined contribution plans, because these are both easier to administer and easier to explain to participants and employers. Only arithmetic, rather than actuarial science, is required to perform calculations under a defined contribution plan, and the contribution formula is simple. In addition, employers are more inclined to sponsor defined contribution arrangements because the investment risk is borne by participants.

However, defined benefit top-hat arrangements are particularly useful when the top-hat arrangement is intended to be a true supplement to an executive's other sources of retirement income or is designed to replace some portion of the executive's preretirement income. For example, if an employer and an executive wish to design a program that will ensure the executive's receipt of aggregate retirement income, from all employer-derived sources, of 60 percent of final average compensation at age 65, the ideal top-hat plan is a defined benefit arrangement that provides a benefit under the following formula: 60 percent of final average compensation, less amounts payable from the employer's tax-qualified and other top-hat deferred compensation plans (to the extent derived from employer contributions), less one half of the Social Security benefits payable to the participant (that is, less the portion of Social Security attributable to Social Security taxes paid by the employer).

The decision of whether to utilize a defined contribution or defined benefit top-hat arrangement must be made based on the facts and circumstances of each case.

For important considerations for tax-exempt and government employers, see chapter 10.

Q 2:9   What is a top-hat welfare plan and when would one be used in executive compensation planning?

A top-hat welfare plan, like a top-hat deferred compensation plan, provides benefits for a select group of its employer-sponsor's management or highly compensated employees. However, whereas a top-hat deferred compensation plan provides deferred compensation benefits to these individuals, a top-hat welfare plan provides "welfare" benefits, e.g., health, life insurance, disability insurance, and so on. Top-hat welfare plans can be a very effective way to provide key employees with welfare benefits superior to those made available to the employer's rank-and-file employees.

Unlike sponsors of top-hat deferred compensation plans, sponsors of top-hat welfare plans are not required to make a one-time DOL filing in order to be exempt from ERISA's reporting and disclosure requirements (see Q 2:20).

Because of the myriad of nondiscrimination rules applicable under the Internal Revenue Code to welfare benefit arrangements, top-hat welfare plans should be established only after careful consideration of the tax issues involved.

ERISA Considerations

Q 2:10 Are top-hat plans subject to the requirements of Title I of ERISA?

A plan that provides employees with deferred compensation benefits paid at retirement generally would be a "pension plan" under ERISA. However, if the plan is maintained by an employer primarily for the purpose of providing deferred compensation for a select group of management or highly compensated employees and is unfunded (i.e., is a top-hat plan), the plan is exempt from Parts 2, 3, and 4 of Title I of ERISA (pertaining to participation, vesting, funding, and fiduciary responsibilities). Although a top-hat plan is subject to ERISA Title I, Part 1 (pertaining to reporting and disclosure) and ERISA Title I, Part 5 (pertaining to enforcement and preemption), the Part 1 requirements are easily satisfied under an alternative compliance approach available under the DOL Regulations (see Q 2:18), and the Part 5 requirements are implicated only rarely [ERISA §§ 4, 201(2), 301(a)(3), 401(a)(1)].

Q 2:11 What does the term "primarily" mean for purposes of the top-hat plan rules?

ERISA defines a top-hat plan as an unfunded plan maintained by an employer "primarily" for the purpose of providing deferred compensation for a select group of management or highly compensated employees.

The DOL has taken the position that the term "primarily" refers to the purpose of the plan (that is, the primary purpose of the plan must be to provide deferred compensation benefits). The word "primarily" is not intended to imply that, as long as the plan is maintained for a group primarily composed of management and highly compensated individuals, nonmanagement and/or non-highly compensated individuals also may participate. Therefore, a plan that extends coverage beyond "a select group of management or highly compensated employees" would not constitute a top-hat plan for purposes of ERISA. [DOL Adv Op 90-14A, May 8, 1990]

Q 2:12   What does the phrase "select group of management or highly compensated employees" mean for purposes of the top-hat plan rules?

Neither ERISA nor the Regulations thereunder define the phrase "select group of management or highly compensated employees." In addition, the few DOL rulings concerning this phrase have been withdrawn and may not be relied upon. However, it is instructive to examine the way in which these withdrawn rulings and the cases that have considered the top-hat plan definition have dealt with the various components of the definition.

Select group. In the withdrawn rulings, the DOL focused on the size of the select group in relation to the employer's total workforce and the select group's average salary in relation to the average salary of the remainder of the employer's workforce.

In one of the withdrawn rulings, the DOL determined that an unfunded plan covering key executives and managerial employees selected by the employer's compensation committee, comprising fewer than 4 percent of the employer's active employees and having average annual compensation 68 percent higher than the average for all of the employer's management employees was a top-hat plan. [DOL Adv Op 75-64, Aug 1, 1975]

Similarly, courts that have addressed this issue have focused on the percentage of the select group in relation to the employer's total workforce. For example, one court found that a deferred compensation plan covering *only* 4.6 percent of an employer's total number of employees covered only a "select group." Another court found that a group comprising almost 20 percent of an employer's workforce was too large to be considered a "select group" for purposes of the top-hat plan rules. Another court found that a plan that covered only employees who had worked for the employer's former parent company (consisting of nonsupervisory clerical positions (37.5 percent), line supervisors (25 percent), and upper management (37.5 percent)), whose salaries ranged from $12,000 to $336,000, was not for the benefit of a select group. [Belka v Rowe Furniture Corp, 571 F Supp 1249 (D Md 1983); Darden v Nationwide Mutual Insurance Company, 717 F Supp 388 (ED NC 1989), 922 F 2d 203, 208 n3 (4th Cir 1991); Starr v JCI Data Processing, Inc, 757 F Supp 390 (D NJ 1991)]

Or. The term "or" in the phrase "management or highly compensated" also has been the subject of interpretation. The DOL has informally acknowledged that this word is disjunctive rather than conjunctive and, as a result, an employee could be either management or highly compensated and be eligible for coverage under a top-hat plan. However, the DOL has not announced a formal position on this issue.

Management. This term also is as yet undefined. The legislative history of ERISA cites as an example of a top-hat plan a deferred compensation plan that was established solely for the officers of a corporation. The DOL has ruled that a plan that covered all employees on the employer's executive payroll was not a plan maintained primarily for the purpose of providing deferred compensation for a select group of management or highly compensated employees in view of the broad range of salaries and positions held by the participants. [HR Rep No 93-1280, 93rd Cong, 2d Sess 296 (1974) reprinted in 1974 US Code Cong & Ad News 5038, 5076-5077; DOL Adv Op 85-37A, Oct 25, 1985]

The DOL generally takes a somewhat limited view of the employees who may be considered management for purposes of the top-hat plan rules. As an example, the DOL stated in one of its withdrawn rulings that the top-hat definition was met where:

1. A plan covered key executives and managerial employees selected by the employer's compensation committee,
2. The number of participants eligible in any single year was limited to an absolute number, and

3. Fewer than 4 percent of the employer's active employees were covered by the plan.

In another withdrawn ruling, the DOL stated that the top-hat plan definition was met where:

1. The participants earned at least a particular stated amount,
2. The participants were classified as key employees by the plan's administrative committee, and
3. The participants were exempt from the Fair Labor Standards Act as administrative, supervisory, or professional employees.

[DOL Adv Op 75-64, Aug 1, 1975; DOL Adv Op 75-63, July 22, 1975]

Highly compensated employees. The DOL's position with respect to this term also is unclear. The Department of the Treasury, in the preamble to its Section 414(q) Regulations, stated that it "would like to clarify its understanding that Section 414(q) is not determinative with respect to provisions of Title I of ERISA, other than those provisions that explicitly incorporate such section by reference (e.g., Section 408(b)(1)(B) of ERISA)." Furthermore, the preamble noted that "[t]he Departments of Treasury and Labor concur in the view that a broad extension of section 414(q) to determinations under sections 201(2), 301(a)(3), and 401(a)(1) of ERISA would be inconsistent with the tax and retirement policy objectives of encouraging employers to maintain tax-qualified plans that provide meaningful benefits to rank-and-file employees."

Practice Pointer. In view of these uncertainties, employers should consider carefully, after consultation with ERISA counsel, which managerial or highly compensated employees should be covered under a top-hat plan.

Q 2:13   May the Code Section 414(q) definition of highly compensated employee be used to define an employer's top-hat group?

Although the term "top-hat employee" remains undefined, it is clear from the intent of the statute as discussed in the legislative history to ERISA, and it is the often-expressed informal position of the DOL, that a top-hat plan sponsor may not use the definition of highly compensated employee found in Code Section 414(q) to define the members of its top-hat group. This is because the 414(q) definition is an arbitrary, bright-line test that applies to all employers and does not take into account the relative pay level or the management responsibilities of particular so-called highly compensated employees.

For example, for 1995, all employees who earn more than $66,000 and who are in the top 20 percent of an employer's payroll generally would be considered highly compensated employees under Code Section 414(q). However, the DOL would argue—and correctly, most commentators believe—that many employees in this group are not those whom Congress intended to be eligible to participate in a top-hat plan because they do not need the protections of ERISA; that is, they are not employees who, because of their positions as members of a select group of management or highly compensated employees, are able to negotiate the details of their own compensation arrangements and protect themselves with respect to their pension and welfare benefits without the intervention of the ERISA regulators.

Q 2:14   Is a top-hat plan a funded or an unfunded plan for purposes of Title I of ERISA?

A top-hat plan, by definition, must be an unfunded plan. [ERISA §§ 201(2), 301(a)(3), 401(a)(1)] A plan generally will be unfunded if plan benefits are payable out of the employer's general assets and any participant in the plan has no greater rights in these assets than those of a general unsecured creditor of the employer.

Conversely, a plan generally will be considered "funded" if the plan's assets are segregated or otherwise set aside so that the assets are maintained for the exclusive purpose of providing a source for the payment of plan benefits. [GCM 33373, Nov 21, 1966, as modified by GCM 35196, Jan 16, 1973, which was modified by GCM 35326, May 3, 1973; GCM 39230, Jan 20, 1984]

At least one court has noted that the distinction between a funded and an unfunded plan turns on whether there is a separate "res" or property that is set apart or segregated from the employer's general funds to which the employees may look for plan benefits. [Dependahl v Falstaff Brewing Corp, 653 F 2d 1208 (8th Cir 1981), *cert denied,* 454 US 968, 102 S Ct 512 (1981); Belsky v First National Life Insurance Company, 653 F Supp 80, *aff'd,* 818 F 2d 661 (8th Cir 1987); Darden v Nationwide Mutual Insurance Company, 717 F Supp 388 (ED NC 1989), 922 F 2d 203, 208 n3 (4th Cir 1991)]

> **Practice Pointer.** In *Dependahl,* a case that has been criticized and that probably would not be similarly decided today, the employer purchased and owned life insurance policies on the lives of key employees whose named beneficiaries were to receive annuity income benefits under the plan upon the employees' deaths. The court found that this arrangement was a funded plan because the employees were able to look to property separate from the employer's general assets if the employer failed to pay the promised benefits.

Dependahl was subsequently distinguished in *Belsky,* which involved a compensation arrangement that provided for the employer to purchase life insurance policies on the participants. The employer was the sole owner and beneficiary under these policies, and the plans specifically set forth that any assets acquired by the employer in connection with its liabilities under the agreement would not be held in trust for the employee's benefit. Instead, such assets would be general, unrestricted, unpledged assets of the employer. The *Belsky* court distinguished the *Dependahl* decision by noting that, in *Dependahl,* the plan mandated that the employer would acquire assets to finance the liabilities provided for by the plan so that the benefits were paid through a specific insurance policy that was tied directly to the plan benefits.

Q 2:15   Is it significant whether or not a plan is funded or unfunded for purposes of Title I of ERISA?

Yes. Under Title I of ERISA, whether a plan is funded or unfunded is significant. An unfunded plan otherwise meeting the top-hat requirements is exempt from the ERISA provisions pertaining to participation and vesting, funding, and fiduciary responsibilities pursuant to the exemptions contained in ERISA Sections 201(2), 301(a)(3), and 401(a)(1), and may enjoy the extremely simplified alternative method of compliance with ERISA's reporting and disclosure rules which is available under DOL regulations.

Conversely, if a nonqualified plan is funded, it will not qualify as a top-hat plan and it will be required to comply with all of the provisions of Title I of ERISA, leaving the plan almost as inflexible and expensive to operate as the employer's ERISA-governed, tax-qualified plans. [DOL letter to Richard H. Manfreda, Chief, Individual Income Tax Branch, IRS, Dec 13, 1985]

Q 2:16   Will a plan be considered funded by the DOL if an employer purchases life insurance to provide a source of funds from which to pay benefits provided under the plan?

Not necessarily. The DOL has indicated that an employer may purchase life insurance policies to provide a source of funds from which to pay benefits under a plan, and the plan will be considered unfunded if the following conditions are met:

1. The employer is the owner and beneficiary of the insurance policies;

2. The policies are part of the employer's general assets and are subject to the claims of the employer's creditors;

3. Neither the plan nor any participant or beneficiary would have any preferred claim against the policies or any beneficial ownership interest in the policies;

4. The employer may not represent to any participant or beneficiary that the policies will be used solely to provide plan benefits or that the policies represent security for the payment of benefits;

5. The benefits may not be limited or governed by the amount of insurance proceeds the employer receives; and

6. The plan neither requires nor allows employee contributions.

[DOL Adv Op 81-11A, Jan 15, 1981; DOL letter to Richard H. Manfreda, Chief, Individual Income Tax Branch, IRS, Dec 13, 1985]

The requirements of this DOL Opinion go beyond those which should ensure unfunded status for a plan maintained in connection with a life insurance policy. In essence, if all the incidents of ownership of the policy are owned by the employer (that is, if items 1-4, listed above, are met), the plan should be determined to be unfunded.

Q 2:17   Will a rabbi trust that is used in connection with a top-hat plan cause the plan to be funded?

The DOL stated in a 1985 letter to the IRS that the existence of a rabbi trust (see chapter 4) maintained in connection with a top-hat plan will not cause the plan to be a funded plan for purposes of Title I of ERISA. The DOL stated that the positions adopted by the IRS regarding the tax consequences to trust beneficiaries of the creation of, or contributions to, a rabbi trust would be accorded significant weight by the DOL. In a 1990 Advisory Opinion, the DOL also stated that, "in the absence of an ERISA regulation defining a 'top-hat' plan, it is the view of the Department that the positions adopted by the [IRS] with respect to deferred compensation arrangements should be accorded weight in determining whether a 'top-hat' plan is unfunded for purposes of Title I." [DOL letter to Richard H. Manfreda, Chief, Individual Income Tax Branch, IRS, Dec 13, 1985; DOL Adv Op 90-14A, May 8, 1990]

Q 2:18   Are there any regulations interpreting the ERISA definition of a top-hat plan?

No. The DOL has not issued regulations that address top-hat plans. The DOL intended to issue proposed regulations for top-hat plans by early 1992, but has announced that the proposed regulations project has been put on hold.

If the DOL regulations ultimately are issued, they will probably discuss the terms "unfunded," "select group," "management," "highly compensated," "or," and "primarily," as used in ERISA to describe a top-hat plan. It is not clear whether these regulations would affect existing plans or would apply only to plans established after the date the regulations are issued.

Q 2:19 Is a top-hat plan generally subject to the reporting and disclosure requirements of ERISA?

Yes. A top-hat plan generally is subject to the reporting and disclosure obligations under Part 1 of Title I of ERISA that require, among other things, the annual filing of a Form 5500 series report (Annual Return/Report of Employee Benefit Plan) with the Internal Revenue Service (IRS). The report generally must be filed by the last day of the seventh month after the plan year ends. However, the otherwise applicable ERISA reporting and disclosure requirements may be avoided by a top-hat plan if the requirements of an alternative method of compliance under Section 2520.104-23 of the DOL Regulations, described in Q 2:20, are satisfied. If these requirements are not satisfied, the plan administrator annually must file the appropriate Form 5500 series report and satisfy the other ERISA reporting and disclosure requirements.

If the applicable annual filing requirements are not satisfied, substantial penalties could be imposed. Specifically, Section 502(c)(2) of ERISA authorizes the DOL to assess up to $1,000 a day against plan administrators who fail to file complete and timely annual reports. The DOL has announced that it may impose the following penalties with respect to late filers and nonfilers of the annual report:

1. *Late filers.* Plan administrators who voluntarily file annual reports for 1988 and subsequent reporting years after the due date will be considered late filers and may be assessed $50 a day per plan for the period they failed to file.

2. *Nonfilers.* Plan administrators who fail to file may be assessed a penalty of $300 a day per plan, up to $30,000 a year per plan, until the filing is submitted.

(The DOL previously sponsored an amnesty program for assessing significantly reduced penalties against plan administrators for failing to file timely annual reports. This program provided an opportunity for plan administrators to file past due annual reports and past due top-hat plan alternative compliance filings (see Q 2:20) for 1988 and subsequent plan years and be assessed only $50 a day per filing up to a maximum of $1,000 per filing. This program required plan administrators to file such reports during a grace period which began on March 23, 1992 and ended on December 31, 1992. Recently, the DOL has begun to consider the idea of another amnesty program.)

Q 2:20 Can a top-hat plan use an alternative method of compliance to fulfill the reporting and disclosure requirements of ERISA?

Yes. The ERISA reporting and disclosure requirements may be satisfied by providing the top-hat plan documents to the DOL on request and filing a brief statement with the DOL within 120 days after the plan is adopted. The statement must include the following:

1. The employer's name, address, and IRS employer identification number;

2. A declaration that the employer maintains the top-hat plan primarily for the purpose of providing deferred compensation for a select group of management or highly compensated employees;

3. A statement of the number of top-hat plans maintained by the employer; and

4. The number of employees in each top-hat plan maintained by the employer.

[DOL Reg § 2520.104-23]

Compliance with these requirements is important. The statute and the regulations make clear, and the Third Circuit Court of Appeals has confirmed, that a top-hat plan that does not comply with the requirements contained in this alternative method of compliance is subject to all of the reporting and disclosure requirements of Part 1 of ERISA Title I. [Barrowclough v Kidder, Peabody & Co, Inc, 752 F 2d 923 (3rd Cir 1985)]

In *Barrowclough,* the employer established a deferred compensation plan under which executives earning more than $75,000 per year could elect to defer up to 25 percent of their income. These deferred amounts were maintained in accounts credited to the executive. Under the plan, the employer's obligation to pay a participating executive the amount credited to his or her account was neither funded nor secured. In addition, the plan specifically provided that title to, and beneficial ownership of, the assets in the accounts remained with the employer.

Barrowclough participated in the plan for two years until he was discharged from employment. Subsequently, Barrowclough requested information on when the amounts credited to his deferred compensation account would be paid to him and an accounting of his accumulated deferred compensation. The employer did not comply with the request and Barrowclough filed suit.

The district court concluded that the DOL regulation on the alternative method of compliance eliminated the statutory requirement of the ERISA Title I reporting and disclosure rules that a plan administrator provide an accounting upon request and ruled in favor of the employer. The Third Circuit Court of Appeals reversed the district court, stating that the statute authorizing the regulation and the regulation itself are framed in terms of alternative methods for satisfying the statutory requirements. Therefore, if the employer failed to provide the DOL with the required notice filing or plan documents if requested by the DOL, the employer did not use the alternative method of compliance and, therefore, the statutory requirement to provide an accounting, if requested, continued to apply.

Q 2:21 Is a top-hat plan subject to the participation and vesting rules of Part 2 of ERISA Title I?

No. A top-hat plan is exempt from the ERISA Title I requirements regarding participation and vesting. If, however, a nonqualified plan is funded, the plan must comply with those requirements. [ERISA § 201(2)]

In *Healy v. Rich Products Corporation*, Thomas Healy was a participant in two benefit plans made available by his employer, a deferred compensation agreement (DCA) and an incentive compensation plan (ICP). In 1987, Healy resigned and received a DCA benefit installment and an ICP benefit installment from the employer. Later, he entered into a stock purchase agreement with the employer pursuant to which he sold to the employer all of his shares of stock in the employer and its affiliated companies for $25 million. In connection with this agreement, Healy released the employer from any and all liabilities and claims "except any vested rights under any profit-sharing or pension plans of [the employer] which are subject to the Employee Retirement Income Security Act of 1974, which benefits are not released." Subsequently, the employer failed to pay scheduled DCA and ICP benefit installments to Healy and informed him that no further DCA or ICP benefits would be forthcoming because such benefits had been released.

The court found that both the DCA and the ICP were deferred compensation plans that were unfunded and offered to a select group of management or highly compensated employees (that is, were top-hat plans). As such, the DCA and the ICP were exempt from ERISA's vesting requirements. The terms of both the DCA and the ICP contained circumstances under which an employee would forfeit his or her benefits. The court concluded that because the DCA and the ICP were exempt from ERISA's vesting requirements, the forfeiture clauses in the plans were permissible and Healy's DCA and ICP benefits were not vested rights. Thus, the release of liability included the nonvested benefits under the DCA and the ICP. [Healy v Rich Products Corporation, WD NY, No CIV-89-1526E, Mar 29, 1991]

In *Carson v. Local 1588, International Longshoremen's Association,* Carson was a union business agent who was elected union secretary-treasurer. In 1988, Carson was indicted and convicted of various criminal charges and left his position with the union. Following his termination of employment, the union began paying Carson a monthly pension of $1,387.67. Later, after having paid approximately $9,280, the union ceased to provide Carson with any pension payments after concluding that the payments were not proper. There was no dispute among the parties that the plan was a top-hat plan.

The question was whether Carson's top-hat pension was subject to forfeiture based on alleged violations of portions of ERISA by the union while Carson managed the union. The court noted that, in other cases, the pension plans were separate entities subject to the nonforfeiture and nonalienation provisions of ERISA, and courts have permitted plans to remedy wrongs committed by individuals who were fully protected by these provisions, noting that, even where ERISA provisions apply, courts have held that ERISA does not prohibit equitable exceptions in some circumstances. The court held that in this case, because the plan was a top-hat plan, the nonforfeiture and nonalienation provisions of ERISA's vesting rules did not apply, and that the claims by the union, if proven, could estop Carson from receiving a pension under the plan. The court noted that if other cases have allowed exceptions to ERISA's statutory vesting scheme to remedy wrongs committed by participants in plans afforded the full array of ERISA's vesting protection, then Carson's top-hat pension plan, which was exempt from ERISA's vesting rules, must also be subject to equitable principles of law, such as estoppel. [Carson v Local 1588, International Longshoremen's Association, 769 F Supp 141 (SD NY 1991)]

Q 2:22 Are top-hat plans subject to the funding rules of Part 3 of ERISA Title I?

No. Top-hat plans are exempt from the ERISA Title I requirements regarding funding. If, however, the nonqualified plan is funded, the plan must comply with those provisions. [ERISA § 301(a)(3)]

Q 2:23 Are top-hat plans subject to the fiduciary responsibility rules of Part 4 of ERISA Title I?

No. Top-hat plans are exempt from the ERISA Title I fiduciary provisions. If, however, the nonqualified plan is funded, it must comply with the ERISA fiduciary provisions. [ERISA § 401(a)(1)]

Q 2:24 Is a top-hat plan subject to the enforcement and administration provisions of Part 5 of ERISA Title I?

Yes. A top-hat plan is subject to the enforcement and administration provisions contained in Part 5 of ERISA Title I. In *Barrowclough* (see Q 2:20), the court held that a participant in a top-hat plan could bring a suit in federal court for breach of the terms of the plan under Part 5 of Title I of ERISA. [Barrowclough v Kidder, Peabody & Co., Inc., 752 F 2d 923, 935 (3d Cir 1985); Nagy v Riblet Products Corporation, DC N Ind No. § 90-202, Dec 20, 1990, decision reexamined Feb 6, 1991, and Apr 2, 1991]

Accordingly, a top-hat plan is subject to ERISA Section 503 regarding required plan claims procedures. Therefore, the plan must provide adequate notice in writing to any participant or beneficiary whose claim for benefits under the plan has been denied. The written notice must set forth the specific reasons for the denial, be written in a manner calculated to be understood by the participant, and afford a reasonable opportunity to any participant whose claim for benefits has been denied for a full and fair review by the appropriate named fiduciary of the decision denying the claim. [ERISA § 503; DOL Reg § 2560.503-1]

Q 2:25   What standard of review will courts apply in reviewing a top-hat plan's denial of a benefit request by a participant?

It depends on the language of the top-hat plan. In *Firestone Tire and Rubber Co. v. Bruch*, the Supreme Court concluded that a denial of benefits challenged under ERISA Section 502(a)(1)(B) must be reviewed under a *de novo* standard (that is, the court must make a full review and substitute its own decision for that of the plan administrator or other fiduciary), unless the benefit plan expressly gives the plan administrator or other fiduciary discretionary authority to determine eligibility for benefits and to construe the plan's terms, in which case the court must use a deferential standard of review under which the court simply determines that the decision was not arbitrary and capricious. The Court added that, if an ERISA plan gives discretion to a plan administrator or fiduciary who is operating under a conflict of interest, that conflict must be weighed as a factor in determining whether there is an arbitrary and capricious abuse of discretion. [Firestone Tire and Rubber Co v Bruch, 489 US 101, 109 S Ct 948, 103 L Ed 2d 80 (1989)]

Q 2:26   Is a top-hat plan subject to Title IV of ERISA, which pertains to plan termination insurance?

No. However, a funded nonqualified plan could be subject to Title IV of ERISA. [ERISA § 4021(b)(6)]

Q 2:27   Why are top-hat plans exempt from most of the provisions of ERISA?

The DOL has stated that, in "providing relief for 'top-hat' plans from the broad remedial provisions of ERISA, Congress recognized that certain individuals, by virtue of their position or compensation level, have the ability to affect or substantially influence, through negotiation or otherwise, the design and operation of their deferred compensation plan, taking into consideration any risks attendant thereto, and, therefore, would not need the substantive rights and protections of Title I." However, the DOL has added that this view may not necessarily apply to *all* management or highly compensated employees. For example, a key executive of a subsidiary company may be subject to the compensation restrictions of the company's parent corporation. [DOL Adv Op 90-14A, May 8, 1990]

Q 2:28   Will federal courts enforce top-hat plans as contracts under the federal common law under ERISA?

In the recent case of *Carr v. First Nationwide Bank* [ND Cal 1993], a federal court held for the first time that participants in a top-hat plan have a federal ERISA common law right to have their top-hat plan benefits protected.

In *Carr*, the employer had argued that, because top-hat plans are exempt from most of ERISA's requirements, top-hat plan participants cannot sue under ERISA to enforce their top-hat plan rights.

The court rejected this argument and held that there exists under ERISA a "common law doctrine of unilateral contract" under which an employer-sponsor of a top-hat plan could unilaterally bind itself (as had First Nationwide) to provide a specific top-hat plan benefit and under which plan participants may sue under ERISA to enforce the employer-sponsor's unilateral promise.

In light of the *Carr* decision, top-hat plan sponsors should be aware that plan participants likely will have recourse under ERISA to the federal courts if plan benefits are reduced in a manner not clearly permitted by the plan's terms.

Q 2:29   How does a top-hat plan differ from an excess benefit plan?

Participation in an excess benefit plan is not limited to a select group of management or highly compensated employees. In addition, an excess benefit plan is required to be maintained solely for the purpose of providing benefits in excess of the limits contained in Code Section 415. [ERISA § 3(36); see chapter 3]

Tax Considerations

Q 2:30   Are contributions to an unfunded nonqualified plan treated differently, for tax purposes, from contributions to a funded executive deferred compensation plan?

Yes. Contributions to an unfunded nonqualified plan generally are not deductible by an employer and are not includible in a participating employee's income until the benefits are actually distributed or made available to the employee, which is generally at some future date. Employer contributions to a funded nonqualified plan, however, are generally deductible by the employer and includible in the employee's income in the year the contribution is vested in the employee. [IRC §§ 83, 402(b), 404(a)(5)]

Tax Consequences to the Employer

Q 2:31   When may an employer deduct its contribution to a top-hat plan?

Generally, an employer is entitled to deduct its contribution to a top-hat plan in the year in which an amount attributable to the contribution is includible in the participating employee's gross income, provided that the ordinary and necessary expense and reasonable compensation requirements of the deduction rules are met and that separate accounts are maintained for each participating employee. [IRC §§ 83(h), 162, 212, 404(a)(5); Ltr Rul 9030035, April 30, 1990]

Tax Consequences to the Employee

Q 2:32   When are contributions to a top-hat plan includible in the employee's gross income?

Generally, amounts contributed to an unfunded executive deferred compensation plan are includible in the employee's gross income at the time these amounts are paid or made available to the employee. If the executive deferred compensation plan is considered to be funded, the amounts contributed generally are includible in the employee's gross income in the year the contribution is made. However, contributions to a funded plan that are subject to a substantial risk of forfeiture generally are not includible in the employee's gross income until the contributions have vested and are no longer subject to a substantial risk of forfeiture. [IRC §§ 83, 402(b), 451; Ltr Rul 9030035, Apr 30, 1990]

Q 2:33   Are top-hat plan benefits and deferrals considered compensation for purposes of an employer's tax-qualified retirement plans and welfare benefit plans?

It now appears clear that including a top-hat plan participant's nonqualified plan contributions or salary deferrals in the participant's compensation for purposes of a tax-qualified deferred compensation plan is a violation of the rules of Code Sections 401(a)(4) and 414(s) requiring that compensation definitions in tax-qualified plans not discriminate in favor of highly compensated employees. However, amounts received by an employee under a top-hat plan and included in gross income in the year of receipt may be included in the tax-qualified plan's compensation definition. [Treas Reg §§ 1.415-2(d)(3)(i) and 1.414(s)-1(c)(2)] A number of the "safe harbor" Code Section 414(s) definitions permit the inclusion of top-hat plan distributions. Of course, because top-hat plan distributions usually occur after termination of employment or during the year of termination of employment (when recognizable tax-qualified plan compensation would be limited to the Code Section 401(a)(17) limit of $150,000), most or all top-hat plan amounts are never recognized under tax-qualified plans.

Although not as clear, it is arguable that the same rule applies to those types of welfare benefits that are subject to nondiscrimination rules (self-funded health plans, cafeteria or Section 125 plans, group term life insurance plans, dependent care assistance plans, and so on).

Therefore, employers should review both the terms of their qualified plan documents and the administrative procedures used thereunder to ensure that this rather subtle form of impermissible discrimination is not taking place. Also, if the employer desires top-hat plan distributions to be recognized under the qualified plan, it should review the qualified plan's definition of compensation to determine that the definition includes top-hat plan distributions in a manner permitted by Code Section 414(s). In addition, participants in nonqualified plans should be advised to consider that their non-qualified plan interests may not be taken into account for purposes of determining their benefits under the employer's qualified deferred compensation and welfare plans. Of course, any qualified retirement plan participant earning in excess of the Code Section 401(a)(17) limit on compensation (excluding top-hat plan distributions and salary deferrals) would be unaffected by these issues.

Q 2:34   Are top-hat plans subject to laws other than ERISA?

Although top-hat plans generally are exempt from state laws because of ERISA's preemption provisions, top-hat plans are subject to other applicable federal laws to the extent they are not inconsistent with ERISA (for example, the Age Discrimination in Employment Act, the Americans with Disabilities Act, and the Civil Rights Acts).

Case Study 2-1

Note: See Case Study 1-1 at the end of chapter 1.

The board members of ABC Corporation want to know whether the corporation may maintain a deferred compensation plan for a limited group selected by *A, B, C,* and *D*. Specifically, *A, B, C,* and *D* wish to include themselves and *F, H,* and *K*, the management team members who have the most long-term value to the corporation (and to its competitors), and possibly, the two outside directors.

The advisor explains that under a top-hat plan, not only may an employer limit participation in the nonqualified plan to a select group, but that unless the select group is composed exclusively of members of the employer's management or highly compensated employees, the plan may fail to be a top-hat plan and therefore become subject to ERISA. This would make the plan inflexible and expensive and difficult to operate. (The advisor adds that, because the outside directors are not employees of ABC, ERISA is not implicated with respect to their participation in a nonqualified plan.)

The advisor notes that *A, B, C,* and *D* clearly are members of this top-hat group. The advisor adds that *F* should qualify for membership in the top-hat group and that *H*, although not as highly compensated as *F*, should as well. The advisor warns *A, B, C,* and *D* that the Department of Labor (which has not issued authoritative guidance on this point) *might* consider *K*'s compensation too low to make her a member of the top-hat group, but that her management responsibilities as Vice President of Human Resources should be sufficient to qualify her for inclusion in the top-hat group. The advisor confirms that *G* and *I* may be excluded from the plan without legal effect, but that the exclusion of *J*, who is 60 years old and one of two minority group members on the management team, might not be wise, given the impact of various civil rights laws on top-hat plans.

The advisor informs *A, B, C,* and *D* that in order for the plan to enjoy the benefits of the available exemption from most of ERISA (unless the plan is limited to being an "excess benefit plan"), it will need to be "unfunded" as defined in ERISA and the tax laws, and ABC will need to make a one-time, simple filing with the Department of Labor within 120 days after the establishment of the plan.

A nonqualified plan is considered to be "unfunded" if no assets are set aside for the exclusive purpose of paying benefits under the plan. Maintaining this unfunded status is important not only so that the plan can obtain the top-hat plan exemption from most of ERISA, but in order to avoid earlier-than-desired taxation of plan participants under the economic benefit doctrine. However, even though assets may not be set aside for the exclusive purpose of paying plan benefits (at least not without incurring unwanted taxes), measures may be taken to add security that plan benefits will be paid when promised, such as the use of rabbi trusts, split-dollar life insurance, corporate-owned life insurance, surety bonds, and letters of credit.

Finally, the advisor reminds *A, B, C,* and *D* that contributions by the corporation to a top-hat plan would not be deductible until included in plan participants' incomes, that the plan would need to be designed and operated so as to avoid the unwanted application of the constructive receipt doctrine, and that earnings in any trust maintained in connection with the plan would be taxable as earned.

For more on ABC's excess benefit plan options see Case Study 3-1 at the end of chapter 3.

Chapter 3

Excess Benefit Plans

Excess benefit plans generally are used to provide "make-whole" benefits to employees whose benefits under the employer's qualified retirement plan(s) are limited by Code Section 415. This chapter examines excess benefit plans—what an excess benefit plan is, who establishes it, what the Code Section 415 limitations are, whether an excess benefit plan can be unfunded and the effect of such a characterization for ERISA purposes, the tax consequences, both to employers and employees, of establishing funded and unfunded excess benefit plans, and other related considerations such as the effect of the recently reduced Code Section 401(a)(17) compensation limitation on qualified retirement plan benefits.

Overview

Q 3:1   What is an excess benefit plan?

An excess benefit plan generally is a nonqualified plan that provides "make-whole" benefits to employees whose benefits under the employer's qualified retirement plan(s) are limited by the application of Code Section 415. ERISA Section 3(36) defines an "excess benefit plan" as:

> A plan maintained by an employer solely for the purpose of providing benefits for certain employees in excess of the limitations on contributions and benefits imposed by section 415 of the Internal Revenue Code of 1986 on plans to which that section applies, without regard to whether the plan is funded. To the extent that a separable part of a plan (as determined by the Secretary of Labor) maintained by an employer is maintained for such purpose, that part shall be treated as a separate plan which is an excess benefit plan.

The amount of the benefit that is provided to any one employee under an excess benefit plan generally is the difference between the amount the employee would have received under the employer's qualified retirement plan without applying the Section 415 limitations and the amount actually received under the qualified retirement plan. However, a plan may qualify as an excess benefit plan if its benefits are in excess of the Section 415 limitations and are determined without reference to the participants' qualified plan benefits but with reference to the Section 415 limitations (for example, a nonqualified plan that simply states that each qualified plan participant whose qualified plan benefits are limited by Section 415 will receive a nonqualified plan contribution of $10,000 per year). Note that, although the ERISA definition of excess benefit plan requires that such a plan be maintained solely for the purpose of providing benefits in excess of the Code Section 415 limits, the definition also permits separable excess benefit plan provisions ("as determined by the Secretary of Labor") to be combined with other types of provisions in a single arrangement. This concept was discussed in *Petkus v. Chicago Rawhide Manufacturing Company* [763 F Supp 357 (ND Ill 1991)].

In that case, the employee claimed that he had been improperly denied certain pension benefits promised him under the employer's SERP. The employee, believing the plan to be an unfunded excess benefit plan that was not governed by ERISA, informed the court that the court might no longer have subject matter jurisdiction over the matter because it involved only a state law contract dispute between nondiverse parties. However, the employer maintained that, because the plan contained provisions in addition to its Code Section 415 make whole provision, the plan was not an excess benefit plan exempt from ERISA and, therefore, was subject to ERISA's jurisdictional provisions. (The plan provided make-whole benefits with respect to Code Sections 401(a)(17)–415.)

The court referenced the portion of ERISA Section 3(36) that provides:

> [T]o the extent that a separable part of a plan (as determined by the Secretary of Labor) maintained by an employer is maintained for [excess benefit plan purposes] that part shall be treated as a separate plan which is an excess benefit plan.

(Note that whether or not part of a plan is "separable" is determined by the Secretary of Labor. As yet, there has been no further guidance on how to determine whether an excess benefit provision of a nonqualified plan is separable from other features of the plan. Presumably, a good faith, reasonable determination that the excess benefit feature is distinct enough to be separable will be upheld.)

According to the court, this ERISA provision supported the employee's view that the "solely" language of ERISA Section 3(36) does not necessarily preclude a particular plan from being an excess benefit plan that is exempt from ERISA, simply because the overall arrangement of which the plan is a part makes provision for other benefits, even benefits that might otherwise and independently be subject to ERISA.

Notwithstanding the conclusion of the court in *Petkus*, designers of excess benefit plans should consider the possible impact of the "as determined by the Secretary of Labor" requirement of the excess benefit plan definition before combining a separable excess benefit plan provision with other nonqualified plan provisions.

Q 3:2   Have any recent cases discussed the excess benefit plan definition?

Yes. In *Gamble v. Group Hospitalization and Medical Services* [CA 4th, No. 94-1020, (Oct 21, 1994)], the Fourth Circuit Court of Appeals ruled that a plan that was both unfunded and designed exclusively to provide benefits in excess of the limits of Code Section 415 was an excess benefit plan as defined in ERISA Section 3(36).

In *Gamble,* the employer-sponsor of the plan had encountered financial difficulties and had ceased making payments under the plan because it had been ordered to do so by the insurance commissioners of Virginia and the District of Columbia.

Because of the court's determination that the plan was an unfunded excess benefit plan as defined in ERISA Section 3(36), the court held that the plan was exempt from all of ERISA's requirements and, therefore, that the court lacked jurisdiction under ERISA to hear the participant's ERISA claim for benefits under the plan. The court added, however, that the participant was free to bring a state contract law claim for benefits under the non-ERISA-governed unfunded excess benefit plan. (The participant had argued unsuccessfully that the plan was designed to make the participant whole not only for losses under Code Section 415 but for losses under Code Section 401(a)(17), thereby causing the plan to be an ERISA top-hat plan rather than an unfunded excess benefit plan exempt from all of ERISA.)

Q 3:3   Who establishes an excess benefit plan?

The employer establishes and maintains the excess benefit plan. [ERISA § 3(36)]

Q 3:4   What are the limitations imposed by Code Section 415?

Code Section 415 provides limits on the contributions and benefits under qualified retirement plans. In general, Code Section 415(b) provides an annual limit on the benefits that may be paid to a participant in a qualified defined benefit pension plan equal to the lesser of (1) $90,000, indexed for cost of living increases ($118,800 in 1994), or (2) 100 percent of the participant's average "compensation" for the three consecutive calendar years during which the participant both was an active participant in the plan and had the greatest aggregate compensation from the employer.

In general, Code Section 415(c) provides an annual limit on the sum of employer contributions, employee contributions and forfeitures which may be allocated to the account of a participant in a qualified defined contribution retirement plan equal to the lesser of (1) $30,000 (to be indexed), or (2) 25 percent of the participant's "compensation" from the employer.

Q 3:5 How does a plan qualify as an excess benefit plan?

In order to qualify as an excess benefit plan, the sole purpose of the plan must be to provide benefits to participants that may not be provided through the employer's qualified retirement plans because of the limitations imposed by Code Section 415 on the participants' qualified retirement plan benefits.

Q 3:6 Why would an employer establish an excess benefit plan?

An employer may be interested in establishing an excess benefit plan for several reasons, including:

1. Attracting personnel;

2. Retaining employees;

3. Providing employees with an incentive for better service and increased productivity;

4. Creating goodwill between the employer and the plan participants;

5. Encouraging early retirement for some highly paid employees by providing them with greater benefits than those permitted under the employer's qualified retirement plans; and

6. Compensating participants for the loss (because of the Code Section 415 limits) of benefits otherwise earned under the employer's qualified retirement plans.

Q 3:7   Are there advantages to the employer and the employee in establishing an excess benefit plan?

Yes. An excess benefit plan offers advantages to the employer because it can be drafted to meet the specific needs of the employer. This is because an excess benefit plan generally is not governed by any strict statutory or regulatory framework (although funded excess benefit plans must meet certain ERISA requirements, see Q 3:16). An excess benefit plan offers advantages to the employee because it provides benefits in addition to the benefits provided under the employer's qualified retirement plan.

Q 3:8   What are the concerns for participants in an unfunded excess benefit plan?

The major concern for participants in an unfunded excess benefit plan (see Qs 3:11, 3:12) relates to the unsecured nature of the participants' benefits. A participant has the status of a general, unsecured creditor of the employer with respect to his or her unfunded excess benefit plan benefits, and, as a result, the participant may be concerned that he or she will never receive benefits under the plan, especially if the employer's financial condition is questionable.

Q 3:9   What are the most significant considerations for employers who establish excess benefit plans?

Unlike qualified retirement plans, an employer who establishes an excess benefit plan does not receive an income tax deduction for its contributions to the excess benefit plan until the contributions are includible in income by the participants. This often will not occur until years after the date on which the contribution is made. (See Qs 3:21–3:23 for more detail regarding the employer's deduction.)

Another concern for employers that relates to every excess benefit plan is that the plan's purpose, by definition, is limited to providing benefits to participants that may not be provided to them through the employer's qualified plans because of the limitations imposed by Code Section 415. A plan that is not designed carefully may provide other integrated, nonseparable benefits and therefore may cease to qualify as an excess benefit plan. However, such a plan may qualify as a top-hat plan (thereby avoiding many, if not all, of ERISA's requirements), as long as it satisfies the requirements applicable to top-hat plans (see chapter 2.) [ERISA § 3(36)]

ERISA Considerations

Q 3:10   Is an excess benefit plan subject to the various ERISA Title I requirements relating to participation, vesting, funding, fiduciary responsibilities, reporting and disclosure, enforcement, preemption, and so on?

Whether an excess benefit plan is subject to certain requirements under Title I of ERISA depends upon whether the plan is funded or unfunded. ERISA Section 4(b)(5) provides that an excess benefit plan is exempt from all the requirements of Title I of ERISA if it is unfunded. However, if the excess benefit plan is funded, the plan is subject to certain requirements under ERISA (see Q 3:16). [ERISA §§ 4(b)(5), 201(7), 301(a)(9)]

Q 3:11   Can an excess benefit plan be unfunded?

Yes, an excess benefit plan may be unfunded. To be considered unfunded, the benefits payable under the excess benefit plan must be payable from the employer's general assets, those assets must be available to pay the claims of the employer's general creditors, and a participant's rights to receive payments under the plan must be no greater than the rights of a general unsecured creditor of the employer. In addition, an excess benefit plan will be considered unfunded if the benefits payable under the plan are paid from assets held in a rabbi trust (see chapter 4). [DOL Adv Op 89-22A, Sept 21, 1989; DOL letter to Richard H. Manfreda, Chief, Individual Income Tax Branch, IRS, Dec 13, 1985]

Q 3:12   What does the term "unfunded" mean with regard to excess benefit plans?

Although ERISA does not define the term "unfunded," courts have held "unfunded" to mean that plan benefits are payable from the employer's general assets. The key to the term "unfunded" is that the assets that will be used to provide benefits under the plan are general assets of the employer. As a result, the participants in an unfunded excess benefit plan hold the status of general, unsecured creditors of the employer. In addition, no right or claim to unfunded excess benefit plan benefits by a participant or a participant's beneficiary may be assignable or alienable, nor may any right or claim be taken by the participant's or beneficiary's creditors by attachment, execution, levy, or other legal or equitable proceedings, except to the extent required by law. [Dependahl v Falstaff Brewing Corp, 653 F 2d 1208 (8th Cir 1981), *cert denied*, 454 US 968, 102 S Ct 512 (1981); Belka v Rowe Furniture Corp, 571 F Supp 1249 (D Md 1983); GCM 39230, Jan 20, 1984; Ltr Rul 8921048, Feb 24, 1989]

Q 3:13   Can an excess benefit plan be funded, and, if so, what funding techniques may be used?

Yes, an excess benefit plan may be funded. The funding of an excess benefit plan is accomplished by creating a separate fund or *res* to which participants may look for payment. The key to a funded plan is that assets are set aside for the exclusive purpose of providing benefits to participants, and those assets cannot be reached by the employer or its general creditors. Specific methods of funding an excess benefit plan include:

1. The establishment of a "secular trust" (see chapter 5); and
2. The purchase by the employer of insurance policies to be used exclusively to pay plan benefits (see chapters 6 and 7).

[Dependahl v Falstaff Brewing Corp, 653 F 2d 1208 (8th Cir 1981), *cert denied*, 454 US 968, 102 S Ct 512 (1981); GCM 39230, Jan 20, 1984]

Q 3:14   What does the term "funded" mean with regard to excess benefit plans?

In general, a plan is considered to be funded if assets are segregated or otherwise exclusively set aside as a source to which participants may look for payment of their plan benefits. [Dependahl v Falstaff Brewing Corp, 653 F 2d 1208 (8th Cir 1981), *cert denied*, 454

US 968, 102 S Ct 512 (1981); GCM 33373, Nov 21, 1966, as modified by GCM 35196, Jan 16, 1973, which was modified by GCM 35326, May 3, 1973]

Q 3:15   Are there favorable consequences when an excess benefit plan is considered to be unfunded?

Yes. If an excess benefit plan is considered to be unfunded, the plan is exempt from all requirements imposed by Title I of ERISA, including reporting and disclosure, participation and vesting, and funding and fiduciary responsibilities. [ERISA § 4(b)(5)]

Q 3:16   Are there unfavorable consequences when an excess benefit plan is considered to be funded?

Yes. Even if an excess benefit plan is considered to be funded, the plan is partially exempt from the ERISA Title I requirements. A funded excess benefit plan is exempt from Parts 2 and 3 of ERISA Title I, pertaining to participation, vesting, and funding rules. However, funded excess benefit plans are subject to the reporting and disclosure requirements of Part 1 of ERISA Title I, the fiduciary responsibility requirements, including the written plan requirements, of Part 4 of ERISA Title I, and the enforcement provisions of Part 5 of ERISA Title I. [ERISA §§ 101(a), 201(7), 301(a)(9), 401(a)] In addition, the designer of a funded excess benefit plan must consider the impact of the economic benefit doctrine and Code Sections 402(b) and 83 on the tax incidents of the plan (see Q 3:26).

Q 3:17   Is an excess benefit plan subject to the participation, vesting, and funding requirements imposed by Title I of ERISA?

No, an excess benefit plan, whether funded or unfunded, is not subject to either the participation and vesting rules of Part 2 of ERISA Title I or the funding rules of Part 3 of ERISA Title I. [ERISA §§ 4(b)(5), 201(7), 301(a)(9)]

Q 3:18 Is an excess benefit plan subject to the reporting and disclosure requirements imposed by Title I of ERISA?

It depends upon whether the excess benefit plan is funded or unfunded. If the excess benefit plan is funded, it will be subject to the reporting and disclosure requirements of Part 1 of ERISA Title I. However, if the excess benefit plan is unfunded, it will not be subject to those reporting and disclosure requirements. [ERISA §§ 4(b)(5), 101(a)]

Q 3:19 Is an excess benefit plan subject to the enforcement and administration provisions of Part 5 of ERISA Title I?

If the excess benefit plan is unfunded, it will not be subject to the enforcement and administration provisions, including the claims provisions under Section 503, of Part 5 of Title I of ERISA. However, if the excess benefit plan is funded, it will be subject to those requirements. [ERISA § 4(b)(5)]

Tax Consequences to the Employer

Q 3:20 How is an employer that establishes an excess benefit plan treated for tax purposes?

The employer's tax treatment depends upon whether the excess benefit plan is unfunded or funded (see Qs 3:21, 3:22).

Q 3:21 How is an employer that establishes an unfunded excess benefit plan treated for tax purposes?

The employer generally is not entitled to deduct a contribution made under an unfunded excess benefit plan in the year in which the contribution is made. Instead, the employer is entitled to deduct its contribution under the plan in the year in which an amount attributable to the contribution is includible in a participating employee's gross income. Generally, the employer may deduct the amount of the contribution, plus the amount of any earnings, that are distributed to the participant. [IRC § 404(a)(5); Ltr Rul 9025018, Mar 22, 1990; see Q 4:36]

Q 3:22 How is an employer that establishes a funded excess benefit plan treated for tax purposes?

An employer that sponsors a funded excess benefit plan is entitled to deduct its contribution to the plan in the year in which an amount attributable to the contribution is includible in a participating employee's gross income. Thus, the employer generally is entitled to deduct a contribution in the year in which the participant becomes vested in the contribution. [IRC § 404(a)(5); Treas Reg § 1.404(a)-12(b)(1); see Q 5:29]

In other words, the participant's rights to benefits held under the plan are subject to a substantial risk of forfeiture, the participant generally will not include the contribution in income until the substantial risk of forfeiture no longer applies, and the employer generally will not be entitled to a deduction until that time. [IRC §§ 83, 404(a)(5)]

In addition, the employer must maintain separate accounts for each participant in each funded plan covering more than one participant in order to be entitled to a deduction. [IRC § 404(a)(5); Treas Reg § 1.404(a)-12(b)(3); Wigutow v Comm'r, 46 TCM 1616 (1983), TC Memo 1983-620]

Q 3:23 Do the rules pertaining to "reasonable compensation" under Code Sections 162 and 212 apply to compensation received from an excess benefit plan?

Yes. Generally, an employer will be able to deduct amounts contributed to or paid under an excess benefit plan only if the requirements of Code Sections 162 or 212 are met. This means that a deduction is permitted only to the extent that the excess benefit plan contribution or payment is both reasonable in amount and an ordinary and necessary expense paid or incurred in carrying on a trade or business. [IRC §§ 83(h), 404(a)(5); Treas Reg § 1.83-6(a)(1)]

In the past, courts have generally scrutinized the reasonableness of the amounts contributed or paid under a nonqualified plan by looking to the employee's compensation package as a whole. Therefore, employers should ensure that each employee's nonqualified plan benefits are reasonable in amount when combined with the other elements of the employee's compensation package so the employer will be allowed the full deduction. [Treas Reg § 1.404(a)-12; Wigutow v Comm'r, 46 TCM 1616, 1630 (1983), TC Memo 1983-620]

Tax Consequences to the Employee

Q 3:24   How is an employee who benefits from an excess benefit plan treated for tax purposes?

The tax treatment of the employee depends upon whether the excess benefit plan is unfunded or funded (see Qs 3:25, 3:26).

Q 3:25   How is an employee who benefits from an unfunded excess benefit plan treated for tax purposes?

Generally, amounts contributed to an unfunded excess benefit plan are includible in the employee's gross income at the time these amounts are paid or made available to the employee. [IRC §§ 83, 402(b), 451; Rev Rul 60-31, 1960-1 CB 174 as modified by Rev Rul 64-279, 1964-2 CB 121 and Rev Rul 70-435, 1970-2 CB 100; Cowden v Comm'r, 32 TC 853 (1959), *rev'd and remanded,* 289 F 2d 20 (5th Cir 1961); *opinion on remand,* 20 TCM 1 134 (1961), TC Memo 1961-229]

However, to avoid having benefits under an excess benefit plan taxed prematurely under the doctrine of constructive receipt, employers must exercise caution with respect to the plan provisions specifying the manner of payment. For example, excess benefit plan provisions often make plan benefits payable at the same time and in the same manner as payments under the related qualified retirement plan. This type of provision may cause the employee unexpectedly to be in constructive receipt of income under the excess benefit plan if, for example, the qualified plan provides that the participant may make or change elections or have the right to "cash-out" his or her benefit in a lump sum after the date on which the excess benefit plan benefits first are payable. [See, e.g., Martin v Comm'r, 96 TC 39 (1991)]

Q 3:26 How is an employee who benefits from a funded excess benefit plan treated for tax purposes?

The employee is taxed at the time of the funding of the plan to the extent that the employee's plan interest is vested. In other words, if the employee's benefits are subject to a substantial risk of forfeiture and the benefits are not transferable, the employee will not be taxed on the contributions made to fund the plan until the contributions are no longer subject to the substantial risk of forfeiture or are transferable. [IRC §§ 83, 402(b)]

Q 3:27 What is a "substantial risk of forfeiture"?

In general, a substantial risk of forfeiture exists when the employee's rights to the excess benefit plan amounts are conditioned upon (1) the future performance, or nonperformance, of substantial services by any person, or (2) the occurrence of a condition related to a purpose of the transfer, and the possibility of forfeiture is substantial if the condition is not satisfied. [See, e.g., IRC § 83, Treas Reg § 1.83-3(c)]

Other Considerations

Q 3:28 How does the $150,000 compensation limitation contained in Code Section 401(a)(17) affect an excess benefit plan?

Prior to the enactment of TRA '86, the Code Section 415 limits were the primary limits on the permissible contributions and benefits under qualified retirement plans. TRA '86 added Code Section 401(a)(17), which imposed, in addition to the Code Section 415 limits, a limit on the amount of a participant's compensation ($200,000 indexed to $235,840 for 1993) that could be taken into account for purposes of a qualified retirement plan. OBRA '93 reduced this limit to $150,000 (indexed), effective in 1994. (See Q 1:27.) Under the statutory scheme, the Code Section 401(a)(17) limit is applied first to reduce the participant's compensation to the appropriate limit, the plan's formula then is applied to that reduced compensation, and the Code Section 415 limits then are imposed on the results.

Therefore, an excess benefit plan may be used only to make the participant whole for contributions or benefits lost under the last step of the foregoing process.

Example 1. A participant in a qualified defined contribution retirement plan providing for a 25 percent of compensation annual contribution has 1994 compensation of $300,000.

Without regard to the Code Sections 415 and 401(a)(17) limits, the participant would receive a contribution of $75,000 for 1994 (that is, $300,000 × 25 percent).

Under the statutory scheme, however, the participant's compensation is first reduced to the $150,000 limit of Code Section 401(a)(17). This reduced compensation is then multiplied by the 25 percent contribution formula, resulting in a preliminary contribution amount of $37,500. In other words, the effect of the Code Section 401(a)(17) limit is to reduce the participant's contribution by $37,500 (from $75,000 to $37,500). This shortfall may not be compensated for in an excess benefit plan because the shortfall is caused by Code Section 401(a)(17), not Code Section 415. (However, this shortfall may be compensated for in a top-hat plan which is not an excess benefit plan; that is, in an unfunded nonqualified plan generally subject to more of ERISA's rules than is an excess benefit plan (see chapter 2).

After calculating the participant's preliminary $37,500 contribution amount under the plan's formula, based on the reduced Code Section 401(a)(17) compensation, the Code Section 415 limits are applied. These limits will reduce the $37,500 amount to the lesser of (1) $30,000 or (2) 25 percent of Code Section 401(a)(17) compensation ($37,500) (that is, $150,000 × 25 percent). In other words, the Code Section 415 limits will reduce the preliminary contribution amount of $37,500 to $30,000, resulting in a shortfall of $7,500 to the participant. This $7,500 shortfall may be compensated for in an excess benefit plan because the shortfall is caused by Code Section 415.

Example 2. A participant in a qualified defined contribution retirement plan providing for a 25 percent of compensation annual contribution has 1994 compensation of $200,000.

Disregarding the limits imposed by Code Sections 415 and
401(a)(17), the participant would receive a contribution of
$50,000 for 1994 ($200,000 × 25 percent).

Under the statutory scheme, however, the participant's contribution
amount is calculated by first reducing the compensation amount to
the new, lower $150,000 limit under Section 401(a)(17) as amended
by OBRA '93. It is this reduced figure to which the 25 percent
contribution formula is applied, resulting in a preliminary contribution
amount of $37,500. The effect of the Code Section 401(a)(17) limit is
to reduce the participant's contribution by $12,500 (from $50,000 to
$37,500). This shortfall may not be compensated for in an excess
benefit plan because the shortfall is caused by Section 401(a)(17)
rather than by Section 415. (However, this shortfall may be compensated for in a top-hat plan, as in Example 1, above.)

After the Section 401(a)(17) limit is applied and the preliminary
contribution amount is calculated based on the reduced compensation, the Section 415 limits are applied. This reduces the preliminary amount of $37,500 to the lesser of:

1. $30,000 or

2. 25 percent of the $150,000 compensation limit set by Section
   401(a)(17) (that is, $37,500).

The Section 415 limit reduces the preliminary contribution
amount of $37,500 to $30,000: a shortfall of $7,500 for the
participant. As in Example 1, above, this shortfall may be
compensated for in an excess benefit plan because the shortfall
was caused by Section 415.

Employers should carefully consider the impact of the $150,000
Code Section 401(a)(17) limit of OBRA '93 on their excess benefit,
top-hat, and qualified plans.

**Q 3:29 Can an excess benefit plan be designed to be used in
connection with either a qualified defined contribution
retirement plan or a qualified defined benefit pension
plan?**

Yes. An employer may establish an excess benefit plan which
is used in connection with a qualified defined contribution retire-

ment plan. Such an excess benefit plan might provide for a contribution based upon the amount of the contribution that would have been made for the employee under the qualified plan but for the limitations under Code Section 415, over the amount actually contributed under the qualified plan for the employee (see Q 3:28).

The employer may also establish an excess benefit plan to be used in connection with a qualified defined benefit pension plan. Such an excess benefit plan might provide for a benefit equal to the difference between the annual benefit that would have been payable under the qualified plan to the employee under the qualified plan without regard to the benefit limitation under Code Section 415, over the annual benefit actually payable under the qualified plan to the employee after compliance with the benefit limitation. [See Ltr Ruls 8949060, Sept 12, 1989; 8921048, Feb 24, 1989; 8607022, Nov 15, 1985]

Q 3:30   Are any excess benefit plans subject to Title IV of ERISA, which provides rules concerning plan termination insurance?

No. No excess benefit plans are subject to the requirements of ERISA Title IV. [ERISA § 4021(b)(8)]

Q 3:31   If an excess benefit plan is subject to ERISA, what standard of review will a court apply when reviewing the excess benefit plan's denial of a benefit request by a participant?

It depends upon the language of the excess benefit plan. In *Firestone Tire and Rubber Co. v. Bruch,* the Supreme Court concluded that a denial of benefits challenged under ERISA Section 502(a)(1)(B) must be reviewed under a *de novo* standard (i.e., the court must make a full review and substitute its own decision for that of the plan administrator or other fiduciary) unless the benefit plan expressly gives the plan administrator or other fiduciary discretionary authority to determine eligibility for benefits or to construe the plan's terms. If the plan expressly gives this discretionary authority, the court must use a *deferential* standard of review that simply requires the court to determine that the decision was not arbitrary and capricious. The Court added that if an ERISA plan gives discretion to a plan administrator or fiduciary who is operating under a conflict of interest, that conflict must be weighed as a factor in determining whether there is an arbitrary and capricious abuse of discretion. [Firestone Tire and Rubber Co v Bruch, 489 US 101, 109 S Ct 948, 103 L Ed 2d 80 (1989)]

Case Study 3-1

Note: See Case Studies at the end of chapters 1 and 2.

A, *B*, *C*, and *D* ask their advisor to explain the concept of excess benefit plans. The advisor summarizes the concept by stating that the sole purpose of an excess benefit plan, funded or unfunded, is to provide participants with benefits in excess of those available under tax-qualified plans because of Code Section 415. As an example, the advisor reminds the group that the total annual contributions to a participant's account in the 401(k) plan may not exceed the lesser of $30,000 or 25 percent of the participant's compensation. The advisor notes that if, under the 401(k) plan contribution formula, *A* would receive an annual contribution of $32,000, this contribution would need to be reduced to $30,000 and the uncontributed $2,000 could be contributed to an excess benefit plan. However, any reduction of *A*'s 401(k) plan annual contribution because of, for example, the $7,000 (indexed) limit on salary reduction contributions, the $150,000 limit (indexed) on compensation which may be considered, or the average deferral percentage test may not be compensated for with an excess benefit plan.

The advisor emphasizes that, although the acceptable purpose of an excess benefit plan is rather limited, its primary advantages are that it may be funded (subjecting it to certain, but not all, ERISA requirements) and that its participants need not be limited to the top-hat group. However, participants in a funded excess benefit plan will pay taxes on their benefits when they vest.

The advisor then adds that, unlike the situation with a tax-qualified plan, ABC's contributions to any excess benefit plan would not be deductible until included in the gross incomes of participants, that participants would not receive any favorable tax treatment on distributions from the plan, and that earnings on any fund maintained in connection with the plan would be taxable as earned.

A, B, C, and D conclude that, although an excess benefit plan may be worth considering, its limitations make it incapable of satisfying all of the corporation's deferred compensation goals. The group agrees to keep the concept in mind and to devote the next meeting to a discussion of the concept of rabbi trusts.

Will a rabbi trust be the answer for ABC's highly compensated employees? See Case Study 4-1 at the end of chapter 4.

Chapter 4

Rabbi Trusts

A rabbi trust is a trust established by an employer to provide a source of funds that can be used to satisfy the employer's obligations to employees under one or more nonqualified plans. This chapter examines rabbi trusts—why a rabbi trust is established, whether the use of a rabbi trust in connection with a nonqualified plan will cause the plan to be funded, whether it is significant if a plan is funded or unfunded for tax and ERISA purposes, the criteria for obtaining a favorable letter ruling from the IRS concerning a rabbi trust, what rights employees' and employers' creditors have in the assets that are held in the rabbi trust, and the tax consequences, for both employers and employees, of using a rabbi trust in connection with a nonqualified plan.

Overview

Q 4:1   What is a rabbi trust?

A rabbi trust is a trust established by an employer to provide a source of funds which can be used to satisfy the employer's obligations to employees under one or more nonqualified plans. The trust is referred to as a rabbi trust because the first IRS letter ruling regarding this type of trust was issued to a rabbi whose congregation had established such a trust for him. In that ruling, the IRS determined that the rabbi (or his beneficiary) was not taxed on the funds in the trust until the funds were distributed to the rabbi (or his beneficiary) upon the rabbi's death, disability, retirement, or termination of employment. [Ltr Rul 8113107, Dec 31, 1980] Note that Letter Ruling 8113107 does not deal with a number of rabbi trust issues dealt with in subsequent rulings (for example, participant investment direction, hardship withdrawals, and mandatory employer funding obligations). Note also that although a rabbi trust is established to provide a source of funds which can be used to satisfy the employer's obligations under a nonqualified plan, these funds will be subject to the claims of all of the employer's creditors, including the nonqualified plan participants, in the event of the employer's bankruptcy or insolvency (see Q 4:5).

Q 4:2   Who establishes a rabbi trust?

The employer, as "settlor" or "grantor" of the trust, establishes a rabbi trust by entering into a trust agreement with a trustee (which is usually a bank or trust company). The plans for which benefits are paid from the trust can be top-hat plans (see chapter 2) or excess benefit plans (see chapter 3).

Practice Pointer. It is important to note the roles of the various parties under the nonqualified plan and trust agreements. The nonqualified plan is an agreement between the employer and the employee to provide deferred compensation benefits. The trust, however, is an agreement between the employer and the trustee under which the trustee holds contributions and earnings thereon for the purpose of satisfying employer obligations under the nonqualified plan. Some commentators believe that, even though participants receive payments from the trust and may be treated as third-party beneficiaries under state law, the participants should not be specific parties to the trust agreement (see Q 4:15, Model Rabbi Trust Provision). However, the more reasoned view is that, in order to provide maximum protection for the participants, they should be the named beneficiaries of the trust with full trust beneficiary rights under state trust law. Because of the continuing bankruptcy risk to trust assets, naming participants as full trust beneficiaries should not affect the tax attributes of the trust which are discussed later.

Q 4:3   Why would an employer establish a rabbi trust?

A common purpose for establishing a rabbi trust is to provide both actual and psychological assurance to participants that their respective benefits under the unfunded nonqualified plan will not be endangered by a solvent employer's cash flow demands, an un-friendly takeover of the employer, or an unfriendly change in the management of the employer. The assets in the trust must always be subject to some risk, however, because they must be subject to the claims of the employer's creditors (prioritized according to applicable bankruptcy law rules) in the event of the employer's bankruptcy or insolvency. (See Q 4:15, Model Rabbi Trust Provisions 1 and 5.) A rabbi trust also may be established by the employer, for its own purposes, to ensure that assets will be available for distribution to participating employees, thereby reducing or eliminating a financial strain on the employer, when it is time for distributions to occur. A third purpose may be to provide a vehicle of sufficient size to permit diversified investments of deferred amounts. [Ltr Rul 8418105, Jan 31, 1984]

Q 4:4   Can a single rabbi trust benefit more than one employee?

Yes. A rabbi trust may be established in connection with a non-qualified plan that permits more than one employee to benefit under the plan or in connection with a series of separate deferred compensation agreements with employees. [Ltr Rul 8845053, Aug 17, 1988] However, a separate account must be maintained for each employee.

Also, a rabbi trust may be used in connection with one or more nonqualified plans. For example, several affiliated corporations may have plans that use the same rabbi trust. Where several corporations participate in the same rabbi trust arrangement, identified subtrusts should be established so that if one corporation becomes bankrupt or insolvent, only the assets held in that corporation's subtrust will be used to satisfy the claims of that corporation's creditors and the remaining subtrusts will not be affected. (See Q 4:15, Model Rabbi Trust Provisions 1 and 5.)

ERISA Considerations

Q 4:5   Will the use of a rabbi trust in connection with a nonqualified plan cause the plan to be funded for tax or ERISA Title I purposes?

No. The establishment of a rabbi trust will not cause a participant's rights in the underlying nonqualified plan to be "funded" for tax purposes (under the economic benefit doctrine, or Code Sections 83 or 402(b))—thereby resulting in taxation to the participant when his or her interest in the trust becomes vested—because the funds in the trust have not been set aside *solely* for the benefit of the participant; that is, the funds in the trust are set aside for the benefit of the participant and the employer's bankruptcy and insolvency creditors.

In addition, the DOL has stated that the transfer of assets to a rabbi trust does not cause a nonqualified plan to be funded for purposes of Title I of ERISA. In 1985, the IRS asked the DOL to clarify whether the establishment of a rabbi trust in connection with a nonqualified plan caused the plan to be a funded plan for purposes of Title I of ERISA. The DOL stated that "[I]t has been the working premise of the Department that a 'top-hat' plan or excess benefit plan would not fail to be 'unfunded' solely because there is maintained in connection with such plan a 'rabbi trust' of the kind described in your letter." The DOL indicated that the positions adopted by the IRS regarding the tax consequences to trust beneficiaries of the creation of, or contributions to, a rabbi trust should be accorded significant weight by the DOL in determining whether a nonqualified plan is funded for ERISA Title I purposes. That is, if a nonqualified plan is found by the

IRS to be unfunded for tax purposes, the DOL is likely to conclude that the nonqualified plan is unfunded for ERISA Title I purposes. [Letter from Elliot I. Daniel, Assistant Administrator for Regulations and Interpretations, Pension and Welfare Benefits Administration to Richard H. Manfreda, Chief, Individual Income Tax Branch, Internal Revenue Service, Dec 13, 1985]

The DOL repeated its position on this issue in 1989 in response to a request for a determination as to whether the operation of a rabbi trust caused an excess benefit plan to be other than unfunded under ERISA Section 4(b)(5). The DOL stated that the plan would not fail to be unfunded solely because of the establishment and operation of the rabbi trust. [DOL Adv Op 89-22A, Sept 21, 1989; See also DOL Adv Op 90-14A, May 8, 1990]

In a 1991 letter to Kenneth E. Kempson, Acting Associate Chief Counsel (Technical) of the Office of Chief Counsel of the IRS, the DOL responded to his request for an advisory opinion as to whether a rabbi trust described in a draft Revenue Procedure would be considered unfunded for the purposes of the excess benefit and top-hat plan exemptions under Sections 4(b)(5), 201(2), 301(a)(3), and 401(a)(1) of Title I of ERISA. Specifically, Mr. Kempson requested an advisory opinion as to whether the establishment and operation of the model trust described in the draft Revenue Procedure, with the inclusion of one of the alternative mandatory employer contribution provisions, would cause an underlying excess benefit or top-hat plan to be other than unfunded for purposes of the exemptions under Sections 4(b)(5), 201(2), 301(a)(3), and 401(a)(1) of Title I of ERISA. (The draft Revenue Procedure was published by the IRS as Revenue Procedure 92-64, 1992-33 IRB 11, see Q 4:15.)

The DOL responded that it was the opinion of the DOL that a plan would not fail to be unfunded for purposes of Sections 4(b)(5), 201(2), 301(a)(3), and 401(a)(1) of ERISA solely because there was maintained in connection with the plan a rabbi trust that conformed to the model trust described in the draft Revenue Procedure. (See Q 4:15 for a discussion of the Model Rabbi Trust Revenue Procedure.) [DOL Adv Op 91-16A, Apr 5, 1991]

Q 4:6   Is it significant whether a rabbi trust causes a plan to be unfunded or funded for tax or ERISA Title I purposes?

Yes. If a plan is funded for tax purposes, participants would be taxed currently on any vested benefits under Code Sections 83 or 402(b) and/or the economic benefit doctrine (see Q 2:32). If a plan is funded for ERISA Title I purposes, the plan generally will have to satisfy the requirements contained in Title I of ERISA pertaining to participation and vesting, funding, and fiduciary requirements. If a plan is unfunded, the plan may be exempt from these tax effects and from these ERISA requirements.

Q 4:7   Which ERISA requirements apply to unfunded plans that are used to provide deferred compensation for employees?

Generally, unfunded nonqualified plans maintained by an employer primarily for the benefit of a select group of management or highly compensated employees (i.e., top-hat plans) are exempt from the participation and vesting, funding, and fiduciary responsibility rules of Title I of ERISA. These unfunded plans also are exempt from the plan termination insurance provisions under Title IV of ERISA, but are not exempt from the reporting and disclosure requirements of Part 1 of Title I of ERISA. However, Section 2520.104-23 of the DOL Regulations contains an alternative method of compliance with these latter requirements. Under this regulation, the reporting and disclosure requirements will be satisfied by the timely, one-time filing of a statement with the Secretary of Labor containing information identifying the plan and other limited information required by the regulation. [ERISA §§ 201(2), 301(a)(3), 401(a)(1), 4021(b)(6)]

An excess benefit plan as defined under ERISA Section 3(36) (described in Q 3:1) that is unfunded is exempt from all ERISA Title I and Title IV provisions. [ERISA §§ 4(b)(5), 4021(b)(8)]

Q 4:8   Which types of nonqualified plans are affected by whether or not they are considered to be funded for purposes of Title I of ERISA?

Under Title I of ERISA, whether a plan is funded is significant only if the plan is an ERISA pension plan. Generally, if the deferral period under a nonqualified plan is five years or less, and the plan does not systematically defer compensation until participants' termination of employment or beyond, it is not a pension plan subject to ERISA.

Q 4:9 How are funded and unfunded top-hat plans treated for purposes of Title I of ERISA?

A top-hat plan is an unfunded plan maintained by an employer primarily for the purpose of providing deferred compensation to a select group of management or highly compensated employees (see chapter 2). Pursuant to ERISA Sections 201(2), 301(a)(3), and 401(a)(1), these plans are exempt from Parts 2, 3, and 4 of ERISA Title I, which pertain to participation and vesting, funding, and fiduciary requirements. If a nonqualified plan is funded, the plan will fail to qualify for these exemptions, and the plan will be required to comply with all of the provisions of Title I of ERISA. [DOL letter to Richard H. Manfreda, Chief, Individual Income Tax Branch, IRS, Dec 13, 1985]

Typically, nonqualified plans cannot satisfy Title I of ERISA because they have design goals that would be restricted or prohibited under ERISA.

Q 4:10 How are funded and unfunded excess benefit plans treated for purposes of Title I of ERISA?

An excess benefit plan is defined in ERISA Section 3(36) as "a plan maintained by an employer solely for the purpose of providing benefits for certain employees in excess of the limitations on contributions and benefits imposed by Section 415 of the Internal Revenue Code of 1986 on plans to which that section applies, without regard to whether the plan is funded" (see chapter 3). Under ERISA Section 4(b)(5), a plan that is both unfunded and an excess benefit plan is exempt from all of ERISA Title I coverage. If an excess benefit plan is funded, however, the plan will fail to qualify for the exemption from all of ERISA Title I under ERISA Section 4(b)(5). The plan will be exempt only from Parts 2 and 3 (the participation, vesting, and funding requirements) of Title I of ERISA pursuant to the exemptions in ERISA Sections 201(7) and

301(a)(9). The reporting and disclosure requirements of Part 1 of that Title and the fiduciary responsibility requirements, including the written plan requirements, of Part 4 do, however, apply to the plan. [Letter from Elliot I. Daniel, Assistant Administrator for Regulations and Interpretations, Pension and Welfare Benefits Administration to Richard H. Manfreda, Chief, Individual Income Tax Branch, Internal Revenue Service, Dec 13, 1985; DOL Adv Op 89-22A, Sept 21, 1989]

In a 1991 advisory opinion, the DOL responded to a request by Kenneth E. Kempson, Acting Associate Chief Counsel (Technical) of the Office of Chief Counsel of the Internal Revenue Service for an advisory opinion as to whether the establishment and operation of a model rabbi trust described in a draft Revenue Procedure, with the inclusion of one of the alternative mandatory employer contribution provisions, would cause an underlying excess benefit or top-hat plan to be other than unfunded for purposes of the exemptions under Sections 4(b)(5), 201(2), 301(a)(3), and 401(a)(1) of Title I of ERISA. The DOL responded with the opinion that a plan would not fail to be unfunded for purposes of Sections 4(b)(5), 201(2), 301(a)(3), and 401(a)(1) of ERISA solely because there was maintained in connection with the plan a rabbi trust that conformed to the model trust described in the draft Revenue Procedure. (See Q 4:15 for a discussion of the Model Rabbi Trust Revenue Procedure.) [DOL Adv Op 91-16A, Apr 5, 1991; see Q 4:5]

Note that plans that provide any benefits other than Code Section 415 make-whole benefits (such as benefits intended to compensate employees for benefits lost because of the Code Section 401(a)(17) limit on compensation that may be taken into account by qualified plans) will not qualify as "excess benefit plans." (See chapter 3.)

Q 4:11   Will the IRS issue rulings on rabbi trusts?

Yes. The IRS will issue rulings on rabbi trusts that are used in connection with nonqualified plans. [Rev Proc 92-64, 1992-33 IRB 11, Aug 17, 1992]

Q 4:12   Is it necessary to obtain a favorable ruling from the IRS in order to establish a rabbi trust?

No. Although obtaining a favorable ruling from the IRS will provide employers and employees with some comfort in determining their tax liability with respect to a rabbi trust, favorable tax treatment can be established without a ruling. This is especially true now that the IRS has issued model rabbi trust language. In addition, seeking an IRS ruling on a rabbi trust is often an exercise in futility, because the IRS will not rule favorably on certain common rabbi trust provisions which clearly are supportable under existing tax law.

Q 4:13   Is it necessary to comply with all the IRS requirements for issuing a favorable ruling on a rabbi trust in order to establish a successful rabbi trust?

No. The IRS has promulgated strict ruling requirements—which, in many cases, fairly may be characterized as overly conservative—to ensure that trusts that receive favorable rabbi trust rulings are not likely to violate any of the myriad tax laws or doctrines that apply to these arrangements. Therefore, a rabbi trust may be designed and established that does not satisfy all of the IRS requirements for a favorable rabbi trust ruling but that qualifies for the desired tax treatment. Of course, careful consideration must be given to deviations from the IRS's ruling criteria, discussed in Qs 4:14–4:16.

IRS Considerations

Q 4:14   Are there specific criteria that are necessary to obtain a favorable rabbi trust ruling from the IRS?

Yes. The IRS has published two revenue procedures that provide guidance regarding the specific criteria that are necessary to obtain a favorable rabbi trust private letter ruling. [Rev Procs 92-64 and 92-65, 1992-33 IRB 11 and 16 (Aug 17, 1992)] (Summaries of the revenue procedures are provided in Qs 4:15 and 4:16, and the revenue procedures are reproduced in Appendix A.) However, the IRS states in Revenue Procedure 92-64 that, in appropriate but rare cases, favorable rulings could be issued to trusts not satisfying the specific criteria of the revenue procedures.

Q 4:15   Which guidelines will the IRS apply when reviewing a rabbi trust agreement?

On July 28, 1992, the IRS issued Revenue Procedures 92-64 and 92-65. [Internal Revenue Bulletin 1992-33] Revenue Procedure 92-64 contains a model rabbi trust that is intended to serve as a safe harbor for taxpayers that adopt and maintain rabbi trusts in connection with nonqualified plans. Revenue Procedure 92-65 amends Revenue Procedure 71-19, 1971-1 C.B. 698 with respect to the conditions under which the IRS will issue private letter rulings concerning the application of the doctrine of constructive receipt to nonqualified plans. The remaining portion of this question summarizes the features of Revenue Procedure 92-64.

Scope. The model trust provided in Revenue Procedure 92-64 is a safe harbor for taxpayers who adopt and maintain rabbi trusts in connection with nonqualified plans. Thus, if the model trust is used, an employee will not be in constructive receipt or incur an economic benefit solely on account of the adoption or maintenance of the trust. Note, however, that the use of a model rabbi trust is not a safe harbor with respect to the tax consequences to the taxpayer under the underlying nonqualified plan. However, a taxpayer who desires a private letter ruling with respect to the tax consequences of the underlying nonqualified plan may request such a ruling independently or in connection with a request for a ruling concerning the related rabbi trust.

Revenue Procedure 92-64 also contains general guidelines as to when the IRS will issue nonqualified plan/rabbi trust private letter rulings. Under these guidelines, the IRS will continue to rule on nonqualified plans that do not use a trust. (See Q 4:16.) The IRS also will rule on nonqualified plans that use the model trust. The IRS will not, however, rule on nonqualified plans that use a trust other than the model trust except in rare and unusual circumstances. [Rev Proc 92-64, 1992-33 IRB 11, § 3]

Special Ruling Requirements. Revenue Procedure 92-64 provides that the IRS will issue private letter rulings with respect to a nonqualified plan using a rabbi trust, or the rabbi trust alone, only if the following requirements are satisfied:

IRS's RABBI TRUST LETTER RULING REQUIREMENTS

1. If the taxpayer desires a ruling with respect to a nonqualified plan, the taxpayer must submit a copy of the plan. (The plan must comply with the IRS ruling guidelines with respect to nonqualified plans as described in Revenue Procedure 71-19, 1971-1 CB 698, and Revenue Procedure 92-65, 1992-33 IRB 16. See Q 4:16.)

2. The trust must conform to the model language provided in Section 5 of Revenue Procedure 92-64. These provisions must be adopted *verbatim* except where substitute language is expressly permitted.

3. The taxpayer must make the following representations:

    (a) The trust conforms to the model trust language contained in Revenue Procedure 92-64, including the order in which the sections of the model trust language appear.

    (b) The trust does not contain any inconsistent language in substituted portions or elsewhere that conflicts with the model trust language. Note, however, that the trust provisions may be renumbered if appropriate. Also, language in brackets in the model may be omitted and blanks in the model may be completed. In addition, the taxpayer may add sections to the model language, provided that the additions are not inconsistent with the model language.

    (c) The trust is a valid trust under state law and all the material terms and provisions of the trust, including the creditors rights clause, are enforceable under the appropriate state laws.

    (d) Taxpayers who desire a ruling on the underlying nonqualified plan must include a representation that the plan, as amended, is not inconsistent with the terms of the trust and must follow the guidelines contained in Revenue Procedure 92-65. (See Q 4:16.)

4. The taxpayer must submit a copy of the trust, and must underline or otherwise clearly mark all language substituted for model language and all language which is additional to the model language. Also, the taxpayer must indicate the location of the investment authority provision required by Revenue Procedure 92-64.

5. The trustee of the trust must be an independent third party that may be granted corporate powers under state law, such as a bank trust department or other similar party. [Rev Proc 92-64, 1992-33 IRB 11, §§ 3, 4]

Model Rabbi Trust. The model trust provisions provided in Section 5 of Revenue Procedure 92-64 contain all of the provisions necessary for operation of the trust except for provisions describing the trustee's investment powers. Provisions for investment powers should be agreed to by the employer and the trustee and provided in the trust. However, in order for the arrangement to be characterized, for tax purposes, as a trust rather than as an agency account, the trustee must be given some investment discretion, such as the authority to invest trust assets within broad guidelines established by the employer.

Practice Pointer. It appears that rabbi trusts under which the trustee has no investment discretion (so-called agency accounts) are not covered under the model rabbi trust (see Q 4:25).

The model trust provisions contain (i) required provisions, (ii) optional provisions, and (iii) alternative provisions. In order to qualify as a safe harbor trust, the required provisions must be contained, *verbatim*, in the trust. The trust must provide one or more (as appropriate) of the alternative provisions. The trust may contain any of the optional provisions or may contain substitute language, provided that the substitute language is not inconsistent with the optional provisions. A summary of the core features of the model rabbi trust provisions is provided below:

SUMMARY OF MODEL RABBI TRUST PROVISIONS

1. *Establishment:* The trust must provide that the employer wishes to establish a trust and to contribute assets to the trust that will be held in the trust, subject to the claims of the

employer's creditors in the event of the employer's insolvency, until paid to participants and their beneficiaries.

2. *Status Under ERISA:* The trust must provide that it is the intention of the parties that the trust constitute an unfunded arrangement and that the trust will not affect the status of the underlying nonqualified plan, for purposes of Title I of ERISA, as an unfunded plan maintained for the purpose of providing deferred compensation for a select group of management or highly compensated employees.

3. *Purpose:* The trust must provide that it is the intention of the employer to make contributions to the trust to provide itself with a source of funds to assist it in meeting its liabilities under the underlying nonqualified plan.

4. *Type of Trust:* The trust must state the duration of its existence. The trust may provide that it is (i) revocable, (ii) irrevocable, or (iii) irrevocable upon (a) a change of control, (b) a specified number of days following the issuance of a favorable IRS private letter ruling, or (c) upon approval by the employer's board of directors. The trust also must provide that it is intended to be a grantor trust of which the employer is a grantor within the meaning of Code Sections 671-677 and that the trust shall be construed accordingly.

5. *Participant's Rights:* The trust must provide that:

   (a) The principal of the trust and any earnings thereon shall be held separate and apart from other funds of the employer and shall be used exclusively for the purposes of plan participants and beneficiaries and general bankruptcy and insolvency creditors as set forth in the trust. The trust also must provide that plan participants and their beneficiaries will have no preferred claim on any trust assets, or any beneficial ownership interest in any assets of the trust. (Note that the latter requirement, although often repeated by the IRS, is fundamentally inconsistent with the entire purpose of establishing the trust and, therefore, probably should not be taken too literally.)

   (b) Any rights created under the plan and the trust will be mere unsecured contractual rights of plan participants and their beneficiaries against the employer. (Again, this requirement is fundamentally inconsistent with the fact that plan participants and beneficiaries have rights under state law as beneficiaries of the trust.)

(c) Any assets held by the trust will be subject to the claims of the company's general creditors under federal and state law in the event of insolvency.

6. *Funding:* The trust must indicate how and when the employer will make contributions to the trust. The trust may provide either that the trust will be funded from time to time by the employer in its sole discretion or that the trust is required to be funded upon a change of control of the employer or within a specified number of days after the trust has become irrevocable (that is, a springing rabbi trust). If the funding is in the employer's discretion, neither the trustee nor any plan participant or beneficiary may have any right to compel additional deposits.

If the trust is required to be funded upon a change of control, the trust must objectively define the term "change of control." An option in the model trust defines the term as follows:

> [T]he purchase or other acquisition by any person, entity or group of persons within the meaning of section 13(d) or 14(d) of the Securities Exchange Act of 1934 (Act), or any comparable successor provisions, of beneficial ownership (within the meaning of Rule 13d-3 promulgated under the Act) of 30 percent or more of either the outstanding shares of common stock or the combined voting power of the employer's then outstanding voting securities entitled to vote generally, or the approval by the stockholders of the employer of a reorganization, merger, or consolidation, in each case, with respect to which persons who were stockholders of the employer immediately prior to such reorganization, merger or consolidation do not, immediately thereafter, own more than 50 percent of the combined voting power entitled to vote generally in the election of directors of the reorganized, merged or consolidated employer's then outstanding securities, or a liquidation or dissolution of the employer or of the sale of all or substantially all of the employer's assets.

Practice Pointer. Note that the term funded, as used in Section 6, refers merely to an obligation to transfer assets to the trust. The nonqualified plan maintained in connection with the trust still is treated as unfunded for tax and ERISA Title I purposes.

  7. *Payment Schedule:* The trust must provide the following provisions relating to the payment of benefits to participants:

    (a) The employer will deliver to the trustee a payment schedule that indicates the amounts payable with respect to each plan participant or provide a formula for determining the amounts payable.

    (b) The payment schedule also must provide the form in which benefits will be paid and the time of commencement of benefits.

    (c) The amount and payment of participants' benefits must be determined under the plan and any claim for benefits must be considered and reviewed under procedures contained in the plan.

    (d) The employer may pay benefits directly to the participants and will notify the trustee if it does so.

    (e) If the amounts held in the trust are not sufficient to pay benefits under the plan, the employer will make the balance of each payment as it becomes due.

  8. *Trustee Responsibility:* The trust must provide that the trustee will cease payment of benefits to plan participants and their beneficiaries if the employer is insolvent.

  9. *Definition of Insolvency:* The trust must provide that the employer will be considered insolvent for purposes of the trust if the employer is unable to pay its debts as they become due or if the employer is subject to a pending proceeding as a debtor under the U.S. Bankruptcy Code. The trust also may provide that the employer is insolvent if the employer is determined to be insolvent by a federal and/or state regulatory agency (for example, if the employer is a bank which generally is not subject to the U.S. Bankruptcy Code).

10. *Notice Requirement:* The trust must provide that the board of directors and the chief executive officer (or the highest ranking officer) of the employer will have the duty to inform the trustee

in writing of the employer's insolvency. If a person claiming to be a creditor of the employer alleges in writing to the trustee that the employer has become insolvent, the trustee will determine whether the employer is insolvent and, pending such determination, the trustee will discontinue payment of benefits to plan participants or their beneficiaries. The trustee may resume the payment of benefits to plan participants or beneficiaries only after the trustee has determined that the employer is not insolvent or is no longer insolvent.

11. *Employer Stock:* The trust may permit the trustee to invest in securities (including stock or rights to acquire stock) or obligations issued by the employer. If, however, the trust may invest in company stock, the trust also must provide either that the trust is revocable or that the employer will have the right at any time, and from time to time in its sole discretion, to substitute assets of equal fair market value for any assets held by the trust. This right must be exercisable by the employer in a nonfiduciary capacity without the approval or consent of any person in a fiduciary capacity.

In a 1992 letter to William J. Kilberg of Gibson, Dunn & Crutcher, the DOL responded to his request for an advisory opinion concerning whether a rabbi trust which is designed to invest primarily in employer stock would be considered to be unfunded for purposes of the excess benefit and top-hat plan exemptions under Sections 4(b)(5), 201(2), 301(a)(3), and 401(a)(1) of Title I of ERISA. According to the opinion, the employer establishing the rabbi trust would make cash contributions to the trust at its sole discretion which would be invested primarily in the employer's common stock, purchased by the trustee on the open market. Dividends on the stock would be reinvested in the employer's common stock. The trustee would have full voting rights with respect to the stock. The opinion also notes that Mr. Kilberg submitted a copy of a private letter ruling that the employer received from the IRS concerning the trust. The opinion further notes that the conclusions reached by the IRS on the tax issues indicate that the employer's contributions to the trust will not result in current taxation to plan participants (that is, that the plan is unfunded for tax purposes). The DOL determined that the plan will not fail to be unfunded for purposes of ERISA Sections 4(b)(5), 201(2), 301(a)(3), and 401(a)(1) solely because of the establishment and operation of the trust described in the opinion. [DOL Adv Op 92-13A, May 19, 1992] The IRS has issued at least one private letter ruling, 9235006, approving a rabbi trust that permits the investment of rabbi trust assets in employer stock.

Revenue Procedure 92-64 became effective on July 28, 1992. Accordingly, ruling requests with respect to rabbi trusts used in connection with nonqualified plans and subject to the claims of the employer's bankruptcy and insolvency creditors that were submitted to the IRS subsequent to that date must comply with the terms of the revenue procedure. Also, the revenue procedure does not affect any private letter rulings that were issued prior to the effective date. If, however, a plan or trust that was the subject of such a ruling is amended and the amendment affects the rights of participants or other creditors, the ruling generally will not remain in effect.

Q 4:16 What general guidelines will the IRS apply when reviewing a nonqualified plan in conjunction with a rabbi trust?

Revenue Procedure 92-65, 1992-33 I.R.B. 16, which amplified Revenue Procedure 71-19, 1971-1 C.B. 698, contains the IRS ruling position concerning the application of the doctrine of constructive receipt to certain aspects of nonqualified plans. This revenue procedure, along with Revenue Procedure 71-19, provides the guidelines that the IRS applies when reviewing these aspects of a nonqualified plan. A summary of those guidelines and other IRS informal ruling requirements are as follows:

IRS's NONQUALIFIED PLAN LETTER RULING REQUIREMENTS

1. *Plan Type:* The plan must be an unfunded top-hat plan or an excess benefit plan as discussed in chapters 2 and 3.

2. *Employees:* Chapters 2 and 3 discuss in general terms the classes of employees who may participate in a top-hat plan or an excess benefit plan. In addition to those requirements, the IRS will decline to issue nonqualified plan rulings with respect to two classes of individuals, unidentified independent contractors and controlling shareholders of a company who are

allowed to participate in a plan. Under prevailing law, a controlling shareholder, because of his or her ability to control the employer and, therefore, to accelerate his or her plan payments or waive conditions thereon, generally may not effectively defer compensation for tax purposes from the controlled corporation by the use of a nonqualified plan.

3. *Status Under ERISA:* The plan must state that it is the intention of the parties that the plan and trust agreement be treated as unfunded for tax purposes and for purposes of Title I of ERISA.

4. *Initial Election:* If a nonqualified plan provides for an election to defer payment of compensation, the election must be made before the beginning of the period of service for which the compensation is payable, regardless of any forfeiture provision in the arrangement. [Rev Proc 71-19, 1971-1 CB 698, § 3.01, see also, Rev Proc 92-65, 1992-33, IRB 16] Typically, the term "period of service" refers to a calendar year, although the IRS position provides that a bonus plan may be based on the company's fiscal year. Therefore, in order to receive a favorable ruling, the IRS requires that an election to defer normally must be made prior to the end of a calendar (or fiscal) year in order to defer compensation earned in the next calendar (or fiscal) year.

Practice Pointer. There are two exceptions to the IRS ruling position rule on the timing of initial deferral elections. First, in the year in which the plan is first implemented, eligible participants may make an election, after the beginning of the calendar year, to defer compensation for services to be performed subsequent to the election, as long as the election is made within 30 days after the date the plan is first effective for the participants. Second, in the first year in which a participant becomes eligible to participate in the plan, the newly eligible participant may make an election, after the beginning of the calendar year, to defer compensation for services to be performed subsequent to the election as long as the election is made within 30 days after the date the employee becomes eligible. [See Rev Proc 92-65, 1992-33 IRB 16, § 3.01]

5. *Subsequent Elections:* If a plan provides for an election other than the initial election to defer compensation, the subsequent

election must be made prior to the beginning of the period of service (generally, the calendar or fiscal year) to which the deferred compensation relates or contain a substantial forfeiture provision that remains in effect throughout the entire period of deferral. The imposition on a right to deferred compensation of a substantial forfeiture provision, as described by the IRS, should be considered carefully because it must impose a significant limitation or duty upon the employee that requires a meaningful effort by him or her to fulfill, and there must be a definite possibility that the event which will cause the forfeiture actually could occur. [Rev Proc 71-19, 1971-1 CB 698, § 3.02] For example, if a corporation transfers to an employee 100 shares of stock in the corporation, at $90 per share, and the employee is obligated to sell the stock to the corporation at $90 per share if the employee terminates employment with the corporation for any reason prior to the expiration of a two-year period of employment, the employee's rights to the stock are subject to a substantial risk of forfeiture during the two-year period. [Treas Reg § 1.83-3(c)(4) Ex 1; see also, Ltr Rul 9030028, Apr 27, 1990]

The following examples illustrate common subsequent election provisions that often cause the IRS not to rule favorably on a nonqualified plan:

(a) A plan provision that permits the employee to choose or change the time or form of the payment of benefits at some specified time after the beginning of the period of service but before the receipt of such benefits.

(b) Any election concerning the time or form of benefits payable from an ongoing excess benefit plan where benefits are based, in part, on past service.

(c) An excess benefit plan provision that links the time and/or form of payment of benefits to a similar election made by the participant with respect to his or her qualified plan benefits. This is a constructive subsequent election under the excess benefit plan if the qualified plan permits elections after the beginning of the period of service under the excess benefit plan.

[Ltr Rul 8844031, Aug 8, 1988, revoking Ltr Rul 8735047, June 3, 1987]

Note that these IRS ruling positions are more conservative than the prevailing case law.

Practice Pointer. The subsequent election rules do not apply to elections to direct investments or choose beneficiaries or to hardship withdrawal requests. Consequently, these elections and requests can be made at any time before or after the beginning of the period of service.

6. *Change in Amounts Deferred:* If a plan provides for an election to change the amount deferred, the election must be made before the period of service during which the compensation affected by the election is to be earned. The IRS takes the informal position that this should be done on a yearly basis, although prevailing case law would appear to permit changes at any time, as long as they apply only to compensation not yet payable. The IRS takes the informal position that a plan may permit a participant to revoke his or her election to defer, but such revocation must be done with respect to amounts yet to be earned and the plan must provide that the participant may not elect to defer again until the next calendar year. This latter IRS position is not supported by existing case law.

7. *Payment of Benefits:* The plan must specifically define the time and form for payment of deferred compensation in each event (such as termination of employment, regular retirement, disability retirement, or death) that entitles a participant to receive benefits. The plan may specify the date of payment or provide that payments will begin within 30 days after the occurrence of the stated event. [See Rev Proc 92-65, 1992-33 IRB 16, § 3.01]

8. *Triggering Events:* The IRS will rule on plans that provide benefits upon retirement (normal, early, or late), death, complete and permanent disability, termination of employment, unforeseeable emergency of the participant, or termination of the plan. The plan may not permit a participant to choose between triggering events. For example, the following provisions both contain proper triggering events, but the first provision is acceptable to the IRS, while the second provision is treated as a subsequent election and is unacceptable:

(a) The participant will begin receiving benefits upon the later of the participant's obtaining age 65 or the participant's termination of employment.

(b) The participant will begin receiving benefits, at the participant's election, upon either obtaining age 65 or terminating employment with the employer.

The IRS will not issue a favorable ruling with respect to a plan that contains a triggering event other than the events described above. In particular, the IRS will not rule with respect to deferrals for a term of years (unless the term of years definitely will expire after the participant's retirement age) or until a change in control of the employer has occurred. However, if properly structured and administered, these latter designs should not result in adverse tax consequences.

Practice Pointer. The IRS has ruled favorably, however, when a plan provided that benefits would be payable in the event of retirement, death, or "termination of employment that occurs in connection with a change of control in the company." This is acceptable because termination of employment is the trigger for benefits, and the change of control is merely a condition to the triggering event. [Ltr Rul 9103018, Oct 19, 1990]

9. *Emergency Withdrawal Provisions:* The plan may provide for payment of benefits in the case of an unforeseeable emergency. The term "unforeseeable emergency" must be defined in the plan as an unanticipated emergency that is caused by an event beyond the control of the participant or beneficiary and that would result in severe financial hardship to the individual if early withdrawal were not permitted. The plan must further provide that any early withdrawal approved by the employer is limited to the amount necessary to meet the emergency (presumably considering any taxes due on the distribution). Language similar to that described in Treasury Regulation Section 1.457-2(h)(4) and (5) may be used for this purpose. Other definitions of unforeseeable emergency which are sufficiently unambiguous and beyond the control of the participant also should be effective.

10. *Investment Discretion:* The IRS will rule with respect to a plan that permits a participant to choose investments for the

amounts credited to his or her nonqualified plan account. Also, a plan may provide that a participant can change the investments for amounts already deferred. This will not be treated as a subsequent election. The IRS adds that the plan should provide, however, that the employer shall at all times be the owner and beneficiary of assets held for the participant. (See Q 4:26) However, in a rabbi trust setting, it should be sufficient for the legal owner to be the trustee and the beneficial owner to be the participant (with the employer being treated as the owner for tax purposes).

11. *Loan Provisions:* The plan may not provide that a participant may borrow money from the employer with the participant's account balance as security. Also, the plan may not provide that, upon termination of employment, the employer may offset any indebtedness against the participant's account. Such provisions arguably give the participant more than an unfunded promise to be paid and may cause problems under the economic benefit doctrine.

12. *Nature of the Obligation:* The IRS requires that the plan provide that participants have the status of general unsecured creditors of the employer and that the plan constitute a mere promise by the employer to make benefit payments in the future. If the plan refers to a trust, the plan also must provide that any trust created by the employer and any assets held by the trust to assist the employer in meeting its obligations under the plan will conform to the terms of the model trust as described in Revenue Procedure 92-64.

13. *Nonassignability:* The plan must provide that a participant's or beneficiary's rights under the plan are not subject in any manner to anticipation, alienation, sale, transfer, assignment, pledge or encumbrance, attachment or garnishment by creditors of the participant or the participant's beneficiary. This is necessary in order to avoid problems under the economic benefit doctrine.

14. *Termination:* A plan may provide for an acceleration of benefits in the event of a termination of the plan as long as:

    (a) Everyone is paid benefits in the same manner; and

(b) Participants may not control the decision as to whether the plan should be terminated. (As a result, a plan with a participant who controls the employer may not be able to use this triggering event.)

Note that the above reflects the IRS's ruling positions, positions which are, in some cases, more conservative than the prevailing case law. For example, elections to defer made after the beginning of a calendar year should be effective, as long as they apply only to compensation not yet earned or, under a more aggressive but supportable view, not yet payable.

Q 4:17 What kinds of rulings can an employer receive from the IRS with respect to a rabbi trust?

The following are the five parts, typically, of an IRS rabbi trust ruling:

1. The employer will be treated as the owner of the trust, for tax purposes, under Code Section 677 and Section 1.677(a)-1(d) of the Regulations. Under Code Section 671, the employer must include all of the income, deductions, and credits of the trust in computing its own taxable income and credits.

2. Placing assets in the trust will not be a transfer of property for purposes of Code Section 83(a), or a transfer to a nonexempt trust under Code Section 402(b).

3. The adoption of the plan and trust and the contributions to the trust and earnings thereon will not cause any amount to be included in the gross income of a participant or beneficiary under the constructive receipt doctrine or the economic benefit doctrine.

4. Under Code Section 451, amounts distributable from the trust (as provided for in the plan) to a participant or beneficiary who uses the cash receipts and disbursements method of accounting will be includible in gross income for the year in which the amounts actually are received or otherwise made available. [Ltr Rul 9050014, Sept 13, 1990]

5. Contributions by the employer to the trust will be deductible by the employer under Code Section 404(a)(5) only in the taxable year in which those amounts are includible in the gross

income of the participant, to the extent that they are ordinary and necessary expenses within the meaning of Code Section 162. [Ltr Rul 9021056, Feb 27, 1990]

Practice Pointer. If the agreement between the employer and the trustee is treated as creating an agency relationship instead of a trust (see Q 4:24), the employer will not receive a trust ruling under Code Section 671 as described above. Instead the employer will receive a ruling that the employer will be treated as the owner, for tax purposes, of assets held by the trustee and will include all of the income, deductions, and credits of the assets in computing its own taxable income and credits. [Treas Reg § 1.61-13(b)] Such a trustee is not a "fiduciary" within the meaning of Code Section 7701(a)(6), and, therefore, will not be required to file a Form 1041, U.S. Fiduciary Income Tax Return. [Ltr Rul 9016061, Jan 23, 1990]

Q 4:18   Can a rabbi trust ruling be subject to any conditions?

A rabbi trust ruling may be subject to some or all of the following conditions:

1. The IRS expresses no opinion as to the consequences of the underlying nonqualified plan under Title I of ERISA.

2. Rulings on nonqualified plans using the model rabbi trust will provide that the IRS expresses no opinion on the consequences under Subchapter C of chapter 1 of Subtitle A of the Code or under Sections 1501–1504 on the trust's acquisition, holding, sale, or disposition of stock of the grantor. [Rev Proc 92-64, 1992-33 IRB 11]

3. The ruling is applicable only if the creation of the trust does not cause the plan to be other than unfunded for purposes of Title I of ERISA.

4. The ruling is applicable only if the trust provisions requiring use of trust assets to satisfy claims of the company's general bankruptcy and insolvency creditors are enforceable by those creditors under federal and state law. (This caveat raises at least theoretical issues when the applicable state bankruptcy law gives the employer's employee-creditors priority for some purposes over other creditors of the employer.)

5. This ruling may not remain in effect if the terms or operation of any applicable documents are changed. [Ltr Rul 9050014, Sept 13, 1990]

Q 4:19   Has the IRS received any comments on the model rabbi trust published in Revenue Procedure 92-64?

Early in 1995, the IRS reported that it had received five comments on the model rabbi trust published in Revenue Procedure 92-64. According to the IRS, four of the comments were of a technical nature and the fifth noted that, under the federal statute governing financial institutions, the definition of insolvency contained in the model rabbi trust is inapplicable to employers governed by that statute and should be replaced for those rabbi trust employer-sponsors with the special insolvency definition in that statute. The IRS did not provide any detail on the four technical comments or disclose whether it plans to make changes to the model rabbi trust to reflect any of the five comments.

Q 4:20   Can state bankruptcy law preferences result in rabbi trusts being funded for ERISA and tax purposes?

As noted at item 4 of Q 4:18, the IRS has noted, and the DOL has concurred, that if, under applicable state bankruptcy law, an employee-participant in a nonqualified plan would have a priority over other general unsecured creditors of the employer with respect to assets in a rabbi trust maintained in connection with the nonqualified plan, the plan could be determined to be funded, with the attendant adverse tax and ERISA consequences discussed above. However, this point has never been developed or applied by the IRS or the DOL.

Because virtually all states give employees a limited bankruptcy preference over other creditors with respect to recently earned wages, this IRS/DOL position does cause at least a theoretical concern about some of the assets in any particular rabbi trust. However, at present, neither the regulators nor commentators and practitioners have altered their use or view of rabbi trusts because of this issue. Employers using rabbi trusts in connection with their nonqualified plans should monitor any developments on this issue and react appropriately.

Q 4:21   Can an employer use a vesting schedule in a nonqualified plan that is used in connection with a rabbi trust?

Yes. A vesting schedule may be used in a nonqualified plan. Of course, even when the employee becomes vested in his or her benefits under the plan, the assets of any underlying rabbi trust will continue to be subject to the claims of the employer's creditors in the event of the employer's insolvency or bankruptcy. What this means is that an employee will have a vested interest in a promise to be paid, secured only by the rabbi trust. This is a less valuable interest than a vested interest in a qualified plan, the assets of which are beyond the reach of all of the employer's creditors. [Ltr Rul 8834015, May 25, 1988]

Q 4:22   Are the assets held in a rabbi trust subject to assignment by the employee or attachment by his or her creditors?

No. Legal title to the assets held in a rabbi trust is owned by the trustee, beneficial title is owned by the participants, and, pursuant to the terms of the trust, the assets are subject to the claims of the employer's general bankruptcy and insolvency creditors. The trust must provide that the assets may not be anticipated, assigned (either at law or in equity), alienated, pledged, encumbered, or subjected to attachment, garnishment, levy, execution, or other legal or equitable process, except in the employer bankruptcy/insolvency situation. [GCM 39230, Jan 20, 1984; Ltr Ruls 8843045, Aug 3, 1988; 8743065, July 29, 1987; 8711033, Dec 12, 1986]

Q 4:23   What rights do employees have in the assets that are held in a rabbi trust?

Employees have the rights of contingent, state trust law beneficiaries with respect to the assets held on their behalf in a rabbi trust. In other words, they are entitled to the same protections under state fiduciary laws as the beneficiaries of any trust (for example, the right to have the trustee hold trust assets, as a fiduciary, solely for their benefit pursuant to the terms of the trust, the right to hold the trustee liable for certain trust losses, the right to demand trust accountings, and so forth).

Q 4:24   Can individuals direct the investment of assets held in a rabbi trust?

Yes. As discussed in Q 4:16, the IRS will issue favorable rulings on plans that permit participants to direct the investment of amounts held in their accounts. For example, in one ruling, the IRS indicated that the assets of a rabbi trust may be invested by the trustee in its discretion, taking into account, to the extent the trustee deems advisable, instructions from the participants. The IRS also ruled favorably on a plan that allowed semiannual changes in the self-directed investment election. In another ruling, the IRS indicated that plans may provide for participant directed investments. Under this arrangement, participants were permitted to direct that amounts attributable to their deferred compensation be invested in certain investment vehicles, such as U.S. Treasury Notes, a fixed income fund, an equity fund, a money market fund, or life insurance. The IRS also ruled favorably on an arrangement that permitted participants to direct amounts credited to their accounts to be invested in one or more hypothetical investment funds.

Note that taxable employers may want to consider limiting the investment vehicles available as choices under a plan to tax-exempt investments, such as municipal bonds, so that the tax (payable by the employer) on the earnings may be avoided. [Ltr Ruls 8952037, Sept 29, 1989; 8834015, May 25, 1988; 8804023, Oct 30, 1987; 8607022, Nov 15, 1985; 8507028, Nov 20, 1984]

Note, however, that the model rabbi trust contained in Revenue Procedure 92-64 provides that, in order for the arrangement to be characterized as a trust, as opposed to an agency account, for tax purposes, the trustee must be given some investment discretion such as the authority to invest within broad guidelines established by the parties (for example, to invest in government securities, bonds with specific ratings, or stocks of Fortune 500 companies). [See Rev Proc 92-64, 1992-33 IRB 11, § 5.01.] Except for the fact that trustees of agency accounts need not file annual Form 1041s with the IRS, this distinction is immaterial, for tax purposes, to employers.

Q 4:25 Has the IRS expressed concerns where participants have the discretion to direct plan investments?

Yes. The IRS has, in the past, expressed concerns about participants having unbridled discretion over directing plan investments. These concerns are not currently being articulated and would appear to be without support under current law. The IRS's historical concerns where a participant has unbridled investment discretion are as follows:

1. Whether the participant would be viewed as having more rights than a mere "unfunded, unsecured promise to be paid," so that the rabbi trust arrangement would not be treated as unfunded for purposes of Title I of ERISA.

2. Whether the rabbi trust should be treated as a trust for tax purposes or, in the alternative, as an agency account.

With regard to the first concern, if the trust is considered funded and the plan is not an excess benefit plan, the plan generally will have to comply with all the requirements in Title I of ERISA (see Q 4:7). However, the impact of a characterization of a rabbi trust arrangement as a mere agency account is not as obvious. In addition to the differing applications of the Form 1041 filing rules as discussed above, if the arrangement is found to be an agency account, investment cannot be made in a bank's common trust funds.

Therefore, although many employers do not care whether their arrangement is characterized as a trust or an agency account, trustees that intend to invest the assets of the account in a common trust fund would disapprove of an agency account ruling.

Resolution of this issue involves a determination regarding whether the trustee has sufficient discretionary powers so that the agreement may be classified as a trust for tax purposes. If the trustee does not have sufficient discretionary powers, the trustee will be treated, for tax purposes but not for state law purposes, as acting as an agent for the employer and not as a trustee. Because a trustee for a rabbi trust typically has very little general discretionary authority, the discretion to determine the investments of the trust often is determinative on this point. Accordingly, plans that gave the trustee no investment discretion are viewed as agency accounts. In fact, there were several rulings issued in recent years that provided that the establishment of a rabbi trust created an agency account, for tax purposes. [See Ltr Ruls 9021056, Feb 27, 1990; 9016061, Jan 23, 1990; 8942040, July 24, 1989] The result of a determination that an agency account exists is that, instead of receiving a rabbi trust ruling under Code Section 671, the employer would receive an agency account ruling. Note that the rulings are identical in all other respects.

Note that the model rabbi trust contained in Revenue Procedure 92-64 provides that the trustee must be given some investment discretion, such as the authority to invest within broad guidelines established by the employer. This revenue procedure apparently is intended to apply to rabbi trust arrangements that previously could have received agency account private letter rulings. Accordingly, it is unclear whether the IRS will continue to entertain agency account ruling requests. [Rev Proc 92-64, 1992-33 IRB 11, § 5.01]

Q 4:26 What rationale has the IRS used to resolve whether an employer's rabbi trust arrangement should be treated as a trust or agency account?

The authority and rationale used by the IRS for providing an agency account ruling, as opposed to a trust ruling, are described below.

Section 301.7701-4(a) of the Regulations provides, in general, that the term "trust," as used in the Code, refers to an arrangement created either by a will or by an *inter vivos* declaration whereby a trustee takes title to property for the purpose of protecting or con-serving it for the beneficiaries under the ordinary rules applied in chancery or probate courts. This definition, however, is not viewed as the sole test of whether an arrangement is a trust for tax purposes. Instead, it is seen as an effort to distinguish ordinary trusts, which are taxable under Section 641, from business trusts, which are not so taxable. [United States v De Bonchamps, 278 F 2d 127 (9th Cir 1960) *(en banc)*]

One court that dealt with whether an agreement between a tax-payer and a bank created a trust or an agency account relationship ruled that an agency account relationship was created. In that case, the bank could not invest or dispose of any trust corpus without the consent of the settlor and was relieved of all liability for any decline in the value of the corpus. The settlor had the power to vote any corporate stock held by the bank and could remove the bank and select a successor at any time. The court stated that, while an agent undertakes to act on behalf of its principal and is subject to the principal's control, a trustee usually has discretionary powers and acts for a term. Accordingly, because the bank did not have discretionary powers, the court held that the agreement created an agency relationship rather than a trust. [United States v Anderson, 132 F 2d 98 (6th Cir 1942); see also City Nat Bank & Trust Co v United States, 109 F 2d 191 (7th Cir 1940)]

Conversely, Revenue Ruling 69-300 involved a bank that was appointed custodian of certain property by a court order, which vested the bank with broad discretionary powers of administration and management. Therefore, the IRS held that a trust was created. [Rev Rul 69-300, 1969-1 CB 167; see also Rev Rul 76-265, 1976-2 CB 448]

Finally, if, under the terms of a rabbi trust agreement, the trustee of the rabbi trust (1) does not have discretionary authority to invest or make payments to participants or their beneficiaries, (2) is relieved of liability for actions that are directed by the employer, and (3) can resign or be removed at any time, then the rabbi trust agreement is likely to be treated, for tax purposes, as creating an agency account. [Ltr Rul 9016061, Jan 23, 1990]

Practice Pointer. Note, however, that the model rabbi trust, which is contained in Revenue Procedure 92-64, 1992-33 I.R.B. 11, provides that a trust must provide the trustee with some investment discretion. Therefore, it is unclear as to whether the IRS will continue to entertain agency account rulings.

Q 4:27   Can an employer exercise discretion regarding how or when benefits are distributed to an employee?

Sometimes. The IRS has indicated that it will not issue rulings on nonqualified plans that permit employers to exercise discretion with respect to the time or manner of payment of benefits to an employee. The reason for this position is that it is impossible for the IRS to determine at the time that a letter ruling is issued how the employer discretion will be exercised. If the discretion is exercised in a manner that is consistent with the wishes of an employee, issues are raised relating to the constructive receipt doctrine and Revenue Procedure 71-19 (see Q 4:16, IRS's Nonqualified Plan Letter Ruling Requirement 5) that concern whether the employee, rather than the employer, made the subsequent election. [Rev Proc 92-65, 1992-33 IRB 16; Ltr Rul 8830069, May 5, 1988, modifying Ltr Rul 8739031, June 29, 1987]

However, such a plan provision, if it is implemented by the employer in its discretion and is not subject to employee manipulation, should not adversely affect the tax status of the arrangement.

Q 4:28 In the IRS's view, are there any exceptions to the IRS rule that prohibits discretion regarding the payment of benefits?

Yes. The IRS has indicated that an employer may exercise discretion regarding the distribution of benefits to an employee if the discretion is exercised in the event of an unforeseeable emergency. The term "unforeseeable emergency" must be defined in the plan as an unanticipated emergency that is caused by an event beyond the control of the participant or beneficiary and that would result in severe financial hardship to the individual if early withdrawal were not permitted. The plan must further provide that the early withdrawal approved by the employer is limited to the amount necessary to meet the emergency. Language similar to that described in Section 1.457-2(h)(4) and (5) of the Treasury Regulations may be used. [Rev Proc 92-65, 1992-33 IRB 16]

Section 1.457-2(h)(4) of the Treasury Regulations defines an unforeseeable emergency as:

1. A severe financial hardship to the participant caused by a sudden and unexpected illness or accident of the participant or a dependent of the participant (as defined in Code Section 152(a));
2. A loss of the participant's property due to casualty; or
3. Other similar extraordinary and unforeseeable circumstances caused by events beyond the participant's control.

The circumstances that will constitute an unforeseeable emergency generally depend upon the facts and circumstances of each case. Payment may not be made to the extent the hardship may be relieved by insurance or other similar reimbursement or compensation, liquidation of assets (to the extent liquidation would not itself cause severe financial hardship), or a cessation of deferrals under the plan. College tuition or the costs of purchasing a home are not considered unforeseeable emergencies.

Section 1.457-2(h)(5) of the Regulations provides that the amount withdrawn as a result of a financial hardship must be limited to the amount reasonably needed to satisfy the emergency.

Practice Pointer. There are other IRS regulations that contain guidelines for hardship distributions. These regulations provide guidance with respect to qualified plans under Code Section 401(k). [Treas Reg § 1.401(k)-1(d)(2)(ii)] Although these regulations generally are more generous than the Section 457 Regulations, and although the definitions in the 401(k) regulations, as well as other definitions, should be sufficient to protect the tax status of the plan, the IRS will rule only with respect to provisions that are similar to those in the Section 457 Regulations.

Q 4:29   What is a "springing rabbi trust"?

A springing rabbi trust is a trust that has little or no assets or is revocable until an event occurs, such as a change in the control of the employer, which requires the trust to be funded or become irrevocable. [Ltr Rul 8907034, Nov 21, 1988]

Q 4:30   Will the IRS issue a favorable ruling on rabbi trusts which are funded or become irrevocable only upon the occurrence of some future event (i.e., springing rabbi trusts)?

Yes. The IRS has changed its ruling position with respect to springing rabbi trusts. In fact, the model rabbi trust contained in Revenue Procedure 92-64 provides specifically that a springing rabbi trust—a trust that will become funded or become irrevocable only upon the occurrence of some future event—may be used.

In a 1991 letter to Kenneth E. Kempson, Acting Associate Chief Counsel (Technical) of the Office of Chief Counsel of the IRS, the DOL responded to his request for an advisory opinion as to whether a nonqualified plan using the model rabbi trust (under which there was a springing rabbi trust feature) would be considered unfunded for purposes of the excess benefit and top-hat plan exemptions under Sections 4(b)(5), 201(2), 301(a)(3), and 401(a)(1) of Title I of ERISA. It was the opinion of the DOL that a plan would not fail to be unfunded for purposes of Sections 4(b)(5), 201(2), 301(a)(3), and 401(a)(1) of ERISA solely because there was maintained in connection with the plan a rabbi trust that conformed to the model trust. [DOL Adv Op 91-16A, Apr 5, 1991]

Q 4:31   Will the IRS issue a favorable ruling on provisions that accelerate the distribution of benefits to employees?

No. The IRS will not issue a favorable ruling on a trust that contains a provision that accelerates the distribution of benefits upon the occurrence of some event, such as a change in control of the employer or a change in the employer's financial situation, because it is concerned that such provisions may frustrate the rights of an employer's bankruptcy and insolvency creditors. However, if the events are not related to any employer credit risk, such accelerations should not adversely affect the tax status of the arrangement. (However, see Practice Pointer to Q 4:16, Plan requirement 8.)

> **Practice Pointer.** The IRS had ruled that a rabbi trust and an underlying severance agreement that provided that an eligible executive was entitled to receive severance benefits if his employment with the employer terminated after a change in control of the employer satisfied the standards for a favorable ruling. However, the IRS subsequently stated that this ruling was incorrect and revoked the ruling. [Ltr Rul 8844031, Aug 8, 1988 revoking Ltr Rul 8735047, June 3, 1987]

Q 4:32   What is the procedure for applying for an IRS ruling on a rabbi trust?

An employer that seeks a private letter ruling with respect to the tax consequences of a rabbi trust must comply with the requirements contained in Revenue Procedure 92-64, 1992-33 I.R.B. 11. Under this revenue procedure, an employer generally may obtain a private letter ruling with respect to the tax consequences of a nonqualified plan submitted on its own. Also, the employer may obtain a private letter ruling with respect to the nonqualified plan that is maintained in connection with a rabbi trust if the trust complies with the model trust provisions contained in that revenue procedure. An employer generally may not obtain a private letter ruling with respect to a trust that does not comply with model provisions contained in the revenue procedure except in rare and unusual circumstances. The requirements of Revenue Procedure 92-64 are discussed in detail in Q 4:15. Also, an employer must comply with the general private letter ruling procedures contained in Revenue Procedure 94-1. Under this revenue procedure, the application for a ruling must be accompanied by:

1. A request for ruling(s) (see Q 4:17);

2. A complete statement of all of the facts relating to the transaction;

3. A statement as to whether the identical issue is in a prior return of the taxpayer;

4. A statement of relevant authorities in support of the taxpayer's views;

5. A declaration under penalty of perjury;

6. A statement of proposed deletions;

7. A power of attorney (if the taxpayer has an authorized representative); '

8. The user fee required for such a request. Currently, the user fee for obtaining a rabbi trust letter ruling is $3,000 (unless the taxpayer is eligible for the reduced fee of $500); and

9. A checklist contained in Revenue Procedure 94-1. [Rev Proc 94-1, 1994-1 IRB 10; Rev Proc 90-17, 1990-1 CB 479, and IRS Ann 90-125, 1990-48 IRB 8]

Practice Pointer. Revenue Procedure 94-1 is updated each year. Therefore, if a taxpayer is preparing a ruling request in 1995, Revenue Procedure 95-1 [1995-2 IRB 59] should be observed, and so on.

Tax Consequences to the Employer

Q 4:33   Who is the owner of a rabbi trust?

For tax purposes, the employer is treated as the owner of a rabbi trust. If the assets of a trust can be used to discharge the employer's legal obligations, such as its obligations to its general creditors in the event of its bankruptcy or insolvency, or the employer retains certain administrative powers with respect to the trust funds, the trust generally will be taxable as a grantor trust and the employer will be treated as the grantor and owner of the trust and its assets. [IRC §§ 674, 675, 677(a); Treas Reg § 1.677(a)-1(d); Ltr Ruls 8849030, Sept 9, 1988; 8842008, July 21, 1988]

Q 4:34   Must the employer include the rabbi trust's income, deductions, and credits when calculating its income tax liability?

Yes. An employer must include the rabbi trust's income, deductions, and credits when calculating its income tax liability because, for tax purposes, the employer is treated as the grantor and the owner of the trust and its assets. When the grantor of a trust is regarded as the owner of any portion of a trust, the grantor's taxable income and credits include the items of the trust's income, deductions, and credits that are attributable to that portion of the trust. [IRC §§ 671 and 677(a); Treas Reg §§ 1.677(a)-1(d); Ltr Ruls 8845053, Aug 17, 1988; 8842008, July 21, 1988; 8703061, Oct 22, 1986]

Q 4:35   When can the employer deduct a contribution to a rabbi trust?

Employers can deduct rabbi trust contributions in the year in which they are includible in the gross income of the recipient, but only to the extent such payments are ordinary and necessary business expenses. Generally, if more than one employee participates in a plan, separate accounts must be maintained for each employee in order for the employer to deduct the contributions to the plan (however, see Q 4:37). [IRC §§ 162, 212, 404(a), 404(a)(5); Treas Reg § 1.404(a)-12(b); Ltr Rul 9012050, Dec 27, 1989]

Q 4:36   May an employer deduct the earnings in a rabbi trust when it deducts its contributions to the rabbi trust?

For deduction purposes, payments from a rabbi trust generally are treated as if they were made directly by the employer to the employee because the employer is considered the owner of a rabbi trust. As a result, the employer may deduct the full amount paid to a participant (that is, the employer's contributions, plus income) when this amount is includible in the gross income of the participant (subject to the ordinary and necessary and separate account requirements discussed in Q 4:35). [IRC § 404(a)(5); Treas Reg § 1.404(a)-12(b); Ltr Rul 9025018, Mar 22, 1990]

Q 4:37   Must an employer maintain separate accounts for the participating employees to receive a deduction?

The answer seems to be no. As a practical matter, if more than one employee participates in a plan, separate plan accounts must be maintained for each employee. However, the IRS has indicated that contributions to a rabbi trust are not treated as transfers of property under Code Section 83(a) (see Q 4:41) and are not considered contributions to a nonexempt trust under Code Section 402(b) (see Q 4:42). Also, because a rabbi trust does not cause a plan to be considered funded, deductions should be permitted irrespective of whether separate rabbi trust accounts are established for each employee. [IRC § 404(a)(5), Treas Reg § 1.404(a)-12(b)(3)]

Additionally, the IRS has indicated in at least one Letter Ruling that amounts payable to employees under a rabbi trust are deductible by the employer without regard to whether separate accounts are maintained under the deferred compensation plan for each participant. [Ltr Rul 9012050, Dec 27, 1989]

Tax Consequences to the Employee

Q 4:38   When are the funds held in a rabbi trust included in an employee's income?

The funds held in a rabbi trust are includible in the gross income of the employee (or the employee's beneficiary) when the benefits are paid or made available to the employee (or beneficiary) without substantial limitations or restrictions. [GCM 39230, Jan 20, 1984; Ltr Ruls 8845007, Aug 11, 1988; 8743029, July 27, 1987]

Q 4:39 Are contributions to a rabbi trust includible in an employee's income under the constructive receipt doctrine?

No. Contributions to a rabbi trust should not be taxable to the employee when made under the constructive receipt doctrine if the employee's right to receive the contributions is subject to substantial limitations or restrictions. Generally, a taxpayer includes the amount of any item of gross income in his or her gross income for the taxable year in which he or she receives it, unless, under the taxpayer's method of accounting, it is properly included in a different period. Generally, the employee, as a cash method taxpayer, includes amounts in gross income when they are actually or constructively received. [IRC § 451(a); Treas Reg § 1.451-1(a)]

Generally, income, although not actually reduced to a taxpayer's possession, is constructively received by the taxpayer in the taxable year during which it is:

1. Credited to his or her account;

2. Set apart for him or her; or

3. Otherwise made available to him or her.

However, income is not constructively received if the taxpayer's control of its receipt is subject to substantial limitations or restrictions. [Treas Reg § 1.451-2(a)]

The funds held in a rabbi trust must at all times be subject to the claims of the employer's bankruptcy and insolvency creditors (see Q 4:15, Model Rabbi Trust provisions 1 and 5). Thus, the creation of the trust will not result in constructive receipt by the employees of the amounts the employer contributes to the trust.

In *Goldsmith v. United States,* a physician agreed to have amounts withheld from his compensation pursuant to a deferred compensation arrangement with a hospital. The hospital purchased an insurance policy on the life of the doctor to finance the plan. The insurance policy identified the hospital as the owner and beneficiary of the policy. The court held that the financing of the plan through the purchase of the insurance policy did not result in constructive receipt by the physician of the withheld amounts. According to the court, the purchase of the insurance was merely a method of investment by the hospital. "No trust, escrow or other such arrangement affecting the withheld sums was constituted such as would invalidate the deferment by giving the taxpayer a security interest in the sums deferred."

The physician had no rights in the withheld sums either against the hospital or the insurance company. The hospital was the owner and beneficiary of the policy, and the physician could rely only on the credit of the hospital and the strength of its promise. In the event of the hospital's bankruptcy, the physician would be an unsecured, general creditor of the hospital, and his claim against the hospital's assets would rest on no firmer ground than those of other similarly situated hospital creditors. [Goldsmith v United States, 586 F 2d 810 (Ct Cl 1978)]

The leading revenue ruling in this area is Revenue Ruling 60-31. In example 2 of the ruling, a corporation established a nonqualified plan for certain officers and key employees. A separate account was established for each participant and, each year, the corporation credited amounts to the separate accounts. Each account also was credited with the net amount realized from investing any portion of the amount in the account. The corporation merely had a contractual obligation to make the payments when due and had not intended that the amounts in each account be held by the corporation in trust for the participants. In example 3 of the ruling, a publisher contracted with an author to provide that royalties in excess of a certain amount would be carried over by the publisher into succeeding accounting periods, and the publisher was not required either to pay interest to the author on any excess sums or to segregate such sums in any manner. The IRS determined that the amounts credited to the accounts under these examples were not constructively received in a taxable year prior to the taxable year of actual receipt. The mere promise to pay, not represented by notes or secured in any way, was not regarded as a receipt of income within the meaning of the cash receipts and disbursements method of accounting. [Rev Rul 60-31, 1960-1 CB 174 as modified by Rev Rul 64-279, 1964-2 CB 121, Rev Rul 70-435, 1970-2 CB 100; Rev Rul 71-419, 1971-2 CB 220; Rev Rul

69-650, 1969-2 CB 106; Rev Rul 69-649, 1969-2 CB 106; Ltr Ruls 8708063, Nov 28, 1986; 8641039, July 15, 1986]

In a recent case, *Martin v. Commissioner*, the employer adopted an unfunded shadow stock plan for its key employees in order to improve an old plan that provided units representing hypothetical shares of common stock to the employees who entered into separate agreements with the employer. Under the old plan, a participant's benefits were payable only in ten equal, annual installments. The new plan provided for payments in a lump sum unless participants elected to receive ten equal, annual installments. In 1981, two participants elected annual installments and, later that year, terminated employment. The Tax Court considered whether the addition or availability of the lump-sum option resulted in constructive receipt even though, in the cases of the two participants, the installment option was elected. The IRS argued that the participants had an unqualified right to receive a lump sum distribution under the plan resulting in the constructive receipt of lump sum plan benefits upon the termination of their employment. However, the court held that, because the participants elected the installment payment method before they were entitled to any payments, the participants did not constructively receive the entire amount of their benefits upon termination of employment. [Martin v Comm'r, 96 TC No 39 (June 18, 1991)].

This holding, although consistent with prior case law in this area, represents a set-back for the IRS given the IRS's recently expressed views.

Q 4:40 Are contributions to a rabbi trust includible in an employee's income under the economic benefit doctrine?

No, contributions to a rabbi trust are not includible in the participating employee's income under the economic benefit doctrine because the funds held in a rabbi trust are treated for tax purposes as owned by the employer and as not set aside for the employee because they are subject to the claims of the employer's general bankruptcy and insolvency creditors.

Under the economic benefit doctrine, if any economic or financial benefit, such as unconditionally setting aside a fund or granting a currently assignable right, is conferred on an individual as compensation in a taxable year, it is taxable to the individual in that year.

The economic benefit doctrine was applied in *Sproull v. Commissioner* in 1945. In that case, a corporation created a trust of $10,500 for its president. The trustee was directed to invest the money and pay one-half of it to the president in 1946 and pay the remainder to the president in 1947. The court considered the doctrine of constructive receipt but determined that it did not apply because the president was not able to reduce any part of the trust fund to actual possession in 1945 because of the time limitation set on payment in the trust instrument.

The court determined, however, that the creation of the trust in 1945 had conferred an economic or financial benefit upon the president in 1945 so that the sums paid into the trust were taxable to the president in 1945. The court explained that, in 1945, the employer had completed its part of the transaction by irrevocably paying out the $10,500 for the president's benefit, and the president had to do nothing further to earn the benefit. The court said that this fact distinguished the case from those in which the exact amount of compensation is subject to a future contingency or subject to the possibility of return to the employer. The court also noted that the trustee's only duties were to hold, invest, and accumulate the funds, and distribute the funds to the president; that no one else had any interest in or control over the funds held in the trust; and that the president could have assigned or otherwise disposed of his beneficial interest in the trust. [Sproull v Comm'r, 16 TC 244 (1951), *aff'd per curiam*, 194 F 2d 541 (6th Cir 1952)]

Under the economic benefit doctrine, an employee has currently includible income from an economic or financial benefit received as compensation, even though not in cash form. The economic benefit doctrine applies when assets are unconditionally and irrevocably paid into a fund or trust to be used for an employee's sole benefit or are assignable by the employee. Thus, in general, because contributions to a rabbi trust are not assignable and are treated, for tax purposes, as owned by the employer and are subject to the claims of the employer's bankruptcy and insolvency creditors, no sole purpose, irrevocable fund is created, the economic benefit doctrine does not apply to the amounts contributed to the trust, and no amounts are currently includible in the employee's income. [GCM 39230, Jan 20, 1984; Ltr Ruls 8743029, July 27, 1987; 8711033, Dec 12, 1986]

Q 4:41   Does the creation of a rabbi trust result in a transfer of property to an employee that triggers tax under Code Section 83?

No. If contributions made to a rabbi trust are subject to the claims of the employer's general bankruptcy and insolvency creditors, the contributions will not be considered to be a transfer of property under Code Section 83. In general, Code Section 83 provides rules for the taxation of property transferred to an employee in connection with the performance of services. This property generally is not taxable to the employee until it has been transferred to the employee or becomes substantially vested in the employee. Section 1.83-3(a)(1) of the Regulations provides that a transfer of property also occurs when a person acquires a beneficial ownership interest in the property.

Section 1.83-3(b) of the Regulations provides that a taxpayer's right to property is substantially vested for purposes of Section 83 when it is either transferable or not subject to a substantial risk of forfeiture. Section 1.83-3(c) of the Regulations provides that a substantial risk of forfeiture exists where rights in property that are transferred are conditioned upon the future performance, or nonperformance, of substantial services by any person, or the occurrence of a condition related to a purpose of the transfer, and the possibility of forfeiture is substantial if such condition is not satisfied. Section 1.83-3(d) of the Regulations provides that the rights of a person in property are transferable if the person can transfer any interest in the property to any person other than the transferor of the property, but only if the rights in the property of the transferee are not subject to a substantial risk of forfeiture. Accordingly, property is transferable if the person performing the services or receiving the property can sell, assign, or pledge his or her interest in the property to any person other than the transferor of the property and if the transferee is not required to give up the property or its value if the substantial risk of forfeiture materializes.

Section 1.83-3(e) of the Regulations provides that, for purposes of Code Section 83, the term "property" includes real and personal property other than money or an "unfunded and unsecured" promise to pay money or property in the future. "Property" also includes a beneficial interest in assets, including money, transferred or set aside from the claims of the creditors of the transferor.

Contributions to a rabbi trust are subject to the claims of the employer's bankruptcy and insolvency creditors and, as a result, those contributions do not meet the definition of property for purposes of Code Section 83. Therefore, there is no transfer of property within the meaning of Code Section 83 when amounts are contributed to a rabbi trust. [Ltr Ruls 8842008, July 21, 1988; 8641039, July 15, 1986]

Q 4:42   Does a contribution to a rabbi trust result in a contribution of property to a "nonexempt trust" under Code Section 402(b)(1) that triggers tax to the employee?

No. If there is no transfer of property under Code Section 83 because contributions to a rabbi trust are treated, for tax purposes, as owned by the employer and subject to the claims of the employer's bankruptcy and insolvency creditors, there can be no contribution of property to a nonexempt trust under Code Section 402(b)(1). This is because Code Section 402(b)(1) provides that employer contributions to a nonexempt trust are included in the gross income of the employee in accordance with Code Section 83, except that the value of the employee's interest in the trust is substituted for the fair market value of the property for purposes of applying Section 402(b)(1).

Section 1.402(b)-1(a)(1) of the Regulations provides that contributions made on behalf of an employee by an employer to a nonexempt trust will be included as compensation in the gross income of the employee for the year during which the contribution is made, but only to the extent that the employee's interest in the contribution is substantially vested at the time the contribution is made. The regulation then refers to Section 1.83-3(b) of the Regulations for the definition of the term "substantially vested." Section 1.83-3(b) of the Regulations provides that property is substantially vested when it is either transferable or not subject to a substantial risk of forfeiture.

If contributions to a rabbi trust are not considered property that is substantially vested within the meaning of Section 1.83-3 of the Regulations, then those contributions will not be considered property that is substantially vested within the meaning of Section 1.402(h)-1 of the Regulations. Therefore, if a contribution to a rabbi trust is subject to the claims of the employer's bankruptcy and insolvency creditors, the contribution will not constitute a contribution to a nonexempt trust under Code Section 402(b)(1).

Q 4:43 May a participant in a rabbi trust, without adverse tax consequences, purchase an insurance policy to ensure payment from the rabbi trust?

Generally, yes. In Letter Ruling 9344038, the IRS held that an employee's purchase of a policy from an insurer to secure future payment of nonqualified plan benefits from a rabbi trust established by the employee's employer did not result in the conferring of an economic benefit on the employee by anyone other than the employee and, therefore, did not result in taxation to the employee.

The IRS stressed that the employee's negotiation and purchase of the policy was made without the involvement of the employer, that premiums were paid solely by the employee, that no collateral agreement existed between the employer and the insurer, and that the insurer obtained no information from the employer other than information that was publicly available.

The employer stated in its ruling request that it might, but it was not obligated to, reimburse the employee for the premiums paid. The IRS responded that, if the employer reimbursed the employee for premiums paid on the policy, the reimbursement amounts would be includible in the employee's income when paid.

Finally, the IRS held that the employee's payment of the premiums on the policy was a nondeductible personal expense of the employee.

Case Study 4-1

Note: See Case Studies at the end of chapters 1 through 3.

The advisor opens the meeting by reminding A, B, C, and D that a rabbi trust (and, in most cases, the other securitization devices to be discussed) may be used in connection with a top-hat plan or an excess benefit plan. As a preliminary matter, the advisor notes that these trusts are called "rabbi" trusts because the first IRS ruling on the concept involved a deferred compensation arrangement between a rabbi and his congregation. The advisor adds that, in essence, a rabbi trust is simply a grantor trust under the Code; that is, a trust in which the party establishing the trust (here, the corporation) retains sufficient rights under the trust (here, the right to have the trust's assets used to satisfy the corporation's bankruptcy and insolvency creditors) to result in the trust being treated, for most tax law purposes, as property of the party establishing the trust.

In other words, the corporation would establish an actual trust with, for example, a bank as trustee, and deposit amounts equal to plan participants' deferred compensation into the trust. Unless the corporation became bankrupt or insolvent, a possibility which A, B, C, and D believe is very unlikely, the trust's assets would be used for the exclusive purpose of paying participant benefits under the top-hat or excess benefit plan.

The advisor adds that, because the rabbi trust would be considered, for most tax purposes, to be property of the corporation, the plan would not be considered to be funded for tax or ERISA purposes and, therefore, would enjoy the desired tax treatment and exemption from most of ERISA. However, the trust would exist for all state law purposes, thereby providing participants with significant protections.

A, B, C, and D find this securitization option particularly attractive, especially in light of their confidence that the corporation's bankruptcy/insolvency is most unlikely and in light of the possibility that the corporation may be acquired by unrelated parties. The group also believes that the existence of the trust will make the plan seem substantial to the other participants.

A asks whether it would be wise to seek an IRS ruling on any rabbi trust which is established. The advisor suggests that, although an IRS ruling would provide considerable tax comfort to the corporation and the participants, the requirements that must be met in order to receive a favorable IRS ruling are rather restrictive and the risk of proceeding without a ruling—if one proceeds with caution—is extremely small. The group concludes, therefore, that, if a rabbi trust is used, an IRS ruling will not be sought. *B* asks whether the benefits for certain participants in the arrangement can be subject to a vesting schedule, and whether all participants can be permitted to direct the investment of their accounts in the rabbi trust, adding "lustre" and visibility to the plan. The advisor answers yes to both questions, but suggests that, in order to avoid administrative complexity, participant investment choices be limited to a menu of options (e.g., a family of mutual funds) selected by the corporation and acceptable to the trustee.

C asks whether the trustee will be required to file annual tax returns for the trust. The advisor notes that, under current IRS interpretations, if the trustee has no investment discretion concerning trust assets, no annual trust tax returns are required because the IRS treats the trust as an "agency account." On the other hand, if the trustee has investment discretion, an annual trust tax return would be required. The advisor reminds the group that taxes on trust earnings would be paid by the corporation and not the trust in either event, that contributions to the trust are not deductible until included in participants' incomes (at which time the corporation's deduction will equal the amounts includible in participants' incomes), and that participants receiving distributions from the trust do not receive any favorable tax treatment.

D asks if participants may have the right to withdraw amounts from the rabbi trust. The advisor responds by noting that the arrangement is subject to the doctrine of constructive receipt. In other words, if a participant has a right to receive amounts under the arrangement, he or she will be treated as having received them and will be subject to tax. Therefore, a withdrawal option (except one limited to events, such as financial hardship, beyond the participant's control) will eliminate the tax advantages of the arrangement. The group tentatively concludes that a rabbi trust will be used to provide a source for plan benefits, but wants to delay a final decision until the next meeting, at which the advisor promises to explain the concept of a secular trust.

See Case Study at the end of chapter 5 for an overview of secular trusts.

Chapter 5

Secular Trusts

A secular trust is an irrevocable trust that holds assets to be used for the exclusive purpose of paying for an employee's nonqualified plan benefits. This chapter examines secular trusts—whether the use of a secular trust in connection with a nonqualified plan will cause the plan to be funded for tax and ERISA purposes, whether it is significant if a nonqualified plan is funded or unfunded for tax and ERISA purposes, whether the IRS will issue favorable letter rulings on secular trusts and the criteria for receiving such a favorable IRS ruling, and the tax consequences, for both employers and employees, of using a secular trust in connection with a nonqualified plan.

Overview

Q 5:1   What is a secular trust?

A secular trust is an irrevocable trust, usually established in fact by the employer, but treated for tax purposes as established by the employee for the benefit of providing a source from which nonqualified plan benefits are paid. The employees' nonqualified plan benefits are held by the trustee of the secular trust for the exclusive benefit of the employees until they are paid under the nonqualified plan. A significant feature of a secular trust is that participants generally have a nonforfeitable and exclusive right to the contributions made to the trust and to the earnings on those contributions. The contributions generally are includible in the participants' income in the year they are made to the trust, and the earnings on the contributions generally are includible in the participants' income as they are earned. [Ltr Ruls 8843021, July 29, 1988; 8841023, July 9, 1988]

Q 5:2   Who establishes a secular trust?

The employer establishes the secular trust for the benefit of its employees, although for tax purposes, the participating employees are treated as having established the trust. The IRS has ruled that an employer may not be treated as the owner of a secular trust under the grantor trust rules (see Q 5:25). [Ltr Ruls 8841023, July 9, 1988; 8843021, July 29, 1988; 9206009, Nov 11, 1991; 9207010, Nov 12, 1991; 9212019, Dec 20, 1991; and 9212024, Dec 20, 1991]

Q 5:3   Why is a secular trust established?

In general, a secular trust is established in connection with a nonqualified plan to provide a source of funds from which the nonqualified plan benefits will be paid. The establishment of the secular trust provides security to the nonqualified plan participants that their benefits under the nonqualified plan will not be endangered by an unfriendly takeover of the employer or any other unfriendly change in the management of the employer. In addition, the establishment of a secular trust provides security to the participants that their nonqualified plan benefits will not be endangered by the employer's inability to pay the benefits at a future time because of financial difficulty. A secular trust can offer this security because, unlike assets held in a rabbi trust, the assets held in a secular trust are not subject to the claims of the employer's bankruptcy and insolvency creditors, but must be used for the exclusive purpose of paying benefits due under the nonqualified plan. A secular trust also may be established to ensure the employer that assets will be available for distribution to participants when distributions are due, thereby eliminating the requirement of future cash flow planning by the employer. [Ltr Ruls 8843021, July 29, 1988; 8841023, July 9, 1988; 8418105, Jan 31, 1984]

Q 5:4 Can a single secular trust benefit more than one individual?

It should be possible to establish a single secular trust in connection with a nonqualified plan that benefits more than one individual. However, the IRS occasionally has expressed concerns about this issue. [Ltr Ruls 8843021, July 29, 1988; 8841023, July 9, 1988; 9031031, May 8, 1990]

Q 5:5 What is a secular annuity?

A secular annuity is an annuity, purchased by the employer in connection with a nonqualified plan, that is titled in the name of a plan participant rather than in the name of the employer. Although the use of a secular annuity places the nonqualified plan funding asset beyond the reach of the employer's general and insolvency creditors, the elimination of this insolvency risk causes the immediate taxation to the employee of the value of the annuity as soon as the employee's interest in it is no longer subject to a substantial risk of forfeiture. That is, as soon as the employee vests in his or her interest in the annuity, its full present value will be taxable to the employee.

Like a secular trust, a secular annuity might have to be structured as an employee grantor secular annuity in order to avoid the double taxation of the inside buildup, or cash value growth, under the annuity product. This is because, if a corporate employer were determined to be the owner of the annuity or its inside buildup, before the transfer of the annuity or the inside buildup to the employee, Code Section 72(u) would tax the employer on the inside buildup, and Code Section 83 would tax the employee on the value of the annuity (including its inside buildup) when the employee became vested in his or her interest under the annuity.

Q 5:6   What is a heavenly trust?

Heavenly trusts combine the features of rabbi trusts and secular trusts, either in a single document or in complementary separate documents, in an attempt to eliminate the insolvency risk associated with rabbi trusts while eliminating the current taxation feature of secular trusts.

In its simplest form, a heavenly trust operates as follows. First, the employer establishes a rabbi trust and explains to participants that, should the employer become insolvent, the nonqualified plan participants will simply be general creditors of the employer, and rabbi trust assets will be available to satisfy the claims of all of the employer's general creditors. Next, the employer establishes a secular trust to secure nonqualified plan participants' interests in the event of the employer's insolvency. The employer explains to participants that their interests in the secular trust are contingent only because they are enforceable only upon the unlikely event of the employer's insolvency. Therefore, the employer argues to the IRS, the participants' interests under the secular trust are "subject to a substantial risk of forfeiture" because of the substantial likelihood that the employer will not become insolvent, and thus no amounts will ever be paid to participants out of the secular trust.

In other words, the employer argues to the IRS that participants not be taxed on their rabbi trust interests unless they receive them, because of the insolvency risk under the rabbi trust. Similarly, the employer argues that participants not be taxed on their secular trust assets unless they actually receive them, because of the "substantial" risk that they will never receive those assets, due to the improbability that the employer will become insolvent.

The IRS has stated repeatedly that it would not agree with the above analysis of the tax effects of a heavenly trust because the combination of the rabbi trust and secular trust elements serves to eliminate any risk to the nonqualified participants of receiving their plan interests and, for practical purposes, makes their nonqualified plan interests funded for tax purposes and therefore immediately taxable under the economic benefit doctrine, Code Section 83, and/or Code Section 402(b). Most commentators concede that the IRS's position likely would prevail if the issue were litigated.

ERISA Considerations

Q 5:7 Will the use of a secular trust in connection with a nonqualified plan cause the plan to be funded for purposes of Title I of ERISA?

The establishment of a secular trust by an employer would cause the underlying nonqualified plan to be funded for ERISA purposes. This is a major difference under ERISA between secular and rabbi trusts (see chapter 4). Generally, a "funded" ERISA plan is created when an amount is set aside irrevocably by the employer for the benefit of an employee. Because a secular trust established by an employer is an irrevocable trust established with a third party to hold assets for the exclusive benefit of participating employees, and neither the employer nor its creditors can reach those assets, the underlying plan would be treated as a funded plan for ERISA purposes. [GCM 37256, Sept 15, 1977; GCM 33373, Nov 21, 1966 as modified by GCM 35196, Jan 16, 1973, which was modified by GCM 35326, May 3, 1973; Ltr Rul 8841023, July 9, 1988] However, if an employee-grantor secular trust is treated for ERISA purposes as having been established by the employee (as it is for tax purposes), the existence of the trust should not cause the underlying plan to be funded for ERISA purposes (see Q 5:13).

Q 5:8 What is the significance of whether or not a secular trust causes the underlying plan to be funded for purposes of Title I of ERISA?

Generally, if a plan is funded, the plan will have to satisfy the requirements contained in Title I of ERISA, which pertain to participation and vesting, funding, and fiduciary requirements. On the other hand, if a plan is unfunded, the plan may be exempt from these requirements.

Q 5:9   Which ERISA Title I requirements must be met by funded nonqualified plans?

A funded nonqualified plan generally is subject to the following requirements under Title I of ERISA:

1. *Reporting and disclosure* requirements, including the summary plan description requirements under ERISA Section 102 and the annual report requirements under ERISA Section 103;
2. *Participation and vesting* requirements, including compliance with the joint and survivor annuity requirements under ERISA Section 205;
3. *Funding* requirements, unless the plan is funded exclusively by insurance contracts; and
4. *Fiduciary responsibility* requirements, including the written plan requirement, the exclusive benefit rule, and the prohibited transaction rules.

[ERISA Title I, Parts 1, 2, 3, and 4]

Q 5:10   Which types of nonqualified plans are affected because a secular trust causes nonqualified plans to be funded for purposes of Title I of ERISA?

Under Title I of ERISA, whether or not a nonqualified plan is funded is significant with respect to both top-hat plans and excess benefit plans.

Q 5:11   How are funded and unfunded top-hat plans treated for purposes of Title I of ERISA?

A top-hat plan is a plan that is *unfunded* and maintained by an employer primarily for the purpose of providing deferred compensation for a select group of management or highly compensated employees. These plans are exempt, pursuant to the exemptions in ERISA Sections 201(2), 301(a)(3), and 401(a)(1), from Parts 2, 3, and

4 of Title I of ERISA, which pertain to participation and vesting, funding, and fiduciary responsibilities. If a plan that is maintained by an employer primarily for the purpose of providing deferred compensation for a select group of management or highly compensated employees is funded, the plan will not qualify for those ERISA exemptions. Thus, secular trusts that are established in connection with nonqualified plans will cause those nonqualified plans to be subject to Title I of ERISA. (See chapter 2.)

Q 5:12 How are funded and unfunded excess benefit plans treated for purposes of Title I of ERISA?

An excess benefit plan is defined in ERISA Section 3(36) as "a plan maintained by an employer solely for the purpose of providing benefits for certain employees in excess of the limitations on contributions and benefits imposed by Section 415 . . . on plans to which that section applies, *without regard to whether the plan is funded*" (emphasis supplied). Under ERISA Section 4(b)(5), a plan that is both unfunded and an excess benefit plan is exempt from all of ERISA Title I coverage. If an excess benefit plan is funded, however, the plan will not qualify for the exemption from all of Title I. Instead, a funded excess benefit plan is exempt, pursuant to the exemptions in ERISA Sections 201(7) and 301(a)(9), only from Parts 2 and 3 of Title I of ERISA. Thus, excess benefit plans that are funded through secular trusts are subject to reporting and disclosure requirements and fiduciary obligation requirements. However, they are exempt from ERISA's participation and vesting requirements, including the joint and survivor annuity rules, and ERISA's funding requirements. [DOL letter to Richard H. Manfreda, Chief, Individual Income Tax Branch, IRS, Dec 13, 1985; DOL Adv Op 89-22A, Sept 21, 1989] (See chapter 3.)

Q 5:13 Will the ERISA Title I requirements apply if a secular trust is deemed to be established and maintained by an employee?

Probably not. If the secular trust is deemed to be established and maintained by the employee, the requirements under ERISA Title I should not apply. This is because ERISA Section 4(a) provides that Title I of ERISA will apply only to employee benefit plans established or maintained by an employer, an employee organization or by both.

Thus, if the secular trust is deemed to be established and maintained by the employee, ERISA Title I should not apply. [ERISA § 4(a); see DOL Adv Op 81-86A, Nov 13, 1981]

Q 5:14   Is there a possible exception to coverage under Title I of ERISA where only one individual is covered under the secular trust and underlying deferred compensation arrangement?

Possibly. If only one executive is covered under the secular trust and underlying deferred compensation arrangement, the agreement to provide deferred compensation to the individual may be considered an individual contract and not an "employee pension benefit plan" as described in ERISA Section 3(2). ERISA Section 3(2) defines the terms "employee pension benefit plan" and "pension plan" to include any plan, fund, or program that is established or maintained by an employer or by an employee organization, or by both, to the extent that the plan, fund, or program provides retirement income to employees, or results in a deferral of income by employees for periods extending to the termination of covered employment or beyond. This is true regardless of the method of calculating contributions, benefits, or distributions.

The DOL has determined on at least two occasions that an agreement between a company and a single employee was an individual contract and not an employee pension benefit plan within the meaning of ERISA Section 3(2). [ERISA § 3(2); DOL Reg § 2510.3-2; DOL Adv Op 76-110, Sept 28, 1976; DOL Adv Op 76-79, May 25, 1976] However, another DOL opinion and several cases suggest that even one participant arrangements can be "pension plans" under ERISA. [See DOL Adv Op 79-75A, Sept 29, 1979; Pane v RCA Corp, 868 F 2d 631 (3d Cir 1989) (relying on Fort Halifax Packing Co, Inc v Coyne, 482 US 1, 107 S Ct 2211 (1987)] Therefore, employers should proceed with caution before characterizing a one participant arrangement as a non-ERISA plan.

Q 5:15   Is a participant's interest in an employee grantor secular trust protected in the event of the participant's bankruptcy or insolvency?

This issue has not been settled. Although a participant's interest in an employee grantor secular trust should be protected in the event of the employer's bankruptcy or insolvency, in the event of the employee's bankruptcy or insolvency, the trust may be deemed by a bankruptcy court to be a "self-settled" trust subject to the claims of the employee's creditors, rather than a "spendthrift trust" not subject to creditor claims.

Q 5:16   Is a participant's interest in a Code Section 402(b) "nonexempt trust" protected in the event of the participant's bankruptcy or insolvency?

This issue is unsettled. However, unlike the case with an employee grantor secular trust—where the employee, in fact, has had the unfettered opportunity to receive the compensation and, instead, has elected to deposit it into the trust—with a Code Section 402(b) nonexempt trust, the employer typically deposits the amounts into the trust without giving the employee the option to receive the amounts currently. Therefore, it is possible that the Code section 402(b) trust would be deemed by a bankruptcy court to be a spendthrift retirement trust beyond the reach of the employee's bankruptcy creditors.

IRS Considerations

Q 5:17   Will the IRS issue rulings on secular trusts?

Yes. The IRS will issue rulings on secular trusts that are established in connection with nonqualified plans.

Q 5:18   Are there criteria for receiving a favorable IRS ruling on a secular trust?

Yes. Although the IRS has issued favorable rulings on secular trusts used in connection with nonqualified plans, it has not issued a model secular trust (like its model rabbi trust) establishing standards that a secular trust must meet in order to receive a favorable IRS ruling. However, the IRS has ruled favorably on secular trusts established in connection with nonqualified plans that satisfied the following requirements:

1. The assets of the trusts were not available either to the employer or to the creditors of the employer in the event of the employer's bankruptcy or insolvency;

2. The participating individuals were fully vested in the assets transferred to the trusts;

3. The participating individuals were permitted to elect to receive the amounts in cash as they were earned or have them paid into the trusts; and

4. The trusts were irrevocable.

The IRS also has indicated that separate accounts must be established in the secular trust for each participating individual. [IRC § 404(a)(5); Ltr Ruls 8843021, July 29, 1988; and 8841023, July 9, 1988; see Ltr Rul 9031031, May 8, 1990]

Q 5:19   Is it necessary to obtain a favorable ruling from the IRS in order to establish a secular trust?

No, although obtaining a favorable ruling from the IRS will provide taxpayers with some comfort in determining their tax liability with respect to the secular trust. However, a secular trust that is entitled to the intended tax treatment can be established without a ruling from the IRS.

Q 5:20   May the assets that an employer transfers to a secular trust be subject to the claims of the employer's creditors?

Generally, no. By definition, except in the case of assets transferred to the trust to defraud creditors, neither the employer nor its creditors has any interest in the assets held in a secular trust, and an employee's benefits held in a secular trust will not be endangered by the employer's inability to pay benefits due to the employer's bankruptcy or insolvency. This protection is one of the primary benefits of establishing a secular trust. [Ltr Ruls 8843021, July 29, 1988; 8841023, July 9, 1988; 9031031, May 8, 1990]

Q 5:21 Are employees fully vested in the benefits held on their behalf in a secular trust?

Generally, an employee is fully vested in the benefits held on his or her behalf in a secular trust. However, if a vesting schedule is used with respect to a secular trust, the employee would not be required to include employer contributions and trust earnings in income until the employee becomes vested in them. Note that, because a non-qualified plan maintained in connection with a secular trust treated as established by the employer is subject to the vesting requirements under Part 2 of Title I of ERISA, the employee can avoid the recognition of all income for a period no longer than the permissible ERISA vesting periods (i.e., five years of service for "cliff" vesting or seven years of service for graduated vesting). Finally, if the employee should incur a forfeiture of his or her benefits, the forfeited amounts may not be returned to the employer. The forfeited amounts may be allocated to the remaining participants, but this may produce benefits greater than intended and may not be satisfactory to the employer. [Ltr Ruls 8843021, July 29, 1988; 8841023, July 9, 1988 and 9031031, May 8, 1990]

Q 5:22 What rights does the employee have in the assets that are held in a secular trust?

Generally, as an unconditional state trust law beneficiary of the secular trust, the employee is entitled to the entire amount held in his or her account under the secular trust and neither the employer nor the employer's creditors has any interest in such assets. [Ltr Ruls 8843021, July 29, 1988; 8841023, July 9, 1988; 9031031, May 8, 1990]

Q 5:23 When is an employee entitled to the benefits held in a secular trust?

Generally, benefits will be distributed from the secular trust to the employee in accordance with the terms of the underlying nonquali-fied plan that is established in connection with the trust. Often, benefits may be paid to the employee or the employee's beneficiary upon the employee's retirement, disability, death, termination of employment, or some other stated event. [Ltr Ruls 8843021, July 29, 1988; 8841023, July 9, 1988; 9031031, May 8, 1990]

Q 5:24   What is the procedure for applying for an IRS ruling on a secular trust?

The procedure is the same as the procedure for applying for any IRS private letter ruling. This procedure is contained in the annual IRS Revenue Procedure dealing with requests for IRS private letter rulings (Revenue Procedure 94-1 for ruling requests initiated in 1994). The procedure involves, among other things, general instructions for requesting letter rulings, supplemental instructions applicable in certain cases, and instructions for requesting limited retroactivity of rulings.

Tax Consequences to the Employer

Q 5:25   Can the employer be treated as the grantor and owner of a secular trust?

For a number of years, it was unclear whether the IRS would treat the employer or the participant as the grantor and owner of a secular trust. However, in 1988 and 1992, the IRS issued a series of private letter rulings which clarified this issue. [Ltr Ruls 8843021, 8841023, 9206009, 9207010, 9212019, 9212024].

The IRS indicated in the two 1988 rulings that it will treat an employee as the grantor and owner of a secular trust in certain circumstances. Under these rulings, the participants had the right to elect either to receive compensation in cash as it was earned or to have the compensation contributed to the trusts established by or on behalf of the participants for the participants' benefit. The trusts were irrevocable and the employers and the creditors of the employers had no interest in the assets of the trusts. (Instead, the employers generally would act as administrators of the trusts and have the power to appoint and remove the trustees, consent to amendments, and direct the trustees to pay certain amounts to the participants.)

The IRS determined that, under Code Sections 83 and 451, payments by an employer, pursuant to a participant's election, under a nonqualified plan to a trust were included in the participant's income in the year the payments were made to the trust. The IRS also determined that the participant would be treated as the owner of the trust under the grantor trust rules. The payments by the employer were deductible in the year paid, if the reasonable compensation requirements were met. The income on the amounts in the trust was distributed to the participant or accumulated for future distribution to the participant. Because the participant is treated as the owner of such a trust under the grantor trust rules, the participant is taxed currently on any investment income in the trust. The employer is not permitted a deduction for such income.

Prior to the issuance of the four 1992 IRS letter rulings cited above, some practitioners argued that, if an employer established a secular trust and provided that the income from trust assets would, in the discretion of the employer, be reallocated to employees at some later date, the employer would be treated as the grantor of the trust under the grantor trust rules. Furthermore, some practitioners asserted that the employer could receive a current deduction not only with respect to its contributions, but also for the amount of investment income that was "received" by the employer (that is, taxed to the employer under the grantor trust rules) and reallocated to participants. This current employer deduction for investment income was viewed as an attractive feature of an "employer grantor secular trust."

In the 1992 rulings, the IRS rejected the above analysis and held, instead, that when an employer—rather than an employee—is treated as having established a secular trust, the trust is not an employer grantor trust, but is, instead, a Section 402(b) taxable trust (i.e., a separate,taxpaying entity).

Under this analysis, the IRS concluded that the employee would be taxed on the contributions to the secular trust and the earnings thereon as soon as they were vested, that the trust, as a separate taxpayer, also would pay tax on the earnings in the trust (to the extent they were not distributed) in the year earned, and that the employer would receive a deduction only for its contributions, and not for the earnings on those contributions. The IRS added that the Section 72(q) 10 percent early distribution penalty tax would also apply to such arrangements. Finally, the IRS held that, where the investment income of the secular trust was held in suspense accounts, the separate account requirement of Section 404(a)(5) would not be satisfied and the employer would not receive a deduction until the requirement was satisfied.

Obviously, the combined effect of the various elements of this 1992 IRS position make the traditional, employer-established secular trust economically unwise, if not completely unworkable. Therefore, in order to maintain a secular trust that is cost-effective, the secular trust must be designed to be an "employee-grantor secular trust."

Q 5:26   What is an employee-grantor secular trust?

Under an employee-grantor secular trust, the employee-participants are given the right to elect to have employer contributions paid directly to them or contributed to the secular trust. By using this approach, the participants are treated as the grantors of the trust and, therefore, trust earnings are taxed only once, at the participant level, and not at the trust level.

Q 5:27   When can a contribution to a secular trust be deducted by the employer?

Code Section 404(a)(5) provides that an employer's contribution to a nonqualified plan is deductible in the taxable year in which an amount attributable to the contribution is includible in the gross income of the employees participating in the plan, to the extent such contributions are ordinary and necessary expenses. [IRC §§ 162, 212, 404(a); see Ltr Ruls 9012050, Dec 27, 1989; 8841023, July 9, 1988; 9031031, May 8, 1990]

Q 5:28   Is an amount designated as interest on amounts held in a secular trust currently deductible by the employer under Code Section 163?

If the secular trust is an employee grantor secular trust, interest on amounts held in the secular trust would not affect, or be deductible by, the employer in any event. Even if the secular trust were deemed to be an employer grantor secular trust, amounts designated as interest on amounts held in the trust would be currently deductible by the employer only in the Ninth Federal Circuit, and perhaps only temporarily there. The Tax Court ruled, in *Albertson's, Inc. v. Commissioner,* that the interest credited to a participant's account under a nonqualified plan is not interest within the meaning of Code Section

163 and, therefore, is not deductible under that Section. The court stated that the interest is part of the deferred compensation for the participants and therefore is deductible only as permitted under Code Sections 404(a)(5) (for employees) and 404(d) (for independent contractors).

However, on appeal, the Ninth Circuit Court of Appeals reversed the Tax Court and held for the taxpayer. Most commentators—even those who represent taxpayers—side with the IRS and the Tax Court and expect that the Appeals Court's opinion will not be followed in other federal judicial circuits and expect the opinion to be overturned by the Supreme Court, or by the Ninth Circuit on reconsideration. Therefore, employers should exercise extreme caution before taking deductions based on the Appeals Court decision.

Q 5:29   How much of a contribution to a secular trust can the employer deduct?

The amount of the deduction available under Code Section 404(a)(5) is equal to the amount of the contribution and not the entire amount taxable to the employee which is attributable to the contribution. [Treas Reg § 1.404(a)-12(b)(1)] That is, earnings on the contribution are not deductible by the employer, even when they are includible in the income of the employee.

Q 5:30   Must separate accounts be maintained for each participating individual in order for an employer to receive a deduction for contributing to a secular trust?

Yes. Separate accounts must be maintained for each participating individual in the case of a funded nonqualified plan in which more than one employee participates. This requirement may create a problem for anyone seeking to establish a defined benefit nonqualified plan in connection with a secular trust because a defined benefit plan ordinarily does not involve individual accounts. Note that while the requirement of separate accounts does not require that a separate trust be maintained for each employee, it does require that a separate account be maintained for each employee to which employer contributions are allocated, along with any income earned thereon. [IRC § 404(a)(5); Treas Reg § 1.404(a)-12(b)(3)]

Tax Consequences to the Employee

Q 5:31   Can the participating employee be treated as the grantor and the owner of a secular trust?

Yes. The participating employee may be treated as the grantor and the owner of a secular trust. In fact, in light of the IRS's 1992 secular trust private letter rulings, this may be the only economically efficient method by which to establish a secular trust. To create such a secular trust, the participating employees must have the right to elect to receive cash payments when earned or to have the payments contributed to the trust.

Q 5:32   When are funds held in a secular trust considered income to the participating employee?

Contributions to a secular trust are includible in the employee's income in the year they are made to the trust or, if later, in the year they become vested. [Ltr Ruls 8843021, July 29, 1988; 8841023, July 9, 1988; see also Ltr Rul 9031031, May 8, 1990]

Q 5:33   Are contributions to a secular trust includible in an employee's income under the constructive receipt doctrine?

If there are no substantial limitations upon an employee's right to receive the amounts to be contributed to, or which have been contributed to or earned by, the secular trust, the funds are includible in the employee's income under the constructive receipt doctrine. Generally, a taxpayer includes the amount of any item of income in his or her gross income for the taxable year in which he or she receives it, unless, under the taxpayer's method of accounting, it is properly included in a different period. Generally, an employee, as a cash method taxpayer, includes amounts in gross income when they are actually or constructively received. [IRC § 451(a); Treas Reg § 1.451-1(a)]

Generally, income, although not actually reduced to a taxpayer's possession, is constructively received by the taxpayer in the taxable year during which it is:

1. Credited to his or her account;
2. Set apart for him or her; or
3. Otherwise made available to him or her.

However, income is not constructively received if the taxpayer's control of its receipt is subject to substantial limitations or restrictions. [Treas Reg § 1.451-2(a)]

Q 5:34   Are vested contributions to a secular trust includible in the employee's income under the economic benefit doctrine?

Yes. Vested contributions to a secular trust are includible in the participating employee's income under the economic benefit doctrine because such contributions are placed irrevocably in trust for the participant's exclusive benefit and are not subject to the claims of the employer or the employer's creditors.

Under the economic benefit doctrine, if any economic or financial benefit is conferred on an individual as compensation in a taxable year, it is taxable to the individual in that year, even though not in cash form. The economic benefit doctrine applies when assets are unconditionally and irrevocably paid into a fund or trust to be used for the employee's sole benefit. Thus, in general, because vested contributions to a secular trust are not subject to the claims of the employer or the employer's creditors and the participating employee is fully vested in the benefits under the secular trust, the economic benefit doctrine would require that vested amounts contributed to the trust be includible in the employee's income when contributed.

Q 5:35   Will the creation of a secular trust result in a transfer of property to an employee triggering tax under Code Section 83?

The IRS, in certain of its rulings on secular trusts, has indicated that payments by an employer, pursuant to a participant's election, under a nonqualified plan to a secular trust established by the participant will be includible in the participant's gross income in the year paid pursuant to Code Sections 83 and 451. In general, Code Section 83 provides rules for the taxation of property transferred to an employee in connection with the performance of services. This property generally is not taxable to the employee until it has been transferred to the employee or becomes substantially vested in the employee. Section 1.83-3(a)(1) of the Regulations provides that a transfer of property occurs when a person acquires a beneficial ownership interest in the property.

Section 1.83-3(b) of the Regulations provides that a taxpayer's right to property is substantially vested for purposes of Section 83 when it is either transferable or not subject to a substantial risk of forfeiture. Section 1.83-3(c) of the Regulations provides that a substantial risk of forfeiture exists where rights in property that are transferred are conditioned upon the future performance, or nonperformance, of substantial services by any person, or the occurrence of a condition related to a purpose of the transfer, and the possibility of forfeiture is substantial if such condition is not satisfied. Section 1.83-3(d) of the Regulations provides that the rights of a person in property are transferable if the person can transfer any interest in the property to any person other than the transferor of the property, but only if the rights in such property of such transferee are not subject to a substantial risk of forfeiture. Accordingly, property is transferable if the person performing the services or receiving the property can sell, assign, or pledge his or her interest in the property to any person other than the transferor of the property and if the transferee is not required to give up the property or its value if the substantial risk of forfeiture materializes.

Section 1.83-3(e) of the Regulations provides that, for purposes of Code Section 83, the term "property" includes real and personal property other than money or an unfunded and unsecured promise to pay money or property in the future. Property also includes a beneficial interest in assets, including money, transferred or set aside from the claims of the creditors of the transferor.

Vested contributions to a secular trust are not subject to the claims of the employer's creditors and, because the participating employee's rights to the contributions are not subject to a substantial risk of forfeiture, the participating employees are fully vested in these contributions. The IRS has held that there is a transfer of property within the meaning of Code Section 83 when contributions are made to a secular trust and payments to the trust are includible in the participant's income in the year paid. [Ltr Ruls 8841023, July 9, 1988; 9031031, May 8, 1990]

Q 5:36 Does the creation of a secular trust result in a contribution of property to a nonexempt trust that triggers tax to the employee?

Yes, unless the trust is established as an employee grantor secular trust (see Qs 5:25, 5:26, and 5:38). If the secular trust is an employer-established secular trust, an employee generally will be subject to tax under Code Section 402(b)(1) on contributions made on his or her behalf to the secular trust. Code Section 402(b)(1) provides that employer contributions to a nonexempt trust are included in the gross income of the employee in accordance with Code Section 83 (see Q 5:35), except that the value of the employee's interest in the trust will be substituted for the fair market value of the property for purposes of applying Section 83. Distributions from the trust are taxed in accordance with Code Section 72, relating to annuities; including the ten percent early distribution penalty tax. Under these rules, a portion of the distribution will be a return of the participant's investment, which will not be taxable.

Section 1.402(b)-1(a)(1) of the Regulations provides that contributions made on behalf of an employee by an employer to a nonexempt trust will be included in the gross income of the employee for the year during which the contribution is made, but only to the extent that the employee's interest in the contribution is substantially vested at the time the contribution is made. The regulation then refers to Section 1.83-3(b) of the Regulations for the definition of the term "substantially vested." Section 1.83-3(b) of the Regulations provides that property is substantially vested when it is either transferable or not subject to a substantial risk of forfeiture.

If contributions to an employer-established secular trust are considered property that is substantially vested within the meaning of Section 1.83-3 of the Regulations, then those contributions will be considered property that is substantially vested within the meaning of Section 1.402(b)-1 of the Regulations (see Q 5:35). Therefore, a contribution to an employer-established secular trust which is not subject to a substantial risk of forfeiture is taxable to the employee at the time the contribution is made under Code Section 402(b)(1). If the contribution is subject to a substantial risk of forfeiture, the employee will be subject to tax under Section 402(b)(1) when there is no longer a substantial risk of forfeiture.

Code Section 402(b)(2) provides that, if one of the reasons a trust is not exempt from tax under Code Section 501(a) is the failure of the plan of which it is a part to meet the requirements of Code Section 401(a)(26) or Code Section 410(b), then a highly compensated employee, as defined under Code Section 414(q), shall not include in gross income the amount determined under Code Section 402(b)(1). Instead, the highly compensated employee includes in gross income, for the taxable year with or within which the taxable year of the trust ends, an amount equal to the vested accrued benefit of the employee (less the amounts previously taxed) as of the end of the taxable year of the trust. Under this provision, because most participants in a nonqualified plan will qualify as highly compensated employees, the plan would not meet the Code Section 410(b) requirements and these highly compensated participants would be taxed on the benefits under the plan not previously taxed. Thus, under Section 402(b)(2), unless the secular trust is an employee grantor secular trust, the employee would be taxed currently on the contributions to the trust (except to the extent they are subject to a substantial risk of forfeiture) and trust earnings would be taxed currently to the employee and to the trust as a taxable entity. Note that, if Section 402(b)(2) applies and the employee is taxed currently on both the contributions to the trust and the earnings, the employee should not, under Section 72, have to pay additional tax on the distributions from the trust.

Q 5:37   If contributions to a secular trust are includible in an employee's income, is the employee typically provided with funds to be used to pay the resulting tax liability?

Often, yes. Participating employees often receive from their employers a "grossed-up bonus" to cover the tax owed on the contribution and the bonus. As an alternative, the secular trust may be designed to pay to participating employees an amount from the secular trust equal to the tax owed on the contribution and the distribution.

Q 5:38 How is the income of a secular trust treated for tax purposes?

The tax treatment of the income on the assets held in a secular trust depends upon the manner in which the trust is created.

In rulings regarding secular trusts, the IRS has treated employee-grantor secular trusts as trusts within the meaning of Treasury Regulations Section 301.7701-4(a) and has treated the participants as the grantors of the trusts. The IRS has stated in these rulings that, because all income will be distributed to the grantor or accumulated for future distribution to the grantor, each participant, as the grantor, will be treated as the owner of the trust under Code Section 677. Therefore, pursuant to Code Section 671, each participant is required to include the income, deductions, and credits of the trust in computing his or her taxable income. [IRC §§ 671, 677; Ltr Ruls 8843021, July 29, 1988; 8841023, July 9, 1988]

The IRS recently ruled that the rules of Code Sections 402(b) and 404(a)(5) preclude a Section 402(b) employees' trust from being treated as owned by the employer under the grantor trust rules. Under Section 404(a)(5), an employer's deductions for contributions to a Section 402(b) employees' trust over the life of the trust are limited to the amount of the employer's contributions to the trust, and may never include trust income. Application of the grantor trust rules to treat the employer as the owner of an employees' trust would compel the employer to include income of the trust in the employer's income even though Section 404(a)(5) prohibits the employer from ever deducting the trust income. Also, if the employer was treated as the owner of a Section 402(b) employees' trust, the timing under Section 404(a)(5) of the employer's deduction of the amount of the contribution to match the timing of the employee's inclusion in income would result in a deduction by the employer of contributions to the trust, while the employer was still considered to be the owner of the underlying assets for federal income tax purposes. Accordingly, the IRS ruled that the tax consequences of a Section 402(b) employees' trust are "fundamentally inconsistent" with the treatment of the employer as the owner of the trust under the grantor trust rules. Therefore, the grantor trust rules may not be applied to treat the employer as the owner of any portion of a Section 402(b) employer-established employees' trust [Ltr Ruls 9206009, Nov 11, 1991; 9207010, Nov 12, 1991; 9212019, Dec 20, 1991; 9212024, Dec 20, 1991; see Q 5:25]

Q 5:39   Is it possible to protect income earned in the trust from taxation by investing in tax-exempt investments?

Yes. Because the employee-grantor is treated, for tax purposes, as the owner of the assets in an employee-grantor secular trust, tax on a secular trust's income may be avoided by investing trust assets in municipal bonds or some other tax-free investments.

Q 5:40   Will the funding of a secular trust create any adverse tax consequences under Code Section 280G, which provides rules for "golden parachutes"?

Possibly. The funding of a secular trust within a certain period of time prior to a change in the ownership or control of the employer may result in a "parachute payment" within the meaning of Code Section 280G (see chapter 9 regarding parachute payments).

Q 5:41   Are distributions of benefits from a secular trust pursuant to the terms of a nonqualified plan subject to the premature distribution rules of Code Section 72(q)?

Possibly. According to two recently published IRS letter rulings, the income inclusion rules of Sections 72 and 402(b) apply with respect to the distribution of benefits from a secular trust and, therefore, the ten percent penalty for early distributions from "annuity contracts" also applies. However, taxpayers may be able to argue successfully that the Section 72(q) penalty would not apply if all the participant's income is taxed in the year in which it is earned and/or that Section 72(q) was never intended to apply to nonqualified plans (especially those funded by employee grantor secular trusts). [Ltr Ruls 9212019, Dec 20, 1991; 9212024, Dec 20, 1991; see Q 5:25.]

Q 5:42   What are the tax incidents of permitting an executive to transfer his or her rabbi trust interest to a secular trust?

In Letter Ruling 9337016, the IRS commented on a situation in which employees were permitted to elect to have amounts held on their behalf in a rabbi trust transferred to a newly established secular trust. The IRS held that, regardless of whether a particular employee exercised this transfer right, the mere existence of the transfer right caused the employee to realize taxable income, in an amount subject to the transfer right, in the year in which the transfer right is first exercisable. The IRS held that the employees were in constructive receipt of the amount subject to the transfer right because there were no substantial limitations or restrictions on the employees' rights to have the amounts transferred to the fully vested secular trust which—unlike the rabbi trust—was exempt from the claims of the employer's bankruptcy and insolvency creditors.

Case Study 5-1

Note: See Case Studies at the end of chapters 1 through 4.

A opens the meeting by reminding the group of its interest in the rabbi trust concept and asks the advisor to describe the differences between a rabbi trust and a secular trust. The advisor responds by stating that, unlike a rabbi trust, secular trust assets are held for the exclusive purpose of paying plan benefits and, like the assets in a tax-qualified plan's trust, may not be reached by any creditors of the employer, including bankruptcy/insolvency creditors.

B asks why anyone would utilize a rabbi trust if a secular trust is available. The advisor responds that, under the economic benefit doctrine contained in Code Sections 83 and/or 402(b), participants in plans using secular trusts are taxed on contributions and any taxable earnings as soon as they vest, rather than when the benefits are actually or constructively received (as is the case with rabbi trust situations), and that the employer may deduct the contributions as they are made. *C* points out that, therefore, plans using secular trusts to secure vested benefits do not provide "deferred" compensation at all. The advisor notes that, in essence, this is correct, although actual access to the already-taxed compensation may be deferred and grossed-up bonuses may be paid to participants by the employer to eliminate the economic effect of the current taxes on the participants.

The advisor adds that the use of an employer-established secular trust in connection with a nonqualified plan may cause the plan to be funded for ERISA purposes, thereby losing some of the advantages of maintaining the underlying plan.

In light of their consensus that bankruptcy/insolvency is an unlikely event for ABC, the group concludes that a secular trust is not indicated at this time. However, they agree that, should the corporation's financial circumstances change, this option should be revisited. This meeting ends with *A* noting that *D* will bring a friend in the insurance business to the next two meetings to discuss some insurance-related deferred compensation options.

See Case Study at the end of chapter 6 for a discussion of split-dollar life insurance.

Chapter 6

Split-Dollar Life Insurance

A split-dollar life insurance plan typically is an arrangement in which the benefits and the costs of a life insurance policy are split between an employer and an employee. A split-dollar life insurance plan can provide current life insurance protection to the employee and a cash accumulation to the employer for funding a future obligation of the employer, such as a deferred compensation arrangement or future key employee buy-out. Split-dollar life insurance plans use cash-value policies, such as whole or universal life policies, and not term life policies. This chapter examines a number of varieties of split-dollar life insurance plans (including reverse split-dollar life insurance), the tax consequences for employers and employees who use split-dollar life insurance plans, and the extent to which ERISA applies to split-dollar life insurance plans.

Overview

Q 6:1   What is a typical example of a split-dollar life insurance plan?

In a typical split-dollar life insurance plan (referred to as the "P.S. 58 method" in the following questions), an employer and an employee join together in purchasing an insurance policy on the life of the employee and enter into an agreement that requires the employer and employee to split:

1. The cost of the policy's premium, and
2. The policy's benefits, such as cash value and death proceeds.

The employer generally pays the portion of the annual premium that exceeds what is known as the P.S. 58 or Table I (see Appendix B) cost of the term life insurance benefit under the policy (that is, the cost of the term life insurance benefit as calculated from a table in the IRS regulations, rather than the actual cost of the benefit). In return, the employer is entitled to receive, from the policy proceeds (at the death of the employee or upon the surrender (roll-out) date of the policy), an amount equal to the policy's cash surrender value. The employee pays the portion of the annual premium that equals the policy's P.S. 58 cost. In return, the employee is entitled to receive term life insurance protection and has the right to name a beneficiary of the policy proceeds in excess of the policy's cash surrender value that are payable at his or her death.

One problem with this method arises if the policy is terminated in the first few years after initiation. If this occurs, the cash value may not be sufficient to fully reimburse the employer for its cash outlay. The employer may wish to insert a plan provision that requires the employee to reimburse the employer for any shortfall in the cash value if, for example, the early termination of the policy is caused by the employee's termination of employment. [Rev Rul 64-328, 1964-2 CB 11; GCM 32941, Nov 20, 1964]

Q 6:2   What are some other examples of split-dollar life insurance plans?

In addition to the typical P.S. 58 method split-dollar life insurance plan, there are many other examples of split-dollar life insurance methods. The type of plan that should be used depends on the circumstances of the particular setting and the goals which the employer and employee wish to achieve. New variations on the split-dollar life insurance concept are constantly emerging. The following list includes the primary categories of split-dollar life insurance methods that are currently used in addition to the P.S. 58 method.

1. *Cash Value Method.* Under this type of split-dollar life insurance plan, the employer pays that portion of each annual premium equal to the annual increase in the policy's cash surrender value and the employee pays the balance. Because increases in the policy's cash surrender value are small in the policy's early years, the employee will pay a substantial portion of the premium during those years. However, over the life of the policy, the employee's share of the premium decreases and, in some cases, may eventually drop to zero. This method ensures that the cash value always will be sufficient fully to reimburse the employer for its cash outlay. [Rev Rul 64-328, 1964-2 CB 11]

2. *Level Contribution Method.* Under the level contribution method, the employee pays a level portion of the insurance premium for a specified number of years (typically from 5 to 10 years). The employer pays the portion of the premium that exceeds the level premium paid by the employee. This method is used to avoid the substantial early years' payments by the employee that occur under the cash value method. However, if the policy is terminated within the first few years, this method could result in the inability fully to reimburse the employer for its cash outlay.

3. *Employer-Pays-All Method.* Under this form of split-dollar life insurance plan, the employer pays the entire annual premium due on the policy. The employee pays no portion of the premium but receives term life insurance protection and has the right to name a beneficiary of that portion of the death proceeds that exceeds the amount necessary to reimburse the employer for its cash outlay. As under the P.S. 58 method and the level contribution method, if the policy is terminated in the first few years, the cash value may not be sufficient to fully reimburse the employer for its cash outlay.

4. *Equity Method*. Under the different forms of split-dollar life insurance plans described above, the employer often is entitled to the entire cash value of the policy. Any of those different forms, however, can be structured to give the employee an interest in the cash value (equity) of the policy. For example, the P.S. 58 method can be structured so that the employer will receive a reimbursement of its cash outlay and any excess cash value will be split between the employer and the employee or transferred to the employee at the policy's surrender (roll-out) date (see Q 6:19).

Q 6:3   Can a split-dollar arrangement be used in situations other than between employers and employees?

Yes. While a split-dollar arrangement usually involves an employer and an employee, such an arrangement may also be structured between individuals, a shareholder and a corporation, or an individual and any entity having an insurable interest in the individual. [Rev Rul 79-50, 1979-1 CB 138]

Q 6:4   What is a reverse split-dollar life insurance plan?

In general, a reverse split-dollar life insurance plan is a plan in which the normal split-dollar interests of the employer and those of the employee are reversed. Under the typical reverse split-dollar life insurance plan, the employer pays the portion of the policy premium equal to the policy's P.S. 58 cost and the employee pays the remaining portion of the policy premium.

Generally, under this type of plan, the employer receives life insurance protection on the employee and is the beneficiary of that portion of the death proceeds that exceeds the policy's cash surrender value. The employee is entitled to receive, from the policy's proceeds, an amount equal to the policy's cash surrender value.

Thus, in a typical reverse split-dollar life insurance plan, an employee acquires an insurance policy on his or her life and files an endorsement with the insurance company designating the employer as the beneficiary of the specified portion of the death benefits, in exchange for the employer's agreement to pay that portion of the premium equal to the P.S. 58 cost. The employee owns the cash surrender value of the policy and may use the cash value as a source of supplemental retirement benefits. There are few IRS rulings regarding these arrangements and it is not entirely clear how these arrangements are taxed.

Q 6:5   How is a split-dollar life insurance plan implemented?

In general, there are two methods for implementing a split-dollar life insurance plan: the endorsement method and the collateral assignment method.

1. *Endorsement Method.* Under this method, the employer owns the insurance policy and is responsible for the payment of the annual premiums. An endorsement is filed with the insurance company that requires the appropriate payment to the employer from the death or other proceeds. The endorsement also designates the beneficiary and prohibits a change in the designation unless the employee (or a third party) consents to the change. An existing corporate owned life insurance (COLI) policy on the life of the employee can be used, which may be important if the employee no longer is insurable. [Rev Rul 64-328, 1964-2 CB 11]

2. *Collateral Assignment Method.* Under this method, the employee owns the policy and is responsible for the payment of premiums. The employer's payments essentially are considered advances made on behalf of the employee. The employee assigns the appropriate portion of the policy to the employer as collateral for the repayment of these advances. [Rev Rul 64-328, 1964-2 CB 11] For federal tax purposes, the IRS has taken the position that the employer's payments are not loans and that the tax consequences applicable to both the endorsement method and the collateral assignment method are the same. [Rev Rul 64-328, 1964-2 CB 11]

Q 6:6   What are some examples of situations where a split-dollar life insurance plan is warranted?

Split-dollar life insurance plans often are used to provide current life insurance protection to an employee in amounts that the employee otherwise could not afford. In addition, a split-dollar life insurance plan may be established for the following purposes:

Funding a nonqualified plan. The employer establishes an unfunded nonqualified plan to provide deferred compensation for a select group of management or highly compensated employees. At the same time, the employer and each employee who participates in the nonqualified plan implement a split-dollar life insurance plan using the cash value method (that is, the employer pays the premiums for the annual increase in the policy's cash surrender value). Each year, the employer credits a participating employee's nonqualified plan account with an amount equal to some portion or all of the premiums paid by the employer for such year with respect to the life insurance policy purchased in connection with the employee's split-dollar life insurance plan.

When a distribution event (such as retirement) occurs under the nonqualified plan, the employer pays the employee the benefits that the employee is eligible to receive under the nonqualified plan from the employer's general assets. Then, when the life insurance policy becomes payable because of the employee's death, the employer receives, from the proceeds of the policy, an amount equal to the cash surrender value, or, if less, a portion thereof equal to the employer's cash outlay under the split-dollar life insurance plan. This arrangement allows the employee to receive insurance benefits under the split-dollar life insurance plan and additional deferred compensation under the nonqualified plan. This arrangement also permits the employer to fund the benefits payable under the nonqualified plan with the proceeds received under the split-dollar life insurance plan. Under certain circumstances, it may be possible for the employer to receive payment under the split-dollar life insurance plan at the same time as the employer pays benefits under the nonqualified plan.

Funding stock purchase agreements. The employer establishes an ESOP or a buy-sell arrangement under which the employer has a future obligation to purchase the employer's stock from management or highly compensated employees. (Under the ESOP, the employer's obligation to purchase its own stock will extend to all participants, but the most significant obligations will occur with respect to the highly compensated participants who will hold the largest blocks of the employer's stock under the plan.) The employer and each member of the select group of management or highly compensated employees implement a split-dollar life insurance plan under which the employer is entitled to more than just a return of its cash outlay (for example, the entire cash value of the policy and/or a portion of the death proceeds of the policy). Upon the event which triggers the employer's obligation to purchase its own stock (typically the retirement or death of the employee), the employer uses the excess cash value or death proceeds of the policy to make the purchase.

Funding severance benefits. The employer establishes a severance benefit program under which certain highly compensated employees will receive cash payments upon termination of employment. The amount of the severance payment increases as the employee's length of service with the employer and compensation increase. The employer and each employee covered by the severance program who is age 50 or younger implement a split-dollar life insurance plan using the cash value method, which provides that the employer is entitled to the entire cash value of the policy, even if the cash value exceeds the employer's cash outlay. Upon the termination of employment of an employee covered under the severance program, the employer uses the cash value of that employee's split dollar policy to pay the severance benefit.

Providing benefits to shareholders. Under any of the benefit programs described above, the employer has an obligation to use its general assets to pay deferred compensation, buy its own stock or pay severance benefits. Without some type of funding of these obligations, shareholders could be affected adversely because of a drain on corporate assets caused by the obligations. Also, the use of a split-dollar life insurance plan to fund the obligations can avoid a decrease in stock price that may occur if other corporate assets are depleted to fund the obligations.

A split-dollar life insurance plan is not always the appropriate method for providing the benefits described above (e.g., where the employer is tax-exempt and therefore gains no advantage, and perhaps may sacrifice return, by investing funds in an insurance product), but it should be considered as one option.

Q 6:7   Is documentation required to establish a split-dollar life insurance plan?

Yes. In addition to the documentation requirements under ERISA (explained later in this chapter) to implement a split-dollar life insurance plan, the employer and the employee must designate in writing their respective obligations under the policy and their respective rights to receive policy proceeds.

ERISA Considerations

Q 6:8   Is a split-dollar life insurance plan subject to ERISA?

Yes, a split-dollar life insurance plan generally is considered an "employee welfare benefit plan" under ERISA Section 3(1). ERISA Section 3(1) defines an employee welfare benefit plan as:

> [A]ny plan, fund, or program . . . established or maintained by an employer or by an employee organization, or by both, to the extent that such plan, fund, or program was established or is maintained for the purpose of providing for its participants or their beneficiaries, through the purchase of insurance or otherwise . . . benefits, in the event of sickness, accident, disability, death or unemployment . . . (other than pensions on retirement or death, and insurance to provide such pensions).

Shortly after the enactment of ERISA, the DOL determined that a specific split-dollar life insurance plan was an employee welfare benefit plan because the split-dollar life insurance plan was established and maintained by an employer for the purpose of providing death benefits to participants and their beneficiaries through the purchase of insurance. Because the plan was an employee welfare benefit plan within the meaning of ERISA Section 3(1), the plan was held to be subject to the ERISA Title I provisions regarding reporting, disclosure, and fiduciary requirements. [DOL Adv Op 77-23, Feb 14, 1977]

Typically, a split-dollar life insurance plan is a top-hat plan and is exempt from ERISA's reporting and disclosure requirements because it benefits only employees who are members of a select group of management or highly compensated employees. A top-hat plan classification, however, will not exempt the split-dollar life insurance plan from ERISA's requirements that the plan be in writing, designate a named fiduciary (who is responsible for administering the plan), and contain a specified claims procedure. A split-dollar life insurance plan also should be exempt from ERISA's bonding requirements for plan assets. The DOL recently determined that the cash value of a split-dollar life insurance plan did not constitute plan assets. [PWBA Op Ltr 92-22A, Oct 27, 1992]

Note that it may be successfully argued that an individual contract or arrangement between an employer and one employee that involves a split-dollar life insurance arrangement is an individual contract and does not constitute an employee welfare benefit plan within the meaning of ERISA Section 3(1). [See generally DOL Adv Ops 76-79, May 25, 1976; 76-110, Sept 28, 1976] Also, a split-dollar life insurance plan will not be subject to ERISA if it is a "governmental plan" under ERISA Section 3(32) or a "church plan" under ERISA Section 3(33).

Q 6:9 Is the cash value portion of a split-dollar life insurance plan a "plan asset" for purposes of ERISA?

Under a typical split-dollar life insurance plan, the cash value portion of the policy will not be a "plan asset" for purposes of ERISA. Therefore, the fiduciary obligations imposed under ERISA will not apply with respect to the management of the cash value portion of the policy. [DOL Adv Op 92-22A, Oct 27, 1992]

Q 6:10 Do any of ERISA's fiduciary standards apply to a split-dollar life insurance plan?

ERISA's general standards of fiduciary conduct apply to the selection and retention of the policy, if the plan is subject to ERISA. Therefore, the employer should not select a policy without regard to the cost of the pure insurance portion of the policy and the financial soundness and claims paying ability of the insurer. [ERISA §§ 404, 406; DOL Adv Op 92-22A, Oct 27, 1992]

Q 6:11   Can an employer deduct the portion of the insurance premium it pays under a split-dollar life insurance plan?

No. Because the employer is either an indirect or direct beneficiary under a split-dollar policy, it is not entitled to a deduction for its share of the annual premiums. In addition, the employer apparently is not entitled to a deduction for the P.S. 58 costs included in the executive's gross income, although not all commentators agree with this conclusion. [IRC §§ 264(a)(1) and 162; Treas Reg § 1.264-1; Rev Rul 64-328, 1964-2 CB 11; Rev Rul 66-110, 1966-1 CB 12; Rev Rul 70-148, 1970-1 CB 60]

Q 6:12   Are there any variations of a split-dollar life insurance plan that allow the employer to deduct its costs under the plan?

Variations of split-dollar arrangements continue to appear on the market which claim to provide the employer with a method to deduct some or all of its costs under a split-dollar life insurance plan. One such arrangement is a "leveraged split-dollar life insurance plan." A leveraged split-dollar life insurance plan is designed to provide a deduction for the interest payments on a loan of up to $50,000 to the employer, the proceeds of which are used to purchase the policy. Under this arrangement, the employer borrows $50,000 from the insurance company and immediately contributes this amount to the insurance company as an advance payment of premiums. This initial deposit is used for the first $50,000 of premiums for the policy. The employer's annual payments are limited to the interest payments on the "loan" until the $50,000 has been absorbed as premium payments. The argument under this arrangement is that the interest payments on the $50,000 of indebtedness used to purchase life insurance covering an officer, employee, or other financially interested party are deductible under Code Section 264(a)(4). The question this arrangement raises is whether the "loan" is a bona fide loan for purposes of the tax law.

Tax Consequences to the Employer

Q 6:13   Is the employer taxed on the policy's cash value if the policy is terminated during the employee's life?

Possibly. The employer has reportable income to the extent that the cash surrender value proceeds it actually receives exceed the premiums it actually paid. Generally, the proceeds paid to the employer first are treated as a return of the employer's basis, and no portion of the proceeds are included in the employer's gross income until the proceeds paid to the employer exceed the employer's basis. However, if:

1. The policy was issued after 1984,

2. There is a cash distribution to the employer within the first 15 years after the policy was issued, and

3. There is a reduction in policy benefits (for example, death proceeds) as a result of the distribution, the distribution will be treated first as income and not as a return of basis. [IRC §§ 72(e), 7702(f)(7); Treas Reg § 1.72-11(c)]

Q 6:14 Is the employer taxed on its share of the proceeds that are payable upon the employee's death?

Generally, no. The employer's share of the policy's death benefit proceeds is not included in its gross income. However, if the policy used under the split-dollar life insurance plan was "transferred for value" (for example, an employee-owned policy is transferred to the employer and the employee is not an officer or shareholder of the employer), the employer's share of the death proceeds in excess of the employer's basis in the policy is included in the employer's gross income. [IRC § 101; Rev Rul 64-328, 1964-2 CB 11]

Q 6:15 Is the employer taxed on any dividends that are paid by the insurance company on the policy?

No. If, under the typical forms of split-dollar life insurance plans, the dividends (1) are used to reduce the employer's payment for the year, (2) are paid directly to the employer, (3) are used to increase the policy's cash value or (4) are used in any other way to benefit the employer, the dividends are not included in the employer's gross income.

Q 6:16   Are the tax consequences to the employer and to the employee different under a reverse split-dollar life insurance plan?

Although the IRS has not ruled on this issue, it appears that, under a reverse split-dollar life insurance plan, the tax consequences to the employer and the employee are reversed.

Tax Consequences to the Employee

Q 6:17   Does the employee recognize income under the typical split-dollar life insurance plan?

Yes. The IRS has ruled that a typical split-dollar insurance arrangement confers an economic benefit on the employee. The economic benefit is the value of any current life insurance protection enjoyed by the employee, plus any other benefits the employee may receive under the policy, such as cash dividends. The amount that is includible in the employee's gross income each year is equal to the excess of the total economic benefit received by the employee under the plan for the year, minus the amount, if any, paid by the employee under the plan for that year. The value of any current life insurance protection enjoyed by the employee is equal to the lesser of the P.S. 58 cost or the insurer's individual initial issue one-year term life insurance rates.

Q 6:18   If a policyholder's dividend is paid by the insurance company, does the employee recognize income?

Generally, yes. Where a policyholder's dividend is paid directly to the employee, the amount of this dividend must be included with the other benefits received by the employee under the split-dollar life insurance plan for purposes of determining the amount includible in the employee's gross income. In addition, the economic benefit of the dividend is includible in the employee's gross income if the dividend is used to purchase additional one-year term insurance, or paid-up life insurance in which the employee has a nonforfeitable interest, for a period of more than one year. The value of this economic benefit may be the amount of the dividend or the P.S. 58 cost of the additional life insurance, depending on the circumstances. [Rev Rul 66-110, 1966-1 CB 12]

Q 6:19 How is the employee taxed if the employee has an interest in the policy's cash value?

Under a traditional split-dollar life insurance plan, the employee has no interest in the policy's cash value. However, the plan can provide that the employee will accrue an interest in the cash value over the policy's life or that an interest in the cash value will be transferred to the employee upon the scheduled termination date (roll-out date) of the plan. This type of split-dollar life insurance plan typically is called the equity method, because the cash value, or equity, of the policy is split between the employer and the employee.

Under the equity method, as long as the employee's interest in the policy's equity is subject to "a substantial risk of forfeiture," the employee does not include any portion of the equity in income. Although the inclusion of equity in income for tax purposes has not been resolved definitively, most commentators believe that, in the year that the employee's interest in the equity (or a portion thereof) is no longer subject to a substantial risk of forfeiture, that amount should be includible in the employee's gross income. Subsequent increases in the employee's vested interest in the equity likewise would be included in the year in which they occur.

In one ruling, the IRS reviewed a split-dollar life insurance plan described as a split-dollar roll-out plan. Under the arrangement, the employer would apply for a paid-up-at-age-65 participating insurance policy on the life of an employee, pursuant to which the employer would have ownership rights in the death benefit under the policy (measured by the aggregate premiums that it pays) and the balance of the death benefit would be owned by the employee. The plan provided that, during the first seven years of the policy, the employee would pay only the P.S. 58 cost portion of the premium and the employer would pay the balance of the premium. At the beginning of the eighth year of the policy, the employer would borrow out of the policy an amount equal to its aggregate premium payments and then transfer full ownership of the policy, subject to the loan, to the employee. In the event of termination of employment by the employee (for any reason other than death) prior to the transfer of full ownership of the policy at the beginning of the eighth year, the employee would forfeit all rights under the arrangement. Thus, the policy was subject to a substantial risk of forfeiture until the eighth year of the policy.

The IRS, relying on Code Section 83, ruled that, upon the transfer of a policy to the employee, the amount included in the employee's gross income is the net cash surrender value of the policy transferred to the employee less the amount the employee contributed to the net cash surrender value. Thus, the contributions made by the employee provided the employee with a basis in the policy which the employee could use to offset income. The IRS also ruled, based upon Code Section 83(h), that the employer would be entitled to a deduction under Code Section 162 equal to the amount included in the gross income of the employee. At the same time, the employer would be required to recognize any gain to the extent described in Treasury Regulations Section 1.83-6(b). [Ltr Rul 83-100-27, Dec 3, 1982]

Q 6:20   Is the employee taxed on his or her share of the death benefits?

No. The employee's estate's, or named beneficiary's, share of the policy's death benefit proceeds is exempt from income tax. [IRC § 101(a); Rev Rul 64-328, 1964-2 CB 11]

Q 6:21   Are death benefit proceeds paid to an employee's estate or beneficiary includible in the employee's gross estate for federal estate tax purposes?

Generally, yes. The death benefit proceeds are includible in the employee's gross estate where these proceeds are payable to that estate. Similarly, these proceeds are includible in the employee's gross estate where they are payable to a beneficiary and the employee is considered to possess any incidents of ownership in the policy at the time of death. In general, an employee will be deemed to have incidents of ownership in the policy if the employee has the power to change the beneficiary. Also, the IRS has ruled that when an employee owns more than 50 percent of the employer and the employer holds at the employee's death the right to borrow against the cash surrender value of a life insurance policy on the employee's life, the portion of the policy proceeds payable (other than to or for the benefit of the employer) is includible in the employee's gross estate under Code Section 2042(2). However, if the employee has no incidents of ownership in the policy, and does not own more than 50 percent of the employer (or, if the employee does own more than 50 percent of the employer, the employer has no incidents of ownership in the policy), the death benefit proceeds will not be includible in the employee's gross estate. [IRC § 2042; Treas Reg § 20.2042-1(c)(2); Rev Rul 82-145, 1982-2 CB 213; Schwager v Comm'r, 64 TC 781 (1975); Estate of Tomerlin v Comm'r, TC Memo 1986-148, 51 TCM 831 (1986)]

Q 6:22   Does an assignment of an employee's rights and obligations under a split-dollar arrangement to another party result in a new split-dollar arrangement?

Yes. The IRS has determined that an assignment of an employee's rights and obligations to another party constitutes a termination of the split-dollar life insurance plan and results in a new contractual relationship based upon a new contract by all interested parties. The concept behind the taxation of split-dollar life insurance plans is that an employee has received an economic benefit from his or her employer, the value of which is included in the gross income of the employee. It is the employer-employee relationship that gives rise to the tax consequences of such an arrangement. Although the terms of an employer's agreement with one employee may be the same as the terms of an earlier agreement with another employee, and the insurance policy utilized in the later agreement may be the same as that which was utilized in the earlier one, the agreements necessarily constitute separate arrangements by virtue of the fact that they involve different employees. [IRS Action on Decision CC-1982-008, Mar 29, 1982; see Rev Rul 90-109, 1990-2 CB 191]

In *Sercl v. United States* [684 F 2d 597 (8th Cir 1982)], George Sercl entered into a split-dollar arrangement with his company on November 4, 1964, allowing him to rely on Revenue Ruling 55-713 with respect to the tax consequences of the arrangement. He assigned all of his rights and obligations under the split-dollar arrangement to his son on February 1, 1971, in connection with his subsequent retirement from the company. His son contended that he stepped into his father's arrangement and he, too, relied on Revenue Ruling 55-713. The court did not agree and found that a new split-dollar arrangement was created which fell outside the protection of the grandfather clause of Revenue Ruling 64-328 (see Q 6:23 regarding the grandfather clause).

Q 6:23   Is there a grandfather rule that allows employees to continue to rely on Revenue Ruling 55-713 with respect to the tax consequences of a split-dollar arrangement?

Yes. In Revenue Ruling 55-713, the IRS stated that, under a split-dollar arrangement, no realization of taxable income by the employee would result from the payment of a portion of the premium by the employer, and the employer would receive no deduction for such payment. The ruling stated:

> In the instant case, the substance of the insurance arrangement between the parties is in all essential respects the same as if Y corporation makes annual loans without interest, of a sum of money equal to the annual increases in the cash surrender value of the policies of insurance taken out on the life of B. The mere making available of money does not result in realized income to the payee or a deduction to the payor.

In 1964, the IRS issued Revenue Ruling 64-328, which revoked Revenue Ruling 55-713. Revenue Ruling 64-328 departed entirely from the interest-free loan concept. The ruling looked to the substance of the arrangement to discern whether or not any economic benefit was received by the employee under the split-dollar arrangement. As described in Q 6:20, pursuant to Revenue Ruling 64-328, the employee must include in gross income the value of the economic benefit received by the employee, less any amount paid by the employee, under the arrangement for the year. However, Revenue Ruling 64-328 stated that this new interpretation regarding split-dollar life insurance plans would apply only to policies purchased under split-dollar arrangements, or used to establish such arrangements, after November 13, 1964. [Rev Rul 55-713, 1955-2 CB 23; Rev Rul

64-328, 1964-2 CB 11; Bagley v United States, 348 F Supp 418 (D Minn 1972); Sercl v United States, 684 F 2d 597 (8th Cir 1982)]

Q 6:24   What are the tax consequences of a reverse split-dollar life insurance plan?

The IRS has issued few rulings on the tax consequences to the employer or to the employee with respect to reverse split-dollar arrangements. However, certain tax issues should be noted.

There may be potential tax consequences to a corporate employer with regard to accumulated earnings and alternative minimum taxes. With respect to the employee, if the actual cost of the term insurance is less than the P.S. 58 cost, the excess will increase the policy's cash value and this increase may be considered imputed income that would be includible in the employee's income when vested or transferable. In addition, the employee's estate may be required to include all proceeds payable under the policy if the employee has any incidents of ownership in the policy at death. [IRC §§ 56, 83, 531-537, 2042; Treas Reg § 1.83-1(a) (2); see Estate of Levy v Comm'r, 70 TC 873 (1978)]

In a ruling issued by the IRS on reverse split-dollar life insurance plans, the IRS addressed the federal estate tax consequences applicable to such plans. In this ruling, an individual, who owned 7.4 percent of the common stock of the company, purchased a life insurance policy on his life and used the policy to enter into a split-dollar life insurance plan with the company.

Under the terms of the split-dollar agreement, the shareholder was entitled to exercise all ownership rights granted to the policy owner by the policy, subject to the company's interest in any prepaid and unearned premium. The company was entitled to designate itself as a beneficiary of the policy to the extent of a certain dollar amount plus any prepaid and unearned premium, and the shareholder was required to effectuate the company's designation under the policy. The company was entitled to claim this amount from the death proceeds. The balance of any death proceeds were to be paid according to any other policy beneficiary designation made by the shareholder. The premiums on the policy were to be paid by the shareholder to the insurance company. The company was required to reimburse the shareholder for the P.S. 58 cost portion of the premium paid by the shareholder. The shareholder agreed not to sell, assign, surrender or otherwise terminate the policy. The split-dollar life insurance plan would terminate (1) upon written notice by either party to the other, but only if no premium was owed; (2) by mutual consent of both parties; or (3) upon termination of the shareholder's employment with the company.

The IRS ruled that the entire policy proceeds would be included in the shareholder's gross estate under Code Section 2042(2) because the shareholder possessed incidents of ownership in the policy that were exercisable either alone or in conjunction with the company.

The IRS recognized, however, that, because of the contractual obligation pursuant to which a portion of the proceeds would be paid to the company, the shareholder's estate would be entitled to a deduction under Code Section 2053(a)(4) for any proceeds paid to the company pursuant to the split-dollar agreement. [Ltr Rul 9026041, Mar 30, 1990]

Q 6:25   Has the IRS issued any rulings on the estate tax implications of split-dollar life insurance plans involving a corporation and its majority shareholder?

In Letter Ruling 9511046, the IRS ruled on the estate tax aspects of a split-dollar life insurance plan involving a corporation and its majority shareholder. The ruling concerned a transaction in which the corporation and the independent trustee of an irrevocable life insurance trust established by the majority shareholder of the corporation entered into a collateral assignment split-dollar life insurance plan. The IRS ruled that the security interest of the corporation in the split-dollar policy under the collateral assignment did not constitute an incident of ownership in the policy that could be attributed to the majority shareholder through his ownership of the corporation, thereby causing the value of the policy death benefits to be included in the majority shareholder's estate.

Note that the ruling did not deal with the perhaps more interesting question of the attribution to the majority shareholder of the inside build-up in the split-dollar life insurance policy during his life, because of his control of the corporation and, through the corporation, the life insurance policy.

Case Study 6-1

Note: See Case Studies at the end of chapters 1 through 5.

D opens the meeting by introducing an insurance professional with extensive experience in the nonqualified deferred compensation area. A asks the insurance professional to describe insurance-related deferred compensation options.

The insurance expert introduces the concept of split-dollar life insurance, stating that split-dollar life insurance provides a means for an employer and an employee working together to acquire for the employee amounts of life insurance, which can be used to provide death benefits, cash value build-up, or both, not otherwise realistically available to the employee. This is accomplished by splitting the premium cost of the insurance between the employer and the employee (with the employer paying the bulk of the cost). The ultimate return on the policy is used to reimburse the employer for some or all of its outlay.

The insurance professional notes that there are a number of variations on the split-dollar theme, but D has specifically inquired about the "P.S. 58 cost" variation. The insurance expert explains this variation with the following example:

Example: D, age 33, is insurable and requires $1,000,000 in death benefit protection under a life insurance policy, but cannot afford the premiums of $1,000 per year. D's employer, corporation P, is willing to pay most of the $1,000 per year for D's benefit, but would like, ultimately, to recoup its premium outlays. Corporation P and D enter into an agreement under which the $1,000,000 policy is purchased, D pays that portion of the annual $1,000 premium equal to the P.S. 58 cost ($90 while he is 33 years old) and corporation P pays the remainder of the premium ($910 while D is 33 years old). The agreement provides that, if D dies, the $1,000,000 death benefit is paid to Corporation P to the extent of the premiums it has paid and the remainder of the $1,000,000 death benefit is paid to the beneficiary designated by D.

B asks if the cash value build-up in the insurance policy, to the extent it exceeds corporation P's premium payments, may be used to provide deferred compensation benefits to D. The insurance advisor notes that this typically is referred to as "equity" split-dollar life insurance and often is used by employers and employees. The advisor explains that there is a risk that any vested cash value build-up under the policy will be taxable to D as it accrues, under the theory that D has not paid for any portion of that cash value build-up but has recognized an economic benefit equal to the value of the build-up.

A and B are particularly excited about the split-dollar life insurance concept, because they believe they are underinsured from an estate planning point of view. The insurance advisor informs them that, unfortunately, split-dollar life insurance is available only to participants who plan to work for at least 15 additional years, and neither A nor B would qualify.

The advisor notes that any premiums the corporation pays will not be deductible, but that any death proceeds received by the corporation to reimburse it for its premium outlays or received by the beneficiary designated by the participant will not be taxable.

The group asks the insurance advisor to prepare a written split-dollar proposal, using the P.S. 58 cost method, for $1,000,000 of coverage each for C, D, and E, to be discussed at the next meeting, and to prepare an overview of the corporate-owned life insurance concept for discussion at that time.

For a discussion of corporate-owned life insurance see the Case Study at the end of chapter 7.

Chapter 7

Corporate-Owned Life Insurance

This chapter examines corporate-owned life insurance (COLI) as a funding vehicle for nonqualified plans. Topics include how this insurance is structured, who owns and benefits from the insurance, tax considerations such as whether a deduction is allowed for the premiums for, and interest on loans from, such insurance, and whether a nonqualified plan that is funded with COLI is subject to ERISA.

Overview

Q 7:1   What is corporate-owned life insurance?

Corporate-owned life insurance (COLI) is exactly what its name implies—a life insurance policy that is owned by the employer, which insures the lives of one or more employees of the employer. A COLI policy generally covers the lives of several executive employees of the employer and can be used for a variety of purposes that may or may not bear any relation to the anticipated actual financial loss to the employer on the death of the covered employees. For example, a COLI policy may bear little relation to the employer's financial loss when it is used to fund the employer's obligation under a buy-sell agreement or a nonqualified plan that is due upon the death of the executive insured by the COLI policy. However, a COLI policy may be directly related to the employer's financial loss when the insured is a key employee and the death proceeds are to be retained by the employer to meet the financial loss to the employer caused by the death of the employee.

Q 7:2   How are COLI policies structured?

Generally, an employer purchases cash value life insurance policies on individual employees and pays the premiums for the policies. The premium payments eventually can be met through loans from the cash value that accumulates under the policy. If structured properly, the cash value that accumulates under the policy will not be subject to tax as it accumulates. In addition, subject to certain restrictions, the interest paid on any loan against the cash value is deductible by the employer. In many cases, COLI policies are used to "fund," on a tax-preferred basis, executive benefits unrelated to the death of the insured. As explained in the following questions and answers, the employee is the insured under the COLI policy but has no other rights or obligations with respect to the policy.

Q 7:3   Who is the owner and beneficiary of a COLI policy?

The employer is the owner and beneficiary of the policy. The employer retains all rights to the benefits under the policy (for example, the death proceeds and the cash-value build-up). [Rev Rul 68-99, 1968-1 CB 193; Rev Rul 72-25, 1972-1 CB 127]

Q 7:4   Does the employee have any interest in a COLI policy?

No. Although the employee is the insured under a COLI policy, neither the employee nor any beneficiary of the employee has any interest in the COLI policy. [Rev Rul 68-99, 1968-1 CB 193; Rev Rul 72-25, 1972-1 CB 127]

Q 7:5 Who pays the premiums for the COLI policy?

The employer pays the premiums for the COLI policy. The employee has no obligation to pay any portion of the premiums for the COLI policy.

Q 7:6 Is the employer permitted to borrow against the COLI policy?

Yes. An employer is permitted to borrow against the COLI policy. These borrowed funds then may be used to pay COLI premiums and/or to fund nonqualified plans.

Q 7:7 May withdrawals be made from the COLI policy to pay benefits to an employee pursuant to a nonqualified plan?

Yes. To the extent the cash value of the COLI policy is not required to be left in the policy in order to maintain the policy in force, the cash value may be withdrawn by the employer and used to pay benefits to an employee pursuant to a nonqualified plan.

Tax Considerations

Q 7:8 Is the employer allowed a deduction for the premiums paid on a COLI policy?

No. No deduction is allowed for premiums paid on any life insurance policy covering the life of any officer or employee of the employer, or of any person financially interested in any trade or business carried on by the employer, when the employer is directly or indirectly a beneficiary under the policy. Because the employer is the direct beneficiary under a COLI policy, the employer is not allowed a deduction for premiums paid for it. [IRC § 264(a)(1); Rev Rul 70-148, 1970-1 CB 60]

Q 7:9 Is the interest on loans to the employer from a COLI policy deductible?

Possibly. If four of the first seven years' policy premiums are paid without borrowing from the policy, interest paid by the employer on loans to the employer from the COLI policy is deductible, subject to the following condition: For policies purchased after June 20, 1986, no deduction is allowed for interest on loans totaling more than $50,000 per insured individual under policies covering the lives of officers, employees, or any individual who is financially interested in any trade or business of the employer. An employer, therefore, can purchase separate COLI policies on any number of its employees and, if the four-out-of-seven requirement is met, can deduct the interest on a loan of up to $50,000 from each policy. [IRC § 264(a); Ltr Rul 9041052, July 17, 1990]

Q 7:10 Is the cash value build-up under a COLI policy subject to taxation?

If the COLI policy is structured properly, the policy's cash-value build-up is not taxed currently. Life insurance policyholders are allowed to accumulate cash value in the policy free of taxation as long as the policyholder allows the cash value to accumulate inside the contract. [Theodore H. Cohen, 39 TC 1055 (1963), acq. 1964-1 (Part 1) CB 4]

Q 7:11 Are COLI policy withdrawals, loan proceeds, and surrenders of dividend additions subject to taxation?

In general, no. (However, see Q 7:13.) An employer's withdrawals of cash value or surrender of dividend additions under a life insurance policy generally are treated as a nontaxable recovery of the employer's investment in the contract (that is, premiums paid reduced by dividends and any prior cash distributions). However, withdrawals or dividend addition surrenders that exceed the employer's investment in the contract will be treated as income to the employer. Loans generally are not treated as distributions under the policy and, therefore, are not subject to taxation. [IRC § 72(e); see Pub L No 97-248 § 265; HR 4961, as reported by the Senate Finance Committee, § 267; 1982 US Code Cong & Ad News 781, 1084]

Q 7:12   What is a modified endowment contract?

A modified endowment contract is defined as any contract that satisfies the definition of a life insurance contract under Code Section 7702, that was entered into on or after June 21, 1988, and that fails to meet the seven-pay test (described below). In addition, a modified endowment contract includes any life insurance contract that is received in exchange for a modified endowment contract. [IRC § 7702A(a)] In essence, a modified endowment contract is a life insurance contract that fails to enjoy all of the tax benefits traditionally associated with life insurance contracts. For this reason, modified endowment contract status is to be avoided where possible.

A contract fails to satisfy the seven-pay test if the cumulative amount paid under the contract at any time during the first seven contract years exceeds the sum of the net level premiums that would have been paid on or before the first seven contract years if the contract provided for paid-up future benefits after the payment of seven level annual premiums. Thus, in order for a contract to satisfy the seven-pay test, the contract must provide greater insurance protection per premium dollar during the first seven years of the contract than is required under the general definition of life insurance. [IRC § 7702A(b)]

If there is a material change in the benefits or other terms of a modified endowment contract, the contract is considered a new contract that is subject to the seven-pay test, adjusted to take into account the policy's cash value as of the date that the material change takes effect. Material changes include the exchange of a life insurance contract for another life insurance contract, the conversion of a term life insurance contract into a whole life insurance contract, and an increase in the future benefits provided under a life insurance contract. Note, however, that a material change does not include the following:

1. An increase in the future benefits provided under a contract if the increase is attributable to the payment of premiums necessary to fund the lowest death benefit payable in the first seven contract years, or the crediting of interest or other earnings with respect to those premiums, and
2. A death benefit increase attributable to a cost of living adjustment that is based on an established broad-based index, if the

increase is funded ratably over the remaining period during which premiums are required to be paid under the contract.

[IRC § 7702A(c); 1988 US Code Cong & Ad News 5048, 5162-5165]

If a contract fails to satisfy the seven-pay test, the contract will be treated as a modified endowment contract only with respect to distributions made during the year in which the failure takes effect and during any subsequent contract year, and, pursuant to regulations prescribed by the Secretary of the Treasury, with respect to distributions made in anticipation of the failure (for example, any distribution that is made within two years before the failure).

(Note that the legislative history of Code Section 7702A indicates that the assignment or pledge of any portion of a modified endowment contract is not treated as a distribution if the assignment or pledge is solely to cover the payment of burial expenses or prearranged funeral expenses and the maximum amount of the death benefit provided under the contract does not exceed $25,000.) [IRC § 7702A(d); 1988 US Code Cong & Ad News 5048, 5162]

Q 7:13   Is the tax treatment of withdrawals, surrender of dividend additions, and loans affected if the COLI policies are treated as modified endowment contracts?

Yes. Cash withdrawals from and surrenders of dividend additions under COLI policies treated as "modified endowment contracts" are treated as distributions of policy income. In other words, they first are included in the employer's taxable income, and then treated as nontaxable investment in the contract recovered by the employer. In addition, loans under modified endowment contracts and loans secured by modified endowment contracts are treated as amounts received under the policy and first are included in the employer's taxable income and then treated as recovery of the employer's investment in the contract. Also, an additional 10 percent income tax is imposed on certain amounts received under modified endowment contracts to the extent that the amounts received are includible in gross income. [IRC §§ 72(v), 7702A; H Conf Rpt No 100-1104 reprinted at 1988 US Code Cong & Ad News 5048, 5156-5166]

Q 7:14   Is the tax treatment of withdrawals, surrender of dividend additions, and loans affected if changes are made to the COLI policy?

Possibly. If the benefits or other terms of a COLI policy are changed (except certain changes such as automatic increases in benefits as cash value increases), a redetermination should be made as to whether the policy continues to meet the definition of an insurance contract under Code Section 7702. For example, if the change to the policy is a reduction in benefits that occurs during the 15-year period commencing on the issue date of the policy, and the change is accompanied by a cash distribution to the employer, the cash distribution is treated as a return of policy income that is first included in the employer's taxable income and then treated as a return of the employer's investment in the contract. The amount that is included in the employer's income is limited by recapture rules under Code Section 7702. If the COLI policy fails to meet the definition of an insurance contract under IRC Section 7702 for other reasons, the cash value build-up may be included in the employer's taxable income even if no distributions are made to the employer. [IRC § 7702].

Q 7:15   Are the death benefits payable to the employer under a COLI policy excludable from income?

Yes. The employer's gross income does not include amounts received under a COLI policy if the amounts are paid because of the death of the insured. However, if the COLI policy was "transferred for value" to the employer, a portion of the death benefits may be included in the employer's taxable income. [IRC section 101(a)]

A transfer of a COLI policy to a rabbi trust should not be considered a transfer for value because the employer, after the transfer, still is considered the owner of the policy. The IRS has considered a situation in which an employer proposed to transfer certain COLI policies to a rabbi trust. After the transfer, the trustee would become the owner and beneficiary of the policies. The IRS ruled that as long as the insured, terms, conditions, benefits, and beneficial interests of the policies (other than naming a trustee as beneficiary and nominal owner of the policies) at all times remain the same before and after the transfer to the trust, the transfer of the policies to the trust will not be treated as a transfer for value under Code Section 101(a)(2) and the regulations thereunder because, for income tax purposes, the employer remains the owner of the policies transferred to the trust. Thus, the transfer does not prevent the exclusion of death benefits from the employer's taxable income under Code Section 101(a).

On the other hand, a transfer of a COLI policy to a secular trust may be considered a transfer for value. Another example of circumstances which would result in a "transfer for value" is a transfer of an employee-owned policy to the employer if the employee is not a shareholder or officer of the employer. [See Goldsmith v US, 586 F 2d 810 (Ct Cl 1978), and Frost v Commissioner, 52 TC 89 (1969); Ltr Rul 9041052, July 17, 1990]

Q 7:16   Are amounts paid to an employee under a nonqualified plan that is "funded" by a COLI policy deductible by the employer?

Yes. Generally, an employer will be able to deduct the amounts paid or made available to an employee or the employee's beneficiary under a nonqualified plan in the year in which the amounts are includible in the income of the recipient, to the extent the payments are ordinary and necessary business expenses. The fact that the source of the funds used to pay the deferred compensation is a COLI policy does not change this result. [IRC §§ 162, 404(a)(5); Ltr Rul 9041052, July 17, 1990] However, Code Section 280G (i.e., the so-called "golden parachute" rules) may limit the amount that may be deducted (see chapter 9).

ERISA Considerations

Q 7:17   Will the use of a COLI policy cause a top-hat plan to be subject to additional ERISA provisions?

Generally, no. The use of a COLI policy in connection with a top-hat plan should not affect the extent to which the arrangement is subject to ERISA. If the employer is the owner and beneficiary of the policy and premiums are paid directly out of the employer's general assets (the policy is considered to be an asset of the employer) the plan should be considered unfunded for ERISA purposes. It will therefore be exempt from Parts 2, 3, and 4 of Title I of ERISA, which pertain to participation and vesting, funding, and fiduciary responsibilities, pursuant to the exemptions in ERISA Sections 201(2), 301(a)(3), and 401(a)(1). [Belka v Rowe Furniture Corp, 571 F Supp 1249 (D Md 1983)]

Other Considerations

Q 7:18   **If a key employee terminates employment without any right to benefits under a nonqualified plan, is it possible for a life insurance policy to provide the employer with an option to change the insured from one key employee to another key employee?**

Yes. However, the IRS has ruled that if a life insurance policy provides the employer with an option to change the insured, the exercise of the option is a sale or other disposition of the policy under Code Section 1001 and the nonrecognition provisions of Code Section 1035 do not apply (i.e., if a gain is realized as a result of the sale or exchange, the gain must be included in the employer's taxable income). The IRS indicated that a change in contractual terms effected through an option provided in an original contract is treated as an exchange under Code Section 1001 if there is a sufficiently fundamental or material change causing the substance of the original contract to be altered through the exercise of the option. Under these circumstances, the old contract is treated as if it actually were exchanged for a new one.

Under the ruling, a corporation exercised an option in its insurance policy that permitted the corporation to change the insured from the original insured under the policy to a new insured. The IRS concluded that this resulted in a change in the fundamental substance of the original contract because the essence of a life insurance contract is the life that is insured under the contract. Thus, according to the IRS, the corporation's exercise of the change-of-insured option is substantively the same as an actual exchange of contracts and is a sale or other disposition for purposes of Code Section 1001.

The IRS also noted in the ruling that Section 1.1035-1 of the Regulations excludes from coverage by Code Section 1035 those exchanges of policies that do not relate to the same insured and thus prevents policyholders from indefinitely deferring the recognition of gain with respect to the policy value. If the corporation had assigned a life insurance policy on the original insured to the insurance company as consideration for a new life insurance policy on a new insured, any gain realized on the exchange would have been ineligible for nonrecognition treatment under Code Section 1035. Therefore, the IRS concluded that the corporation cannot avoid the same-insured limitations of Code Section 1035 by inserting terms into its original documents that obviate the need for an actual exchange but nevertheless effect a de facto exchange of the original contract for a new contract on a different insured.

As a result, the exercise of an option in an insurance policy to change the insured constitutes a sale or other disposition of the policy under Code Section 1001, and this disposition does not qualify as a tax-free exchange of insurance policies under Code Section 1035. The IRS also indicated that the result would be the same if the corporation insured a person holding a particular position and, thus, no formal substitution was required to be made when a new person occupies that position. [Rev Rul 90-109, 1990-2 CB 191]

Q 7:19 Are proposals being considered by Congress that would adversely affect the benefits of establishing a COLI policy on the life of a key employee?

No. Although substantive changes have been made to or considered with respect to the rules applicable to COLI policies over the past several years, currently there are no proposals under serious congressional consideration that would affect adversely the benefits of COLI policies.

Q 7:20 Are there risks with respect to the use of a COLI policy to fund nonqualified plans?

Yes. If a COLI policy is the only source of funds for the payment of the employer's obligations under a nonqualified plan and the insurance company experiences extreme financial difficulties, the employer may be unable to access the policy's cash value to pay the plan's benefits. In addition, the estimated earnings under the policy may be substantially less than the actual earnings under the policy, leaving the employer with insufficient cash value to pay plan benefits when they are due. Therefore, when considering the use of COLI policies, an employer should evaluate carefully (1) the insurance company's financial stability and earnings history and (2) whether, under the employer's particular circumstances, a COLI policy is the best alternative. (For example, if the employer is a tax-exempt entity, a tax-preferred product such as a COLI policy may not be the best investment alternative.)

Q 7:21 If a corporate employer owns a COLI policy, are there alternative minimum tax issues that the employer should consider?

Yes. If a corporate employer is the owner of a life insurance policy, the annual inside build-up and death proceeds are among the factors that may subject the employer to an alternative minimum tax (AMT).

Code Section 56(g) provides that in computing the AMT of most C corporations, alternative minimum taxable income is increased by 75 percent of the excess, if any, of adjusted current earnings (ACE) over preadjustment alternative minimum taxable income. ACE generally includes items of economic income that are excluded from gross income for regular tax purposes, as well as certain adjustments to deductible items.

ACE includes cash-value build-up on a life insurance contract. Solely for ACE purposes, the taxpayer's adjusted basis in the contract is increased by the amount of income included in ACE. [Treas Reg §§ 1.56(g)-1(c)(5)(ii), 1.56(g)-1(c)(5)(iii)]

Term life insurance contracts having no surrender value are treated differently. A current deduction is allowed in determining ACE to the extent premiums paid on the term contract are allocable to coverage provided in the year of payment. However, premiums not allocable to coverage provided in the year of payment are added to the taxpayer's ACE basis in the term contract. [Treas Reg § 1.56(g)-1(c)(5)(vi)(A)]

The excess of the contractual death benefit of a life insurance contract over the taxpayer's ACE basis in the contract at the time of the insured's death is included in ACE. [Treas Reg §§ 1.56(g)-1(c)(5)(v), 1.56(g)-1(c)(5)(vi)]. ACE also includes the amount of any outstanding policy loan treated as forgiven or discharged by the insurance company upon the death of the insured.

Distributions under a life insurance contract are included in ACE in accordance with regular tax principles but with a special adjustment to reflect the difference between the taxpayer's ACE basis and the adjusted basis for regular tax purposes. [Treas Reg § 1.56(g)-1(c)(5)(iv)].

C corporation employers might respond to potential AMT problems in several ways. First, a material AMT problem involving COLI is likely to arise only upon the death of the insured. Because the taxable portion of the death proceeds effectively is taxed at 15 percent (75 percent of the 20 percent corporate AMT rate), the *C* corporation simply might add approximately 15 percent to the face amount of insurance purchased to cover the AMT. An alternative would be to consider whether an *S* election might be appropriate for the corporation, because the ACE adjustment does not apply to *S* corporations. [IRC § 56(g)(6)].

Q 7:22   Has the IRS made any recent statements about the use of COLI in connection with nonqualified plans?

On August 7, 1995, *The Wall Street Journal* reported that the IRS is taking a renewed interest in COLI arrangements, especially in the Midwest, and that it may be considering mounting a coordinated examination program in this area. Apparently, the IRS is interested in auditing select employers to check whether their COLI programs, especially those maintained to fund retiree medical benefits, satisfy the various applicable tax rules (the three out of seven rule, the market interest limitation, and so on).

Although no formal announcement has been made about an IRS audit program in this area, employers with COLI programs would be wise to have those programs reviewed in order to identify potential compliance problems prior to any IRS examination.

Case Study 7-1

Note: See Case Studies at the end of chapters 1 through 6.

D asks the insurance advisor to provide the group with an overview of the COLI concept and to discuss how it can be used in connection with a nonqualified plan.

The advisor explains that, unlike the case with split-dollar life insurance, the employee whose life is insured by a COLI policy has no rights in the policy or its proceeds. Instead, a COLI policy simply is an asset of the employer, the proceeds of which are expected to be used by the employer to satisfy its obligations under a nonqualified plan. The advisor notes that, for example, if the corporation had a deferred compensation obligation to D with a projected cost of $100,000, the corporation could invest assets in an insurance policy projected to have a value of $100,000 and could use the insurance policy's value to pay the obligation.

The insurance advisor stresses that, with COLI, the corporation would be both the owner and the beneficiary of the policy and would retain all rights in the policy. In essence, the policy would be a tax-favored investment, with a tax-free (except for alternative minimum tax) death benefit element, to be used by the corporation as a place to set aside assets to meet its future obligations under the nonqualified plan. The corporation would not be permitted to deduct its premium payments on the policy, but would be able to deduct the nonqualified plan payments when made. The cash value build-up on the policy generally would accrue tax-free, as well, subject to alternative minimum tax concerns. Finally, subject to the $50,000 limit, interest paid on policy loans used to carry the policy, or used for other purposes, would be deductible by the corporation.

A asks the advisor to discuss stock-based deferred compensation techniques at the group's next meeting.

See Case Study at the end of chapter 8 for a discussion of stock-based plans.

Chapter 8

Stock Plans

Stock plans provide officers, directors, employees, and other service providers of the sponsoring corporation with incentives based on the market or financial performance of the stock of the corporation, often on a tax-deferred basis. This chapter examines stock plans—the persons who may participate in those plans, the types of stock plans (including incentive stock options (ISOs), nonstatutory stock options (NSOs), discounted stock options (DSOs), restricted stock, phantom stock, and employee stock purchase plans (ESOPs), the tax incidents of stock plan sponsorship and participation, the federal and state securities law aspects of stock plans, and the accounting aspects of stock plans. Further, it examines some new developments—including the $1 million deduction limit for executive compensation and other developments—that are likely to affect the popularity of stock plans.

Overview

Q 8:1   What are stock plans?

Stock plans provide officers, directors, employees, and independent contractors with compensation, either in the form of stock of the sponsoring corporation or a cash incentive based upon the performance of the stock of the corporation. By providing participants with incentives based upon the market or financial performance of the stock, stock plans are intended to encourage the participants to work harder to ensure the financial success of the corporation. Because the economic value of the benefits to the participants increases as the value of the sponsor's stock increases, these plans tie the interests of the participants with those of the corporation's stockholders. Also, because benefits under these plans often involve taxation to the participant at a time after the date of the grant of rights under the plans, and result in capital gains treatment, rather than ordinary income tax treatment, of realized income, these plans also often offer tax advantages to the participant, as compared to the current payment of cash compensation to the participant for services rendered. The difference between the 28 percent capital gains rate and ordinary income tax rates is particularly meaningful now that OBRA '93 has increased the top marginal ordinary income tax rate to 39.6 percent.

Q 8:2   Who may benefit under stock plans?

Stock plans generally may be designed to benefit anyone. This contrasts favorably with many other types of nonqualified plans in which participation must be limited to a "select group of management or highly compensated employees" (and must satisfy other requirements) in order to avoid many of ERISA's substantive rules. This expanded participation and ease of administration occurs because stock plans generally are not subject to ERISA. However, by

design, these plans typically benefit officers, directors (both employee and nonemployee) and key employees of the corporation or
its subsidiaries. Stock plans also may be structured to benefit wider
groups of individuals such as rank-and-file employees, consultants
and other individuals outside the corporation. Certain types of stock
plans can benefit only certain classes of individuals (for example,
employees), and the availability of relief from certain federal and
state securities law requirements also often is affected by the types
of individuals who receive benefits under the particular stock plan
(for example, sophisticated individual investors, service providers, or
residents of a particular state).

Q 8:3   Are there different types of stock plans?

Yes, there are numerous types of stock plans. For purposes of this
chapter, the following stock plans will be discussed:

1. *Incentive Stock Options (ISOs)*. ISOs are rights granted by the
   sponsoring corporation to an employee to purchase shares of
   stock of the corporation at a certain price for a specified period
   of time, notwithstanding an increase in the value of the stock
   after the date the option is granted. ISOs satisfy certain statutory requirements set forth in Code Section 422, and possess
   certain unique and generally favorable (from the employee's
   perspective) tax incidents.

2. *Nonstatutory Stock Options (NSOs)*. NSOs are rights granted by
   the sponsoring corporation to participants (who need not be
   employees) to purchase shares of the corporation's stock at a
   certain price for a specified period of time. NSOs do not meet
   the statutory requirements of Code Section 422, either because
   they are not designed to satisfy it, or they are so designed but
   do not satisfy Code Section 422 operationally, and therefore do
   not qualify for the favorable tax treatment (from the optionee's
   perspective) afforded to ISOs.

3. *Discounted Stock Options (DSOs)*. DSOs are nonstatutory stock
   options that are granted at an exercise price that is considerably
   below the fair market value of the underlying stock on the date
   of grant.

4. *Restricted Stock.* Restricted stock is stock of a corporation issued to participants, either at no cost or at a nominal cost, in connection with the performance of services for the corporation. The stock is referred to as restricted because, at the date of grant, it is subject to forfeiture if certain conditions are not met (for example, continued employment or service). The participants will, however, often have certain incidents of ownership in the restricted stock beginning on the date of grant (for example, the right to receive dividends).

5. *Stock Appreciation Rights (SARs).* SARs are rights to be paid an amount equal to or based upon the difference between the value of a specified number of shares of stock (typically, the stock of the sponsoring corporation or a related entity) on the date the SARs are granted and the value of the stock on the date the SARs are exercised by the participant in the future. This amount usually is paid in cash or in shares of the related stock, but the amount may be paid in promissory notes or some other form of consideration.

6. *Phantom Stock.* Phantom stock is a right to a future bonus based on the performance of phantom (rather than real) shares of a corporation's stock over a specified period of time. Phantom stock frequently carries dividend equivalent rights which are payable during the participation period. The right to receive the bonus typically is subject to certain conditions such as continued employment or service.

7. *Employee Stock Purchase Plans.* Employee stock purchase plans provide employees with options to purchase shares of the sponsoring corporation's stock at fixed intervals, often through payroll deduction and at some discount.

Incentive Stock Options

Q 8:4   What are ISOs?

An ISO is a right (that is, an option) granted by the sponsoring corporation to the corporation's employees to purchase shares of the corporation's stock, generally at a price fixed on the date of grant, for a specified period of time. The option price may increase periodically, and the exercise of the option may be conditioned on the occurrence of certain events. In order for an option to be considered an ISO for tax purposes, the option must satisfy certain requirements set forth in Code Section 422.

Q 8:5 What are the requirements for ISOs under Code Section 422?

The requirements for ISOs under Code Section 422 are as follows:

1. The ISO may be granted only to an employee of the issuing corporation, its parent or a subsidiary. [IRC § 422(b)]

2. The option must be granted pursuant to a plan that specifies the total number of shares that may be issued under options and the employees (or class of employees) who are eligible to receive the options. In addition, the plan must be approved by the corporation's stockholders within twelve months before or after the date the plan is adopted. [IRC § 422(b)(1)] (As a corollary to this rule, stockholder approval also is required for later amendments to the plan that increase the number of shares that may be issued under options or that change the employees or class of employees eligible to receive options.)

3. The option cannot, by its terms at the time it is granted, provide that it will not be treated as an ISO. [IRC § 422(b)]

4. The ISO, by its terms, cannot be exercisable after the expiration of ten years from the date the option is granted. [IRC § 422(b)(3)]

5. The option must be granted within ten years after the earlier of (1) the date on which the plan was adopted or (2) the date on which the plan was approved by stockholders. [IRC § 422(b)(2)]

6. The ISO, by its terms, cannot be transferable by the optionee other than by will or the laws of descent and distribution. During the optionee's lifetime, the option may be exercised only by the optionee. [IRC § 422(b)(5)]

7. The option exercise price must not be less than the fair market value of the stock on the date of grant, which must be determined without regard to any restriction other than a

restriction which, by its terms, will never lapse (for example, restrictions on transfer because of federal securities laws generally cannot be factored into the fair market valuation). [IRC §§ 422(b)(4), 422(c)(7)] The fair market value determination need not be precise, nor even correct, but it must be made in good faith.

8. If the optionee owns stock comprising more than 10 percent of the total combined voting power of all classes of stock of the corporation (or parent or subsidiary thereof), the option exercise price must not be less than 110 percent (rather than 100 percent) of the fair market value of the stock and the option may not be exercisable after the expiration of five years (rather than ten years) from the date the option is granted. [IRC § 422(c)(5)]

9. Options will not be treated as ISOs to the extent that the total fair market value (determined at the time of grant) of the stock with respect to which the ISOs are exercisable for the first time by any individual during any calendar year exceeds $100,000. This determination is made taking into account all plans of the corporation, its parent and subsidiary corporations. [IRC § 422(d)] For ISOs granted before 1987, a carry-over rule applies to a portion of the amount from previous years by which the amount of first exercisable options failed to reach the $100,000 limit.

10. The optionee cannot make a "disqualifying disposition" of the stock within two years from the date the option is granted or one year from the date the option is exercised, or the favorable tax aspects (from the optionee's perspective) associated with an ISO will be lost (and the option generally will be treated as an NSO for tax purposes). Also, the optionee must exercise the option while an employee or within three months of termination of employment for the ISO to retain the favorable tax characteristics. [IRC § 422(a)] A special exception to this last rule provides that an ISO may be exercised within one year of termination of employment by reason of disability, and an ISO may be exercised during its entire term by the estate or heirs of a deceased employee.

Any modification, extension or renewal of an ISO which results in greater rights to the optionee generally is considered a grant of a new option for purposes of the above preceding rules. This will require, for example, that the exercise price satisfy the ISO fair market value requirements based on the value of the underlying stock on the date of modification, extension, or renewal. [IRC § 424(h)]

Q 8:6   May an ISO contain terms that are more restrictive or in addition to the terms set forth in Code Section 422?

Yes. An ISO may contain additional terms and conditions that are not inconsistent with the specific provisions of Code Section 422(b). For example, the option term may be set at any period that is less than ten years from the date of grant, and often the term is set at five years. The exercise dates for the option may be deferred so that only a portion of the option is exercisable each year, or the option may provide that a portion of the option lapses if it is not exercised within a particular period. The option exercise price may increase each year, or the exercise price may change based on financial or other perform-ance measures, as long as the exercise price is never less than the fair market value of the stock at the time of grant. The option may expire immediately upon termination of employment, rather than permit any post-employment exercise. Although most ISOs require payment of cash at the time of exercise of the option, the option may allow an employee to use employer stock as the consideration for exercise of the option. [IRC § 422(c)(4)]

Q 8:7   What is the tax treatment of ISOs?

An ISO optionee is not subject to federal income taxation at the time the option is granted or exercised. [IRC § 421(a)] (However, the optionee may be subject to alternative minimum tax (AMT) in the year of exercise because the exercise gives rise to an adjustment of AMT income equal to the difference between the fair market value of the stock at the exercise date and the exercise price of the option for purposes of applying the Code Section 83 rules. A discussion of the AMT rules is beyond the scope of this book.) [IRC § 56(b)(3)]

If the stock is not disposed of within two years from the date of grant or one year from the date of exercise, the optionee will be taxed at the time of the ultimate sale of the stock acquired under the option, generally at capital gains rates, on the difference between the option exercise price and the amount realized upon the sale. (An AMT tax credit will be available to offset this tax inclusion if the optionee paid AMT upon his or her exercise of the ISO.) If a "disqualifying disposition" occurs (that is, a disposition within the two-year and one-year time periods), the optionee will be subject to ordinary income tax in the year of the disposition. In such an event, the optionee is taxed, in the year of disposition, generally on the lesser of (a) the difference between the fair market value of the stock at the time of exercise and the exercise price, or (b) the difference between the disqualifying disposition sales price and the exercise price. [IRC § 421(b)] If (a) is less than (b), the difference between the fair market value at the time of exercise and the sales price is taxed at long or short term capital gains rates, as applicable. [IRC § 83(a)]

The corporation is not entitled to any deduction from gross income with respect to the grant or exercise of the ISO or the disposition by the employee of the underlying stock if the relevant holding periods are met by the optionee. [IRC § 421(b); Treas Reg § 1.421-8(a)(1)] If the optionee makes a disqualifying disposition, however, the corporation that employs the optionee is entitled to a deduction for a compensation expense equal to the amount of ordinary income recognized by the optionee. [IRC § 421(b)]

Q 8:8   What are the other advantages and disadvantages of ISOs?

For the optionee, ISOs have the advantage of deferral of taxation. The optionee does not recognize income or capital gains until a disposition occurs. If the optionee does not make a disqualifying disposition, taxes are measured in the year of sale at capital gains rates (see Q 8:7). On the other hand, if the optionee makes a disqualifying disposition, taxes are incurred in the year of sale at ordinary income and capital gains rates. There is no withholding obligation on the corporation at the time of exercise of the option (because there is no income tax obligation), nor at the time of disposition of the underlying stock (even in the case of a disqualifying disposition), so compensating an optionee with ISOs has cash flow benefits to the corporation not present in other stock compensation arrangements with respect to which tax withholding is required.

Planning Pointer. As a result of reductions over the past decades of favorable capital gains rates relative to income tax rates and the application of AMT to ISO exercises, the favorable tax treatment of ISOs has been substantially limited if not eliminated in some cases. Thus, because the sponsoring corporation does not receive a tax deduction (absent a disqualifying disposition by the optionee), the increased cost to the corporation of granting ISOs instead of NSOs, and the greater flexibility of NSOs because of the inapplicability of Code Section 422 to NSOs, often counsels in favor of granting NSUs instead of ISOs.

Nonstatutory Stock Options

Q 8:9   What are NSOs?

An NSO is a stock option that does not meet the requirements of an ISO under Code Section 422, either because the NSO is not designed to satisfy Code Section 422 or because the NSO was so designed but does not satisfy Code Section 422 operationally. Therefore, NSOs do not qualify for the special tax treatment applicable to ISOs. NSOs may be issued pursuant to a plan, or individually, as approved by a corporation's board of directors (or a committee thereof) and the exercise price of an NSO may be set at, above, or below the fair market value of the underlying stock on the date of grant. There is no tax law limitation on the duration of NSOs, nor is there any limitation on the aggregate amount of NSOs that may first become exercisable by an optionee in any year. Therefore, the corporation has more flexibility with the grant of NSOs than it does with the grant of ISOs. It should be noted, however, that option plans, by design, may limit any of those flexible characteristics of NSOs. In addition, some state securities laws restrict the price and duration of options to executives of corporations which intend to register a public offering of stock under state law, and some durational requirements imposed under the federal securities laws as a condition to enjoying certain exemptive relief (such as relief under the rules of Section 16 of the Securities Exchange Act of 1934 (see Q 8:44)) cause NSO sponsors to limit the duration of NSOs.

Q 8:10   What is the tax treatment of NSOs?

Unlike ISOs, which have no ordinary income component for tax purposes (but rather have only a capital gains component), NSOs have both an ordinary income component and a capital gains component. Under Code Section 83, the ordinary income taxation to the employee (and the deduction by the employer) with respect to an NSO depends on whether the NSO itself has a readily ascertainable market value (that is, generally, whether or not the option itself, rather than the underlying stock, is actively traded on an established market). This is because Code Section 83 does not apply to a transfer of an option without a readily ascertainable fair market value, and no other provision of the Code requires inclusion of such a transfer. If the NSO has a readily ascertainable fair market value, the optionee must recognize ordinary income in the year in which the NSO is granted, generally in an amount equal to the excess of the NSO's fair market value over the amount (if any) the optionee paid for the NSO. Because, in such a case, the income is recognized at the time of grant and the ordinary income/compensation element is thus closed, the eventual exercise of the NSO will not be a taxable event.

If the NSO does not have a readily ascertainable fair market value (which is usually the case), then there are no tax consequences to the optionee (or to the sponsoring corporation) at the time of the grant of the NSO. However, the recipient of an NSO without a readily ascertainable fair market value is taxed upon the exercise of the NSO on an amount equal to the difference between the fair market value of the stock received upon exercise of the NSO and the exercise price.

Therefore, unlike an ISO, an NSO does not defer income beyond the date the option is exercised. On the other hand, consistent with the ordinary income character of the compensation, the employer corporation is entitled to a deduction for part of the benefit conferred. If the sponsoring corporation wishes to deduct an amount equal to the income recognized by the optionee, it must withhold from the optionee's wages an amount equal to the estimated tax on that income. Upon the sale of the stock by the optionee, the difference between the amount realized in the sale and the fair market value of the stock on the date of exercise is taxable as a capital gain (or loss).

The corporation on whose behalf the services were rendered by the optionee will receive a deduction at the same time and in the same amount as the optionee's ordinary income inclusion. [IRC § 83(h)] The corporation generally will not be allowed any deductions unless it makes proper withholdings with respect to the income recognized by the optionee. [Treas Reg § 31.3402(a) 1(c), as amended]

Under final regulations issued by the IRS on July 19, 1995, the corporation will be allowed a deduction even if it fails properly to withhold with respect to the income subject to recognition by the optionee, as long as the optionee in fact includes the includible amount in his or her gross taxable income. The optionee will be deemed to have included an amount in gross income if the corporation provides a timely Form W-2 or 1099, as appropriate, to the optionee. [Treas Reg § 1.83-6(a)]

Q 8:11 What are the other advantages and disadvantages of NSOs?

The sponsoring corporation has flexibility in structuring NSOs because they are not subject to the limitations imposed on ISOs by Code Section 422. For example, the optionee may receive NSOs in unlimited amounts and at prices below the fair market value of the stock on the date of grant. Also, the corporation receives a tax deduction on the exercise of the option (unlike the case with ISOs), and, if the option is granted at fair market value, there is no corresponding charge to earnings (as there is with ISOs). However, this latter accounting benefit is in imminent danger of elimination (see Q 8:50).

Disadvantages to the use of NSOs include the fact that the optionee is taxed at the time of exercise, so there is no deferral of income recognition beyond the exercise date (as is the case with ISOs). Likewise, in order to enjoy its NSO deduction, the corporation is required to withhold with respect to the income recognized by the optionee, resulting in a cash demand on the corporation.

Q 8:12   Can features be added to NSOs to offset the withholding and tax burdens?

Yes. The most significant problem associated with NSOs from the perspective of the optionee is the liquidity needs created by the requirement to withhold and pay taxes as of the exercise date in situations where the optionee may not intend to dispose of the stock immediately. Practitioners have devised at least three methods of dealing with the withholding and payment burdens.

Method 1. The corporation can provide a cash bonus on exercise, which can be used to pay the tax generated by the exercise of the NSO. Under the arrangement, the optionee is granted a cash bonus by the corporation at the date of exercise in an amount sufficient to pay the tax on the exercise of the option plus the tax on the bonus itself. The corporation would be entitled to a tax deduction at the date of exercise for both the spread between the option price and fair market value of the option stock at the time of exercise and the amount of the bonus. This mechanism, however, results in a cash cost to the corporation.

Method 2. Alternatively, the corporation can alleviate the income tax withholding burden by withholding a number of shares otherwise issuable upon exercise of the option equal to the amount of withholding due (generally 20 percent of the income recognized, for federal income tax purposes). In addition, shares already owned by the optionee may be used to satisfy the withholding requirement. (Note: For officers and directors of a corporation with securities registered pursuant to the Securities Exchange Act of 1934, the election to have shares withheld must be made during specified window periods. (See Q 8:44 for more details.)

Method 3. Finally, stock appreciation rights (SARS) can be issued in tandem with the NSOs. As discussed below, these rights permit the optionee to receive in cash the increase in value of specified shares of stock between the grant date and the exercise date. By making these rights run concurrently with NSO rights, the optionee may exercise a sufficient number of SARs at the time of NSO exercise to satisfy the withholding and tax liability burdens and the burden of coming up with sufficient cash to pay the exercise price of the NSO, thus alleviating the liquidity problems associated with the NSOs.

Discounted Stock Options

Q 8:13   What are DSOs?

A DSO is a term given to an NSO that has an exercise price as of the date of grant which is substantially lower than the fair market value of the underlying stock as of that date. DSOs frequently are used partially as a substitute for current cash compensation and partially as an equity compensation device. Instead of receiving the cash compensation that would be payable currently, an individual may elect to receive DSOs, which, like NSOs, generally are taxed upon exercise with the DSO exercise price typically set at a point below fair market value and relating to the amount of compensation foregone.

> **Example.** An optionee might forego a $25,000 increase in salary in a year in exchange for an option to purchase 100,000 shares of the employer's stock for $75,000 at a time when the stock is valued at $1 per share.

DSOs allow the optionee to defer the recognition of income until the time, and in the amounts, determined by the optionee, provided that the value of the stock is in excess of the exercise price at the date of the exercise.

Q 8:14   What is the tax treatment of DSOs?

As a general matter, the tax treatment for a DSO should be the same as for an ordinary NSO. That is, there should be no tax upon the grant of the DSO, and the difference between the market value of the stock at the time of exercise over the option exercise price should be taxed at that time as ordinary income. [IRC § 83(a)] However, the IRS has suggested that possible constructive receipt issues may exist in cases where the exercise price is so low that it is not considered a substantial obstacle to the ultimate receipt of the underlying stock, resulting, because of the lack of a substantial risk of forfeiture, in current taxation under Code Section 83. Thus, it may be advisable to make an election to defer compensation in the form of DSOs prior to the time that the individual has performed the services for which the compensation will be payable, at least to protect the optionee from adverse tax consequences in the year of deferral. As with NSOs, the corporation receives a deduction at the same time and in the same amount as the optionee's ordinary income recognition and the corporation has a withholding obligation as a condition of this deduction. [Treas Reg § 31.3402(a)-1(c)]

Under final regulations issued by the IRS on July 19, 1995, the corporation will be allowed a deduction even if it fails properly to withhold with respect to the income subject to recognition by the optionee, as long as the optionee in fact includes the includible amount in his or her gross taxable income. The optionee will be deemed to have included an amount in gross income if the corporation provides a timely Form W-2 or 1099, as appropriate, to the optionee. [Treas Reg § 1.83-6(a)]

Q 8:15   What are the other advantages and disadvantages of DSOs?

With DSOs, the corporation is able to pay compensation without dipping into cash, while it retains the ability to take a deduction at the exercise date equal to the difference between the market price of the DSO stock at the time of exercise and the option exercise price.

The principal risk for the optionee is the constructive receipt tax risk (for deeply discounted options—see Q 8:14) and that the deferred compensation will be lost to the extent that the market price of the stock drops after the grant date.

From the corporation's standpoint, DSOs create greater dilution than in the case of at-market options. This is because the purchase (that is, the option) price for the same share of stock is less in the case of a DSO than in the case of an at-market option, resulting in a greater reduction in net tangible book value of the issuer's stock in the case of the exercise of a DSO than in the exercise of an at-market option. In addition, unlike ordinary NSOs granted at market price, there is a charge to earnings for the amount of the discount at the time of grant (although there is no corresponding deduction for the corporation at that time). [Accounting Principle Board Opinion No 25] However, there is no additional earnings charge for any subsequent increases in stock price.

Restricted Stock

Q 8:16   What is restricted stock?

Restricted stock is stock of a corporation issued, at no cost or at a nominal cost, in connection with the performance of services on behalf of the sponsoring corporation. Typically, the certificates for the shares are issued in the name of the participants but held by the corporation until certain conditions are met. One of the most common conditions imposed by corporations is that the participant continue in the employ of the corporation for a specified period of time. Another possible condition may be that the corporation reach a specified level of earnings. The restricted shares are subject to forfeiture in the event the conditions are not met. The holder of the restricted stock typically has the right to vote the shares and receive dividends and other distributions from the date of grant, although the shares generally are not transferable prior to the fulfillment of the specified conditions.

Q 8:17   What is the tax treatment of restricted stock?

The participant must include in gross income, at the time the shares become transferable (or no longer subject to forfeiture), the excess of the fair market value of the shares over the amount paid for the shares, provided the holder has not made a Code Section 83(b) election to be taxed in the year the restricted stock is granted. [Treas Reg § 1.83-3(c)(1)] The corporation is entitled to a deduction in an amount equal to the amount included in the participant's gross income upon the earliest to occur of:

1. The date the shares become nonforfeitable;

2. The date the participant makes a Section 83(b) election; or

3. The date the corporation cancels the restriction pursuant to Code Section 83(d)(2).

[Treas Reg § 1.83-6(a)]

The corporation must make the appropriate withholding to qualify for the deduction.

Under final regulations issued by the IRS on July 19, 1995, the corporation will be allowed a deduction even if it fails properly to withhold with respect to the income subject to recognition by the restricted stock grantee, as long as the restricted stock grantee in fact includes the includible amount in his or her gross taxable income. The restricted stock grantee will be deemed to have included an amount in gross income if the corporation provides a timely Form W-2 or 1099, as appropriate, to the restricted stock grantee. [Treas Reg § 1.83-6(a)]

Q 8:18   What are the other advantages and disadvantages of restricted stock?

The holder of restricted stock typically enjoys certain benefits of ownership as of the date of grant (for example, dividend rights, voting rights, and appreciation possibility), although the shares are nontransferable and are subject to forfeiture at that time. This is often seen as a particularly attractive aspect of these plans because shares of stock held by employees generally may be expected to vote with management in corporate control matters. The determination of the amount and the time for payment of taxes is deferred (absent a Code Section 83(b) election) until the restrictions lapse or the conditions are fulfilled. If there is a market decline in the stock, the restricted stock will have some value, while stock options, on the other hand, may have no present value in such instances.

Stock Appreciation Rights

Q 8:19   What are SARs?

SARs are rights to be paid an amount equal to the difference between the value of a specified number of shares of stock on the date the SARs are granted and the value of the stock on the date the SARs are exercised. This amount may be paid in cash, stock, a combination of cash and stock, or any other form of consideration. SARs may be granted alone, in tandem with options (where the optionee's exercise of the SAR will cancel the right to exercise the corresponding option), or in addition to options.

Q 8:20   What is the tax treatment of SARs?

There is no taxation upon the grant of a SAR. Instead, the holder of a SAR must include in gross income an amount equal to the consideration received upon exercise of the SAR. [Treas Reg § 1.83-3(e); IRC §§ 61, 83, 451] The sponsoring corporation is entitled to a deduction at the same time and in the same amount as the income that is recognized by the holder of the SAR (generally, upon exercise). [IRC §§ 83(h), 404(a)(5)] The corporation must make the appropriate withholding in order to qualify for the deduction.

Under final regulations issued by the IRS on July 19, 1995, the corporation will be allowed a deduction even if it fails properly to withhold with respect to the income subject to recognition by the SAR holder, as long as the SAR holder in fact includes the includible amount in his or her gross taxable income. The SAR holder will be deemed to have included an amount in gross income if the corporation provides a timely Form W-2 or 1099, as appropriate, to the SAR holder. [Treas Reg § 1.83-6(a)]

Q 8:21   What are the other advantages and disadvantages of SARs?

SARs provide the holder with a cashless way of receiving the benefit of capital appreciation of the corporation's stock, and no tax is owed until the exercise of the SAR. This contrasts favorably with the liquidity problems associated with ISOs (that is, the optionee must have the exercise price), NSOs (that is, the optionee must have the exercise price and pay a tax liability upon exercise) and restricted stock (that is, the participant must pay a tax liability upon vesting). Further, by using SARs, the corporation can provide an equity-based incentive without issuing additional stock, generally eliminating most state corporate law and federal securities law concerns and providing an attractive alternative for closely-held corporations that are reluctant to issue stock to persons other than the current owners.

SARs do not, however, provide voting, dividend, or other rights associated with stock ownership. In addition, the corporation must charge its earnings with a compensation cost over the period during which the SAR is outstanding in an amount equal to the difference between the fair market value of the stock associated with the SAR and the exercise price of the SAR. This generally results in earlier compensation cost recognition than in the case of options or restricted stock. Finally, SARs do not result in stock ownership and thus do not provide performance incentives beyond the exercise date.

Phantom Stock

Q 8:22   What is phantom stock?

Phantom stock is a right to a bonus based upon the performance of phantom (rather than real) shares of a corporation's common stock over a specified period of time. The bonus is typically an amount equal to the difference between the fair market value of the shares of common stock at the date of grant and the fair market value of the stock at the later specified date. The arrangement is similar to a SAR, except that participants do not have a choice with respect to the specified date of exercise, phantom stock typically is not granted in tandem with options, and phantom stock typically carries dividend equivalent rights. The right to receive the bonus typically is subject to certain conditions (such as continued employment or service) and the bonus may be paid in cash, stock, a combination of cash and stock, or another consideration.

Q 8:23   What is the tax treatment of phantom stock?

The tax treatment of phantom stock is substantially identical to the tax treatment of SARs. The participant does not recognize federal income tax upon the grant of the phantom stock rights. The participant is taxed at ordinary income tax rates upon the settlement of the phantom stock rights and is taxed upon dividend equivalent rights as those payments are made. [IRC § 451(a)] The corporation is entitled to a deduction at the same time and in the same amount as the participant's ordinary income recognition in connection with the phantom stock. [IRC § 83(h)] The corporation is required to withhold with respect to the income recognized by the participant in order to enjoy the deduction. [Treas Reg § 31.3402(a)-(1)(c)]

Under final regulations issued by the IRS on July 19, 1995, the corporation will be allowed a deduction even if it fails properly to withhold with respect to the income subject to recognition by the phantom stock grantee, as long as the phantom stock grantee in fact includes the includible amount in his or her gross taxable income. The phantom stock grantee will be deemed to have included an amount in gross income if the corporation provides a timely Form W-2 or 1099, as appropriate, to the phantom stock grantee. [Treas Reg § 1.83-6(a)]

Q 8:24 What are the other advantages and disadvantages of phantom stock?

The same advantages and disadvantages associated with SARs apply to phantom stock rights. The participant does not need to expend cash in order to receive the benefit of phantom stock and no tax is owed by the participant until the settlement of the phantom stock award. The corporation can provide an equity-based incentive without issuing additional stock.

Phantom stock does not provide voting rights associated with stock ownership, but the dividend equivalent rights frequently associated with phantom stock rights cause phantom stock rights to compare favorably to SARs. There typically is no flexibility with respect to the date of exercise of the phantom stock; that is, the bonus is awarded as of a specified date. In addition, like SARs, the corporation must charge its earnings with compensation expense in each period during which the phantom stock is outstanding, based upon the difference between the exercise price (usually zero) and the fair market value of the stock in each such period. The amounts paid as dividend equivalent rights are considered compensation expenses in the applicable period. Moreover, phantom stock awards do not necessarily encourage stock ownership.

Employee Stock Purchase Plans

Q 8:25   What is an employee stock purchase plan?

An employee stock purchase plan is a right (an option) granted by the sponsoring corporation to employees to purchase shares of the corporation's stock at fixed intervals. Frequently, the payment for the stock is accomplished by means of regular payroll deductions. Most employee stock purchase plans are governed by Code Section 423, although the sponsoring corporation could implement an employee stock purchase plan that does not meet the Section 423 requirements. If the requirements of Section 423 are met, the tax consequences to the employee will be similar to those of an ISO. One requirement applicable to employee stock purchase plans qualifying under Section 423 that does not apply to Section 422 ISOs provides that an employee stock purchase plan must make options available to all employees, except certain part-time, seasonal, temporary, and highly compensated employees. Thus, an employee stock purchase plan typically is a broader-based plan than is an ISO plan, the latter typically being maintained only for the benefit of key employees.

Q 8:26   What are the requirements for employee stock purchase plans under Code Section 423?

The requirements for employee stock purchase plans under Code Section 423 are as follows:

1. The plan must provide that options may be granted only to employees of the issuing corporation or of its parent or subsidiary corporation. [IRC § 423(b)(1)]

2. The plan must be approved by stockholders within 12 months before or after the date the plan is adopted. [IRC § 423(b)(2)]

3. Under the terms of the plan, no employee can be granted an option if the employee, immediately after the option is granted, owns stock possessing 5 percent or more of the total combined voting power or value of all classes of stock of the corporation. For purposes of this limitation, stock which the employee has

a right to purchase under outstanding options is treated as stock owned by the employee. [IRC § 423(b)(3)]

4. Under the terms of the plan, options must be extended to all employees of the corporation, except that there may be excluded (1) employees who have been employed less than two years, (2) employees whose customary employment is 20 hours or less per week, (3) employees whose customary employment is for not more than five months in any calendar year, and (4) "highly compensated employees." [IRC § 423(b)(4)]

5. Under the terms of the plan, all employees granted options must be treated similarly, except that the amount of stock subject to options granted to employees may bear a uniform relationship to their compensation. The plan may impose maximum limits on the number of options granted to any employee. [IRC § 423(b)(5)]

6. Under the terms of the plan, the option exercise price must not be less than the lesser of: (1) 85 percent of the fair market value of the stock at the time of grant, or (2) 85 percent of the fair market value of the stock at the time of exercise. [IRC § 423(b)(6)]

7. If, under the terms of the plan, the option exercise price may not be less than 85 percent of the fair market value of the stock at the time of exercise, the maximum term of the option cannot exceed five years. If any other limitation is used (e.g., 85 percent of the fair market value as of the time of grant), the maximum term of the option cannot exceed 27 months. [IRC § 423(b)(7)]

8. Under the terms of the plan, no employee may be granted an option which permits the employee's rights to purchase stock under all employee stock purchase plans of the corporation to accrue at a rate which exceeds $25,000 of fair market value of stock (determined at the date of grant) for each calendar year. [IRC § 423(b)(8)]

9. Under the terms of the plan, the option cannot be transferable by the employee other than by will or the laws of descent and distribution. During the employee's lifetime, the option may be exercised only by the employee. [IRC § 423(b)(9)]

Q 8:27   What is the tax treatment of employee stock purchase plans?

The tax treatment applicable to both the corporation and the employee with respect to options under an employee stock purchase plan is similar to the tax treatment of ISOs. For instance, the employee will not be subject to federal income taxation at the time the option is granted or exercised. [IRC § 421(a)]

However, because of the bargain element (that is, the extent to which the exercise price is less than the fair market value of the stock at the grant date), which is permissible in employee stock purchase plans, the amount of gain is typically greater in the case of employee stock purchase plans than in the case of ISOs.

If the employee does not dispose of the shares acquired under the plan within one year after the shares are acquired and within two years after the option is granted, a disposition of the shares will result in ordinary income to the extent of the lesser of (1) the amount by which the fair market value of the stock at the time the option was granted exceeds the option price, or (2) the amount by which the fair market value of the stock at the time of disposition exceeds the option price. Moreover, if these holding periods are satisfied, any profit/loss realized upon disposition (excluding the bargain element) will be taxed as capital gain (or loss). [IRC §§ 423(a), 421(a)]

If a "disqualifying disposition" (that is, a disposition within the two-year or one-year time periods) occurs, the employee may realize ordinary income. The amount to be treated as ordinary income is the difference between the option price and the price of the stock at the time the option is exercised. Any additional gain or loss realized will be recognized as short-term or long-term capital gain or loss, depending on how long the shares are held. [IRC § 83(a)]

Unlike the optionee of an ISO, an optionee under an employee stock purchase plan is not subject to AMT in the year of exercise of the option (see Q 8:7).

As in the case of ISOs, deferred tax treatment is available only if, at all times during the period beginning with the date of grant and ending on the day not more than three months before the date of exercise, the optionee is an employee of the corporation, its parent or subsidiary. [IRC § 423(a)(2)]

The corporation will receive no deduction for tax purposes except where there is a disqualifying disposition. In the event of a disqualifying disposition, the corporation will be entitled to a deduction in an amount equal to the ordinary income realized by the employee.

Q 8:28 What are the other advantages and disadvantages of employee stock purchase plans?

For the employee, the arrangement has the advantage of deferral of taxation. The optionee does not recognize income or capital gains until a disposition occurs. There is no withholding obligation on the corporation at the time of exercise of the option. The corporation does not receive a tax deduction absent a disqualifying disposition.

Planning Pointer. As a result of the reduction of favorable capital gains rates relative to income tax rates over the past decade, the favorable tax treatment of employee stock purchase plans has been limited substantially. In addition, the corporation does not receive a tax deduction absent a disqualifying disposition by the employee. Thus, the arrangement may cost a corporation more than other alternative incentive arrangements, such as discounted stock option plans.

Securities Aspects of Stock Plans

Q 8:29 What are the securities law considerations for stock plans?

Each of the various stock plans raises both federal and state securities law considerations. The Securities Act of 1933, as amended (the Securities Act), and the Securities Exchange Act of 1934, as amended (the Exchange Act), potentially regulate and may restrict the purchase or sale of securities in certain instances. The Securities Act applies to any purchase or sale of securities of an issuer corporation engaged in interstate commerce, notwithstanding the size of the offering, the size of the issuer, or the size or character of the offer or sale, but these considerations affect the availability of exemptions under the Securities Act. The Exchange Act requires registration of, and regulates an issuer who issues, any class of securities which is held of record by 500 or more persons if the issuer has assets of $5 million or more. The Securities and Exchange Commission (SEC) administers these acts and has promulgated rules and regulations under them. In addition, private parties can, in certain instances, seek to enforce certain provisions of the Securities Act and the Exchange Act. Separate state securities laws may be applicable in each state in which there are employees participating in the stock plan. Although state securities law compliance generally follows federal securities law compliance, this is not always the case, and the exemptions applicable to a particular transaction may be different.

Q 8:30   What registration requirements does the Securities Act impose on stock plans?

The Securities Act applies to the offer and sale of securities and imposes reporting and disclosure obligations in certain instances. The Securities Act requires that every offer and sale of a security be registered with the SEC and that a prospectus be delivered to the offeree, unless the offer and sale are exempt from registration. Section 5 of the Securities Act provides that it is unlawful to offer to sell a security unless an appropriate registration statement has been filed with the SEC, or to sell a security unless the registration statement has become effective. [15 USC §§ 77e(a), 77e(c)] Section 2(1) of the Securities Act defines "security" in terms broad enough to encompass most stock plan interests, and can include options, stock underlying options, "participation interests" in plans and other investment-type interests. [15 USC § 77b(i)] If registration is required, a prospectus or other summary materials satisfying statutory disclosure standards must be delivered to potential investors which describes the issuer, the plan, the securities and the plan of distribution. Other items may have to be disclosed as well, depending upon the form of SEC registration statement used to register the securities. The disclosure obligation can be costly and time consuming, particularly where the issuer is not an Exchange Act reporting company.

In addition, Section 10(b) of the Securities Exchange Act of 1934 and Rule 10b-5 promulgated thereunder prohibit fraud, including the use of untrue statements of material facts or the omission of material facts, in connection with the purchase or sale of any security registered under the Exchange Act, whether or not the transaction was registered or was exempt from registration under the Securities Act of 1933. [15 USC § 78j; 17 CFR § 240.10b-5] To avoid claims for failure to disclose material information, companies often prepare disclosure documents for employees participating in stock plans. These disclosure documents often include current financial statements, descriptions of risks of investing in stock and summaries of business plans. For publicly held Exchange Act reporting companies, optionees have access to the periodic reports filed with the SEC and other publicly available information, which can help them to make informed investment decisions. Even where there may be no formal disclosure document requirements (because exemptive relief from Securities Act registration is available and/or the issuer or class of securities is not subject to the Exchange Act), stock plan participants should have access to the same information about the sponsoring corporation that is available to stockholders in order to vitiate state fraud claims.

Q 8:31   What exemptions or other relief from the registration requirements imposed by the Securities Act are available?

There are various exemptions and other relief from the Securities Act registration requirements that may be available in certain instances. Traditionally, corporations have relied upon the following exemptions from the registration requirements:

1. Section 3(a)(11) of the Securities Act, which provides an intrastate offering exemption that corporations may rely upon when issuing stock to persons within a single state [15 USC § 77c(a)(11)];

2. Section 4(2) of the Securities Act, which provides a private offering exemption for offerings that are not public offerings [15 USC § 77d(2)];

3. Rule 701 under the Securities Act, which provides exemptive relief from the Act's registration requirements for certain compensatory offerings by nonpublic company issuers;

4. The small offering exemptions available for certain offerings by nonpublic company issuers which are limited in amount and with respect to which certain other requirements are satisfied, under Regulation A under the Securities Act and Rule 504 of Regulation D under the Securities Act; and

5. The no-sale rule, which provides that certain transactions do not involve a sale and thus are not subject to Securities Act registration or other requirements in the first instance.

Q 8:32   How does the intrastate offering exemption work?

The intrastate offering exemption requires that all offers be made to offerees residing in the same state as the state where the corporation was incorporated. [17 CFR § 230.147] If, however, the offering is integrated with other offerings by the corporation to out-of-state residents, the exemption is lost. The SEC has indicated that a single offer to an out-of-state resident will invalidate the exemption. [17 CFR § 231.1459] Accordingly, the intrastate offering exemption is not favored except in very small, tightly controlled corporate settings.

Rule 147 under the Securities Act provides a safe harbor for satisfying the intrastate offering exemption under Securities Act Section 3(a)(11). Under Rule 147, the issuer will be deemed to satisfy the small offering exemption if the issuer is incorporated and has its principal office in the state containing all of the offerees, all offerees are residents of that state, 80 percent of the proceeds of the offering are used in that state, 80 percent or more of the revenue of the issuer is derived from operations within that state and 80 percent or more of the issuer's assets (and those of its affiliates, on a consolidated basis) are located within that state.

Q 8:33   How does the private offering exemption work?

The private offering exemption, as interpreted by SEC regulations and interpretations, requires that the offering be made in such a limited fashion as not to constitute an offering to the public (that is, that the offering shall be made to a limited number of sophisticated offerees). The sophistication requirement often is fulfilled where the offeree is an executive officer or director of the corporation (generally, those holding policy-making positions with respect to the issuer), or has a substantial net worth (generally, $1 million) or income (generally, $200,000 per annum). Regulation D, a safe harbor promulgated by the SEC, spells out additional alternatives, including a general qualification for an exemption for offerings to 35 or fewer persons. [17 CFR §§ 230.501-230.508] Many corporations, however, desire to issue stock to consultants and employees who do not meet the sophistication requirements or to a number of persons in excess of the applicable safe harbor limit. Also, depending on the size of the offering and the number of sophisticated and unsophisticated offerees, the issuer may have to prepare and deliver to the offerees a private placement memorandum satisfying somewhat extensive disclosure requirements, at sometimes considerable expense. Therefore, the private offering exemption may not be available for these types of issuances, or may be available only upon meeting substantial and expensive disclosure requirements.

Q 8:34   Are there any exemptions available for small offerings?

Yes. Regulation A under the Securities Act provides an exemption for certain nonpublic company issuer offerings involving less than $5 million in aggregate offering price in a 12-month period if an Offering Circular is delivered to purchasers and a Form 1-A is filed with the SEC. The preparation of an Offering Circular could be an expensive undertaking, and issuers engaging in compensatory offerings that would qualify for Rule 701 (see Q 8:36) exemptive relief typically would follow that latter route. Also, offerings by nonpublic company issuers of less than $1 million are generally exempt under Rule 504 of Regulation D under the Securities Act, and such offerings generally do not require the delivery of information or the filing of a Form 1-A. An issuer engaging in a compensatory offering of less than $1 million may desire to rely on Rule 504, subject to certain integration rules under Rule 504 and Regulation D which require that offerings other than the offering seeking a Regulation D exception be combined with the offering seeking a Regulation D exemption, often causing the Rule 504 offering threshold limitation to be exceeded. These small offering exemptions (that is, Regulation A, Rule 504 and Rule 701) are not available to companies that are subject to the reporting requirements of the Exchange Act.

Q 8:35   If no amount is paid by the employee for the stock, is registration required?

Generally, no. The SEC takes the position that no sale has occurred requiring Securities Act registration if the employee is not required to give up something in exchange for the stock other than the giving up of mere employment services. This no-sale rule typically does not apply if the employee is required to achieve specific personal performance objectives (in contrast to group performance objectives) in order to receive the stock. The no-sale rule usually provides an exemption in the case of a transfer of restricted stock, the grant of a stock option (but not the sale incident to the exercise of the stock option) and, to the extent they constitute securities, the transfer of SARs or phantom stock rights.

Q 8:36   How does the Rule 701 exemption work?

Rule 701 provides a registration exemption for companies that are not subject to the reporting requirements of the Exchange Act, issuing stock or stock options in compensatory transfers, subject to certain amount limitations. [17 CFR § 230.701] Rule 701 exempts from the Securities Act registration requirements certain offers and sales of securities by nonreporting corporations that are made pursuant to employee benefit plans or contracts with employees, consultants or advisers. (Certain offers of securities must be registered, even if the issuer is not required to report, thereafter, under the '34 Securities Act. Also, a '34 Act company conceivably could float an issue of securities that does not need to be registered.) A nonreporting corporation is a corporation that is not subject to the extensive, complex, and regular reporting requirements of the Exchange Act (specifically, one which does not have a class of securities registered under Section 12 of the Exchange Act). The securities may only be issued pursuant to a written compensatory benefit plan for the participation of employees, directors, officers, consultants or advisers or pursuant to a written contract relating to the compensation of those persons. If the securities are issued to consultants or advisers, bona fide services must be rendered and those services must not be in connection with the offer and sale of securities in a capital-raising transaction. [17 CFR § 230.701(b)] The purpose of the exemption is to accommodate the issuance of securities in compensatory circumstances. The exemption is not available for plans whose primary purpose is the raising of capital. [17 CFR § 230.701, Preliminary Note 5]

Rule 701 requires that the corporation provide each participant with a copy of the compensatory plan or written contract. [17 CFR § 230.701(b)(3)] There are no other required disclosures under the Rule, although corporations should be aware of the obligation to provide information consistent with the antifraud provisions of the federal securities laws. Rule 701 further provides that the aggregate amount of securities offered and sold pursuant to the exemption during any 12-month period must be limited to the greatest of:

1. $500,000;

2. 15 percent of the corporation's total assets as of the previous fiscal year end; or

3. 15 percent of the outstanding securities of the class of securities being offered.

The aggregate offering price of the securities to be offered and sold pursuant to (2) or (3) above, however, may not exceed $5 million [17 CFR § 230.701(b)(5)]

Rule 702(T) requires that a one-page Form 701 be filed with the SEC no later than 30 days after the first sale that causes the aggregate sales in a Rule 701 offering to exceed $100,000. The Form 701 must be amended annually within 30 days following the end of the corporation's fiscal year. The failure to file does not invalidate the exemption. [17 CFR § 230.702(T)(a)] Noncompliance with the filing requirement may, however, disqualify a corporation from future use of the exemption. The SEC does have the authority to waive the disqualification upon a showing of good cause by the corporation. [17 CFR § 230.703(T)]

Securities issued pursuant to a Rule 701 offering are restricted securities which generally cannot be resold freely or transferred until 90 days after the sponsoring corporation becomes subject to the reporting requirements of the Exchange Act (that is, becomes a reporting company), but such shares are exempt from most other SEC Rule 144 restrictions applicable to restricted securities; most notably, the two year holding period requirement.

(See the discussion at Qs 8:40, 8:41, 8:42.)

Q 8:37   Do corporations that report under the Exchange Act have an easier time instituting stock plans than corporations that do not report?

Generally, yes. For reporting corporations (that is, those with a class of securities registered under the Exchange Act), the registration requirements are fairly simple, so it often is not necessary to rely on exemptions from the Securities Act registration requirements. After a corporation first becomes subject to the Exchange Act reporting requirements, it may accomplish registration on a short-form registration statement, the Form S-8. [17 CFR § 239.16b] The Form S-8 does not require that a prospectus be filed with the registration statement. Instead, summary information regarding the plan and its tax implications may be used in lieu of a prospectus. The Form S-8 is effective upon filing (that is, there is no waiting period for SEC review and clearance). The registered securities may be resold immediately, as there is no two-year holding period (which is discussed below). However, executive officers and other so-called affiliates of the issuing corporation must use an additional Form S-8 Re-offer Prospectus to sell freely shares acquired by them under a Form S-8. Most reporting companies rely on the Form S-8 for the registration of securities to be issued to employees and directors. Form S-8 is not available when the stock transfer is for capital raising purposes (that is, is noncompensatory).

Compensatory issuances by companies that do not report under the Exchange Act have been facilitated substantially by the promulgation by the SEC of Rule 701 and the Rule 504 and Regulation A small-offering exemptions. In the absence of exemptive relief under Regulation D, Rule 701, Regulation A, or Rule 504, given the unavailability of the Form S-8, the cost of registering shares under a compensatory arrangement by a nonreporting company likely would be prohibitive. Similarly, in the case of an Exchange Act reporting company for which the Form S-8 is not available (for example, because the company has not been satisfying its Exchange Act reporting requirements or because the transaction is not in fact compensatory (but, instead, is intended to raise capital), the cost of using another form of Registration Statement (for example, the Form S-1 or the Form SB-2 for certain small business issuers) to register the securities could be extremely, if not prohibitively, expensive.

Q 8:38   What does the Securities Act actually require to be registered?

The Securities Act requires registration of particular sales of securities, not the securities themselves. That is, the registration or exemption pertains to the particular transaction, not to other transactions involving the same class of securities or subsequent resales of the same security. Thus, even if a transaction is fully registered or qualifies for an exemption, the purchaser also must register the securities when he or she sells them or qualify for an exemption from registration at that time.

Q 8:39   Are there sanctions for a violation of the Securities Act requirements?

Yes. The Securities Act contains major civil sanctions for the violation of its requirements. Section 12 of the Securities Act provides that any person who offers or sells a security in violation of the registration requirements, or any person who offers or sells a security by means of a communication that includes an untrue statement of a material fact or a material omission, is liable to the person purchasing the security from the seller for an amount equal to the consideration paid or for damages (so-called "recision damages"). [15 USC § 77l] Section 17 of the Securities Act generally prohibits fraud in connection with an offer or sale of securities. [15 USC § 77q] Note that Sections 12(2) and 17 apply to every sale of a security, even if the sale is exempt from registration under the Securities Act. Thus, an exemption is relief from registration, but not from the Securities Act's antifraud provisions.

Q 8:40   Can recipients of securities acquired under a stock plan freely resell those securities?

It depends. The ability of the recipient of securities to freely resell the securities is dependent upon whether the securities are restricted securities within the meaning of Rule 144 promulgated under the Securities Act. [17 CFR § 230.144] Securities that have been registered under the Securities Act are not restricted securities and, if those nonrestricted securities are held by so-called "nonaffiliates" of the corporation, those securities are freely transferable without further registration insofar as subsequent transactions involving the securities are exempt under Section 4(1) of the Securities Act, which exempts "transactions by persons other than an issuer, underwriter or dealer." Securities that have not been registered under the Securities Act (for example, securities issued in a private offering) or that are held by an "affiliate" (even if received by the affiliate in a registered offering) are often subject to restrictions on transfer and generally may not be resold unless they are registered or sold pursuant to Rule 144. Rule 144 generally provides a safe-harbor for Securities Act Section 4(1) compliance, on the theory that holding periods and other controls will prevent issuers from evading the registration requirements of the Securities Act through affiliates or private persons acting as conduits.

Q 8:41   What special requirements apply to restricted securities?

If securities are deemed to be restricted securities, each person (whether or not an affiliate of the corporation) will have to hold the securities for a minimum of two years prior to resale, after which time the sale also is subject to the volume limitations and other manner-of-sale requirements contained in Rule 144. Under the volume limitation, the maximum amount of restricted securities (and all other securities of the same class if the seller is an affiliate) that may be sold for the account of the seller during any three-month period is the greater of 1 percent of the outstanding securities of the same class, or the average weekly trading volume for the class during the preceding four calendar weeks. Under the manner of sale requirements, the securities must be sold either in brokers' transactions or in transactions directly with a market maker, and the transaction must satisfy certain other similar requirements. [17 CFR § 230.144(d)] After the securities have been held for three years and the holder is not an affiliate of the corporation and has not been an affiliate within the preceding 90 days, the securities will be transferable without regard to the volume limitations of Rule 144.

In the case of securities that are not deemed to be restricted securities, affiliates can resell the securities without regard to the two-year holding requirement, although the other requirements of Rule 144 (volume and manner of sale restrictions) would apply. An affiliate is a person who directly or indirectly controls, is controlled by, or is under common control with the corporation. As a general rule, directors, officers, and 5 percent stockholders (depending on the ownership structure) are affiliates of a corporation under Rule 144.

To summarize, a nonaffiliate receiving securities in a registered offering (including an offering registered on a Form S-8) may resell those shares freely without registration, because those shares are not restricted securities. Nonaffiliates receiving securities in other than a registered offering (for example, in a private placement transaction under Regulation D) may resell those shares by registering those shares (which in almost all cases is impractical for a nonissuer) or by satisfying the holding period and other requirements under Rule 144. In the case of an affiliate, even if the affiliate receives the securities in a registered transaction, the affiliate can sell the shares only in a registered offering (for example, pursuant to a Form S-8 "re-offer prospectus") or by satisfying the Rule 144 requirements applicable to affiliates holding nonregistered securities. An affiliate receiving restricted securities must satisfy the requirements applicable to restricted security holders and the requirements applicable to the affiliate by virtue of the person's affiliate status (that is, even after the three-year holding period is satisfied, the affiliate must satisfy Rule 144's volume limitations).

Q 8:42   Are securities issued pursuant to Rule 701 treated as restricted securities?

Yes. However, under Rule 701, after a corporation becomes an Exchange Act reporting corporation, the restrictions applicable to the securities as restricted securities under Rule 144 are removed, except for the manner of sale requirements (see Q 8:36). The holders must, however, wait 90 days after the public offering before disposing of such securities. [17 CFR § 230.701(c)(3)] Restrictions applicable to affiliates as such generally continue to apply. Note that as soon as a corporation becomes a reporting corporation it can no longer utilize the Rule 701 exemption to issue additional securities (although all outstanding options or rights granted under Rule 701 and the securities issuable upon their exercise will continue to receive the favorable exemption and resale treatment).

Q 8:43   How does Section 16 of the Exchange Act affect the acquisition or disposition of securities under a stock plan by "insiders"?

Section 16 of the Exchange Act affects the acquisition or disposition by insiders of a corporation of a class of the corporation's Exchange Act registered securities. An insider for purposes of Section 16 is any officer, director or beneficial owner of more than 10 percent of a class of registered securities (that is, securities registered pursuant to the Exchange Act). Section 16(a) requires insiders to report to the SEC their beneficial ownership of any equity securities of the corporation and any changes in the beneficial ownership. [15 USC § 78p(a)] Section 16(b) requires insiders to disgorge any profit from any purchase and sale, or sale and purchase, of the corporation's registered securities within a period of six months. [15 USC § 78p(b)]

Q 8:44   Does the acquisition of stock or options pursuant to a stock plan constitute a purchase for purposes of Section 16(b) of the Exchange Act?

Ordinarily, the acquisition of stock or options pursuant to a stock plan would be deemed a purchase for Section 16(b) purposes. In order to minimize the potential adverse impact of Section 16(b) on stock plans, the SEC adopted Rule 16b-3, which specifically exempts certain transactions that are made pursuant to employee stock plans from the scope of Section 16(b) liability and which provides limited relief from the reporting obligations under Section 16(a) applicable to those transactions. Specifically, Rule 16b-3 exempts from Section 16(b) liability the grant or award of an equity security, including a "derivative security," if the security is held for six months and is issued under a plan that meets the conditions of Rule 16b-3. (In the case of a derivative security, six months must transpire between the date of grant and the date the underlying security is sold.) [17 CFR § 240.16b-3] A derivative security is defined as any option, warrant, convertible security, SAR or similar right with an exercise or conversion privilege at a price related to an equity security, or similar securities with a value derived from the value of an equity security. This definition generally would include ISOs, NSOs, options under employee stock purchase plans, SARs, and phantom stock units, all discussed above. [17 CFR § 240.16a-1(c)] In addition, Rule 16b-3 exempts the expiration, cancellation or surrender to the issuer of a stock option or SAR in connection with the grant of a replacement option or right, and the surrender or delivery to the issuer of shares of its stock as payment for the exercise of an option, warrant or right with respect to shares of the same class. [17 CFR § 240.16b-3(f)]

In order for the stock plan to qualify for the Rule 16b-3 exemptions, the plan must:

1. Be in written form;
2. Provide that options and rights issuable under the plan are nontransferable (other than by will or the laws of descent and distribution or pursuant to a qualified domestic relations order);
3. Be approved by stockholders of the corporation; and
4. Be administered by disinterested persons if discretion can be exercised as to either the selection of insiders as participants, or the grant of stock options or rights to insiders.

The previous (pre-1991) version of Rule 16b-3 did not exempt the acquisition of stock pursuant to the exercise of a stock option. The exercise of a stock option did constitute a purchase for Section 16(b) purposes. The recent revisions to the rules adopted by the SEC provide that the closing of a derivative security position as a result of its exercise will be exempt from sale treatment under Section 16(b) and the acquisition of underlying securities at a fixed exercise price due to the exercise of an option or right will be exempt from purchase treatment under Section 16(b). [17 CFR § 240.16b-6(b)]

In addition, Rule 16b-3 exempts the cash settlement of SARs in certain circumstances. (The SEC previously had indicated that the cash settlement of a SAR could be viewed as the simultaneous purchase and sale of stock.) [17 CFR § 240.16b-3(e)] The cash settlement of an equity security to satisfy the tax withholding consequences of an exercise also generally is deemed to be a SAR.

In order for the cash settlement of SARs to be exempt from Section 16(b) liability:

1. There must be publicly available information regarding the corporation (generally, the corporation must be complying with its Exchange Act reporting obligations);

2. The plan under which the SAR is granted must provide awards pursuant to a formula or be administered by disinterested persons, and those persons must have sole discretion either (1) to determine the form in which payment of the right will be made (i.e., cash, securities, or any combination thereof) or (2) to approve the election of the participant to receive cash in whole or in part in settlement of the right;

3. Both the election by the employee to receive cash in full or partial settlement of the SAR, as well as the actual exercise of the SAR, must be made during a window period of ten business days beginning on the third business day after each release by the corporation to the public of its quarterly or annual financial information. The window period does not need to be satisfied if the exercise date of the SAR is automatic or fixed in advance under the plan and is outside the control of the participant. Thus, phantom stock awards can be structured to avoid the window period requirement; and

4. The SAR must be held for at least six months from the date of grant to the date of cash settlement.

Rule 16a-1(c)(3) excludes from the definition of derivative securities, and thus completely exempts from Section 16's reporting and liability rules, certain cash-only arrangements satisfying the conditions of that Rule. The Rule exempts plans that grant rights which may be redeemed or exercised only for cash (such as rights under most phantom stock plans and cash-only SARs) if the plan (1) is in writing, (2) prescribes a limit on the amount of the awards, (3) provides that the rights are not transferrable, and (4) is administered by disinterested directors or provides benefits pursuant to a formula which precludes the exercise of discretion as to participants and amount of awards. Alternatively, a cash-only plan may be exempt under this Rule if the rights are redeemable or exercisable only upon a fixed date or dates at least six months after the award, or incident to the participant's death, retirement, disability, or termination of employment. [17 CFR § 240.16(a)-1(c)(3)(i)]

Section 16 compliance responsibility and liability fall primarily upon the insider. However, Section 16(a) disclosure violations, which are caused by insiders, must be reported in the employer's annual proxy statement to its shareholders. Because of this somewhat embarrassing disclosure and the complications associated with Section 16 compliance, issuers in almost all cases assume responsibility for Section 16(a) compliance by their insiders and for monitoring and preventing inadvertent Section 16(b) violations, particularly with respect to securities acquired pursuant to the issuer's stock compensation arrangements.

The consequences of not qualifying a stock plan under Rule 16b-3 or some other exemption is that "purchases" and "sales" within the plan will be "matched" with "purchases" and "sales" of securities by the insider outside of the plan (for example, on the open market), and the transactions within the plan would have to be reported monthly to the SEC under Section 16(a). Thus, it generally is considered critical that a stock plan qualify for exemptive relief under Section 16 in a case where the plan benefits insiders.

Q 8:45 Which state laws are applicable to stock plans?

Almost every state has adopted laws governing sales of securities to residents of the state. These so-called blue sky laws generally are rather uniform, but there are a number of significant variations. These laws generally require registration of persons who sell equity securities (so-called broker/dealer registration) and registration of sales of an issuer's securities (so-called securities registration) to a state resident. In almost every state, issuers selling their own securities are deemed not to be subject to the broker/dealer registration requirements. Therefore, equity compensation arrangements typically would not give rise to blue sky broker/dealer registration. (A notable exception is New York, which requires "dealer" registration of issuers selling their own securities to New York State residents.) Also, most states have provided exemptions from the securities registration requirements for transactions for which exemptions are provided under the Securities Act, such as exemptions for sales to sophisticated investors and certain small offerings, for sales of securities which are traded on a national securities exchange, and for securities provided to employees under employee benefit plans.

State blue sky laws typically apply to issuances of securities to a state resident without regard to the public/private status of the issuer or class of securities. The availability of exemptions may be limited in the case of nonpublicly traded equity securities because of the unavailability of certain exemptions which are typical of only public companies, such as those provided for securities registered under the Securities Act and those provided for securities traded on a national securities exchange.

Thus, without regard to the availability of an exemption under the Securities Act or the public/private character of the issuer or class of securities, applicable blue sky requirements should be consulted any time an issuer issues equity securities within any state to the issuer's employees.

Q 8:46   If the particular class of stock is traded on a securities exchange, are any other considerations applicable?

If the particular class of securities granted to employees under a stock plan is traded on a national securities exchange (for example, the New York Stock Exchange, the American Stock Exchange, NASDAQ, and the Pacific Stock Exchange), the exchange may impose special requirements. Usually, these requirements are duplicative of other requirements imposed under applicable law. (For example, a number of the exchanges require shareholder approval for the establishment of stock plans, and shareholder approval also is required for most plans to satisfy for the exemption under Rule 16b-3.) Nevertheless, the requirements of any exchange upon which an issuer's securities are traded should be consulted any time the issuer issues securities to its employees. Also, if the issuance of the issuer's stock under the Plan increases the issuer's outstanding securities above the number of shares previously listed with the exchange, a listing application (or amendment to a previous one) typically would be required.

Q 8:47   How is the compensation cost of a compensatory stock plan measured for accounting purposes?

For accounting purposes, the compensation cost of a compensatory stock plan is measured as the difference between the quoted market price (or other fair market value) at the measurement date and the amount the employee is required to pay for the stock. [APB

Opinion No 25] A corporation thus recognizes no compensation cost where the employee pays an amount at least equal to the quoted market price at the measurement date. [APB Opinion No 25] Because of this rule, grants under some plans (such as stock option plans with an exercise price at the date of grant equal to the fair market value of the underlying shares), generally result in no compensation expense because the measurement of compensation under this formula equals zero. On the other hand, discounted options, restricted stock, phantom stock and stock appreciation rights typically result in a positive compensation cost number. For stock appreciation rights, phantom stock and other variable plan awards, compensation cost should be measured as the amount by which the current quoted market price of the underlying stock exceeds the option price or value specified, subject to maximum limitations, if any, in the plan. [Financial Accounting Standards Board (FASB) Interpretation No 28] Accordingly, variations in the quoted market price between the grant date and the measurement date change the measure of compensation cost. [FASB Interpretation No 28] If a quoted market price from an established market is not available, the corporation should use the "best estimate" of the market value of the stock to calculate compensation cost. [APB Opinion No 25]

Q 8:48 What compensation cost should be charged against the corporation's earnings?

Compensation cost in stock plans should be recognized as an expense in one or more periods in which an employee performs services as part or all of the consideration received by the corporation for stock issued to the employee. [APB Opinion No 25; FASB Interpretation No 28] The service period may be defined in the plan or inferred from the terms or past pattern of the grant or award. [APB Opinion No 25] In the case of SARs or other variable plan awards, the service period should be presumed to be the vesting period unless another period is defined in the plan or some other agreement. [FASB Interpretation No 28] Therefore, in the case of fully vested, at-market options, the compensation cost calculation, which generally equals zero, is applied immediately upon grant. Therefore, under current rules, the grant of at-market options generally escapes compensation cost treatment.

If an employee performs services in several periods before stock is issued for those services, the corporation should accrue compensation cost in each period in which the services are performed. [APB Opinion No 25] If the measurement date is later than the grant or award date, the corporation should record the compensation expense in each period based on the quoted market price of the stock at the end of the period. [APB Opinion No 25; FASB Interpretation No 28]

Compensation costs accrued based on estimates may need to be adjusted in subsequent periods. [APB Opinion No 25] For example, accrued compensation for grants or awards which are forfeited should be adjusted by decreasing compensation expense in the period of forfeiture. [APB Opinion No 25; FASB Interpretation No 28] For SARs and other variable plans, as noted above, variations in the quoted market price change the measure of compensation cost and require an offsetting adjustment to compensation cost in the period in which the changes occur. [FASB Interpretation No 28]

If stock is issued before some or all of the services related to the award are performed, part of the consideration recorded for the stock issued is unearned compensation and should be shown as a separate reduction of stockholders' equity. [APB Opinion No 25] The unearned compensation should be accounted for as expense in the periods in which the employee performs services. [APB Opinion No 25]

A corporation may offer a combination plan that permits employees to elect among different forms of stock compensation, as is the case with a plan which grants NSOs and SARs in tandem. In that case, compensation expense should be accrued based on the terms the employee is most likely to elect based on the facts available for each period. [APB Opinion No 25; FASB Interpretation No 28] A corporation should presume the employee will elect to exercise the SARs, unless past experience or the terms of the combination plan provide evidence that the employee instead will elect to exercise the related stock options. [FASB Interpretation No 28]

In plans not resulting in the accrual of compensation cost, the corporation still may receive a tax deduction for amounts taxable to employees. [APB Opinion No 25] The tax benefit of the excess deduction should not be included in income, but should be added to paid-in capital. [APB Opinion No 25] In rare instances, the tax deduction may be less than the recorded compensation cost. Paid-in capital should then be charged in an amount limited to previous credits for excess deductions, with any remainder included in income tax expense. [APB Opinion No 25]

Timing differences arise when compensation costs are deductible in a period different from the one in which they are reported as costs in measuring net income. [APB Opinion No 25; APB Opinion No 11; FASB Statement of Financial Accounting Standards No 96] When the timing differences arise, deferred taxes should be recorded. [APB Opinion No 25, APB Opinion No 11, FASB Statement of Financial Accounting Standards No 96]

Q 8:49   What are the earnings per share effects of stock plans?

A stock plan can have two effects that negatively impact earnings per share. First, any compensation cost recognized decreases net income, which is the numerator in the earnings per share ratio. Second, to the extent that grants or awards dilute stockholders' equity, they increase the denominator of the earnings per share ratio because of the necessary adjustment to the number of common shares considered outstanding. [APB Opinion No 15; FASB Interpretation No 28; FASB Interpretation No 31]

Q 8:50   Are the accounting considerations for stock plans likely to change?

On June 30, 1993, the FASB issued a proposal, in the form of an exposure draft, which would require companies to recognize compensation cost for all stock-based compensation awards, including stock options with an at-market exercise price as of the date of grant, effective for awards occurring after December 31, 1996. This rather controversial proposal would require corporations to charge earnings with compensation expense equal to the fair market value of the award, not the fair market value of the stock underlying the award minus the exercise price, recognized over the vesting period, if any. This will have the effect of making similar the accounting treatment of stock options and other performance-based awards. The exposure draft did not specify the types of pricing models required to be used for options, but indicated that the exercise price, the expected term of the option, the current price of the underlying stock, expected dividends of the stock and the stock's expected volatility would be reasonable criteria for valuing options for expense recognition purposes.

In a prior draft issued on April 7, 1993, FASB deferred the cost recognition treatment for stock compensation awards until 1997 and thereafter, but, according to that prior draft and the June 30, 1993 proposal, companies will have to provide note disclosures, including disclosures of the effect on net income and earnings per share that would occur if the new rules currently were effective, as if the new recognition requirements had been adopted effective for 1994.

The exposure draft received widespread criticism, primarily on the bases that stock options are not susceptible to accurate valuation and that the exposure draft will discourage equity ownership by corporate executives and other employees. In December of 1994, FASB revised its proposal so as no longer to require expensing of stock options at fair market value, but to require only that an estimate of the value of the stock option (together with a statement concerning the estimation method) be disclosed in a footnote.

Recent Developments

Q 8:51 What recent developments have affected, positively or adversely, the popularity of NSOs, ISOs, or SARs?

The relative popularity of ISOs, NSOs, and SARs fluctuates from time to time based on evolving business, liability, tax, and other conditions. Recently (i.e., since the enactment of the Tax Reform Act of 1986), a number of factors have employers constantly pondering which of those vehicles is the most appropriate at a particular time. For example, the application of the alternative minimum tax to ISOs has tended to decrease the popularity of ISOs. On the other hand, the increase in ordinary income tax rates as compared to capital gains tax rates has tended to have the contrary effect (i.e., increasing the attractiveness of ISOs). The seemingly imminent adoption by the FASB of final accounting rules leveling the playing field between NSOs and ISOs on one hand, and SARs and similar performance based equity compensation arrangements on the other, would seem to eliminate the advantage NSOs and ISOs have had over the performance based arrangements from an accounting perspective. However, recent revisions to the Section 16 exemptions liberalizing the treatment of stock option grants and exercises have increased the attractiveness of those vehicles relative to SARs, which traditionally have received more lenient treatment under Section 16. Finally, because of heightened disclosure with respect to all stock-based compensation and the level of such compensation received by public company executives, SARs, NSOs, ISOs and all other forms of reportable stock-based compensation might also diminish in popularity as compared to cash compensation. (See Q 8:52.)

Q 8:52 What securities disclosure requirements apply to public company issuers that maintain stock plans?

One issue applicable to all employee benefit arrangements maintained by any employer subject to the reporting and disclosure requirements under the Exchange Act is the compensation reporting and disclosure obligations with respect to such arrangements in the public company's proxy and information statements, registration statements and periodic reports under the Exchange Act and registration statements under the Securities Act.

In October 1992, the SEC promulgated final regulations (which were amended in December 1993) concerning the disclosure in public company proxy statements and other reports of the types and value of compensation paid to the company's senior executive officers. These rules generally apply to proxy statements and other reports filed with the SEC on or after January 1, 1993, with certain transitional relief offered for certain disclosures (e.g., for valuing stock options). Although the new disclosure rules have many far reaching implications beyond stock compensation and benefits generally (e.g., performance disclosures relative to comparable companies, Compensation Committee interlocks, etc.), many of the rules focus on the disclosure of the economic value of various distinct benefit types. The following discusses very generally the coverage by these rules of stock-based benefits and the relevant required disclosures.

The new rules require disclosure concerning cash and stock compensation and other benefits of the company's chief executive officer and those of its four other highest-paid executive officers who earn in excess of $100,000 annually.

[1] SUMMARY COMPENSATION TABLE

The new rules require disclosure in tabular form of three distinct types of compensation: cash compensation; long-term incentive compensation; and "all other compensation." Salary and bonus amounts paid during each of the last three years are reportable, whether or not the compensation is deferred and whether or not the compensation is paid in cash. One exception to this deferred compensation disclosure requirement exists where an executive elects to receive non-cash compensation in lieu of salary or bonus under a long-term incentive plan (e.g., a DSO), in which case the amount may be reported on the table as a long-term incentive award rather than cash compensation.

The table also must contain the dollar value for the three years of restricted stock awards, NSOs, ISOs, and SARs awards, long-term incentive payouts (not accruals), and "all other compensation." This latter category would include company contributions to defined contribution plans, life insurance premiums, build up of cash value of life insurance (for example, in a split-dollar life insurance arrangement), interest on deferred compensation in excess of the "market rate" (but not market interest or actual investment performance on deferred compensation), preferential dividends on restricted stock and stock options, and amounts accrued pursuant to any severance or golden parachute arrangements.

[2] STOCK OPTIONS/STOCK APPRECIATION RIGHTS

Although the Summary Compensation Table only requires information concerning stock compensation granted during each of the relevant three years, separate tables require more detail concerning these grants and information concerning awards from prior periods. One table requires a description of the terms and conditions of each grant during the most recent year, the percentage that the amount granted to the particular executive bears to the amount granted to all other employees during the year, and the present value and potential gain to the executive of the grant using specified assumptions as to annual increases in the stock price over the term of the option/SAR or using another accepted method of valuation (for example, the so-called "Black Scholes" valuation model). Another table requires disclosure of all exercises of options and SARs by the executives during the most recent year, the value realized, the number of unexercised options or SARs held at the end of the year and the value of any such options or SARs which are "in-the-money" (i.e., which would yield the executive a gain if currently exercised). An additional table is required if any options were repriced, or cancelled and regranted, during the year.

[3] Long-Term Incentive Plan Awards Table

This table requires disclosure concerning long-term incentive arrangements during the most recent year apart from NSOs, ISOs, SARs, and restricted stock. The table requires a description of the terms and conditions of the long-term incentive award, a general description of relevant performance criteria for receiving the award and estimated future payout amounts for awards not based entirely on stock price.

[4] Alternative 10-K Disclosure

On July 10, 1995, the SEC released proposed regulations permitting certain items otherwise subject to disclosure on a company's proxy or information statements under the rules discussed above to be disclosed instead on the company's Form 10-K Annual Report. These include (i) the table that requires disclosure of exercises of options and SARs by the executives during the most recent year, the value realized, the number of unexercised options or SARs held at the end of the year, and the value of any options or SARs that are "in-the-money"; (ii) the long-term incentive plan awards table; (iii) information on options that were repriced, or cancelled and re-granted, during the year; and (iv) certain non-stock disclosures, such as information concerning defined benefit plans, employment agreements, and change-in-control agreements.

Q 8:53 Are stock plans subject to ERISA?

Generally, no. Most stock compensation arrangements (including conventional NSO plans, ISO plans, restricted stock plans,

SAR plans, and phantom stock plans) are not governed by ERISA because they are not structured to defer the receipt of compensation to the termination of a participant's employment or beyond (and thus are not ERISA-governed pension plans) and do not provide the types of benefits set forth in section 3(1) of ERISA (and thus are not ERISA-governed welfare benefit plans). Non-ERISA employee benefit arrangements generally are governed by the common law of contracts. Thus, from the employer's perspective, it is wise to structure stock plan documents and agreements in a way that reserves to the employer (or other applicable administrative committee) the greatest degree of discretion with respect to the selection of participants, the size of awards, and the ability to terminate and reduce plan benefits. From the participant's perspective, the participant should look for non-forfeitability of benefits accrued under the plan so that the economic substance of the award cannot be diminished by future events. Of course, given the nature of the transaction (which usually does not involve additional services or other consideration from the employee), the employer typically is in the driver's seat as to the nature of the contract and thus controls its terms.

Q 8:54   How are stock compensation plans impacted by the new $1 million deduction limit for executive compensation?

OBRA '93 added Section 162(m) to the Code, which generally prohibits public corporations from deducting compensation in excess of $1 million per year to any of the five executives subject to the SEC executive compensation disclosure rules (see Q 8:53), effective for tax years beginning after 1993. This $1 million deductibility limit generally does not apply to so-called performance-based items of compensation and to other specified forms of compensation. An item of compensation is "performance-based" if it is paid under one or more pre-established performance goals which are established by the employer's compensation committee in writing before the employee performs the relevant services and while the outcome under the goal is substantially uncertain. Regulations promulgated by the IRS under this limitation provide that NSOs, ISOs, SARs, and phantom stock arrangements are deemed to be based on pre-established performance goals if three conditions are satisfied. First, the grant or award must be made by the employer's compensation committee, which must be composed of outside directors. Second, there must be a per-employee limitation on the number of shares for which options or rights may be granted during the specified period, although different amounts of options or rights may be granted to different officers. Third, the exercise price of the option or, if applicable, the amount that forms the original basis of the SAR or phantom stock grant must equal or exceed the underlying stock's fair market value on the date of the grant. (Because of this latter condition, discounted NSOs appear not to be exempt from the calculation of non-deductible compensation.)

Case Study 8-1

Note: See Case Studies at the end of chapters 1 through 7.

A opens the meeting by asking the advisor to provide the group with a broad overview of the ways in which the corporation may use stock-based techniques to provide deferred compensation to executives. A reminds the advisor that the group is not interested in giving up voting control of the corporation to others.

The advisor begins by noting that her remarks will be limited to stock-based techniques with a deferred receipt element. In other words, she will not discuss outright stock grants, stock purchase plans and so on. The advisor also notes that, in lieu of techniques using actual corporation stock, there are stock appreciation plans, phantom stock plans, and other devices which operate by reference to actual corporation stock but do not grant it. A remarks that, given the limited time available, the advisor should limit her remarks to the actual stock-based plans.

The advisor limits her remarks at the meeting to two such techniques, incentive stock options (ISOs), and nonstatutory stock options (NSOs). With these techniques, selected participants are granted the right, exercisable at a specified future time, to purchase corporation stock from the corporation at a specified price. The options may require that the participant be employed by the corporation on the option exercise date and can provide the participant with an option to purchase the stock at discounted prices.

The advisor notes that ISOs provide participants with more favorable tax treatment than do NSOs, but that ISOs result in no deductions for employers, whereas NSOs do.

The group concludes that since negotiations with a potential buyer of the corporation are in progress, this is not an appropriate time to compensate executives with stock-based techniques. However, the group is intrigued with the NSO concept and would like to return to a discussion of it in the future if the negotiations end without resulting in a sale.

The advisor adds that a number of additional technical issues would need to be discussed in detail before proceeding with any stock-based techniques.

Table 8-1 illustrates the relative tax incidents (from both an employer's and an employee's perspective) of the various types of stock plans discussed in this chapter. The Table assumes a fair market value of the stock of $100 on January 1, 1994, $200 on January 1, 1996, and $300 on January 1, 1998.

What happens to A, B, C, D, and E if a corporate take over occurs? See Case Study at the end of chapter 9.

TABLE 8-1. Comparison of Tax Incidents of Stock Plans

	January 1, 1994 *Grant Date*	January 1, 1996 *Vesting Date/* *Exercise Date*	January 1, 1998 *Disposition of* *Stock Date*
Incentive Stock Option Exercise price: $100	Employee receives no income Employer receives no deduction	Employee receives no income Employer receives no deduction	Employee receives $200 capital gains income Employer receives no deduction
Nonstatutory Stock Option* Discounted exercise price: $90	Employee receives no income Employer receives no deduction	Employee receives $110 ordinary income Employer receives $110 deduction	Employee receives $100 capital gains income Employer receives no deduction
Deeply Discounted Stock Option Exercise price: $40	Employee receives no income Employer receives no deduction	Employee receives $160 ordinary income Employer receives $160 deduction	Employee receives $100 capital gains income Employer receives no deduction
Restricted Stock	Employee receives no income Employer receives no deduction	Employee receives $200 ordinary income Employer receives $200 deduction	Employee receives $100 capital gains income Employer receives no deduction
Stock Appreciation Right/ Phantom Stock	Employee receives no income Employer receives no deduction	Employee receives $100 ordinary income Employer receives $100 deduction	N/A N/A
Employee Stock Purchase Plan Discounted exercise price: $85	Employee receives no income Employer receives no deduction	Employee receives no income Employer receives no deduction	Employee receives $15 ordinary income/$200 capital gains income Employer receives no deduction

---

*Assume option has no readily ascertainable fair market value.

Chapter 9

Parachute Payments

Parachute payments are severance agreements that are designed to protect key employees from the effects of a corporate takeover or change in control. This chapter examines parachute payments—why they are used, how they are defined under the Code, which payments and transfers of property are considered "in the nature of compensation" for purposes of the parachute payment rules, how nonqualified stock options are treated for purposes of these rules, when a "change in ownership" occurs for purposes of these rules, which payments are *not* considered parachute payments, and whether an agreement to provide payments in the nature of parachute payments is a plan that is covered by ERISA.

Overview

Q 9:1   What are "golden parachutes"?

Generally, "golden parachutes" are severance agreements that protect key employees from the effects of a corporate takeover or change in control. Payments under golden parachutes are triggered by a change in ownership or control of the corporation. They provide key employees who are terminated, or who, under certain circumstances, resign, as a result of a takeover or change in control with either continued compensation for a specified period following the key employees' departure or a lump sum payment.

Q 9:2   Why do employers use golden parachutes?

Employers provide golden parachutes to key employees for several reasons, including:

1. To provide incentives to sought-after employees to join an employer despite significant risk of a takeover or change in control that could result in employees losing their jobs; and

2. To reduce key employees' incentive to oppose takeovers that are beneficial to the organization, but that may endanger the employees' jobs.

Critics of golden parachutes have argued that they provide little benefit to the employer. They believe that, in many takeover or change in control situations, golden parachutes are used, in part, to dissuade interested buyers from proceeding with the acquisition by increasing the cost of the acquisition. In other situations, critics are concerned that the existence of these arrangements tends to encourage the executives involved to favor a proposed takeover or change in control that might not be in the best interests of the organization and its shareholders.

In response to such criticism, legislation was enacted (codified in Code Sections 280G and 4999) to impose limits on excessive parachute payments. Under these rules, parachute payments greater than or equal to three times the covered executive's annual compensation are presumed excessive for tax purposes, resulting in the employer losing its deduction for some of the payments and the imposition of an excise tax on the recipient of the payments.

Q 9:3   How is a parachute payment defined under the Code?

A parachute payment is, in general, any payment in the nature of compensation that is made to, will be made to, or is for the benefit of, an employee or independent contractor who is a shareholder, an officer, or a highly compensated individual (a "disqualified individual") which is contingent on a change: (1) in the ownership of a corporation, (2) in the effective control of a corporation, or (3) in the ownership of a substantial portion of the assets of a corporation, and which has an aggregate present value of at least three times the individual's base amount. For this purpose, an individual's base amount is the individual's annualized includible compensation for the most recent five taxable years (or appropriate portion thereof). A parachute payment also includes any payment to, or for the benefit of, a disqualified individual that is in the nature of compensation and that is made in accordance with an agreement that violates a generally enforced securities law or regulation. [IRC §§ 280G(b)(2), 280G(c); Treas Reg § 1.280G-1, Q&A 2]

For purposes of this definition, any payment made pursuant to an agreement entered into within one year before a change in control or ownership or in the ownership of a substantial portion of the assets of the corporation, or an amendment of a previous agreement made within that one-year period, is presumed to be contingent on the change unless the contrary is established by clear and convincing evidence. In such cases, the burden rests on the taxpayer to prove to the IRS and, perhaps, to the courts, by the judicial "clear and convincing evidence" standard, that the payment was not, in fact, contingent on the change. [IRC § 280G(b)(2)(C)]

If the aggregate present value of all payments made to or on behalf of a disqualified individual that are contingent on a change of ownership or control is less than the amount equal to three times the individual's base amount, no portion of the payment is a parachute payment. Also, parachute payments that violate securities laws are not included in this computation if they are not contingent on a change in ownership or control. [Treas Reg § 1.280G-1, Q&A 30(a)]

Example. Assume A is an officer of corporation M and that A's base amount is $100,000. A payment of $400,000 that is contingent on a change in the ownership of M is made to A on the date of the change. The payment is a parachute payment because it has an aggregate present value at the date of the event entitling the executive to the payments equal to at least three times A's base amount of $100,000 ($3 \times \$100,000 = \$300,000$). If, however, the payment that is contingent on the change in the ownership of M is only $299,999, no portion of the payment would be a parachute payment because the payment does not have an aggregate present value equal to at least three times A's base amount. [Treas Reg § 1.280G-1, Q&A 30(b)]

Therefore, change of control payments often are carefully structured to be under the three times limit, occasionally using fail-safe forfeiture provisions.

Example. In 1991, the IRS ruled regarding the application of these rules to certain annuity payments an employer made to employee A. According to the ruling, the employer acquired another entity (M) and the acquisition constituted a change in control of M for purposes of Code Section 280G(b). Approximately nine months prior to this change in control, M entered into agreements with certain of its executives, including A.

The agreement with A provided that, in the event of an involuntary termination of employment, as defined in the agreement, at any time after a change in control, or in the event of a voluntary resignation at any time more than six months after a change in control, annuity payments would be made to A and to A's spouse. Pursuant to the agreement, the annuity payments were to be reduced by whatever amount was necessary to avoid the deduction disallowance and excise tax provisions of Code Sections 280G and 4999.

The employee's employment terminated in December 1988 and, pursuant to the terms of the agreement, annuity payments were to begin on February 1, 1989. According to the ruling, the payments met the definition of parachute payments in Code Section 280G(b)(2) except for the fact that the present value of the payments would be limited to 299 percent of A's base amount.

The IRS ruled that, for purposes of the "three times base amount" test of Code Section 280G(b)(2)(ii), the present value of the annuity payments in question was determined on the date of the change of control of M. Therefore, because the present value on that date was less than the three times amount, the IRS concluded that the parachute payment rules did not apply. [Ltr Rul 9202016, Oct 9, 1991]

Q 9:4 What payments are considered to be in the nature of compensation?

Generally, all payments that arise out of an employment relationship or are associated with the performance of services are considered to be payments in the nature of compensation. These payments include wages and salary, bonuses, severance pay, fringe benefits, pension benefits, and other deferred compensation. However, payments in the nature of compensation do not include attorney's fees or court costs paid or incurred in connection with the payment of any amount made to a disqualified individual which is contingent on a change in ownership or control of a corporation. Payments from qualified employee benefit plans also are not considered payments in the nature of compensation. [Treas Reg § 1.280G-1, Q&A 8, Q&A 11(a)]

Q 9:5 Can transfers of property be treated as payments in the nature of compensation?

Yes, a transfer of property can be treated as a payment in the nature of compensation. A transfer of property is considered a payment made (or to be made) in the taxable year in which the property transferred is includible in the gross income of the disqualified individual under Code Section 83 and the regulations thereunder. Thus, a payment generally is considered made (or to be made) when the property is transferred to a disqualified individual and becomes substantially vested in the individual. Further, the amount of the payment is equal to the excess of the fair market value of the transferred property (determined without regard to any lapse restriction, as defined in Section 1.83-3(i)) at the time the property becomes substantially vested, over the amount (if any) paid for the property. [Treas Reg § 1.280G-1, Q&A 11(b), Q&A 12(a); Ltr Rul 9119051, May 13, 1991]

In other words, in general, the amount of the payment is equal to the excess of the fair market value of the transferred property over the amount, if any, paid for the property. For example, assume that, on January 1, 1986, corporation *M* gave to *A*, an officer, in connection with *A*'s performance of services to corporation *M*, a bonus of 100 shares of corporation *M* stock. Under the terms of the bonus arrangement, *A* is obligated to return the corporation *M* stock to corporation *M* unless the company's earnings double by January 1, 1989, or there is a change in the ownership or control before that date. *A* is prohibited from transferring the stock while it is subject to the return restriction. *A*'s rights in the stock are treated as substantially non-vested for the period during which the stock is subject to the return restriction because *A*'s rights are subject to a substantial risk of forfeiture and are nontransferable. On January 1, 1988, a change in the ownership of corporation *M* occurs. On that day, the fair market value of the corporation *M* stock is $250 per share. Because *A*'s rights in the stock become substantially vested on that day, the payment is considered made on that day, and the amount of the payment is $25,000 (100 × $250). [IRC § 280G(d)(3); Treas Reg § 1.280G-1, Q&A 12(d)]

Q 9:6 How are nonqualified stock options treated for purposes of these rules?

For purposes of the parachute payment rules, if an option to which Code Section 422 (pertaining generally to qualified incentive stock options) does not apply has an ascertainable fair market value (whether or not readily ascertainable as defined in Section 1.83-7(b)) at the time the option becomes substantially vested, the option will be treated as property that is transferred not later than the time at which the option becomes substantially vested.

Thus, when an option to which Section 422 does not apply becomes substantially vested, its value is treated, for purposes of the parachute payment rules, as a payment in the nature of compensation. (This is the case even though this treatment is not consistent with the general tax treatment of nonqualified stock options under which there ordinarily is no taxable event until the options are exercised (even though exercisable) unless the option has a readily ascertainable fair market.)

Thereafter, any money or other property transferred to a disqualified individual upon the exercise, or as consideration upon the sale or other disposition, of the option is not treated as a payment in the nature of compensation for purposes of the parachute payment rules. [Treas Reg § 1.280G-1, Q&A 13(a), Q&A 13(b); Ltr Ruls 9104040, Oct 31, 1990; 9119051, May 13, 1991]

Q 9:7 For purposes of the parachute payment rules, are options covered by Code Section 422 treated as payments at the time of grant or at a later time?

The issue of whether, for purposes of the parachute payment rules, an option to which Code Section 422 applies will be treated as a payment at the time of the grant or at a later time specifically has been reserved by the IRS for future regulations. [Treas Reg § 1.280G-1, Q&A 13(c)]

In one ruling, the IRS examined a transaction in which X, Z, and Z-1 (a wholly owned subsidiary of Z) executed an agreement on *date d* which provided that Z-1 would acquire the stock of X from its shareholders, after which Z-1 would merge into X. Under the agreement, X would become a wholly owned subsidiary of Z. The change in the ownership or effective control of X occurred on *date h*.

Also, because Z wanted to acquire all of the equity of X, the agreement provided that, on the effective date of the merger, the holders of all vested and nonvested outstanding options would receive a payment equal to the spread between the option exercise price and the offer price in the merger. The merger occurred on *date m*. All the options were vested at that time except for those granted on *date n*, which were to vest on *date o*. The options were both nonqualified and incentive stock options. The nonqualified options were granted pursuant to a plan adopted by X's board of directors and approved by its shareholders approximately 15 months prior to the change in control of X. Prior to adoption of the plan, X had granted options to employees in every year, except one, of the 13 years prior to the change in control. Further, the options granted within a year prior to the merger were not excessive when compared to those granted in prior years.

The IRS ruled that any nonvested options granted to the employees on *date n* were not presumed to be contingent on the change in the ownership or control of *X* under Section 1.280G-1, Q&A 25 of the Regulations (see Q 9:14). Any nonvested options granted to the employees on *date n*, to which Code Section 422 did not apply, were payments in the nature of compensation, a portion of which was contingent on the change of ownership or control of *X* on the date those options became substantially vested, as defined under Section 1.83-3(b) of the Regulations. The portion of the payments that was treated as contingent on a change of ownership or control of *X* was determined under Section 1.280G-1, Q&A 24(c), of the Regulations (see Q 9:14). The options that were incentive stock options when granted, but which were cashed out, were treated as options to which Section 422 did not apply. [Ltr Rul 9104040, Oct 31, 1990]

In another ruling, the IRS examined a transaction in which approximately 80 percent of *X*'s stock was acquired by a subsidiary of *Y*. As part of the acquisition agreement, *X* was required to cancel all stock option plans. The holders of such options, including both vested and nonvested options, were entitled to a cash payment in exchange for the surrender of their options to acquire shares of *X*. These funds were paid to employees and others who were neither officers nor directors of *X*. However, on the advice of counsel, it was determined that payment would not be made to the officers and directors of *X* until the earlier of six months following the change in control date or the closing of the change in control transaction. The closing of the change in control transaction occurred two weeks before the expiration of the six-month period. At that time, the corporation cashed out the officers and directors, paying them the difference between the fair market value of the stock and the exercise price on the date that the shareholders who were not insiders were cashed out.

Based on these facts, the IRS determined that neither the options nor any stock remained nonvested after the determination was made concerning how much cash *Y* would pay for the options. Thus, for purposes of Code Section 280G(b)(2), the payment in the nature of compensation relative to the nonqualified stock options occurred on the date the determination was made as to how much cash would be paid in exchange for the options. The IRS also determined that the formula in Section 1.280G-1, Q&A 24(c) of the Regulations, if applicable, must be applied on that date. Also, the IRS determined that, in applying the three times base amount test, the present value of the payment that is contingent on the change in control is determined on the date of the change and that any deferred compensation that was not includible in the officers' and directors' incomes is not included in their base amounts. [Ltr Rul 9119051, May 13, 1991]

Q 9:8 When is the present value of a parachute payment determined for the purpose of these rules?

In general, the present value of a parachute payment is determined as of the date on which the change in ownership or control occurs. However, if a payment is made prior to the date on which the change in ownership or control occurs, the present value of a payment is determined as of the date on which the payment is made. [Treas Reg § 1.280G-1, Q&A 31; Ltr Rul 9104040, Oct 31, 1990]

In a 1991 ruling, the IRS determined that, for purposes of the three times base amount test of Code Section 280G(b)(2)(ii), the present value of the annuity payments in question was determined as of the date of the change of control of the acquired entity pursuant to Treasury Regulations Section 1.280G-1, Q&A 31. (See Q 9:3.) [Ltr Rul 9202016, Oct 9, 1991]

Q 9:9 What special rules apply to the determination of the base amount?

The base amount of a disqualified individual generally is the average annual compensation from the corporation which was includible in the individual's gross income during the most recent five taxable years ending before the date of the change in ownership or control. If the individual was not an employee or independent contractor of the corporation with respect to which the change in ownership or control occurs, or a predecessor entity or a related entity as described in Section 1.280G-1, Q&A 21 of the Regulations, for this entire five-year period (or "base period"), the individual's base period is the portion of the five-year period during which the individual performed personal services for the corporation or predecessor entity or related entity. Compensation for a short or incomplete taxable year is annualized before determining the average annual compensation for the base period. For example, assume an officer was employed by a corporation for two years and four months preceding the taxable year in which a change in ownership or control of the corporation occurs. Assume the individual's includible compensation from the corporation was $30,000 for the four month period, $120,000 for the first full year, and $150,000 for the second full year. The individual's base amount is $120,000:

$$((3 \times \$30,000) + \$120,000 + \$150,000) \div 3$$

Also, for purposes of the base amount, amounts that are change of control payments are not taken into account. [IRC §§ 280G(b)(3) and (d); Treas Reg § 1.280G-1, Q&A 34–Q&A 36]

In the case of a disqualified individual who did not perform services for the corporation or predecessor or related entity prior to the individual's taxable year in which the change in ownership or control occurs, the base amount is the annualized compensation which was includible in the individual's gross income for that portion of the taxable year prior to the change in ownership or control, was not contingent on the change in ownership or control, and was not a securities violation parachute payment. [Treas Reg § 1.280G-1, Q&A 36(a)]

The base amount includes only compensation that is includible in gross income. For example, payments in the form of untaxed fringe benefits or untaxed elective deferrals to retirement or welfare benefit plans are not included in the base amount. However, for purposes of determining an individual's status as a highly compensated employee, the elective deferrals are taken into account in determining compensation. [Treas Reg § 1.280G-1, Q&A 34(c), Q&A 21]

Q 9:10   Who is a disqualified individual?

A disqualified individual is, in general, any individual who, at any time during the determination period, performs personal services for a corporation and who is an employee, independent contractor, or other person described in the regulations and who is, with respect to the corporation, a shareholder, an officer, or a highly compensated individual. The period for determining an individual's status as a disqualified individual is the portion of the year of the corporation ending on the date of the change in ownership or control (the change in ownership period) and the preceding 12-month period. For example, a change in ownership of corporation *M*, a calendar year corporation, takes place on June 12, 1991. The disqualified individual determination period of corporation *M* begins on January 1, 1990 and ends on June 12, 1991. [IRC § 280G(c); Treas Reg § 1.280G-1, Q&A 15, Q&A 20; Ltr Rul 9104040, Oct 31, 1990]

Q 9:11   Are all shareholders considered disqualified individuals?

No. Only a shareholder who owns (as determined taking into account the constructive ownership rules of Code Section 318(a)), at any time during the determination period, stock of the corporation having a fair market value that exceeds the lesser of $1 million or 1 percent of the total fair market value of the outstanding shares of all classes of the corporation's stock, is treated as a disqualified individual by reason of being a shareholder for purposes of the parachute payment provisions. An individual who owns a lesser amount of stock may, however, be a disqualified individual because the individual is an officer or a highly compensated individual with respect to the corporation. [Treas Reg § 1.280G-1, Q&A 17]

Q 9:12   Who is an officer for purposes of the parachute payment rules?

Generally, for purposes of the parachute payment rules, an officer is an administrative executive who is in regular and continued service for the corporation. However, whether an individual is an officer with respect to a corporation is determined by all the facts and circumstances in the particular case. [Treas Reg § 1.280G-1, Q&A 18(a)]

An individual who is an officer with respect to any member of an affiliated group that is treated as one corporation in accordance with the rules under Code Section 1504 is treated as an officer of that one corporation. [Treas Reg § 1.280G-1, Q&A 18(b)]

Generally, no more than 50 employees (or, if less, the greater of three employees, or 10 percent of the employees (rounded up to the nearest integer)) of the corporation (or, in the case of an affiliated group treated as one corporation, each member of the affiliated group) are treated as disqualified individuals with respect to a corporation by reason of being officers of the corporation. [Treas Reg § 1.280G-1, Q&A 18(c)]

Q 9:13   Who is a highly compensated individual for purposes of the parachute payment rules?

A highly compensated individual for purposes of the parachute payment rules is any individual who is, or would be if the individual were an employee, a member of the group consisting of the lesser of (1) the highest paid one percent of the employees of the corporation (rounded up to the nearest integer), or (2) the highest paid 250 employees of the corporation, when ranked on the basis of compensation paid during the disqualified individual determination period (i.e., the portion of the year of the corporation ending on the date of the change in ownership or control of the corporation (the change in ownership period) and the 12-month period immediately preceding the change in ownership period). However, no individual whose annualized compensation during this determination period is less than $75,000 is treated as a highly compensated individual. [IRC § 280G(c); Treas Reg § 1.280G-1, Q&A 19(a)]

An individual who is not an employee of the corporation is not treated as being highly compensated with respect to the corporation on account of compensation received for performing services (such as brokerage, legal, or investment banking services) in connection with a change in ownership or control of the corporation if the services are performed in the ordinary course of the individual's trade or business and the individual normally performs similar services for a significant number of clients unrelated to the corporation. [Treas Reg § 1.280G-1, Q&A 19(b)]

In determining the number of employees of a corporation, employees are not counted if they normally work less than $17\frac{1}{2}$ hours per week (as defined under Code Section 414(q)(8)(B) and the regulations thereunder) or if they normally work during not more than six months during any year (as defined in Code Section 414(q)(8)(C) and the regulations thereunder). However, an employee who is not counted for such reasons may nevertheless be a highly compensated individual. [Treas Reg § 1.280G-1, Q&A 19(c)]

Q 9:14 When is a payment contingent on a change in ownership or control?

In general, a payment is considered to be contingent on a change in ownership or control if the payment would not have been made had no change in ownership or control occurred. Property that becomes substantially vested, as defined in Treasury Regulations Section 1.83-3(b), as a result of a change in ownership or control will not be treated as a payment that was substantially certain to have been made whether or not the change occurred. A payment also generally is treated as contingent on a change in ownership or control if the following conditions exist:

1. The payment is contingent on an event that is closely associated with a change in ownership or control (such as the onset of a tender offer, a substantial increase in the market price of the corporation's stock that occurs within a short period prior to a change in ownership or control, the cessation of the listing of the corporation's stock on an established securities market, or the acquisition of more than 5 percent of the corporation's stock by a person or persons acting as a group not in control of the corporation),

2. A change in ownership or control actually occurs, and

3. The event is materially related to the change in ownership or control.

[Treas Reg § 1.280G-1, Q&A 22(a), 22(b)]

An event will be presumed to be materially related to a change in ownership or control if the event occurs within the period that begins one year before and ends one year after the date of change in ownership or control. If the event occurs outside this period, the event will be presumed not to be materially related to the change in ownership or control. [Treas Reg § 1.280G-1, Q&A 22(b)]

A payment that would have been made had no change in ownership or control occurred is treated as contingent on a change in ownership or control if the change accelerates the time at which the payment is made. Also, a payment is treated as contingent on a change in ownership or control even if the employment or independent contractor relationship of the disqualified individual is not terminated (voluntarily or involuntarily) as a result of the change. [Treas Reg § 1.280G-1, Q&A 22(c), 22(d)]

Payments are not, however, treated as contingent on a change in ownership or control if they are made (or are to be made) pursuant to an agreement entered into after the change. However, an agreement that is executed after a change in ownership or control, pursuant to a legally enforceable agreement that was entered into before the change, will be considered to have been entered into before the change. [Treas Reg § 1.280G-1, Q&A 23(a)]

Any payment pursuant to an agreement entered into within one year before the date of a change in ownership or control, or an amendment that modifies a previous agreement in any significant respect, if the amendment is made within one year before the date of a change in ownership or control, is presumed to be contingent on the change unless the contrary is established by clear and convincing evidence. However, even if this presumption is rebutted, the payment still may be treated as contingent on a change pursuant to Treasury Regulations Section 1.280G-1, Q&A 22(b). [Treas Reg § 1.280G-1, Q&A 25; Ltr Rul 9104040, Oct 31, 1990]

In a recent ruling, the IRS responded to the issue of whether the confirmation of a plan of reorganization (under chapter 11 of the United States Bankruptcy Code), which would trigger payment under the employer-debtor's deferred compensation plan, was a "closely associated event" under Treasury Regulations Section 1.280G-1, Q&A 22(b) when, under the reorganization, a creditor of the employer would exchange debt for equity that would represent more than 5 percent of the fair market value of the employer's outstanding stock. The second issue considered by the IRS was whether the representation of creditors on certain creditors' committees would cause them to be viewed as "acting as a group" for purposes of Treasury Regulations Section 1.280G-1, Q&As 27, 28, and 29.

According to the ruling, the employer and substantially all of its active subsidiaries filed separate petitions for reorganization under chapter 11 of the Bankruptcy Code. Since the filing, the employer and its affiliated debtors had continued in the management and operation of their respective businesses and properties as debtors-in-possession. By its filing under chapter 11, the employer believed that it could successfully reorganize and return to profitability.

Various classes of creditors of the employer and its affiliated debtors were represented on creditors' committees appointed by the Bankruptcy Court. These committees exercise a general oversight role regarding the debtors' ongoing operations. The creditors' committees, along with the employer, participated in developing the final plans of reorganization (POR) that would be subjected to a vote of all creditors.

At the time the employer filed for chapter 11 relief, it was anticipated that the reorganization process would last for several years. In an effort to retain and recruit experienced and qualified executives during the pendency of the reorganization process and to retain those individuals for at least a one-year period following the employer's emergence from bankruptcy, a plan was adopted by A (apparently, a related employer) to provide payments for certain employees. The plan provided for the establishment of an unfunded account for each participant upon commencement of participation in the plan. For each year that the participant participated in the plan, the account would be credited with an award. In addition to annual awards, participants eligible to participate in the plan on January 1, 1990, were credited with an initial award. Awards were expressed as a percentage of base salary at the time of the award, ranging from 10 percent to 40 percent. The last year for which an award would be made would be the year in which the employing debtor's plan of reorganization became effective or, if earlier, the year in which a sale of that debtor occurred.

If a participant voluntarily terminated employment with the relevant employer-debtor or was discharged for cause prior to either of the relevant payment dates, the participant's account balance in the plan would be forfeited, with certain exceptions. A participant who was discharged except for cause, or who left with "good reason," prior to the payment date, would become entitled to receive his or her account balance under the plan. "Good reason" generally was defined in the plan as a reduction in the participant's responsibilities or salary.

The IRS noted that Treasury Regulations Section 1.280G-1, Q&A 22 provides guidance concerning when a payment will be contingent on the change in ownership or control of a corporation. Under Treasury Regulations Section 1.280G-1, Q&A 22(a), the general rule is that a payment is treated as contingent on a change in ownership or control if the payment would not, in fact, have been made had no change in ownership or control occurred. A payment generally is to be treated as one which would not, in fact, have been made in the absence of a change in ownership or control unless it is substantially certain, at the time of the change, that the payment would have been made whether or not the change occurred.

The IRS also noted that Treasury Regulations Section 1.280G-1, Q&A 22(b), provides further that a payment generally will be treated as contingent on a change in control if:

1. The payment is contingent upon an event closely associated with a change in control,
2. The change in control actually occurs, and
3. The event is materially related to the change in control.

An event will be presumed to be materially related to a change in control if the event occurs within one year before or after the change in control, and not so related if it occurs more than one year before or after the change.

An event is considered closely associated with a change in ownership or control if the event is of a type often preliminary or subsequent to, or otherwise closely associated with, a change in control. According to Treasury Regulations Section 1.280G-1, Q&A 22(b), events in the following nonexclusive list are considered closely associated with a change in control:

- The onset of a tender offer
- A substantial increase in the market price of the corporation's stock within a short period prior to the change
- The cessation of the listing of the corporation's stock on an established securities exchange
- The acquisition of more than 5 percent of the corporation's stock by a person or group not in control of the corporation

- The voluntary or involuntary termination of the individual's employment
- A significant reduction in the individual's job responsibilities.

Under the plan, participants were entitled to receive a payment from the plan upon the occurrence of a termination of the employment (for example, termination with "good cause"), upon the sale of the employing debtor, upon the change in status of the bankruptcy proceedings from chapter 11 to chapter 7 of the Bankruptcy Code, and upon the confirmation of a plan of reorganization. Of these events, a termination of employment is a "closely associated event" under Treasury Regulations Section 1.280 G-1, Q&A 22(b). The sale of an employing debtor to a person or group also would be a closely associated event if the fair market value of that debtor was significant in relation to the fair market value of the affiliated group prior to the sale.

The IRS ruled that payments from the plan that were triggered by the confirmation of a plan of reorganization would not be considered to be contingent on an event that is "closely associated with a change in ownership or control" under Treasury Regulations Section 1.280G-1, Q&A 22(b). However, the IRS noted that this ruling would not apply if, as a result of the effectiveness of a plan of reorganization, Y, the largest single creditor of the employer, thereafter obtained the ownership or control of the employer as set out under Treasury Regulations Section 1.280G-1, Q&As 27, 28, or 29.

The IRS also ruled that the creditors of the employer would not be considered to be "acting as a group" for purposes of determining whether a change of ownership or control, within the meaning of the Regulations, had occurred as a result of the effectiveness of a plan of reorganization merely by virtue of service or representation on one of the official or unofficial committees of the employer's creditors, or of participation in the formulation of, and voting upon, the employer's (or any of its affiliated debtors') plan of reorganization.

The IRS noted that temporary or final regulations pertaining to one or more of the issues addressed in the ruling have not been adopted. Therefore, the ruling would be modified or revoked by adoption of temporary or final regulations to the extent that the regulations were inconsistent with any conclusion in the ruling. [Ltr Rul 9212025, Dec 23, 1991]

Q 9:15   If a payment is contingent on a change in ownership or control, is the entire payment generally treated as contingent on a change in ownership or control?

Generally, yes. However, if it is substantially certain that the payment would have been made whether or not the change occurred, but the payment is treated as contingent on the change solely because the change accelerates the time at which the payment is made, then the portion of the payment that is treated as contingent on the change in ownership or control is the amount by which the amount of the accelerated payment exceeds the present value of the payment absent the acceleration. [Treas Reg § 1.280G-1, Q&A 24(a), Q&A 24(b)]

> **Example.** Corporation *X* grants a stock appreciation right to a highly compensated individual. After the stock appreciation right vests and becomes exercisable, a change in the ownership of the corporation occurs, and the individual exercises the right. Neither the granting nor the vesting of the stock appreciation right is treated as a payment in the nature of compensation. Even if the change in ownership accelerates the time at which the right is exercised, no portion of the payment received upon the exercise of the right is treated as contingent on the change because the amount of the accelerated payment does not exceed the present value of the payment absent the acceleration. [Treas Reg § 1.280G-1, Q&A 24(e)]

In the case of a payment that is accelerated by a change in ownership or control and that was substantially certain to have been made whether or not the change occurred, if the disqualified individual had continued to perform services, the portion of the payment that is treated as contingent on the change in ownership or control is the lesser of:

1. The amount of the accelerated payment; or
2. The amount by which the total accelerated payment exceeds the present value of the payment that was expected to be made absent the acceleration, plus an amount to reflect the lapse of the obligation to continue to perform services.

The amount that reflects the lapse of the obligation to continue to perform services generally will depend on all of the facts and circumstances. However, in no event is it to be less than 1 percent of the amount of the accelerated payment multiplied by the number of full months between two defining dates. The first date is when the individual's right to receive the payment is not subject to any requirement or condition that would be treated as resulting in a substantial risk of forfeiture (within the meaning of Regulations Section 1.83-3(c)). The second date is when, absent the acceleration, the individual's right to receive the payment would not have been subject to any requirement or condition that would be treated as resulting in a substantial risk of forfeiture. [Treas Reg § 1.280G-1, Q&A 24(c)]

> **Example.** On January 15, 1986, Y corporation gives to a highly compensated individual a bonus of 1,000 shares of the corporation's stock in connection with the individual's performance of services to the corporation. Under the terms of the bonus arrangement, the individual is obligated to return the stock to the corporation if the individual terminates employment for any reason prior to January 15, 1991. However, if there is a change in the ownership or effective control of the corporation prior to January 15, 1991, the individual ceases to be obligated to return the stock. The individual's rights in the stock are treated as substantially non-vested during that period. On January 15, 1989, a change in the ownership of the corporation occurs. On that day, the fair market value of the stock is $500,000.
>
> Because the stock would have become substantially vested in the individual in the absence of the change if the individual had continued to perform services for the corporation through January 15, 1991, it is substantially certain that the payment would have been made in the absence of the change if the individual had continued to work for the corporation. Thus, only a portion of the payment is treated as contingent on the change in ownership or control. The portion of the payment that is treated as contingent on the change is the amount by which the accelerated payment on January 15, 1989 ($500,000), exceeds the present value of the payment that was expected to have been made on January 15, 1991, plus an amount reflecting the lapse of the obligation to continue to perform services. Assuming that, at the time of the change, it cannot be ascertained reasonably what the value of the stock would have been on January 15, 1991, the future value of the stock on January 15, 1991 is deemed to be $500,000, the amount of the accelerated payment. The present value on January

15, 1989 of a $500,000 payment to be made on January 15, 1991 is $406,838. Thus, the portion of the payment treated as contingent on the change is $93,162 ($500,000-$406,838), plus an amount which reflects the lapse of the obligation to continue to perform services. The amount will depend on the facts and circumstances, but in no event will the amount be less than $115,000 (One percent × 23 months × $500,000). [Treas Reg § 1.280G-1, Q&A 24(e), Ex 6]

Q 9:16   When does a change in ownership or control occur?

A change in the ownership or control of a corporation occurs on the date that any one person, or group of persons acting as a group, acquires ownership of stock of the corporation that, together with stock already held by the person or group, possesses more than 50 percent of the total fair market value or total voting power of the stock of the corporation. However, if any one person, or group of persons acting as a group, is considered to own more than 50 percent of the total fair market value or total voting power of the stock of a corporation, the acquisition of additional stock by the same person or persons is not considered to cause a change in the ownership of the corporation (or to cause a change in the effective control of the corporation).

> **Example.** Assume corporation *M* has owned stock having a fair market value equal to 19 percent of the value of the stock of corporation *N* for many years prior to 1986. *M* acquires additional stock having a fair market value equal to 15 percent of the value of the stock of *N* on January 1, 1986, and an additional 18 percent on February 21, 1987. As of February 21, 1987, *M* has acquired stock having a fair market value greater than 50 percent of the value of the stock of *N*. Thus, a change in the ownership of *N* is considered to occur on February 21, 1987 (assuming that *M* did not have effective control of *N* immediately prior to the acquisition on that date). [Treas Reg § 1.280G-1, Q&A 27]

In one ruling, the IRS examined a transaction in which *X*, *Z*, and *Z-1* (a wholly owned subsidiary of *Z*) executed an agreement on *date* d which provided that *Z-1* would acquire the stock of *X* from its shareholders, after which *Z-1* would merge into *X*. Under the agreement, *X* would become a wholly owned subsidiary of *Z*, subject to the approval of appropriate governmental agencies. The agreement also authorized X to enter into employment agreements with employees of X and to cash out all outstanding stock options. On *date e*, *Z-1* acquired approximately 9.9 percent of X's stock from Y, and on *date f*, *Z-1* commenced a tender offer for all the remaining shares of X. Because federal law prohibited Z and its affiliates from acquiring beneficial ownership of as much as 10 percent of the voting securities of X without government approval, *Z-1* established a voting trust to acquire an additional 41.1 percent of X's shares (for a total of 51 percent) pending government approval. *Z-1* subsequently acquired beneficial ownership of and legal title to the additional 41.1 percent of X's shares on *date h*. Z-1 transferred the shares to the voting trust on *date i*. The government subsequently approved the application to permit Z to acquire control of X on *date k* and the voting trust was dissolved on *date l*. The IRS ruled that the change in the ownership or effective control of X occurred on *date h*. [Ltr Rul 9104040, Oct 31, 1990]

A change in the effective control of a corporation is presumed to occur on the date that either (1) any one person, or group of persons acting as a group, acquires (or has acquired during the 12-month period ending on the date of the most recent acquisition by such person or group of persons) 20 percent or more of the total voting power of the stock of the corporation; or (2) a majority of the members of the corporation's board of directors is replaced during any 12-month period by directors whose appointment or election is not endorsed by a majority of the members of the corporation's board of directors prior to the date of the appointment or election. This presumption may be rebutted by establishing that the acquisition or acquisitions of the corporation's stock, or the replacement of the majority of the members of the corporation's board of directors, does not transfer the power to control the management and policies of the corporation from any one person or persons acting as a group to another person or group.

Example. Assume shareholder A acquired percentages of the voting stock of corporation M as follows: 16 percent on January 1, 1985; 10 percent on January 10, 1986; 8 percent on February 10, 1986; 11 percent on March 1, 1987; and 8 percent on March 10, 1987. Thus, on March 10, 1987, shareholder A owns 53 percent of M's voting stock. Because A did not acquire 20 percent or more of the voting stock during a 12-month period, there is no presumption of a change in effective control. Also, under these facts, there is a presumption that no change in the effective control of *M* occurred. If this presumption is not rebutted, a change in the ownership of *M* will be treated as having occurred on March 10, 1987, because *A* had acquired more than 50 percent of *M*'s voting stock as of that date. [Treas Reg § 1.280G-1, Q&A 28]

Another IRS ruling concerned an employer that had filed for reorganization under chapter 11 of the United States Bankruptcy Code. The IRS determined that the organization's creditors would not be considered to be acting as a group for purposes of determining whether a change in ownership or control (within the meaning of Treasury Regulations Section 1.280G-1, Q&As 27, 28, and 29) had occurred. In other words, a change in ownership or control was not ruled to have occurred merely because of the effectiveness of a plan of reorganization or by virtue of service or representation on one of the official or unofficial committees of the employer's creditors, or of participation in the formulation of, and voting upon, the plan of reorganization of the employer or any of its affiliated debtors. [Ltr Rul 9212025, Dec 23, 1991; see Q 9:14]

Also, see *Sutton Holding Corporation v. DeSoto, Inc.* [Del Ct of Chancery Civil Action No 12051, May 14, § 1991] where the court discussed the concept of change in control in the context of a voting contest.

Q 9:17   When does a change in the ownership of a substantial portion of a corporation's assets occur?

A change in the ownership of a substantial portion of a corporation's assets occurs on the date that any one person, or group of persons acting as a group, acquires (or has acquired during the 12-month period ending on the date of the most recent acquisition by such person or persons) assets from the corporation that have a total fair market value equal to or more than one third of the total fair market value of all of the assets of the corporation immediately prior to the acquisition or acquisitions. [Treas Reg § 1.280G-1, Q&A 29(a)]

The IRS has ruled that a severance agreement entered into by an individual and corporation X, which had been acquired by corporation Y and was in the process of being acquired by corporation Z, was not a parachute payment because the sale of corporation X to corporation Z did not represent a change in ownership of a substantial portion of corporation Y's assets. The fair market value of the assets of corporation X immediately prior to the sale of corporation X to corporation Z represented less than one third of the total fair market value of the assets of the affiliated group comprised of corporation Y and its subsidiaries, including corporation X. Therefore, the IRS ruled that, when corporation Y sold corporation X to corporation Z, there was not a change in the ownership of a substantial portion of the assets of corporation Y and, as a result, the payments the individual received or will receive under the severance agreement were not considered parachute payments as described in Code Section 280G [Ltr Rul 9043036, July 30, 1990]

Q 9:18 Are there some types of payments that are not considered parachute payments even though they meet the general rule of Code Section 280G?

Yes. The following types of payments are not considered parachute payments even though they meet the general rule of Code Section 280G:

1. Any payment with respect to a small business corporation (as defined in Code Section 1361(b) but without regard to paragraph (1)(C) thereof) [IRC § 280G(b)(5)(A)(i)];

2. Any payment with respect to a corporation if, immediately before the change in ownership or control, no stock of the corporation is readily tradeable on an established securities market or otherwise (stock is treated as readily tradeable if it is regularly quoted by brokers or dealers making a market in such stock) and the payment was approved by a vote of persons who owned, immediately before the change in ownership or control, more than 75 percent of the voting power of the outstanding stock of the corporation [IRC § 280G(b)(5)];

3. Any payment to or from a tax-qualified retirement plan under Code Section 401(a), an annuity plan described in Code Section

403(a), or a simplified employee pension described in Code Section 408(k) [IRC § 280G(b)(6)]; and

4. Any payment, or portion thereof, which the taxpayer establishes by clear and convincing evidence is reasonable compensation for personal services to be rendered by the disqualified individual on or after the date of the change in ownership or control [IRC § 280G(b)(4)].

[Treas Reg § 1.280G-1, Q&A 5–Q&A 9]

Q 9:19 How does the decision in *Balch v. Commissioner* impact on the characterization of parachute payments?

In the recent Tax Court case of *Balch v. Commissioner* [100 TC 331 (1993), *aff'd* 34 F 3d 480 (7th Cir 1994)], the court considered the taxpayer's claim that certain payments constituted reasonable compensation for services to be performed after the change in control and, therefore, were not parachute payments.

In that case, the corporation amended, prior to the change in control, existing parachute agreements to ensure that the three times limit would not be exceeded. However, after the change of control, the acquiring corporation, pursuant to a prior oral agreement, provided the same executives with cash payments designed to compensate them for their reduced parachute payments.

The IRS argued, and the court agreed, that the cash payments should be added to the amounts paid under the parachute agreements because the cash payments, in fact, were contingent on the change in control and did not constitute reasonable compensation for actual post–change-in-control services provided by the executives.

The *Balch* decision illustrates that taxpayers cannot avoid the effect of the parachute payment rules by arbitrarily characterizing change-in-control amounts as post–change-in-control reasonable compensation.

Q 9:20 When are parachute payments taxable to the recipient?

Generally, parachute payments are includible in the taxable income of the recipient when received.

Q 9:21 Are parachute payments deductible by the employer?

Generally, parachute payments are deductible as reasonable compensation for personal services actually rendered under Code Section 162. However, as previously stated, if a payment in the nature of compensation made to a disqualified individual which is contingent on a change in control or ownership equals or exceeds three times the individual's base amount, then Code Section 280G disallows a deduction for any "excess parachute payment" paid or accrued.

Note that an "excess parachute payment" means an amount equal to the excess of any parachute payment over *one* times the individual's base amount—rather than three times the base amount. Subject to certain exceptions and limitations, an excess parachute payment is reduced by any portion of the payment that the individual establishes by clear and convincing evidence is reasonable compensation for personal services actually rendered by the individual before the date of the change in ownership or control. However, that reasonable compensation first must be applied against the base amount allocated to that payment pursuant to Regulations Section 1.280G-1, Q&A 39(c), Ex. 1. [Treas Reg § 1.280G-1, Q&A 1–Q&A 3]

Q 9:22 What is "reasonable compensation"?

Whether payments are reasonable compensation generally is determined on the basis of all the facts and circumstances of the particular case. Factors relevant to this determination include:

1. The nature of the services rendered;
2. The individual's historic compensation for performing the services; and
3. The compensation of individuals performing comparable services in situations where the compensation is not contingent on a change in ownership or control.

A showing that payments are made under a nondiscriminatory employee plan or program generally is considered to be clear and convincing evidence that the payments are reasonable compensation.

Also, payments of compensation earned before the date of a change in ownership or control generally are considered reasonable compensation for personal services rendered before the date of a change in ownership or control if they qualify as reasonable compensation under Code Section 162. However, severance payments are not treated as reasonable compensation for services rendered before, or to be rendered on or after, the date of a change in ownership or control. Further, any damages paid for a failure to make severance payments are not treated as reasonable compensation for personal services rendered before, or to be rendered on or after, the date of the change. [Treas Reg § 1.280G-1, Q&A 40–Q&A 44; Ltr Rul 9104040, Oct 31, 1990]

Q 9:23 Does an excise tax apply to any "excess parachute payment"?

Yes. Code Section 4999 imposes, in addition to ordinary income taxes, a 20 percent excise tax on the recipient of any excess parachute payment. Note that an "excess parachute payment" means an amount equal to the excess of any parachute payment over *one* times the individual's base amount—rather than three times the base amount. Note also that Code Section 275(a)(6) denies any deduction for the amount of excise tax paid. [Treas Reg § 1.280G-1, Q&A 1]

ERISA Considerations

Q 9:24 Is an agreement to provide parachute payments to employees or former employees of an employer a plan covered by ERISA?

Possibly. If the arrangement otherwise meets the definition of an ERISA pension plan or of an ERISA welfare benefit plan (for example, a severance plan), the arrangement could be covered by ERISA. For example, in *Purser v. Enron Corp.* the court determined that a contract providing for a payment to an employee terminated after a corporate change of control provides severance benefits covered by ERISA.

Similarly, if an arrangement provides for parachute payments to employees and those payments extend for a period beyond two years, it could be argued that the arrangement was an ERISA pension plan.

Q 9:25   What recent cases have discussed the golden parachute rules?

Three recent cases have addressed these rules. In *Cline v. Commissioner* [34 F 3d 480 (CA-7, 1994)], the Seventh Circuit Court of Appeals held that a single golden parachute agreement that was restructured into two separate agreements—one limited to the safe-harbor amounts under Section 280G and the second an oral employment agreement—and that exceeded the limits of Code Section 280G continued to be treated as a single golden parachute agreement exceeding the limitations of Section 280G and subjecting the executive to excise taxes. The court examined the facts surrounding the revision of the single agreement into two related agreements and determined that the payments under each were payable because of the same change of control of the employer.

In *Kulinski v. Medtronic Bio-Medicus, Inc.* [CA-8, No. 93-1186 (Apr 8, 1994)], the Eighth Circuit Court of Appeals held that a golden parachute agreement was not an ERISA-governed top-hat plan and therefore, the court did not have federal jurisdiction under ERISA to hear the executive's claim. According to the court, the golden parachute agreement did not constitute a "plan" that could be an ERISA-governed severance plan, because it did not require the establishment of a separate, ongoing administrative scheme to administer the plan's benefits. Instead, the court concluded that, after a hostile takeover occurred and the executive's employment terminated, "there was nothing for the company to decide, no discretion for it to exercise, and nothing for it to do but write a check." The court added, "Because such a simple mechanical task does not require the establishment of an administrative scheme . . . the plan to provide golden parachutes . . . was not an ERISA plan."

Finally, in *American Medical International, Inc. v. Valliant,* [US Dt Ct ND Cal N. Cr 94-2107-5C (Nov 11, 1994)] a California federal district court held that severance payments made to an executive were golden parachute payments subject to Code Section 280G because they were contingent on a change in control. The executive argued that the payments were not paid on account of a change in control and therefore were not subject to the terms of the agreement, which automatically reduced payments to an amount less than the Code Section 280G limits in those cases. The court held that the amounts paid to the executive after his termination were, in fact, "contingent on a change in control" because they were owed to the employee on an event closely associated with a change in control. Therefore, the court concluded, the payments were subject to the agreement's automatic limiting provisions.

Q 9:26   Are severance pay plans and pension plans subject to the reporting requirements under ERISA?

Generally, yes. ERISA severance pay plans and pension plans are subject to the reporting and disclosure provisions under Title I of ERISA. However, top-hat pension and welfare plans (that is, pension and welfare plans maintained by an employer for the purpose of providing benefits for a select group of management or highly compensated employees) are exempt from all of the reporting and disclosure provisions of Part 1 of Title I of ERISA, except for a one-time filing requirement applicable to top-hat pension plans and a requirement applicable to both types of top-hat plans that they provide plan documents to the Secretary of Labor upon request. [DOL Reg § 2520.104-24] (See chapter 2.)

Other Considerations

Q 9:27   Are there other rules that affect parachute payments?

Yes. The Federal Deposit Insurance Corporation (FDIC) issued proposed rules on October 7, 1991 [56 Fed. Reg. 50529] limiting parachute and indemnification payments to institution-affiliated parties by insured depository institutions, depository institution holding companies, and their subsidiaries and affiliates. The purpose of these proposed rules is to prevent the improper disposition of institution assets and to protect the financial soundness of insured depository institutions, depository institution holding companies, their subsidiaries and affiliates, and the federal deposit insurance funds. Corporations subject to these rules should review them prior to entering into parachute payment arrangements. (See Appendix C for the proposed rules regarding parachute payments.)

Case Study 9-1

Note: See Case Studies at the end of chapters 1 through 8.

At this meeting, *A* asks the advisor to provide the group with a very general overview of the concept of "golden parachutes." The group is particularly interested because they are currently negotiating with a business that is contemplating purchasing the corporation but that is not interested in retaining *A, B, C,* and *D* after the purchase.

The advisor begins by noting that golden parachutes are severance agreements between corporations and selected executives that ease the "termination fall" of the executives, usually by providing substantial severance payments. Payments made under parachute arrangements are triggered by a change in ownership or control of the corporation.

The advisor adds that, generally, if the payments are contingent on a change in ownership or control and they exceed three times the executive's base pay amount (as defined), the amount of the payment exceeding one times the base pay amount is not deductible by the corporation and is subject to income tax plus a 20 percent excise tax. The advisor notes that severance agreements entered into within one year before a change in ownership or control are presumed to be contingent on such a change.

A, B, C, and *D* direct the advisor to prepare drafts of golden parachute agreements for each of them. In order to prevent the cost of acquisition from becoming unattractively high, they decide to limit payments under the agreements to the maximum amount which may be paid without making any portion of the payments nondeductible and subject to the excise tax.

See Case Study at the end of chapter 10 for a discussion of the special rules applicable to the nonqualified plans of tax-exempt and governmental employers.

Chapter 10

Plans of Governmental and Tax-Exempt Entities Under Code Section 457

Code Section 457 provides the rules concerning the taxation of nonqualified deferred compensation arrangements between a state or local government or a nongovernmental, non-church, tax-exempt organization and an individual who performs services for such an entity. This chapter examines both types of Code Section 457 plans (so-called "eligible" and "ineligible" plans). This chapter also examines which deferred compensation plans of governmental and tax-exempt entities are covered by Code Section 457 and the requirements that must be met by eligible plans under Code Section 457. The tax consequences to participants in eligible and ineligible plans under Code Section 457 are discussed, as well as the applicability of ERISA to Code Section 457 plans.

Overview

Q 10:1   To which deferred compensation plans does Code Section 457 apply?

Generally, Code Section 457 applies to any compensation that is deferred (plus income attributable to that deferred compensation) under an arrangement between a state or local government or a non-church, nongovernmental tax-exempt organization and an individual who performs services for such an entity. [IRS Notice 87-13, 1987-1 CB 432, 444]

Q 10:2   Are there exceptions to the general rule of applicability of Code Section 457?

Yes. Code Section 457 does not apply to deferrals under:

1. A plan described in Code Section 401(a) that includes a trust exempt from tax under Code Section 501(a) (that is, a tax-qualified retirement plan such as a defined benefit pension plan, a money purchase pension plan or a profit sharing plan);

2. Any annuity plan or contract described in Code Section 403 (that is, a tax-sheltered annuity plan);

3. That portion of any plan that consists of a property transfer described in Code Section 83 (for example, many life insurance arrangements between employers and employees); and

4. That part of a plan that consists of a trust to which Code Section 402(b) applies (that is, a nonqualified trust).

(See Q 10:17, however, for the effect that contributions to some of these plans may have on contributions to an eligible Section 457 plan.)

Q 10:3   What are the two types of Code Section 457 plans?

The first type of Code Section 457 plan is called an "eligible" deferred compensation plan. Eligible plans must meet specific requirements contained in Code Section 457. If these requirements are met, participants may defer taxes on their elective deferrals and any employer contributions under the plan (and earnings on those deferrals and contributions) until amounts are paid or made available to them. Although technically a nonqualified plan, an eligible plan resembles a tax-qualified plan in that, as long as the plan meets the requirements of Code Section 457, plan participants are not taxed on their plan interests until they actually receive plan distributions.

The second type of Code Section 457 plan is called an "ineligible" deferred compensation plan. Ineligible plans are deferred compensation plans of government and non-church tax-exempt employers that do not meet the Code Section 457 requirements for eligible plans and resemble, in some ways, the nonqualified plans of for-profit employers. Unlike participants in eligible plans, participants in ineligible plans are taxed on their elective deferrals and any employer contributions under the plan when those amounts cease to be subject to a substantial risk of forfeiture. As with eligible plans, earnings on ineligible plan contributions are taxed when amounts are paid or made available under the plan.

Eligible plans typically are used to provide deferred compensation to employees only by government entities that may not sponsor tax-sheltered annuity programs under Code Section 403(b) (that is, government entities other than certain educational organizations) and tax-exempt entities that may not sponsor those programs (that is, tax-exempt entities other than Code Section 501(c)(3) entities). This is because the dollar limit on annual deferrals under an eligible plan is less than the dollar limit on annual deferrals for more attractive 403(b) programs and is offset, dollar for dollar, by deferrals under 403(b) programs. Also, because of the relatively low dollar limit that applies to eligible plans, even those entities that utilize them as part of an executive's deferred compensation package typically supplement them with ineligible plans.

Although ineligible plans have a much broader application for executive deferred compensation planning than eligible plans, eligible plans do have some limited uses and will be discussed below to provide a complete overview of the potentially available nonqualified plan options.

Q 10:4   Is there any exception to the rule that amounts that are deferred under an ineligible Section 457 plan are included in the participant's income when they cease to be subject to a substantial risk of forfeiture?

Yes. TRA '86 provided a special rule for participants in ineligible plans of nongovernmental tax-exempt organizations. Under this special rule, amounts that

1. Were deferred from taxable years beginning before January 1, 1987, or

2. Are deferred from taxable years beginning after December 31, 1986

were grandfathered and not subject to the income inclusion rules applicable to ineligible plans *if* deferrals after December 31, 1986, are made pursuant to an agreement that was in writing on August 16, 1986, that provided for a deferral of either a fixed amount or an amount determined pursuant to a fixed formula for each taxable year covered by the agreement. This exception does not apply with respect to amounts deferred for any taxable year ending after the date on which the amount or formula is modified after August 16, 1986. A technical correction enacted under TAMRA clarified that the relief afforded to amounts deferred after December 31, 1986 is limited to individuals covered under the plan or agreement on August 16, 1986. [§ 1107 of the Tax Reform Act of 1986, Pub L No 99-514, 1986 US Code Cong & Ad News (100 Stat) 2426-2431; TAMRA § 1011(e)(6)(B); see IRS Notice 87-13, 1987-1 CB 432; Ltr Rul 9018052, Feb 6, 1990]

A deferral with respect to an individual is treated as fixed on August 16, 1986, to the extent that a written plan on that date provided for the deferral for each taxable year of the plan and the deferral was determinable on that date under the written terms of the plan as a fixed dollar amount, a fixed percentage of a fixed base amount, an amount to be determined under a fixed formula, or the deferral is the same as the deferral in effect with respect to the individual under the plan on August 16, 1986, even if on that date the written plan did not fix the amount of deferral. [IRS Notice 87-13, 1987-1 CB 432, 445; Ltr Rul 8813026, Dec 30, 1987]

A deferral will not fail to be treated as fixed on August 16, 1986, merely because the written plan also provides for a deferral that is not fixed on that date. Also, a deferral will not fail to be treated as fixed on August 16, 1986, merely because the tax-exempt organization and the individual have the right, under the plan on that date, to renegotiate the plan and thus to alter the deferral (whether or not the plan is part of an employment contract between the organization and the individual) or merely because the individual has the right, under the plan, to vary the amount of the deferral in the future. However, if, at any time after August 16, 1986, these rights actually are exercised to modify the amount, percentage or specified formula, whichever is applicable, deferrals after the effective date of that modification will fail to be treated as fixed on August 16, 1986, and thus will be subject to the income inclusion rules applicable to ineligible plans (assuming that the plan does not meet the requirements imposed on eligible plans). [IRS Notice 87-13, 1987-1 CB 432, 445; Ltr Ruls 8813026, Dec 30, 1987; 9105011, Oct 31, 1987]

Q 10:5   What types of amendments has the IRS permitted to be made to "grandfathered" Code Section 457 plans without causing a loss of grandfathered treatments?

Although the statute is clear that any modification of a grandfathered plan's deferral percentage or dollar amount will cause the plan to lose its grandfathered status, the IRS has been relatively liberal in permitting changes to grandfathered plans without claiming that those changes affect the plans' enjoyment of grandfathered treatment.

For instance, at least informally, the IRS has approved of changes to the distribution options under these plans, the investment indices used to credit earnings under these plans, and so forth. In addition, the IRS has stated informally that a reduction to zero of a deferral percentage or dollar amount does not endanger grandfather treatment.

However, notwithstanding the seemingly generous regulatory posture on the issue, an employer should not make any changes to a grandfathered plan without first consulting its tax advisor.

Q 10:6   Are church plans subject to the provisions of Code Section 457?

No. Plans of churches, as defined under Code Section 3121(w)(3)(A), and qualified church-controlled organizations, as defined in Code Section 3121(w)(3)(B), are not subject to Code Section 457. [IRC § 457(e)(13)]

Q 10:7   Are vacation, sick leave, compensatory time, severance pay, disability pay, or death benefit plans subject to the provisions of Code Section 457?

No. Bona fide vacation leave, sick leave, compensatory time, severance pay, disability pay, and death benefit plans, whether elective or nonelective, are not deferred compensation plans subject to Code Section 457, and benefits thereunder are tax-deferred until actual or constructive receipt.

Q 10:8   May a rabbi trust be used in connection with a Code Section 457 plan?

Yes. A rabbi trust may be used in connection with a plan created under Code Section 457 (see Q 10:36). [Ltr Ruls 9212011, Dec 19, 1991; 9211037, Dec 17, 1991]

Q 10:9   May employers obtain an IRS ruling on their Section 457 plans?

Yes. The procedure for obtaining a ruling on the status of an eligible or ineligible Section 457 plan and the tax consequences to the plan's participants is similar to the procedure described in Q 5:22 for secular trusts. However, the IRS has indicated that no rulings will be issued with respect to the tax consequences to unidentified independent contractors in nonqualified unfunded deferred compensation plans of employers in the private sector under Code Section 451 and of eligible state plans under Section 457. However, a ruling with respect to a specific independent contractor's participation in such a plan may be issued.

Q 10:10   Does Code Section 457 apply to elective and nonelective deferrals?

Yes, for taxable years beginning after 1987, Code Section 457 generally applies to nonelective deferrals as well as to elective deferrals. [IRS Notice 87-13, 1987-1 CB 432, 444; IRS Notice 88-8, 1988-1 CB 477]

Q 10:11   Are nonelective deferred compensation plans covering individuals who are not employees subject to Section 457?

Sometimes not. Section 457 does not apply to nonelective deferred compensation provided to individuals who are not employees if all individuals (who meet applicable initial service requirements) with the same relationship to the plan sponsor are covered under the same plan with no individual variations or options. The following example of the application of this rule is contained in the legislative history of TAMRA: If a doctor who is not an employee receives deferred compensation from a hospital, the deferred compensation is to be considered nonelective only if all doctors who are not employees (who have satisfied any applicable initial service requirements) are covered under the same plan with no individual variations or options. [IRC § 457(e)(12); HR Conf Rep No 1104, 100th Cong, 2d Sess 155 (1988), reprinted in 1988; 1988 US Code Cong & Ad News 5048, 5215]

Q 10:12   Are there transition rules under which the general application of Code Section 457 to nonelective deferrals may be avoided?

Yes. Code Section 457 does not apply to compensation deferred under a written, nonelective deferred compensation plan that was in existence on December 31, 1987, and that was maintained pursuant to a collective bargaining agreement, until the effective date of any material modification to the plan after December 31, 1987. A modification is not treated as material unless it modifies the plan's benefit formula or expands the class of participants beyond those individuals who were participants under the plan on or before December 31, 1987, or beyond those individuals who would have become participants under the terms of the plan as it existed on that date. For purposes of this transition rule, a nonelective plan is defined as a plan that covers a broad group of employees who earn nonelective deferred compensation under a definite, fixed and uniform benefit formula.

This transition rule applies not only to union employees participating in nonelective plans maintained pursuant to collective bargaining agreements, but also to nonunion employee participants under a plan if, on December 31, 1987, participation under the nonelective plan extended to a broad group of nonunion employees on the same terms as the participation provided to union employees, and provided that the union employees constituted at least 25 percent of the total participants in the plan.

Also, Code Section 457 does not apply to amounts deferred under a nonelective deferred compensation plan maintained by a government entity if:

1. The amounts were deferred from periods before July 14, 1988; or

2. The amounts were deferred from periods on or after July 14, 1988, pursuant to an agreement that was in writing on that date that provided for a deferral for each taxable year covered by the agreement of a fixed amount or of an amount determined pursuant to a fixed formula, and the individual with respect to whom the deferral is made was covered under the agreement on that date. This rule does not apply to any taxable year ending after the date on which any modification of the amount or formula is effective. However, this rule does not cease to apply merely because of a modification to the agreement prior to January 1, 1989, that does not increase benefits for participants in the plan. [TAMRA; Pub L No 100-647, § 6064; 1988 US Code Cong & Ad News (102 Stat) 3700-3702; HR Conf Rep at 153-155, reprinted in 1988 US Code Cong & Ad News 5213-5215; see TAM 9121004, Jan 30, 1991; Ltr Rul 9149032, Sept 10, 1991]

Q 10:13 How must nonqualified plans be reported by tax-exempt entities on their annual federal information returns?

Recently, the IRS amended the annual Form 990 informational report used by tax-exempt entities to require reporting on that form of information concerning the nonqualified plans maintained by the tax-exempt entities.

In light of this new disclosure requirement, many tax-exempt entities review the current Form 990 and its instructions prior to finalizing the design of any proposed nonqualified plan in order to determine what disclosures will need to be made concerning the plan and what legal and political issues might be raised by those disclosures.

Eligible Plans

Q 10:14 Does Code Section 457 impose special requirements on eligible plans?

Yes. An eligible plan must satisfy the following requirements:

1. The plan must be established and maintained by an eligible employer (see Q 10:15).
2. Only individuals who perform services for the plan sponsor may be participants (see Q 10:16).
3. The maximum amount that may be deferred by a participant for any taxable year may not exceed the lesser of $7,500 or one third of the participant's "includible compensation," except as permitted under a limited "catch-up" provision (see Qs 10:17–10:19).
4. Compensation may be deferred for any calendar month only if a deferral agreement has been entered into before the beginning of that month (see Q 10:20).
5. Distributions may not be made to a participant or beneficiary earlier than (a) the calendar year in which the participant reaches age $70\frac{1}{2}$; (b) the date the participant separates from service with the employer; or (c) the date the participant incurs an "unforeseeable emergency" (see Qs 10:21–10:24).
6. The plan must meet certain minimum distribution requirements (see Qs 10:25–10:26).
7. The plan must not be funded (see Q 10:36).

[IRC §§ 457(b), 457(d)]

Q 10:15   Who is an eligible employer?

An eligible employer under Code Section 457 is a state, a political subdivision of a state, an agency or instrumentality of a state or political subdivision, and any other organization that is exempt from tax under Subtitle A of the Code. (Note that Subtitle A includes all organizations exempt from tax under Code Section 501, i.e., many more tax-exempt organizations than the religious, educational, and charitable organizations which are tax exempt under Code Section 501(c)(3).)

Q 10:16   Who may participate in an eligible plan?

Only individuals who perform services for the sponsor (including independent contractors) may participate in an eligible plan. Furthermore, although any or all of the employees of a government entity may be permitted to participate in an eligible plan, only a select group of management or highly compensated employees of a non-church tax-exempt organization may participate in an eligible plan (see Q 10:44). [IRC §§ 457(b)(1), 457(e)(2), 457(e)(3)]

Q 10:17   Is there a maximum amount that may be deferred by or on behalf of a participant under an eligible plan?

Yes. The maximum amount that may be deferred by or on behalf of a participant under an eligible plan for a taxable year is the lesser of (a) $7,500, or (b) one third of the participant's includible compensation, subject to rules under Code Section 457(b)(3) which provide for increased limits in certain limited circumstances (see Q 10:18). Furthermore, the maximum amount of compensation that any individual participating in more than one eligible plan may defer under all of those plans during any taxable year may not exceed that limit (see Q 10:35). [IRC §§ 457(b)(2), 457(c)(1)]

The maximum amount that any one individual may defer under an eligible plan or plans also must be reduced by the following:

1. Amounts contributed by or on behalf of the individual under any tax-deferred annuity program for the taxable year (i.e., under a Code Section 403(b) program);

2. Elective deferrals by the participant under any 401(k) plan for the taxable year (except a rural cooperative plan as defined in Code Section 401(k)(7));

3. Elective deferrals by the participant under any simplified employee pension or SEP for the taxable year (except a rural cooperative plan); or

4. Deductible contributions by the participant to a plan described in Code Section 501(c)(18), which involves certain trusts created before June 25, 1959, for the taxable year (except a rural cooperative plan).

[IRC § 457(c)(2)]

If amounts are deferred by or on behalf of a participant in excess of the eligible plan limit, most commentators believe that the amounts deferred in excess of the limit will be considered to have been deferred under an ineligible plan. However, some commentators believe that Code Section 457 may be interpreted to mean that an eligible plan which permits excess deferrals will lose its eligible plan status for all purposes and all deferral amounts. (See Q 10:34.)

If a participant has amounts contributed under a Code Section 403(b) plan, a 401(k) plan, a SEP and/or a Code Section 501(c)(18) trust for a year and has amounts deferred under an eligible plan in the same year, and the total amounts deferred exceed the eligible plan limits, the excess deferrals will be considered made available to the participant in the year of the deferral and subject to taxation. (Note that if an individual participates in both a Section 457 plan and a Section 403(b) or 401(k) plan, the maximum aggregate deferral is $7,500 increased, if applicable, by the catch-up provision (see Q 10:18), but in no event in excess of the Section 403(b) limit or the Section 401(k) limit, as applicable.) [Treas Reg § 1.457-1(b)(2), Exs 5, 6; Ltr Rul 9152026, Sept 27, 1991]

Q 10:18   Are the maximum deferral amounts for eligible plans ever increased for a participant?

Yes. During each of the three taxable years ending before the participant reaches normal retirement age, the participant may defer up to the lesser of $15,000 or the sum of (1) the regular eligible plan limitation for the year (determined without regard to this special limit), and (2) so much of the maximum deferrals for prior years as have not been used previously (the "catch-up" provision). For purposes of the catch-up provision computation, unused deferrals for previous years may be included only for years after 1978 during which the individual was eligible to participate in the plan during all or any portion of the year and which were subject to a limit of $7,500 or one third of the individual's compensation for the year.

A participant may elect the catch-up provision only once to apply to all or any portion of the three-year period. For example, if a participant elects to use the catch-up only for the one taxable year ending before normal retirement age, and, after retirement, the participant renders services for an eligible employer as an independent contractor, the eligible plan may not provide that the participant may use the catch-up for any of the taxable years subsequent to retirement. [IRC §§ 457(b)(2), 457(b)(3); Treas Reg §§ 1.457-1(a)(2), 1.457-2(e), 1.457-2(f)]

For purposes of the catch-up provision, normal retirement age is the age specified in the plan. If no age is specified in the plan, normal retirement age is the later of the latest normal retirement age specified in the basic pension plan of the eligible employer or age 65. A plan may define normal retirement age as any range of ages ending no later than age 70½ and beginning no earlier than the earliest age at which the participant has the right to retire under the eligible employer's basic pension plan without the consent of the eligible employer and to receive immediate retirement benefits without an actuarial or similar reduction because of retirement before some later specified age in the eligible employer's basic pension plan. The plan also may provide that, in the case of a participant who continues to work beyond the ages specified above, the normal retirement age will be the date or age designated by the participant, but that date or age may not be later than the mandatory retirement age provided by the eligible employer, or the date or age at which the participant separates from the service of the eligible employer. [Treas Reg § 1.457-2(f)(4)]

Q 10:19   What constitutes "includible compensation" eligible for deferral under an eligible plan?

Compensation eligible for deferral includes all compensation received by a participant for services performed for the eligible employer that currently is includible in the individual's gross income. Includable compensation does not include amounts excludable under a Code Section 457 plan, and does not include any other amount that is paid by the plan sponsor for services performed for the plan sponsor which is excludable from gross income under the income tax rules of the Code. For example, amounts deferred under a tax-sheltered annuity program under Code Section 403(b) would not be considered includible compensation to the extent those amounts are excludable from gross income. [IRC §§ 457(e)(5), 457(e)(7); Treas Reg § 1.457-2(e)(2)]

Q 10:20   When must an election to defer compensation under an eligible plan be made?

Generally, an agreement providing for deferral under an eligible plan must be entered into before the beginning of any calendar month for which compensation is to be deferred. Nevertheless, an eligible plan may permit a new employee to defer compensation during the first calendar month of his or her employment if the employee enters into an agreement providing for the deferral on or before the first day of employment, even though that date may be after the first day of that month. [IRC § 457(b)(4); Treas Reg § 1.457-2(g)]

Q 10:21   When may benefits under an eligible plan be paid to participants or beneficiaries?

Amounts deferred under an eligible plan cannot be paid or made available to a participant or beneficiary before:

1. The calendar year in which the participant attains age $70\frac{1}{2}$;

2. The date the participant separates from service; or

3. The date the participant is faced with an unforeseeable emergency.

[IRC § 457(d)(1)(A)]

Q 10:22   What does "separated from service" mean for purposes of these rules?

An employee is separated from service if there is a separation from service within the meaning of Code Section 402(e)(4)(A)(iii), relating to lump sum distributions, or because the employee's death or retirement. "Separation from service" is not further defined in the Code or the regulations. The Tax Court, however, has consistently stated that a separation generally will not be found to have occurred "unless there is a change in the employment relationship in more than a formal or technical sense." Therefore, a reduction in work schedule or change in employment status that is anything less than a complete severance from the employer likely will not constitute a "separation from service." Furthermore, a change in the employment relationship such as one caused by a merger, reorganization, liquidation, or other restructuring generally will not constitute a separation from service if the participant continues on the same job for the surviving employer. [Treas Reg § 1.457-2(h)(2); see Rev Rul 81-26, 1981-1 CB 200; Edwards v Comm'r, TC Memo 1989-409, 57 TCM 1217 (1989); Reinhardt v Comm'r, 85 TC 511 (1985)]

Q 10:23   When is an independent contractor considered to have "separated from service" for purposes of these rules?

Generally, an independent contractor is considered to have separated from service upon the expiration of the contract (or all contracts if there is more than one contract) between the independent contractor and the plan sponsor if the contract expiration constitutes a good faith and complete termination of the contractual relationship. If the sponsor anticipates a renewal of the contractual relationship or anticipates the independent contractor becoming an employee, the expiration will not constitute a good faith and complete termination of the contractual relationship. Certain presumptions apply when determining whether a good faith and complete termination of the relationship has occurred. The renewal of a contractual relationship is presumed to have been anticipated by the sponsor if the sponsor intends to contract again for the services provided under the expired contract, and the independent contractor has not been eliminated by either the sponsor or the independent contractor as a possible provider of services under the new contract. The sponsor will be presumed to intend to contract again for services provided under an expired contract if doing so is conditioned only upon the sponsor's incurring a need for the services, the availability of funds, or both.

The separation from service requirement will be satisfied if, with respect to amounts payable to a participant who is an independent contractor, the plan provides that no amount is to be paid to the participant until at least 12 months after the expiration of the contract or, if there is more than one contract, all contracts, under which services are performed for the sponsor, and no amount so payable is paid if the participant performs services for the sponsor as an independent contractor or an employee during that 12-month period. [Treas Reg §§ 1.457-2(h)(2), 1.457-2(h)(3)]

Q 10:24   What is an "unforeseeable emergency" for purposes of these rules?

The regulations define an unforeseeable emergency as:

1. A severe financial hardship to the participant caused by a sudden and unexpected illness or accident of the participant or a dependent of the participant (as defined in Code Section 152(a));

2. A loss of the participant's property due to casualty; or

3. Other similar extraordinary and unforeseeable circumstances caused by events beyond the participant's control.

The circumstances that will constitute an unforeseeable emergency generally depend upon the facts and circumstances of each case. Payment may not be made to the extent the hardship may be relieved by insurance or other similar reimbursement or compensation, liquidation of assets (to the extent the liquidation would not itself cause severe financial hardship), or a cessation of deferrals under the plan. College tuition or the costs of purchasing a home are not considered unforeseeable emergencies. [Treas Reg § 1.457-2(h)(4)]

Finally, withdrawals on account of an unforeseeable emergency must be limited to the amount reasonably needed to satisfy the emergency need. [Treas Reg § 1.457-2(h)(5)]

Q 10:25   When must distributions commence under an eligible plan?

Payment of deferred amounts under an eligible plan must commence not later than the later of:

1. 60 days after the end of the plan year in which the participant or former participant attains, or would have attained, normal retirement age (Q 10:18), or

2. 60 days after the end of the plan year in which the participant separates from service (Q 10:22, Q 10:23).

[Treas Reg § 1.457-2(i)] (See Q 10:26 for the rules after TRA '86.)

Q 10:26   Are there minimum distribution requirements that must be met under an eligible plan?

Yes. An eligible plan must meet the qualified plan distribution requirements of Code Section 401(a)(9) as well as the additional distribution requirements of Code Section 457.

Generally, under Code Section 401(a)(9), distributions must begin no later than April 1 of the calendar year following the calendar year in which the individual attains age $70\frac{1}{2}$. However, in the case of a governmental plan, the required beginning date is the later of the date determined under the prior sentence or April 1 of the calendar year following the calendar year in which the individual retires.

Code Section 401(a)(9) and the regulations thereunder also require certain minimum amounts to be distributed to the participant each year over a certain limited period of time.

In addition, in the case of a distribution beginning before the participant's death, the plan must provide that the amounts payable must be paid at times that are not later than the time determined under Code Section 401(a)(9)(G), relating to incidental death benefits. Amounts that have not been distributed to the participant during his or her life must be distributed after the participant's death at least as rapidly as under the method of distribution being used as of the date of the participant's death and must meet the Code Section 401(a)(9) death distribution rules.

In addition, under Code Section 457, a distribution that does not begin until after the death of the participant must be paid out in its entirety during a period of not more than 15 years, or the life expectancy of the beneficiary if the surviving spouse is the beneficiary.

A distribution payable over a period of more than one year must be made in substantially nonincreasing amounts in payments which are made at least annually. [IRC §§ 457(d)(2), 401(a)(9); Treas Reg §§ 1.401(a)(9)-1, 1.401(a)(9)-2; Ltr Rul 8946019, Aug 17, 1989]

Q 10:27 May an eligible plan permit any elective withdrawals by a participant before the participant otherwise is entitled to a distribution?

Yes, it may, but under very limited circumstances. If the total amount payable to a participant under an eligible plan does not exceed $3,500, and no additional amounts may be deferred by the participant under the plan, the participant may elect to receive the total amount payable after his or her separation from service and within 60 days of the election, even if the otherwise applicable distribution date has not arrived. The Code provides that the mere availability of this election right does not cause the participant's benefits to be treated as "made available" to and taxable to the participant. [IRC § 457(e)(9); IRS Notice 87-13, 1987-1 CB 432]

Q 10:28 Will amounts payable under an eligible plan be considered "made available" to and taxable to a participant or beneficiary if the participant or beneficiary has a right to elect to defer the payment of the amounts beyond the date on which the amounts otherwise will become payable?

No. Amounts deferred under an eligible plan will not be considered made available to and taxable to the participant or beneficiary if under the plan the participant or beneficiary may irrevocably elect, prior to the date on which the amounts become payable, to defer payment of some or all of the amounts to a fixed or determinable future date. [Treas Reg § 1.457-1(b)(1)]

Q 10:29   Can a participant direct the investment of amounts deferred under an eligible plan?

Yes. An eligible plan participant may be permitted to choose among various investment options under the plan. However, any investments must be solely the property of the plan sponsor and must be subject to the claims of its general creditors. [Treas Reg § 1.457-1(b)(1); see Ltr Ruls 9003021, Oct 20, 1989, and 8946019, Aug 17, 1989]

Q 10:30   Will amounts under an eligible plan be considered "made available" to and taxable to a participant if the amounts are used to purchase life insurance contracts as an investment medium?

No. If the plan sponsor (1) retains all of the incidents of ownership of the contracts, (2) is the sole beneficiary under the contracts, and (3) is under no obligation to transfer the contracts or to pass through the proceeds of the contracts to any participant or beneficiary, the purchase of life insurance contracts as an investment medium should not cause the amounts used to purchase the contracts to be considered to be made available to and taxable to the participant. [Treas Reg § 1.457-1(b)(2), Ex 7]

Q 10:31   Can a participant transfer deferred amounts between eligible plans?

Yes. Transfers of amounts from one eligible plan to another eligible plan are permitted, without requiring the participant to include any portion of the amount transferred in the participant's gross income, as long as the transferred amounts are not actually or constructively received by the participant prior to the transfer. A transfer from one eligible plan to another will not be treated as a distribution for any purposes under Code Section 457. [IRC § 457(e)(10); Ltr Rul 8946019, Aug 17, 1989]

Q 10:32   Can amounts deferred under an eligible plan be rolled over to an Individual Retirement Account (IRA)?

No. There is no provision that permits a rollover to an IRA from an eligible plan. Such a transfer would constitute a taxable distribution and an impermissible IRA contribution. [IRC § 457(a); Treas Reg § 1.457-1(a)(1); Rev Rul 86-103, 1986-2 CB 62; TAM 9121004, Jan 30, 1991]

For example, the IRS noted in a 1991 ruling that a Section 457 plan is neither an exempt trust, as described in Section 401(a), nor is it treated as such an exempt trust and that, therefore, the Section 402(a)(6)(F) provision permitting tax-free rollovers of distributions required by a qualified domestic relations order from an exempt trust to an IRA does not apply to any distributions from a Section 457 plan made pursuant to a qualified domestic relations order. (See Q 10:38.) [Ltr Rul 9145010, July 31, 1991]

Q 10:33   Are lump sum distributions from eligible plans eligible for income averaging treatment under Code Section 402?

No. To qualify for the income averaging treatment available under Code Section 402, the lump-sum distributions must be made (1) from a trust which forms a part of a plan described in Code Section 401(a) and which also is exempt from tax under Code Section 501 (i.e., from a tax-qualified retirement plan) or (2) from an annuity plan described in Code Section 403(a). Section 457 plans are not plans under either Section 401(a) or Section 403(a). [Ltr Rul 8119020, Feb 10, 1981; Rheal v Comm'r, TC Memo 1989-525, 58 TCM 229 (1989)]

Q 10:34   What are the consequences if a plan intended to be an eligible plan is administered in a manner inconsistent with the eligible plan requirements?

If a plan maintained by a governmental employer that is intended to be an eligible plan is not administered consistently with the requirements applicable to eligible plans, the plan will be deemed to be an ineligible plan as of the first plan year beginning more than 180 days after notice of the failure is given by the IRS to the sponsor, unless the sponsor corrects the inconsistency before the first day of that plan year. A plan maintained by a tax-exempt organization other than a governmental employer which is intended to be an eligible plan but which does not meet the eligible plan requirements will be treated as an ineligible plan, without notice from the IRS, immediately upon its failure to meet the requirements. [IRC § 457(b)]

Q 10:35   Can an individual participate in more than one eligible plan?

Yes. However, the maximum amount of compensation that an individual may defer for any taxable year under all eligible plans may not exceed $7,500 (except as modified by the catch-up provision). [IRC § 457(c)(1)] (See coordination rules in Q 10:17.)

Q 10:36   Does a participant have any rights in amounts deferred under an eligible plan?

No. All deferrals under the plan, all property and rights purchased with those deferrals, and all income attributable to those deferrals, property, or rights must remain, until made available to participants or their beneficiaries, solely the property and rights of the plan sponsor (without being restricted to the provision of benefits under the plan) subject to the claims of its general creditors. [IRC §§ 457(b)(6), 457(e)(8); Ltr Rul 8946019, Aug 17, 1989] However, a rabbi trust may be used in connection with an eligible plan (see Q 10:8).

Q 10:37   Are amounts deferred under an eligible plan and deposited in depositories insured by the Federal Deposit Insurance Corporation (FDIC) insured up to $100,000 per participant?

Yes. Section 311(b) of the FDIC Improvement Act of 1991, enacted December 19, 1991, provides, in pertinent part, that:

> [E]xcept as provided in clause (ii), for the purpose of determining the amount of insurance due under subparagraph (B), the [FDIC] shall provide deposit insurance coverage with respect to deposits accepted by any insured depository institution on a pro rata or 'pass-through' basis to a participant in or beneficiary of an employee benefit plan . . . including any eligible deferred compensation plan described in section 457 of the Internal Revenue Code of 1986.

Subparagraph (B) provides, in general, that the net amount due to any depositor at an insured depository institution may not exceed $100,000.

The exception described in clause (ii) provides that, after the end of the one-year period beginning on the date of the enactment of the FDIC Improvement Act of 1991, the FDIC will not provide insurance coverage on a pro rata or "pass-through" basis pursuant to clause (i) with respect to deposits accepted by any insured depository institution which, at the time the deposits are accepted, may not accept brokered deposits under Section 29 of the FDIC Act (Section 29 prohibits institutions which do not meet minimum capital requirements from accepting brokered deposits). This exception does not apply if the insured depository institution meets applicable capital standards and the depositor receives a written statement from the institution that the brokered deposits are eligible for insurance coverage on a pro rata or "pass-through" basis. [FDIC Improvement Act of 1991, Pub L No 102-242, § 311(b)(1) 1991 US Code Cong & Ad News (105 Stat) 2236, 2363-64; HR Rep No 330, 102d Cong, 1st Sess 137 (199), reprinted in 1991 US Code Cong & Ad News at 1901, 1950-1951]

Section 311(b)(2) of the FDIC Improvement Act of 1991 provides that deposits in an insured depository institution made in connection with

1. Any individual retirement account described in Code Section 408(a);

2. Any eligible deferred compensation plan described in Code Section 457; and

3. Any individual account plan defined in Section 3(34) of ERISA and any plan described in Code Section 401(d), to the extent that participants and beneficiaries under the Section 401(d) plan have the right to direct the investment of assets held in individual accounts maintained on their behalf by the plan;

must be aggregated and insured in an amount not to exceed $100,000 per participant per insured depository institution. The amount aggregated for insurance coverage consists of the present vested and ascertainable interest of each participant under the plans, excluding any remainder interest created by, or as a result of, the plans. [FDIC Improvement Act of 1991, Pub L No 102-242, § 311(b)(2); 1991 US

Code Cong & Ad News (105 Stat) 2236, 2364-65; H Rep No 102-330, 1991 US Code Cong & Ad News at 1951]

Prior to the enactment of this law, FDIC regulations restricted deposit insurance for eligible Section 457 plans to $100,000 per plan, rather than $100,000 per participant. [55 Fed Reg 20,111 (May 15, 1990); FDIC Improvement Act of 1991, Pub L No 102-242, § 311 (105 Stat) 2236, 2363-2367]

Q 10:38   May an eligible plan make distributions pursuant to a qualified domestic relations order prior to the time distributions are permitted under Section 457(d)(1)(A)?

No. In a 1991 ruling, the IRS responded to a request regarding whether an eligible plan may make distributions pursuant to a qualified domestic relations order prior to the time distributions were permitted under Section 457(d)(1)(A) of the Code. The IRS noted that an eligible plan is an unfunded, nonqualified deferred compensation plan in which the participant has only the plan sponsor's contractual promise that benefits will be paid, as provided in Code Section 457(b)(6). Under Code Section 457(b)(6) and Treasury Regulations Section 1.457-2(j), the participant cannot have any interest in the plan sponsor's assets, and any funds used to pay benefits must be available to the plan sponsor's general creditors. A Section 457 plan would violate these provisions of Section 457 and the regulations thereunder if the participant or anyone else received an interest in the plan sponsor's assets earlier than the earliest date established in Code Section 457(d)(1)(A).

The IRS also noted that under Section 457(d)(1)(A), payments under an eligible plan may not begin until the participant's separation from service, attainment of age $70\frac{1}{2}$, or when the participant has an unforeseeable emergency. An unforeseeable emergency is defined in Treasury Regulations Section 1.457-2(h)(4) as one of the following:

1. A severe financial hardship to the participant resulting from a sudden and unexpected illness or accident of the participant or of a dependent,

2. Loss of the participant's property due to casualty, or

3. Other similar extraordinary and unforeseeable circumstances arising as a result of events beyond the control of the participant.

Because a divorce or separation generally does not give rise to an unforeseeable emergency within the meaning of these regulations, a participant who is working for the sponsor and who is under age 70½ cannot receive payment. The spouse or alternate payee likewise could not receive payment before the participant separates from service or attains age 70½.

Therefore, an eligible plan must make any distribution pursuant to a qualified domestic relations order only at or after the time permitted under Section 457(d)(1)(A) in order to remain an eligible plan. [Ltr Rul 9145010, July 31, 1991]

Ineligible Plans

Q 10:39 How does a participant in or beneficiary of an ineligible plan treat the compensation deferred under that plan?

Compensation deferred under an ineligible plan is included in the gross income of the participant or beneficiary in the first taxable year in which there is no substantial risk of forfeiture of the rights to the compensation. Earnings on amounts deferred under an ineligible plan are includible in gross income when amounts under the plan are paid or made available to the participant or beneficiary.

The tax treatment of any amount made available to a participant or beneficiary under an ineligible plan is determined under the extraordinarily complex rules for annuities contained in Code Section 72. [IRC §§ 457(f) and 72; Treas Reg § 1.457-3(a); Ltr Rul 8946019, Aug 17, 1989]

The application of the ineligible plan rules can be illustrated by the following two IRS rulings. In the first ruling, a school district permitted teachers to defer salary during a four-year period (the deferral period) and to take a paid leave of absence during the year following the deferral period. A teacher would agree to defer 20 percent of salary for each year in the deferral period, and the teacher would receive 100 percent of salary during the leave of absence. If the teacher terminated employment during the four-year deferral period, the teacher would forfeit any right to the deferred salary and would not be entitled to a leave of absence. If the teacher terminated employment during the leave of absence, the teacher would forfeit the right to the remaining monthly payments of salary for the year. The teacher also was required to return to employment for at least one year following the leave of absence. If the teacher failed to return to employment for the full year after the leave of absence, the teacher would be required to repay the salary received during the leave of absence.

The IRS determined that the school district was an eligible employer within the meaning of Code Section 457(e)(1) and that the plan was governed by Section 457. However, because the plan did not limit the amount of deferrals and because it would pay out deferred amounts while the teachers were employed by the school district, the IRS determined that the plan was an ineligible plan subject to the rules of Code Section 457(f). Applying these rules, the IRS determined that, because the teacher would forfeit the deferred amounts unless the teacher worked for four years and for an additional year after the leave of absence, the deferred amounts were subject to a substantial risk of forfeiture until paid, for purposes of Section 457(f), but, when paid to the teacher in year five, the deferred amounts were includible in income in accordance with Code Section 72. [Ltr Rul 9212006, Dec 19, 1991]

In the second ruling, a health care organization exempt from tax under Code Section 501(c)(3) entered into an agreement with an executive that created a supplemental account to which the employer credited 5 percent of the executive's monthly base salary. The executive was not able to make additional contributions to this account. The benefits would vest at the rate of 10 percent per year for ten years, but if the executive terminated employment with the employer at any time within that ten-year period, the executive would forfeit the nonvested portion of his benefits. If the executive did not terminate employment with the employer within this period, payment of his benefits would commence within 60 days of the date of the executive's termination of employment and would be paid out in equal monthly installments over two years. The benefits could not be assigned, alienated or encumbered by voluntary or involuntary action. The employer established a rabbi trust for the purpose of holding assets to fund the employer's obligations under the agreement.

The IRS determined that no plan contributions or benefits were taxable to the executive until the executive vested in those benefits under the terms of the agreement, that the benefits would be includible in income at their value in the year when they were no longer subject to a substantial risk of forfeiture, and that the tax treatment of any amount made available under the agreement would be determined under Section 72. [Ltr Rul 9212011, Dec 19, 1991]

Q 10:40   What have recent IRS Letter Rulings concluded concerning the taxation of "earnings" in ineligible defined compensation plans?

IRS Regulation Section 1.457-3(a)(2) provides that earnings on amounts deferred under an ineligible plan are taxed, pursuant to the rules of Code Section 72, when amounts under the plan actually are paid or made available to the participants. Many commentators have concluded that this regulations section should be interpreted in a straightforward manner and, therefore, that all of the earnings on amounts deferred are taxed under this rule.

However, the IRS occasionally has stated, informally, that, for this purpose, the term "earnings" refers only to amounts earned on the deferred compensation after the deferred compensation is no longer subject to a substantial risk of forfeiture. Under this view, amounts earned before the applicable vesting date are not earnings at all but are part of the principal of the deferred compensation.

In the past, the IRS has issued several Letter Rulings (e.g., Ltr Rul 9329010) that take this position. However, the IRS recently issued Ltr Rul 9444028, which appears to confirm the position of those commentators who believe that IRS Regulation Section 1.457-3(a)(2) stands for the proposition that earnings on amounts deferred under the plan, whether earned prior to or after the vesting date for the deferred amounts, are not taxed until amounts under the plan actually are paid or made available to the participants.

Q 10:41   What is a substantial risk of forfeiture for purposes of Code Section 457?

Compensation is subject to a substantial risk of forfeiture if the right to the compensation is conditioned upon the future performance of substantial services by any individual. The IRS has indicated informally that it would be reasonable to look to the extensive interpretive regulations under Code Section 83 (for example, Treasury Regulations Section 1.83-3(c), which defines situations involving a substantial risk of forfeiture) for guidance concerning the term substantial risk of forfeiture as used under Code Section 457. For example, under the Section 83 rules, the risk of a decline in value is not a substantial risk of forfeiture. Similarly, the fact that deferred amounts are subject to the claims of the employer's creditors does not constitute a substantial risk of forfeiture for purposes of Code Section 83. [IRC § 457(f)(3)(B); Treas Reg § 1.83-3(c)(4); Ltr Ruls 9030028, Apr 27, 1990; 9030025, Apr 27, 1990]

The IRS recently ruled that a substantial risk of forfeiture was considered to exist where an individual was required to complete a minimum of two years of service with the employer. [Ltr Rul 9211037, Dec 17, 1991]

In another ruling, the IRS examined a situation involving a deferred compensation plan established by a school district for its superintendent of schools. The superintendent's employment contract with the school district was for a three-year term and was renewed automatically each year so that the contract period would always be three years. The IRS ruled that because the plan did not limit the amount of deferrals and because the school district could pay out deferred amounts while the superintendent was working for the school district, the plan was an ineligible plan, subject to Code Section 457(f). The IRS also ruled that because the superintendent was required to work at least three years before benefits vested, the superintendent's rights to benefits under the plan were subject to a substantial risk of forfeiture during those three years.

The school district also could vest the superintendent in his benefits anytime on or after three years from the effective date of the plan. The IRS refrained from expressing an opinion on whether a plan sponsor's retention of discretion to vest an otherwise unvested benefit eliminates the substantial risk of forfeiture. [Ltr Rul 9215019, Jan 8, 1992]

Q 10:42   Has the IRS issued any recent rulings concerning the various open issues affecting ineligible plans?

Yes. In a recent Letter Ruling, the IRS discussed in detail the issues of participant investment direction, the definition of substantial risk of forfeiture, and the taxation of pre-vesting earnings as they apply to ineligible plans.

In Letter Ruling 9444028, a tax-exempt employer established an ineligible plan and a related rabbi trust for members of its top-hat group. Under the plan, participants could elect to have their rabbi trust accounts invested among a group of investment options made available under the plan. The employer designated the vesting date for participants' accounts under the plan, and no deferred amounts were permitted to vest before the third January 1 after the calendar year in which the amounts were deferred. A participant's accounts also became vested upon his or her death or disability.

The plan also provided that participants were entitled to distributions of their accounts on their vesting date, and that nonvested amounts would be forfeited by a participant who terminated employment prior to his or her vesting date. However, the plan specifically provided that a participant who forfeits all or a portion of his or her deferred compensation is nonetheless entitled to receive a distribution of the earnings related to the forfeited amount. That is, the plan provided that earnings credited to accounts, both prior to and after the account's vesting date, would be vested in the participant at all times.

The IRS concluded that the minimum vesting period provided under the plan (i.e., the third January 1 after the calendar year of the deferral) created a substantial risk of forfeiture under Code Section 457(f). The IRS reached this conclusion by making reference to IRS Regulation Section 1.83-3(c)(1), noting that Code Section 83 "includes the same definition of substantial risk of forfeiture as [Section 457(f)]." The IRS also concluded that no amount will be considered to be made available to a participant merely because that participant has a right to designate the deemed investment of that amount.

Finally, the IRS concluded that, even though earnings on the deferred amounts were at all times vested—that is, a participant would not forfeit the earnings even if he or she terminated employment prior to his or her vesting date— the earnings would not be taxable to the participant until the taxable year in which the participant becomes entitled to receive the earnings.

Q 10:43 May a participant in an ineligible plan elect to defer his or her vesting date under the plan?

Nothing in Code Section 457(f) or the regulations under Code Section 457 addresses the subject of extensions of vesting dates under ineligible plans. However, in a recent private letter ruling concerning a Code Section 83 arrangement [Ltr Rul 9431021], the IRS held that an agreement between an employer and an employee to extend the period during which the employee was subject to a substantial risk of forfeiture of his rights to property transferred in connection with the performance of services for the employer would be given effect.

Because of the similarity between the language and structure of Code Sections 83 and 457(f), until further guidance is issued on this point, many taxpayers plan to take the position that the conclusions reached in Letter Ruling 9431021 apply to ineligible plans as well as to Code Section 83 arrangements.

Q 10:44 What is the definition of a bona fide severance plan for purposes of Code Section 457(e)(11)?

No definition of bona fide severance plan is provided in Code Section 457(e)(11) or the regulations under Code Section 457. However, the phrase "bona fide severance plan" is defined in the regulations under ERISA Section 3. Generally, under this definition, an arrangement is a bona fide severance plan if: (1) plan benefits are paid only on termination of employment and are not contingent, directly or indirectly, on the participant's retirement; (2) plan benefits are limited to two times the participant's final year's cash plus noncash compensation; and (3) plan benefits are paid only during the 24-month period following the participant's termination of employment.

Until further guidance is provided on this issue, many taxpayers plan to take the position that an arrangement meeting the require-ments for a bona fide severance plan under the ERISA Section 3 regulations should meet the bona fide severance plan definition under Code Section 457(e)(11).

Q 10:45 Is a bona fide severance plan maintained by a governmental or tax-exempt employer subject to the ineligible plan rules?

Under Code Section 457(e)(11), a bona fide severance plan main-tained by a governmental or tax-exempt employer is not subject to the ineligible plan rules. Instead, such a plan presumably is subject to the rules of Code Section 451 and the constructive receipt and economic benefit doctrines. A participant's interest in such a plan presumably is taxed when it is paid or made available to the partici-pant or when it is first funded or assignable by the participant.

ERISA Considerations

Q 10:46 Are the Section 457 plans of governments subject to ERISA requirements?

No. Governmental deferred compensation plans are exempt from ERISA's Section 4(b)(1) requirements.

Q 10:47 Are the Section 457 plans of non-church tax-exempt organizations subject to ERISA requirements?

Unlike plans of state and local governments, plans of other tax-ex-empt organizations may be subject to Title I of ERISA. The IRS has noted that, in the case of a Code Section 457 plan of a tax-exempt organization that is subject to Title I of ERISA, compliance with the exclusive purpose, trust, funding, and certain other rules of Title I will cause the plan to fail to meet the requirements of Code Section 457(b)(6), therefore causing it to fail to be an eligible plan. Specifically, a Code Section 457 plan must be unfunded and all deferred amounts must remain solely the property and rights of the plan sponsor, subject only to the claims of the plan sponsor's general creditors. [IRC § 457(b)(6); DOL News Release 86-527, Dec 19, 1986; IRS Notice 87-13, 1987-1 CB 432, 444; Ltr Rul 8950056, Sept 20, 1989; but see Foil v Comm'r, 920 F 2d 1196 (5th Cir 1990)]

Notwithstanding the foregoing, an ineligible plan maintained by an ERISA-governed tax-exempt organization primarily for the purpose of providing deferred compensation for a select group of management or highly compensated employees within the meaning of ERISA Sections 201(2), 301(a)(3) and 401(a)(1) (the top-hat plan exemption) may qualify for exemption from most of the provisions of Title I. (See chapter 2.)

Case Study 10-1

Note: See Case Studies at the end of chapters 1 through 9.

At the end of the golden parachute discussion, *A* asks the advisor to remain to meet privately. *A* is the Chair of the Executive Compensation Committee of a large, private, tax-exempt, non-church-affiliated hospital. *A*'s committee is increasingly concerned that the hospital's top-notch CEO may be undercompensated and may be enticed away by a competing hospital or a for-profit company. *A* asks the advisor if the hospital could employ certain techniques discussed in the prior meetings.

The advisor cautions that the tax rules applicable to the nonqualified plans of tax-exempt entities are different, and in certain respects less favorable, than the tax rules applicable to for-profit employer nonqualified plans. The advisor notes that, assuming that the CEO fully exploits a 403(b) tax-sheltered annuity program, the committee need not consider so-called eligible deferred compensation plans under Code Section 457. However, the committee will want to consider ineligible deferred compensation plans under Code Section 457, and probably will want to use this type of plan both to provide additional deferred compensation to the CEO and to "handcuff" the CEO to the hospital by imposing a vesting schedule on the CEO's benefits under the plan.

The advisor explains that the imposition of this vesting schedule on the deferrals—which should discourage the CEO from voluntarily leaving the hospital and forfeiting unvested benefits—can be "blamed on the Congress" because of the rules of Code Section 457(f) that tax participants on their plan benefits as soon as they become vested.

The advisor adds that, if the Committee also wishes to provide vested deferred compensation benefits to the CEO, it should examine, for example, a bona fide severance pay plan under Code Section 457(e)(11).

The advisor concludes by stating that certain techniques already discussed for the corporation (for example, rabbi trusts and secular trusts) may be utilized for the CEO as long as appropriate consideration is given to the impact of Code Section 457 on these techniques.

A asks the advisor to attend the Executive Compensation Committee's next meeting to discuss these issues in detail.

See Case Study at the end of chapter 11.

Chapter 11

Withholding Rules for Nonqualified Plans

Various types of withholding rules apply to nonqualified plans. This chapter examines the application of the federal income tax, Federal Insurance Contributions Act (FICA, or Social Security), Medicare tax, Federal Unemployment Taxes Act (FUTA) tax, and Self-Employment Contributions Act (SECA) tax withholding rules to nonqualified plans. It also examines the definition of the term "nonqualified plan" and the term "substantial risk of forfeiture" for purposes of these withholding rules, and the effect of nonqualified plan benefits on Social Security benefits.

Withholding Taxes

Q 11:1   Are interests under nonqualified plans subject to federal income tax withholding?

Generally, yes. Interests (for example, employee deferrals, employer contributions, earnings, rights to certain future distributions, and so forth) of employees participating in nonqualified plans are subject to federal income tax withholding. The broad definition of "wages" in Code Section 3401(a), which contains the federal income tax withholding requirements, includes "all remuneration . . . for services performed by an employee for his employer . . . (including benefits)" and does not exclude nonqualified plan interests from the definition of wages. [Treas Reg § 31.3401(a)-1(b)(1)(i); Rev Rul 82-46, 1982-1 CB 158] However, Code Section 3401(a) does not apply to a self-employed individual (for example, a nonemployee member of the board of directors of the employer). Therefore, although the interests of an individual participating in a nonqualified plan as a self-employed individual are subject to federal income tax, the interests are not subject to federal income tax withholding.

In addition, if an employee's wages are exempt from federal income tax withholding because of a special exemption under Code Section 3401, then the nonqualified plan interests of that employee also should be exempt from withholding (see, for example, Rev Rul 54-122, 1954-1 CB 223, which dealt with the pension of an agricultural laborer whose remuneration for services prior to retirement was exempt from federal income tax withholding).

Q 11:2   When are amounts that are deferred under a nonqualified plan treated as wages for federal income tax withholding purposes?

The timing of the inclusion of amounts that are deferred under a nonqualified plan as wages for federal income tax withholding purposes depends on whether the plan is a nonqualified plan of a taxable employer or a nonqualified plan of a tax-exempt or governmental employer under Code Section 457(f).

Amounts deferred under a nonqualified plan of a taxable employer are included in wages on the date on which the amounts are received, constructively or actually, by the individual. Constructive receipt occurs on the date on which all events have occurred that entitle the individual to the immediate payment of the amount, even if actual payment does not occur on that date. Note that under this type of plan, amounts may become vested before the amounts are included in wages because vesting may occur before all other events have occurred which entitle the individual to payment.

Amounts deferred under a Code Section 457(f) nonqualified plan are included in wages on the vesting date—on which date the amounts no longer are subject to a "substantial risk of forfeiture" (see Q 11:18). Under a Code Section 457(f) plan, the individual cannot delay the inclusion of deferred amounts in wages beyond this vesting date.

Q 11:3 Are contributions to a rabbi trust or other funding mechanism for a nonqualified plan subject to federal income tax withholding?

Contributions to a funding arrangement for a nonqualified plan are subject to federal income tax withholding when the contributions are included in the individual's wages for federal income tax withholding purposes (see Q 11:2). [Rev Rul 79-305, 1979-2 CB 350; see e.g., Rev Rul 56-249, 1956-1 CB 488, amplified by Rev Rul 58-128, 1958-1 CB 89, amplified by Rev Rul 60-330, 1960-2 CB 46, amplified and modified by Rev Rul 77-347, 1977-2 CB 362]

Q 11:4 When must federal income taxes be withheld from nonqualified plan interests?

In general, any interests under a nonqualified plan are subject to federal income tax withholding when they are included in wages for federal income tax purposes (see Q 11:1). To comply with its withholding obligation in the absence of an actual payment to the employee, the employer first should withhold the appropriate amount from any other actual payments the employer is making to the employee (for example, regular wage payments). If no other actual payments are being made, the employer and employee must make the necessary arrangements for the employer to comply with its withholding obligations. [IRC §§ 3405(a), 3405(c)(2); Treas Reg § 35.3405-1, Q&As A-18, A-23]

Q 11:5   Does Code Section 3405 apply to benefits under a nonqualified plan?

No. The withholding provisions of Code Section 3405, which require withholding on payments from deferred compensation plans (such as tax-qualified plans under Code Section 401(a)), to the extent that such payments are includible in the individual's gross income (unless the individual specifically elects not to have amounts withheld), do not apply to nonqualified plan benefits. [IRC §§ 3405(a), 3405(c)(2); Treas Reg § 35.3405-1, Q&As A-18, A-23]

Q 11:6   Does the imposition of the excise tax under Code Section 4999, which applies to excess parachute payments, create a withholding obligation for the employer?

Yes. Under Code Section 4999(c), in the case of any excess parachute payment, which is considered wages under Code Section 3401, the amount of federal income tax deducted and withheld under Code Section 3402 must be increased by the amount of the excise tax imposed under Code Section 4999 on the payment.

Q 11:7   Is withholding of federal income tax required with respect to income realized from the early disposition of stock acquired under an incentive stock option (ISO) or an employee stock purchase plan?

In Revenue Ruling 71-52, the IRS ruled that the income realized by an employee and two former employees from disqualifying dispositions of stock acquired by the exercise of an ISO was not considered wages for federal income tax withholding purposes. In Notice 87-49, the IRS stated it was reconsidering Revenue Ruling 71-52, but that until the results of the reconsideration are announced, the principles of Revenue Ruling 71-52 will continue to apply to a disqualifying disposition of stock acquired by the exercise of an ISO. The IRS added that pursuant to Code Section 7805(b), "any determination that the gross income resulting from such a disqualifying disposition is wages for Federal employment tax purposes will be given prospective effect only."

Although the exemption in Revenue Ruling 71-52 applies to disqualifying dispositions of stock acquired through ISOs, the IRS apparently takes the position that the withholding exemption described in Revenue Ruling 71-52 does not apply to disqualifying dispositions of stock acquired through employee stock purchase plans under Code Section 423. The IRS indicated in a private letter ruling that in the case of an employee who disposes of stock acquired under a Code Section 423 employee stock purchase plan before the expiration of the holding period contained in Code Section 423(a)(1), the employer is allowed a deduction for the amount included in the employee's income pursuant to Code Sections 83(h) and 162 for the year of the disposition only if it withheld federal income taxes from such amount (implying that withholding is required). [Rev Rul 71-52, 1971-1 CB 278; IRS Notice 87-49, 1987-2 CB 355; Ltr Rul 8921027, Feb 22, 1989; Treas Reg § 1.83-6(a)]

FICA Taxes

Q 11:8   Are benefits under a nonqualified plan subject to FICA taxes?

Nonqualified plan interests generally are treated as FICA wages subject to FICA taxes, although certain interests under nonqualified plans in existence on March 24, 1983, may be governed by prior rules. [§ 324(d)(4)(A) of the Social Security Amendments of 1983, Pub L No 98-21, 1983 US Code Cong & Ad News (97 Stat) 126; as amended by § 2662(f)(2), Pub L No 98-369, 1984 US Code Cong & Ad News (98 Stat) 1157-1158; TAM 9050006, Sept 6, 1990]

Distributions from a nonqualified plan that are made to a beneficiary or to an estate following the participant's death, unless previously taxed for FICA purposes, are subject to FICA taxes if paid during the calendar year of the participant's death, but are not subject to FICA taxes if paid after the calendar year of the participant's death. [IRC § 3121(a)(14); Rev Rul 86-109, 1986-2 CB 196]

Q 11:9   When are interests of employees under a nonqualified plan included as wages for FICA purposes and when do they become subject to FICA taxes?

Interests (for example, employee deferrals, employer contributions, earnings, rights to certain distributions, and so forth) of employees under a nonqualified plan are included in FICA wages and become subject to FICA taxes as of the later of:

1. When the services relating to the interests are performed; or

2. When there is no substantial risk of forfeiture of the rights to the interests (see Q 11:18).

[IRC § 3121(v)(2)(A)] (But see Q 11:19 regarding the extent to which the interests are subject to tax.)

After an amount is treated as FICA wages and becomes subject to FICA taxes, that amount is not later treated as FICA wages and subject to FICA taxes. [IRC § 3121(v)(2)(B)] Therefore, if an amount is included as FICA wages under the rule above before it is distributed, that amount will not again be treated as FICA wages when it is distributed.

In a nonqualified salary deferral plan, the amount deferred each year and any earnings that accrue during the year are subject to FICA taxes in the year deferred or earned if they are then vested. When the benefit provided under a nonqualified plan is a promise to pay a fixed amount in the future, and the benefit is included in FICA wages before it is paid, that fixed amount must be discounted to determine the benefit's present value on the date it must be included in FICA wages. [TAM 9050006, Sept 6, 1990] The IRS has stated that the regulations to be issued for this area should address methods for determining a benefit's present value. In the meantime, a good faith, reasonable determination of the present value should be made.

These FICA tax rules were applied in a federal district court case involving a husband and wife, both physicians and shareholder-employees of a professional corporation, who each entered into an employment agreement with the professional corporation. Under these agreements, one spouse was compensated, while the other received little or no compensation. By compensating one spouse and not the other in alternating years, the corporation and the couple paid FICA taxes on only one salary (they paid on only one FICA wage base). After examining the contracts between the physicians and the professional corporation and the rules under Code Section 3121(v)(2), the court concluded that the contractual arrangements should be construed as nonqualified plans because the pattern of payment had the effect of deferring payment of compensation otherwise payable at the expiration of each taxpayer's two-year employment contract.

For example, the husband had a two-year service obligation from May 1, 1984, through May 1, 1986. His wages for this period were not deemed to be earned until his services were completed, and they were subject to forfeiture before that time (that is, the risk of forfeiting these wages ended on May 1, 1986). Any vested amounts were to be paid in 1987. The court concluded that the amounts deferred were deemed to be FICA wages in 1986 under Code Section 3121(v)(2)(A) even though they were not to be paid until 1987. [Hoerl & Associates, PC v US, 785 F Supp 1430, (D Colo 1992)]

The general rule under Code Section 3121(v)(2)(A) stated above also applies to plans of governmental and tax-exempt organizations under Code Section 457(f). However, payments made to, or on behalf of, an employee or his or her beneficiary under or to an "exempt governmental deferred compensation plan" are completely exempt from FICA. An exempt governmental deferred compensation plan includes any plan providing for the deferral of compensation for employees of the United States, a state or political subdivision thereof, or an agency or instrumentality of any of the foregoing. Excluded from this definition are (1) plans to which Code Sections 83, 402(b), 403(c), 457(a), or 457(f)(1) apply; (2) an annuity contract described in Code Section 403(b); and (3) the Federal Employees' Thrift Savings Fund. [IRC §§ 3121(a)(5), 3121(v)(3)(A); Ltr Rul 9024069, Mar 21, 1990, as modified by Ltr Rul 9025067, Mar 27, 1990]

Q 11:10   Does Code Section 421 exclude from wages for FICA tax purposes any income realized from the early disposition of stock acquired under an ISO or under an employee stock purchase plan?

The definition of the term "wages" for FICA tax purposes in Code Section 3121(a) provides that "[n]othing in the regulations prescribed for purposes of chapter 24 (relating to income tax withholding) which provides an exclusion from 'wages' as used in such chapter shall be construed to require a similar exclusion from 'wages' in the regulations prescribed for purposes of this chapter." Therefore, it is possible that the IRS could take the position that while Code Section 421 provides an exclusion of certain compensation items from wages for federal income tax purposes, it does not provide an exclusion of these items from wages for FICA tax purposes.

In Revenue Ruling 71-52, the IRS ruled that the income realized by an employee and two former employees from the disqualifying disposition of stock acquired by the exercise of an ISO was not considered wages for FICA tax purposes. In Notice 87-49, the IRS stated it was reconsidering Revenue Ruling 71-52, but that until the results of the reconsideration were announced, the principles of Revenue Ruling 71-52 will apply to a disqualifying disposition of stock acquired by the exercise of an ISO. The IRS added that pursuant to Code Section 7805(b), "any determination that the gross income resulting from such a disqualifying disposition is wages for Federal employment tax purposes will be given prospective effect only."

The IRS apparently takes the position that the exemption described in Revenue Ruling 71-52 does not apply to employee stock purchase plans under Code Section 423. [Rev Rul 71-52, 1971-1 CB 278; IRS Notice 87-49, 1987-2 CB 355; see Ltr Rul 8921027, Feb 22, 1989]

Q 11:11   Are "excess parachute payment" amounts subject to FICA tax?

Yes, under Code Section 3121(v)(2)(A) excess parachute payment amounts are subject to FICA tax.

SECA Taxes

Q 11:12   Are nonqualified plan interests of self-employed individuals (e.g., nonemployee directors) subject to SECA taxes?

Yes. Nonqualified plan interests of self-employed individuals generally are subject to SECA taxes in the same manner that nonqualified plan interests of employees are subject to FICA taxes. [IRC §§ 1402(a), 1402(b)] (But see IRC § 402(a)(10), Treas Reg § 1.1402(a)-17 regarding certain retirement payments to partners that are exempt from SECA taxes.)

Q 11:13   When are nonqualified plan interests of self-employed individuals included as wages for SECA purposes and when do they become subject to SECA taxes?

Nonqualified plan interests of self-employed individuals generally are included in SECA wages and become subject to SECA taxes at the time they are includible in gross income for income tax purposes. Therefore, a nonqualified plan interest of a self-employed individual is included as wages for SECA purposes and is subject to SECA taxes in the year in which the nonqualified plan interest actually or constructively is received by the self-employed individual. Furthermore, under the Omnibus Budget Reconciliation Act of 1990, after December 31, 1990, income deferred with respect to outside directors will not be subject to SECA taxes until the compensation is paid or constructively received. Previously, income deferred with respect to a corporate director's services performed after January 1, 1988, was subject to tax under SECA at the time the services were performed, unless the director was paid prior to rendering any services. Nonqualified plan interests with respect to outside directors still are included in the Social Security earnings test at the time the services are performed, unless the director is paid prior to rendering any services. [IRC § 1402; Treas Reg § 1.1402(a)-2; see Ltr Rul 8819012, Feb 4, 1988].

FUTA Taxes

Q 11:14   Are interests under a nonqualified plan subject to FUTA taxes?

Nonqualified plan interests generally are treated as FUTA wages and are subject to FUTA taxes; however, certain nonqualified plans in existence on March 24, 1983, may be governed by prior rules. [§ 324(d)(4)(B) of the Social Security Amendments of 1983, Pub L

No 98-21, 1983 US Code Cong & Ad News (97 Stat) 126; as amended by § 2662(f)(2), Pub L No 98-369, 1984 US Code Cong & Ad News (98 Stat) 1157-1158; TAM 9050006, Sept 6, 1990]

Distributions from a nonqualified plan that are made to a beneficiary or to an estate following the participant's death, unless previously taxed for FUTA purposes, are subject to FUTA taxes if paid during the calendar year of the participant's death; however, they are not subject to FUTA taxes if paid after the calendar year of the participant's death. [IRC § 3306(b)(15)]

Q 11:15 When are employees' interests under a nonqualified plan included as wages for FUTA purposes and when are they subject to FUTA taxes?

Employees' interests (for example, employee deferrals, employer contributions, earnings, rights to future distributions, and so forth) under a nonqualified plan are included in FUTA wages and subject to FUTA taxes as of the later of:

1. When the services relating to the interests are performed; or
2. When there is no substantial risk of forfeiture of the rights to the interests (see Q 11:18).

[IRC § 3306(r)(2)(A)] (But see Q 11:19 regarding the extent to which the interests are subject to tax.)

After an amount is treated as FUTA wages and is subject to FUTA taxes, that amount is not later treated as wages. [IRC § 3306(r)(2)(B)]

In a salary deferral nonqualified plan, the amount deferred each year, and any earnings that accrue during the year, are subject to FUTA taxes in the year deferred or earned or, if later, the year in which they become nonforfeitable. When the interest under a nonqualified plan is a right under a promise to pay a fixed amount in the future, and the interest is included in FUTA wages before it is paid, that fixed amount must be discounted to determine the benefit's present value on the date it must be included in FUTA wages. [TAM 9050006, Sept 6, 1990] The IRS has stated that the regulations to be issued for this area will address methods for determining a benefit's present value. In the meantime, a good faith, reasonable determination of the present value should be made.

The general rule stated above also applies to a plan for governmental and tax-exempt organizations under Code Section 457(f). However, payments made to, or on behalf of, an employee or his or her beneficiary under or to an "exempt governmental deferred compensation plan" are completely exempt from FUTA. An exempt governmental deferred compensation plan includes any plan providing for the deferral of compensation for employees of the United States, a state or political subdivision thereof, or an agency or instrumentality of any of the foregoing. Excluded from this definition are (1) plans to which Code Sections 83, 402(b), 403(c), 457(a), or 457(f)(1) apply; (2) an annuity contract described in Code Section 403(b); and (3) the Federal Employees' Thrift Savings Fund. [IRC §§ 3306(b), 3306(b)(5), 3306(r)]

Q 11:16 Does Code Section 421 exclude from wages for FUTA tax purposes the income realized from the early disposition of stock acquired under an ISO or an employee stock purchase plan?

The definition of the term "wages" for FUTA tax purposes in Code Section 3306(b) provides that "[n]othing in the regulations prescribed for purposes of chapter 24 (relating to income tax withholding) which provides an exclusion from 'wages' as used in such chapter shall be construed to require a similar exclusion from 'wages' in the regulations prescribed for purposes of this chapter." Therefore, it is possible that the IRS could take the position that while Code Section 421 provides an exclusion of certain compensation items from wages for federal income tax purposes, it does not provide an exclusion of these items from wages for FUTA tax purposes.

In Revenue Ruling 71-52, the IRS found that the income realized by an employee and two former employees from the disqualifying disposition of stock acquired by the exercise of an ISO was not considered wages for FUTA tax purposes. In Notice 87-49, the IRS stated it was reconsidering Revenue Ruling 71-52, but that until the results of the reconsideration were announced, the principles of Revenue Ruling 71-52 will apply to a disqualifying disposition of stock acquired by the exercise of an ISO. The IRS added that pursuant to Code Section 7805(b), "any determination that the gross income resulting from such a disqualifying disposition is wages for Federal employment tax purposes will be given prospective effect only."

The IRS apparently has taken the position that the exemption described in Revenue Ruling 71-52 does not apply to employee stock purchase plans under Code Section 423. [Rev Rul 71-52, 1971-1 CB 278; IRS Notice 87-49, 1987-2 CB 355; see Ltr Rul 8921027, Feb 22, 1989]

Other Considerations

Q 11:17   For purposes of FICA and FUTA taxes, what does the phrase "nonqualified plan" include?

Generally, the phrase "nonqualified plan" includes any plan or other arrangement that provides for the deferral of compensation other than:

1. A plan that provides payments from a trust described in Code Section 401(a) that is exempt from tax under Code Section 501(a);

2. An annuity plan that is described in Code Section 403(a);

3. A simplified employee pension plan as defined in Code Section 408(a)(8)(other than any contributions described in Section 408(k)(6));

4. An annuity contract as described in Code Section 403(b) (other than a payment for the purchase of a contract which is made by reason of a salary reduction agreement);

5. An exempt governmental deferred compensation plan as described in Code Section 3121(v)(3);

6. A welfare plan as described in ERISA Section 3(2)(B)(ii) that provides cost of living supplemental benefits to any of the pension benefits under plans described above; or

7. A cafeteria plan within the meaning of Code Section 125 (if payments would not be treated as wages without regard to the plan and it is reasonable to believe that Code Section 125 would not treat any wages as constructively received).

[IRC §§ 2131(v)(2)(C), 3306(r)(2)(C)]

Q 11:18   What definition of "substantial risk of forfeiture" is applied for purposes of the withholding of federal income tax and FICA or FUTA taxes from nonqualified plan interests?

The legislative history of the 1983 Social Security Amendments indicates that for purposes of the withholding of federal income tax and FICA or FUTA taxes, Congress intended the phrase "substantial risk of forfeiture" to be interpreted in a manner similar to the interpretation of that phrase under Code Section 83. Generally, under Code Section 83, a substantial risk of forfeiture exists where benefits are conditioned upon:

1. The future performance, or nonperformance, of substantial services by any person; or
2. The occurrence of a condition related to a purpose of the transfer and the possibility of forfeiture is substantial if such condition is not satisfied.

(For further discussion see chapters 1, 4, and 5.) [HR Rep No 98-47, 98th Cong 1st Session, 147 (1983); TAM 9050006, Sept 6, 1990; Treas Reg § 1.83-3(c)]

Q 11:19   Is the inclusion of an interest under a nonqualified plan as wages for FICA and FUTA tax purposes likely to increase significantly the amount of FICA and FUTA taxes paid?

Not necessarily. If, in the year in question, the individual receives other compensation that exceeds the non-Medicare portion of the FICA and the FUTA taxable wage bases, the inclusion of the nonqualified plan interest in FICA and FUTA wages does not significantly affect the amount of FICA and FUTA taxes paid (because the maximum amount of non-Medicare FICA, and FUTA, taxes will have been paid for the year). However, if, in the year in question, the individual receives other compensation that is less than the non-Medicare portion of the FICA, and the FUTA, taxable wage bases, the individual will have to pay additional FICA and FUTA taxes because of the inclusion in wages of the nonqualified plan interest. Under OBRA '93, the Medicare portion of the FICA tax, the wage base for which was $135,000 for 1993, is uncapped beginning in 1994. Therefore, beginning in 1994, individuals and employers whose nonqualified plan benefits previously had not increased their FICA taxes, will be required to pay the Medicare portion of the FICA tax with respect to the nonqualified plan interest earned during the year.

Q 11:20   What is the effect of paying nonqualified plan benefits to a Social Security recipient?

Social Security retirement benefits are meant to replace, in part, income that the retired person no longer will receive. In determining the Social Security retirement benefits to be paid to the retired individual, an annual earnings test is applied to determine to what extent other earnings of the retired individual reduce the individual's Social Security benefits. The annual earnings test applies only to retired or partially retired individuals who are under the age of 70.

Generally, under the Social Security Act, Social Security benefits payable to a recipient who has reached Social Security normal retirement age (age 65 until the year 2000) but who has not reached age 70 are reduced by $1 for every $3 of the recipient's "earned income" above a specified amount. For individuals who have not reached Social Security normal retirement age, Social Security benefits are reduced by $1 for every $2 of "earned income" above a specified amount. [§ 203(f)(3) of the Social Security Act of 1935, as amended]

Annual Earnings Test. In applying the annual earnings test, only certain types of wages are treated as "earned income" when determining the reduction, if any, of Social Security benefits. The following payments from nonqualified plans are not treated as "earned income" for purposes of the annual earnings test:

1. Payments made by an employer under a plan or system to an individual who has reached an age specified in the employer's plan or system and whose employment relationship has terminated because of retirement;

2. Payments made "on account of retirement," meaning additional compensation for services performed prior to retirement from regular employment, whether or not such payments are under an employer's plan or system; and

3. Payments made by an employer for insurance or annuities or into a fund to provide for a payment upon or after "retirement." [§ 203(f)(5)(C) of the Social Security Act of 1935, as amended]

An interest under a nonqualified plan (within the meaning of Code Section 3121(v)(2)(C)) is treated as part of an individual's "earned income" for purposes of the reduction of Social Security benefits at the later of when the services giving rise to the interest are performed or when there is no substantial risk of forfeiture of the interest. Therefore, a person who is receiving Social Security retirement benefits cannot avoid the reduction of those benefits by deferring part of his or her income to a date that is after he or she reaches age 70 unless the deferred income is subject to a substantial risk of forfeiture until that date. [§§ 203(f)(5), 209(a) of the Social Security Act of 1935, as amended]

Q 11:21   How does the $5,000 death benefit exclusion under Code Section 101(b) apply to nonqualified plan benefits?

Up to $5,000 of a death benefit payable to an employee's beneficiary under a nonqualified plan is excludable from the gross income of the beneficiary as long as the employee's right to receive the nonqualified plan benefit is subject to a substantial risk of forfeiture until death. This exclusion is not available if the employee possessed, immediately before his or her death, a right to receive the benefit amounts, without a substantial risk of forfeiture. [IRC § 101(b)(2); Rev Rul 71-361, 1971-2 CB 90].

Q 11:22   Does a governmental early retirement incentive program qualify for the exemption from FICA tax under Code Sections 3121(a)(5)(E) and 3121(v)(3)?

Under Code Sections 3121(a)(5)(E) and 3121(v)(3), the payments made to, or on behalf of, an employee or his or her beneficiary under or to an "exempt governmental deferred compensation plan" are completely exempt from FICA tax. In November 1993, the IRS determined that a school district's early retirement incentive program did not qualify as an "exempt governmental deferred compensation plan" because the benefits under the plan did not accrue until the employee's agreement to retire early and, therefore, the plan did not provide for the deferral of compensation for FICA tax purposes. [TAM 9347006, Nov 1993]

Q 11:23   Are special pension benefits payable on termination of employment due to a takeover treated as nonqualified plan benefits for FICA purposes?

No. Payments under a contract that provides for the payment of special pension benefits only in the event of termination of employment of the employee as a result of a change in control of the employer that significantly and adversely affects the employee, have been determined by the IRS not to be benefits under a nonqualified plan. The IRS determined that the benefits should be treated as severance pay and not as payments under a nonqualified plan of deferred compensation for FICA tax purposes. Therefore, the benefits are subject to FICA tax when paid and are not subject to FICA tax under the rules applicable to interests under a nonqualified plan.

Q 11:24   Is the IRS currently working on regulations that may affect the withholding rules that apply to nonqualified plans?

Yes. The IRS has indicated that it intends to propose regulations under Code Section 3121(v) in 1994. There is a significant amount of interest in this guidance as a result of the change made by OBRA '93 which uncapped the amount of wages subject to the Medicare portion of FICA tax. It is expected that the regulations will address areas such as:

1. The method for valuing accruals under a defined benefit formula nonqualified plan;

2. The possible exemption from FICA tax of benefits under a defined benefit formula nonqualified plan which decrease until Normal Retirement Age, if the benefits are not paid;

3. The method for paying FICA tax for years in which the only "FICA wages" are the interest under the nonqualified plan.

Q 11:25   Has the IRS issued any guidance concerning the withholding rules for nonqualified plans pending the issuance of regulations?

In Notice 94-96, the IRS issued guidance concerning the withholding rules for nonqualified plans pending the issuance of regulations in this area. In general, Notice 94-96 provides that, until regulations are issued, taxpayers may rely on a reasonable, good-faith interpretation of the provisions of Code Section 3121(v).

Case Study 11-1

Note: See Case Studies at the end of chapters 1 through 10.

Prior to making a final decision on the types of nonqualified plans to be employed by the corporation, *A*, *B*, *C*, and *D* ask the advisor to provide them with a general overview of the withholding rules that apply to nonqualified plans. The advisor explains that, generally, interests of employees (but not those of nonemployee directors) under nonqualified plans are subject to federal income tax withholding when they are actually or constructively received and that interests of participants under Code Section 457(f) plans are subject to withholding when they vest. Nonqualified plan participants may not elect to be exempt from these withholding rules.

Generally, nonqualified plan interests also are subject to FICA, SECA, and FUTA tax withholding when they vest. However, the advisor notes that often no FICA, SECA, or FUTA taxes (except Medicare taxes) actually are paid with respect to a participant's nonqualified plan interests because the participant already has reached the wage base against which those taxes are applied for the particular year in question. Furthermore, when they vest, nonqualified plan interests also are treated as earned income for purposes of the reduction of Social Security benefits under the $1 for $3 or $1 for $2 rule.

Chapter 12

Multiple Employer Welfare Benefit Trusts

Code Section 419 multiple employer welfare benefit trusts are recent innovations in deferred compensation planning that attempt to minimize or eliminate some of the adverse tax and funding problems typically associated with traditional nonqualified plans. Multiple employer trusts exist in two basic varieties: death benefit multiple employer trusts and severance multiple employer trusts. This chapter attempts to flesh out some of the law in this area to allow the practitioner to determine whether any arrangement under consideration is suitable for a particular client.

Overview

Q 12:1   What is a multiple employer welfare benefit trust?

A multiple employer welfare benefit trust (also known as a 419 program or 419 trust) is a multiple employer arrangement providing death or severance benefits to eligible employees of ten or more unrelated employers. The program consists of a trust to which ten or more employers contribute to fund death or severance benefits under plans adopted by the several employers.

Sponsors and other promoters of these programs claim that contributions by employers to fund death or severance benefits under the programs will be deductible when made under Code Section 162 and that the programs qualify as "ten or more employer plans" under Code Section 419A(f)(6), with the advance funding deduction limitations of Code Section 419 therefore being inapplicable (see Q 12:18).

Q 12:2   Are employer contributions to a multiple employer welfare benefit trust included in participants' income?

Sponsors and other promoters of multiple employer welfare benefit trusts typically claim that contributions made by the employer to the trust to fund death or severance benefits are intended not to be included in a plan participant's gross income. In death benefit plans, or in severance plans funded by life insurance policies, the participant generally pays taxes annually on current death benefit protection at the PS 58 cost of the death benefit protection (see Q 12:21).

Plan death benefits typically are excludible from beneficiaries' gross income under Code Section 101(a). Severance benefits are includible in the participant's gross income when the participant ceases to have a substantial risk of forfeiture in the severance benefits (for example, when the participant has the ability to voluntarily terminate employment and receive benefits) (see Q 12:21).

Whether these tax results may be achieved legally under the Code is questionable, but many informed practitioners believe these results may be achieved under certain circumstances discussed in this chapter. The IRS has issued very little guidance to date on these programs (see Q 12:22).

Comparison to Other Nonqualified Plans and Qualified Plans

Q 12:3 How may a multiple employer welfare benefit trust be compared to the unfunded, nonqualified deferred compensation plans discussed in this book and to tax-qualified retirement plans?

When comparing multiple employer welfare benefit trusts to unfunded, nonqualified deferred compensation plans and tax-qualified retirement plans, it is useful to examine at least five broad areas: the deductibility of contributions; the income tax treatment to participants of benefits under the plan; the security provided by and tax treatment of any funding vehicle used in connection with the plan; the limitations that apply under the law to such plans; and the comfort that interested parties (primarily employers and employees) have that the tax positions they take with respect to the arrangement are the appropriate tax positions.

Q 12:4 How do tax-qualified retirement plans, nonqualified deferred compensation plans, and multiple employer welfare benefit trusts compare with respect to deductibility of contributions?

Tax-Qualified Retirement Plans. Subject to certain amount limitations found in Code Section 404, contributions to Code Section 401(a) tax-qualified retirement plans (Q plans) are deductible when made by the employer.

Nonqualified Deferred Compensation Plans. Amounts contributed by an employer or accrued by a participant under a nonqualified plan are not deductible by the employer until an amount attributable to the contribution or accrual is included in the participating employee's taxable gross income (see Q 1:19). This means, generally, that the employer pays the tax cost of the program, equal to the time value of income taxes paid by the employer during the pendency of the employee's income tax inclusion event, in order to afford the employee deferred income tax inclusion. This typically provides a disincentive for the employer to permit long-term tax deferral by the employee.

Multiple Employer Welfare Benefit Trusts. Code Section 162 allows an employer a deduction for all ordinary and necessary business expenses, including the provision of welfare benefits to employees, even if the value of the benefit is not included in the participant's gross income until after it is paid or incurred by the employer. Code Sections 419 and 419A provide deduction limitations for certain "welfare benefit funds" to which those sections apply. Those Code Sections generally limit deductible contributions to a "welfare benefit fund" to the benefits paid from the fund during the taxable year in which the contributions are made, plus a limited allowance for reserves. Code Section 419A(f)(6) provides an exception to Code Section 419's advanced deduction funding limitations for certain multiple employer trusts to which no employer normally contributes more than 10 percent of the total contributions made by all employers contributing to the trust (see Q 12:18).

Q 12:5   How do tax-qualified retirement plans, nonqualified deferred compensation plans, and multiple employer welfare benefit trusts compare with respect to income tax treatment to participants?

Tax-Qualified Retirement Plans. A participant is not required to include in his or her gross income benefits under a Q plan until he or she receives those benefits, despite the fact that such benefits are held in a trust and are, subject to the participant's satisfaction of a vesting requirement in most cases, not subject to a risk of forfeiture by the participant. The participant may also roll benefits over to another Q plan or IRA, further deferring income tax on the benefits.

Nonqualified Deferred Compensation Plans. Generally, amounts are not taxed to a nonqualified plan participant until such amounts are "made available" to the participant (see Q 1:16). If the nonqualified plan is properly structured, the participant generally is entitled to receive benefits in the event of his or her voluntary termination of employment (there need not be any substantial risk of forfeiture other than from the employer's bankruptcy) and does not have to include in his or her taxable gross income the benefit entitlement prior to the termination or other benefit entitlement event.

Multiple Employer Welfare Benefit Trusts. Amounts received or accrued by a participant under a welfare benefit plan generally are subject to ordinary income tax inclusion rules, including the rule that benefits held in a trusteed environment that ordinarily would be taxable to the participant upon receipt are earlier includible in his or her gross income on the date on which the benefits cease to be subject to a substantial risk of forfeiture by the participant.

Q 12:6 How do tax-qualified retirement plans, nonqualified deferred compensation plans, and multiple employer welfare benefit trusts compare with respect to the security and taxation of the funding vehicle?

Tax-Qualified Retirement Plans. Q plan assets must always be held in trust beyond the access of the employer's creditors. Assets of the trust appreciate on a tax-deferred basis.

Nonqualified Deferred Compensation Plans. Because of creditor access to nonqualified plan benefits upon the employer's bankruptcy or insolvency, these programs do not provide participants with tremendous comfort that benefits ultimately will be paid upon a benefit entitlement event, although certain arrangements, such as rabbi trusts and insurance arrangements, can be structured to increase (but not completely ensure) benefit security (see Qs 1:6–1:10). Also, if a fund is established to provide a source of funds from which the employer can pay benefits under the nonqualified plan, income on the fund typically is taxed to the employer at the employer's income tax rate.

Multiple Employer Welfare Benefit Trusts. If a trust is used (as is required under Code Section 419A(f)(6)), amounts are insulated from the employer's creditors. If the trust is established as a Code Section 501(c)(9) tax-exempt voluntary employees' beneficiary association (VEBA), assets of the trust will appreciate free of taxation. However, because Code Section 419A(f)(6) plans almost always are funded by insurance policies, the tax-exempt nature of the VEBA typically provides unnecessary tax insulation.

Q 12:7   How do tax-qualified retirement plans, nonqualified deferred compensation plans, and multiple employer welfare benefit trusts compare with respect to limitations?

Tax-Qualified Retirement Plans. Q plan benefits are subject to substantial amount limitations and discrimination rules, including the rule that the plan cover a broad cross section of the employer's employees under Code Section 410(b) and the limitation that the Q plan not recognize annual compensation of any participant in excess of $150,000 (as indexed) under Code Section 401(a)(17).

Nonqualified Deferred Compensation Plans. Employers may discriminate in favor of select employees with respect to nonqualified plans. Indeed, for ERISA-governed employers, these plans typically may be maintained only for a "select group of management or highly compensated employees of the employer" (see Qs 2:10–2:29). Benefits under these plans generally are unlimited, except to the extent that the employer's tax costs provide an economic deterrent to long-term tax deferral of large amounts under a nonqualified plan.

Multiple Employee Welfare Benefit Trusts. Depending upon the type of benefit provided and other design considerations (see Q 12:20), these arrangements may be subject to very stringent or very liberal discrimination limitations. Amount limitations may apply (for example, severance plan benefits typically are limited to no greater than two times the participant's final annual compensation, payable within two years of the participant's severance from employment).

Q 12:8   How do tax-qualified retirement plans, nonqualified deferred compensation plans, and multiple employer welfare benefit trusts compare with respect to the comfort of their tax positions?

Tax-Qualified Retirement Plans. Employers typically receive a determination letter from the IRS that their plan is tax-qualified and, therefore, the employer and employees typically have a high degree of comfort that the tax incidents of the Q plan pertain to the Q plan. That is, if the IRS issues a favorable determination letter in respect to a Q plan and the employer administers the Q plan in accordance with its terms, the employer may claim a deduction for all of its contributions to the Q plan in the year in which the contributions are made.

The employer may also take the tax position that Q plan trust asset appreciation is tax exempt and the employee/participant may defer income tax inclusion on Q plan benefits until he or she receives the benefits and may roll over benefits to his or her IRA or new Q plan without compromising the favorable tax treatment of the receiving vehicle, all virtually without any risk that the tax position would be challenged by the IRS as incorrect.

Nonqualified Deferred Compensation Plans. The law in the nonqualified plan area is fairly well settled, and employers may typically take comfort that traditional nonqualified plan design methods achieve the desired tax results.

Multiple Employer Welfare Benefit Trusts. Very little authoritative guidance is available with respect to the tax incidents of these types of arrangements. Rumors abound concerning informal statements by IRS officials and the issuance of "favorable" formal guidance by the IRS as to the tax incidents of these arrangements. (See Q 12:22 for a discussion of recent IRS guidance concerning these arrangements.) VEBA determination letters provide little or no additional comfort, since these letters merely address the tax-exempt status of the funding vehicle (which usually is not necessary given the vehicle's investment in tax-efficient life insurance policies), and *not* the other deduction/tax inclusion incidents of the arrangement. In any event, informed practitioners may conclude on behalf of their clients that substantial authority exists for a variety of beneficial tax positions taken by employers and employees under certain of these programs.

Multiple Employer Death Benefit Trusts

Q 12:9   What is a multiple employer death benefit trust?

A multiple employer death benefit trust is a trust that provides death benefit coverage to employees of ten or more employers. The employer often may specify, by name or by class, the particular employees who will participate in the plan. (Death benefit plans funded by VEBAs and/or death benefit plans providing postretirement death benefits may not discriminate in favor of highly compensated employees (see Q 12:20).

Q 12:10   Who may participate in a multiple employer death benefit trust?

Participation typically is available to owners of the employer who provide bona fide services to the employer as common-law employees. However, participation should not be available to any employee who has total voting control over the employer, such as a sole proprietor, a sole general partner of a limited partnership, or a sole shareholder of the employer/corporation, even if such a person provides bona fide services to the employer as an employee (see Q 12:21). Participation in the plan *cannot be limited* to owners of the employer, but participation in the plan *can be extended* to owners of the employer (other than sole owners of the employer), as long as one or more common-law employees of the employer are made participants in the plan and the plan's coverage of nonowners is bona fide.

Q 12:11   How is the death benefit determined?

Under most multiple employer death benefit trusts, the employer specifies the death benefit that will be offered to participating employees. The death benefit often will be a multiple of each employee's annual compensation. The multiple of compensation selected generally is uniform for all participating employees of the employer and typically is as high as 14. The definition of compensation for these purposes generally may be any reasonable one and is not limited by any dollar limitation (such as the $150,000 limitation under Code Section 401(a)(17)), except if the trust is established as a VEBA.

A participating employee's beneficiaries generally receive death benefits under these plans only if the employee is an active employee on the date of his or her death. This is because postretirement death benefits cause the application of nondiscrimination requirements (see Q 12:20), and vested death benefits would cause the participant to be taxed on the cash value of the life insurance policies as they accrue. A participating employee who terminates employment with the employer for any reason other than death typically will forfeit his or her entire rights under the plan. The method of using these forfeitures (for example, the cash value of the life insurance policy on the life of the forfeiting employee) is critical to the plan's qualification as a ten-or-more-employer plan and thus the deductibility of amounts contributed under the plan under Code Section 419A(f)(6) (see Q 12:17).

Q 12:12   How is a multiple employer death benefit trust terminated?

A participating employer typically has the authority to terminate its plan by action of its board of directors, partners, or other governing body. Upon an employer's termination of its plan, the employer's allocable share of the assets in the program's trust typically is transferred to participating employees. Note that the method of determining an employer's allocable share is critical to the plan's qualification as a ten-or-more-employer plan and thus is critical to the deductibility of contributions under the plan under Code Section 419A(f)(6) (see Q 12:17).

Multiple Employer Severance Benefit Trusts

Q 12:13   What is a multiple employer severance benefit trust?

A multiple employer severance benefit trust is a trust that provides postemployment severance benefits to eligible employees of ten or more employers that participate in the trust.

Q 12:14   Who may participate in a multiple employer severance benefit trust?

The employer often will specify, by name or by class, the particular employees in its employ who will be participants in the plan. Severance benefit plans funded by VEBAs may not discriminate in favor of highly compensated employees (see Q 12:20).

Participation typically is available to owners of the employer who provide bona fide services as common-law employees to the employer. However, participation should not be available to any employee who has greater than a 50 percent interest in the employer, because the raison d'etre of the severance plan is the continuing risk that the employee may some day be fired by the employer, and any employee with a controlling interest in the employer cannot, in either a practical or a legal sense, be fired.

Q 12:15   How is the severance benefit determined?

The employer will specify a severance benefit that will be offered to participating employees at their involuntary termination of employment. The severance benefit often will be a multiple of the employee's final annual compensation, not in excess of two times the employee's final annual cash plus noncash compensation, and payable within two years of the employee's severance. The multiple of compensation selected generally is uniform for all participating employees of the employer. The definition of compensation for these purposes generally may be any reasonable one and is not limited by any dollar limitation (such as the $150,000 limitation under Code Section 401(a)(17)), except if a VEBA is used to fund the severance benefit.

A participating employee receives severance benefits under the plan only if the employee's termination of employment is involuntary. (Some severance benefit plans attempt to make a participant's voluntary termination of employment look like something other than what it is, sometimes by incorporating certain state law unemployment compensation definitions of "involuntary termination of employment" as the benefit entitlement event definitions which actually capture some events that, in reality, constitute voluntary terminations of employment. Notwithstanding these contrivances, benefits under a severance plan are included in the participant's gross income unless the benefits are subject to the risk that, if the employee voluntarily terminates employment, he or she forfeits all benefits under the plan.) Assets with respect to the severance benefits are in a multiple employer trust and, if the program is properly structured under Code Section 419A(f)(6), are available to pay the benefits of all employees of all employers participating in the trust (see Q 12:16). Therefore, the employer has very little incentive to enforce a voluntary termination of employment forfeiture condition, unless the employer considers that a failure to enforce such a condition would be viewed by the IRS as compromising the bona fides of the plan as a welfare plan (rendering prior contributions nondeductible) and as cause for the affected employee to have income in a prior year (e.g., the year the employer developed the intent not to enforce the condition).

Like death benefit plans, severance plans typically contain a funding policy that recognizes a general need or desire of the employer to fund for severance benefits under the plan on a more accelerated basis than level actuarial funding. Many of these plans fully fund severance benefits payable thereunder at an early date in the plan's existence, making dubious the argument that amounts under the plan are subject to a substantial risk of forfeiture in the participant.

Funding and Deductions

Q 12:16 How are multiple employer death benefit and severance plans funded?

The welfare benefit plan—whether a death benefit or a severance plan—is funded by a trust, the assets of which are beyond the access of the employer's (and anyone else's) creditors.

The trust typically holds cash value, whole life insurance policies on the lives of participating employees. For a death benefit, the face value of each policy typically equals the stated death benefit of the employee/insured under the plan. For a severance plan, the cash value of the policy typically approximates the severance benefit payable under the plan.

The trust will hold assets attributable to plans of ten or more unrelated employers. No employer may normally contribute greater than 10 percent of the aggregate annual contributions to a particular trust by all employers in any calendar year.

If the life insurance policy used to fund a particular employee's death/severance benefit has a value in excess of the benefit, the plan should distribute only the specified death/severance benefit, resulting in an experience gain equal to such excess to the trust. To do otherwise (for example, to permit an employee's death/severance benefit to be defined with reference to the value of the life insurance policy) would violate the employer-specific experience-rating proscription discussed in Q 12:17.

Both types of plans typically contain a funding policy that recognizes the employer's need to fund for benefits under the plan on a more accelerated basis than level actuarial funding. This would include, for example, level funding of death benefits, actuarially assumed to be provided over a 20-year period, over the first five years of the employer's participation in the plan through the purchase by the program's trust of a life insurance policy with a required five-year premium schedule that corresponds to this funding timing.

Q 12:17   May a multiple employer welfare trust maintain experience-rating arrangements on an employer-by-employer basis?

No. Because the plans are designed to permit contributions to the plan to be deductible when made by the participating employer under Code Sections 162 and 419A(f)(6), and not otherwise immediately deductible under any other provision of law, Code Section 419A requires that the trust be a ten-or-more-employer trust and that it not maintain any experience-rating arrangements with respect to individual participating employers. No controlling guidance is available under Code Section 419A as to this non-experience-rating condition.

It is clear from the legislative history to Code Section 419 that the experience-rating proscription is intended to create a relationship between each participating employer and the trust that is similar to the relationship of an insured to an insurer. This is in contrast to the relationship of an employer to a self-funded welfare plan, which typically does involve experience rating, and in which the risk of loss or gain is not shifted to the plan but is retained by the employer.

The regulations under Code Section 419 provide that an arrangement is a "fund" (as opposed to a non-experience-rated arrangement) if the employer or its employees will receive a refund, a credit, or additional benefits if claims under the arrangement are less than assumed for funding or paying administrative costs or because of greater-than-anticipated investment experience attributable to the employer. If the employer or its employees stand to benefit economically if the death/severance of the employer's employees under a death/severance benefit plan occurs at a rate lower than assumed, or if an employer's contributions are reduced or increased because the investment experience of the employer's selected insurance contracts is better or worse than expected, then the arrangement is experience-rated under the only reasonable interpretation of the Code and regulations. Thus, such an arrangement would not qualify under Code Section 419A(f)(6), and the employer's contributions to it would not be deductible.

Under many plans, an employee's forfeiture of benefits directly reduces the employer's contribution obligation or increases benefits to the remaining employees, and positive or negative performance of the life insurance policies on the employees' lives reduces or increases the employer's contribution obligation to the trust. Proponents of these plans argue that where the insurance company underwriting the policies bases the cost of insurance on general actuarial tables rather than the employer's claims experience, the plan is not experience rated. This argument seems disingenuous. Under such a plan, an employee's forfeiture of benefits is tantamount to his or her failure to die while employed or failure to sever employment involuntarily, or lack of (or lower than anticipated) claims experience. The resulting forfeitures increase benefits to the employer's remaining employees or decrease the employer's costs. Similarly, the attribution of actual investment experience of a policy selected by the employer to the employer's contribution obligation cannot reasonably be considered anything but experience rating on an employer-by-employer basis. Such an arrangement thus would fail to qualify for the special deduction timing provisions of Code Section 419A(f)(6).

Code Section 419A(f)(6) trusts are permitted to experience rate at large; that is, *among* all employers. If the trust is characterized by the pooling of forfeitures and investment experience, no experience rating on an employer-by-employer basis occurs in the trust.

Q 12:18   What deduction rules apply to a multiple employer welfare trust?

Contributions to the trust are intended to be deductible in the year they are made by the employer, subject to certain conditions. Code

Section 162 allows a deduction for all ordinary and necessary business expenses paid in carrying on a trade or business, unless a special rule under Code Section 162 or another provision of the Code disallows the deduction or requires the deduction to occur during a period other than when the expense is paid or incurred. Ordinary and necessary expenses paid or incurred in carrying on a trade or business include reasonable salaries or "other compensation paid" for personal services actually rendered by employees of the taxpayer. "Other compensation" includes a variety of welfare benefits provided to employees as compensation for personal services actually rendered, including severance and death benefits. (In *Moser v. Commissioner* [56 TCM 1604 (1989), *aff'd* on other grounds, 914 F2d 1040 (8th Cir 1990)], the Tax Court held that a death benefit provided under a plan qualifies as a benefit contemplated by Code Section 162.) Therefore, amounts paid within a taxable year for the provision of death benefits under a plan are deductible under Code Section 162, unless expressly not deductible, limited, or altered by some other provision of the Code.

Potentially applicable provisions of the Code that would affect the deductibility or timing of deductions for contributions under a multiple employer welfare benefit plan include the following:

- The rules applicable to deferred compensation under Treasury Regulation Section 1.162-10(a) and Code Section 404 (see below);
- The limitations on the amount of deductible contributions to advanced funded welfare benefit plans under Code Sections 419 and 419A (see below);
- The requirement that certain expenditures be capitalized over a period of years rather than being fully deductible in the year paid, under Code Sections 263, 263A, 446, and 461(a) (see Q 12:19); and
- The often-made IRS argument that discriminatory plan contributions are not considered under Code Section 162 to be contributions to a welfare benefit plan (see Q 12:20).

Deferred Compensation Plans. Treasury Regulation Section 1.162-10(a) provides that, notwithstanding that amounts paid or accrued for death or severance benefits generally are deductible under Code Section 162(a), "[s]uch amounts shall not be deductible under section 162(a) if, under any circumstances, they may be used to provide benefits under a stock bonus, pension, annuity, profit-sharing, or other deferred compensation plan of the type referred to in section 404(a)." In such an event, the extent to which the amounts are deductible from gross income is governed by the provisions of Code Section 404 and the regulations issued thereunder. (See also Treasury Regulation Section 1.162-10(c), which provides that the deductibility of amounts paid or accrued under a plan deferring the receipt of compensation is governed by Code Section 404 and the regulations thereunder.)

Under Code Section 404(a), amounts contributed to a funded, non-tax-qualified deferred compensation plan are deductible in the tax year in which an amount attributable to the contribution is includible in the gross income of employees participating in the plan. Therefore, Code Section 404(a) requires that the deduction of amounts contributed under a funded deferred compensation plan coincide with the income tax inclusion event of the employee for whom the contribution is made. Amounts accrued under the typical severance or death benefit plan by an employee (in excess of the reasonable net premium cost of the current term life insurance protection received by the employee) are intended not to be included in the employee's (or anyone's) gross income until paid on the employee's behalf or otherwise made available to the employee. Thus, if the "matching" deduction timing rules of Code Section 404(a) were to apply to contributions to such a plan (if the plan were to be deemed a deferred compensation plan under Code Section 404(a)), amounts contributed to the plan would be deductible by the employer only when those amounts were received by a beneficiary or made available to the employee, which generally would be in a year occurring after the year in which the contribution to the plan is made by the employer (that is, at death, involuntary severance, or plan termination).

However, Treasury Regulation Section 1.404(a)-1(a)(2) provides:

> Code Section 404(a) does not apply to a plan which does not defer the receipt of compensation. Furthermore, Code Section 404(a) does not apply to deductions for contributions under a plan which is solely a dismissal or unemployment benefit plan, or a sickness, accident, hospitalization, medical expense, recreation, *welfare or similar benefit plan*, or a combination thereof. [Emphasis added.]

Under Code Section 404(b)(2)(A), any plan providing for deferred benefits (as opposed to deferred compensation) for employees shall be treated as a plan deferring the receipt of compensation, and thus generally would be subject to the deferred deduction timing rules of Code Section 404.

Welfare Benefit Funds. However, Code Section 404(b)(2)(B) provides that Code Section 404(b)(2)(A) does not apply to any benefit provided through a welfare benefit fund (defined in Code Section 419(e) as any fund that is part of a plan of an employer and through which the employer provides welfare benefits to employees' beneficiaries). The term "fund" for this purpose includes any trust that is not exempt from tax.

Code Sections 419 and 419A provide deduction limitations for certain welfare benefit funds to which those Code Sections apply. Those rules generally limit deductible contributions to a welfare benefit fund to the benefits paid from the fund during the taxable year in which the contribution is made, plus a limited allowance for reserves.

The special deduction limitations of Code Sections 419 and 419A for funded welfare benefit plans do not apply in the case of a funded welfare benefit plan that qualifies as a ten-or-more-employer plan under Code Section 419A(f)(6). A ten-or-more-employer plan is a plan to which more than one employer contributes; to which no employer normally contributes more than 10 percent of the total contributions made to the plan by all employers; and that does not "maintain experience-rating arrangements with respect to individual employers" (see Q 12:17).

Q 12:19 What deduction rules apply to advance contributions to a welfare benefit fund?

Three possible challenges exist to the current deductibility of contributions to a welfare benefit fund that are made on a more accelerated basis than level actuarial funding:

1. Such contributions are not "ordinary" expenses because they create a benefit or asset lasting substantially beyond the close of the tax year in which those contributions were made (and

therefore are in the nature of capital expenditures that are not currently deductible under Code Section 162(a)).

2. The taxpayer's control over the plan causes the plan to be a "private asset reserve" rather than a bona fide welfare benefit plan.

3. In the case of an accrual basis taxpayer, the contribution fails to satisfy the requirement under the Code Section 461(h) "all-events test" that "economic performance" occur with respect to an item of expense before a deduction is allowable for that expense.

Regarding the capitalization argument, the courts have uniformly held that, where the benefits under a plan relate primarily to the well-being of participating employees rather than the well-being of the employer, and where the employer has relinquished sufficient control over the contributions such that the employer cannot direct the disposition of funds prior to their use in paying benefits or paying for benefits, no capitalization of the expenditure is required. This is particularly the case where the employer does not have a contractual obligation to provide in the future the types of benefits provided at the time of the plan's adoption.

Regarding the prepaid expense argument, if a contribution to discharge an employer's obligation to a welfare benefit plan for a particular year relates only to the year in which the payment is made, and if the employer does not have a contribution obligation in a future year that it is discharging in the current year by making the current year's contribution, no definite and determinable future expense obligation is being prepaid within the meaning of the "prepaid expense" doctrine that would require deferred tax deductibility. [See Joel A Schneider, MD, SC v Comm'r, 63 TC 1787 (1992) and Texas Instruments v United States, 551 F2d 599 (5th Cir 1977)]

Under the all-events test, "a liability . . . is incurred, and generally is taken into account for federal income tax purposes, in the taxable year in which all the events have occurred that establish the fact of the liability, the amount of the liability can be determined with reasonable accuracy, and economic performance has occurred with respect to the liability." [Treas Reg § 1.461-1(a)(2)] Treasury Regulation Section 1.419-1T(Q&A-10(e)) provides that, in determining the extent to which contributions to a welfare benefit fund satisfy the requirements of the all-events test, economic performance occurs as contributions to the welfare benefit fund are made.

Q 12:20   May multiple employer welfare arrangements discriminate in favor of highly paid employees?

Sometimes. Cases suggest that plans that are substantially controlled by their employer-sponsor and that benefit exclusively the owners of the employer-sponsor are deferred compensation plans subject to the deduction rules under Code Section 404 (see Q 12:18). [Greensboro Pathology Associates, PA v United States, 698 F2d 1196 (Fed Cir 1982); Citric Orthopedic Medical Group Inc v Comm'r, 72 TC 461 (1979); Sunrise Construction Co Inc v Comm'r, 52 TCM 1358 (1987), aff'd 863 F2d 886 (9th Cir 1988); and Grant-Jacoby Inc v Comm'r 73 TC 700 (1980)]

Otherwise, the imposition by implication or case law of a broad nondiscrimination requirement as a condition of deductibility of contributions to a plan that otherwise qualifies as a welfare benefit plan under Code Section 162 seems to be wholly inconsistent with the intricate statutory scheme governing nondiscrimination in both deferred compensation plans and welfare benefit plans under the Code. These closely related (and sometimes applicable) areas include Code Sections 505(b) and 4976. Other than where these sections apply and where the plan does not benefit only owners, the law does not support the application of nondiscrimination rules to multiple employer welfare benefit plans.

Code Section 505(b) provides that the coverage and benefits of a 419 welfare benefit fund structured as a Code Section 501(c)(9) tax-exempt VEBA must be nondiscriminatory. Clearly, if the plan is not merely a 419 welfare benefit fund but also attempts to qualify for tax exemption as a VEBA, the plan would be subject to these nondiscrimination rules. The fact that Congress imposed specific nondiscrimination standards upon the tax-exempt character of such an arrangement, but not upon the deductibility of contributions to such an arrangement (or the character of the arrangement for deduction purposes), indicates Congress's intent that nondiscrimination requirements do not apply to the deductibility of contributions to a 419 plan not qualifying as a VEBA (or the character of the arrangement for deduction purposes).

Code Section 4976 imposes an excise tax on an employer that maintains a welfare benefit fund (within the meaning of Code Section 419(e), like most 419 death benefit/severance plans) in an amount equal to 100 percent of any so-called disqualified benefit provided under such a fund. A disqualified benefit for this purpose means: (1) a postretirement medical benefit or postretirement life insurance benefit provided by such a fund to certain key employees; (2) a postretirement medical benefit or postretirement life insurance benefit provided to certain highly compensated individuals unless the plan satisfies the nondiscrimination requirements under Code Section 505(b) (without regard to whether the plan is a VEBA); and (3) any portion of a welfare benefit fund reverting to the benefit of the employer.

Income Tax Consequences to Employees

Q 12:21   What are the income tax consequences to participants in a multiple employer welfare benefit arrangement?

Under the typical arrangement, employer contributions to the trust are not intended to be includible in a participating employee's federal gross income beyond the portion of such contributions representing the reasonable net premium cost of the insurance protection the employee receives during the taxable year (that is, only the PS 58 value of the plan's death benefit protection is includible in the employee's gross income).

Treasury Regulation Section 1.61-2(d)(6)(ii) provides that the income tax treatment of contributions made to an employee's trust that is not an exempt trust under Code Section 501(a) is governed by Code Section 402(b) and the regulations thereunder. Code Section 402(b)(1) provides that contributions to a non-tax-qualified employee's trust is included in the employee's gross income in accordance with Code Section 83(a), which provides that

> [i]f, in connection with the performance of services, property is transferred to any person other than the person for whom such

services are performed, the excess of (1) the fair market value of such property . . . at the first time the rights of the person having the beneficial interest in such property are transferrable or are not subject to a substantial risk of forfeiture, whichever occurs earlier, over (2) the amount (if any) paid for such property, shall be included in the gross income of the person who performed such services in the first taxable year in which the rights of the person having the beneficial interest in such property are transferrable or are not subject to a substantial risk of forfeiture.

Thus, an employee must include in his or her federal gross income contributions made by an employer to a death benefit or severance trust for his or her benefit except to the extent that, under the facts and circumstances, the benefits attributable to such contributions are transferable (which the benefits never are), subject to a substantial risk of forfeiture by the employee.

If one were to apply these rules to a common type of multiple employer death benefit trust, one would conceptualize contributions by an employer to a death benefit trust as having two components: (1) the cost of current death benefit protection received during the year by the employee under the plan, and (2) amounts in excess of such cost, which are intended to provide future death benefit protection to the employee.

The death benefit protection (measured by the lower of the PS 58 cost or the insurer's published term rates) an employee receives through participating in the plan during the year is actually received by the employee in that year and therefore is subject to tax.

If the employee terminates employment with the employer for any reason other than death, he or she typically forfeits all rights to such assets. The issue is whether these risks of forfeiture are "substantial risks of forfeiture" under Code Section 83. If the forfeiture rule is enforced or expected to be enforced in the year the employee terminates employment, the risk of forfeiture is substantial, and the employee will not be taxed on excess contributions over the cost of term protection made by the employer on his or her behalf.

Amounts potentially receivable on termination of the plan, but not yet received, would not ordinarily be includible in participating employees' gross income until the employees receive the benefits at termination. Issues might arise in the case of a controlling shareholder/employee who has the unfettered ability to terminate the plan through action of the employer's board of directors or other governing body and thus to cause a termination distribution to the controlling shareholder/employee. In such a case, measures might be taken to create a substantial risk of forfeiture, such as by imposing an enforceable supermajority voting requirement with respect to plan termination or, more effectively, making the plan interminable in such cases.

To apply these rules to a multiple employer severance trust, the question of the existence of a substantial risk of forfeiture under a severance plan, as under a death benefit plan, is a facts and circumstances determination. In order for participating employees to avoid current income taxation on amounts in the trust dedicated to their severance benefit, because of the trust's funded status under the Code, such employees must not have access to the funds in the event of their voluntary termination of employment at any time. Accordingly, under severance plans, participating employees may receive benefits only in the event of an involuntary termination event, including involuntary termination of employment by the employer, death, or disability, but not including retirement or any other voluntary termination of employment.

The incorporation into the plan of objective standards, such as an incorporation of a state-law definition of involuntary termination of employment for unemployment benefits eligibility, does not control the determination as to whether the risk of forfeiture is substantial. For example, if the state law will pay unemployment benefits upon a substantially voluntary termination of employment, the use of the state law's definition of involuntary termination of employment will create no substantial risk of forfeiture of benefits by the employee, and, consequently, will lead to current income tax on benefits held in the trust. Thus, severance plans often require aggressive tax positions to be taken in order to reach the desired tax results, unless the plans are structured as bona fide involuntary reductions in workforce plans designed to protect employees in the event of their being fired.

IRS Guidance

Q 12:22 Has the IRS issued any guidance concerning its position on multiple employer welfare benefit trusts?

Yes. On May 19, 1995, the IRS issued Notice 95-34, detailing certain features of multiple employer welfare benefit trusts that it believes would compromise the advance deduction/deferred income tax treatment typically associated with such plans in their marketing activities.

First, the IRS expresses its disapproval of plans bearing deferred compensation characteristics. Specifically, these include arrangements that purport to be severance plans containing a substantial risk of forfeiture in the event a participant terminates employment voluntarily but actually substantially guarantee payment (see Q 12:21).

Next, the IRS notice addresses the ten-or-more-employer exemption under Code Section 419A(f)(6). Specifically, the IRS formally expresses its hostility to arrangements that act not as a multiplicity of employers in one plan but as separate plans using separate accounting and merely coexisting in one multiple employer trust (see Q 12:17).

Finally, the IRS adds its usual catch-all argument that it has advanced unsuccessfully in many cases in the past with respect to valid, prefunded welfare benefit plans; that is, that "other sections of the Internal Revenue Code" might prevent immediate deductibility of contributions to a multiple employer plan otherwise properly designed under Code Section 419A(f)(6), such as the "prepaid expense" doctrine (see Q 12:19).

Chapter 13

The Life Cycle of a Nonqualified Plan

The life cycle of a nonqualified plan includes the design, adoption, implementation, operation, and termination of the plan. The process involves specific steps that should be taken at each stage of the plan's life cycle. This chapter provides an overview of these steps and suggests considerations that should be taken into account throughout the plan's life cycle.

Overview

Q 13:1 How should an employer begin consideration of a possible nonqualified plan?

Because top-hat nonqualified deferred compensation plans are not subject to the very rigid design strictures and onerous regulatory requirements imposed on plans subject to the tax-qualified retirement plan rules under the Internal Revenue Code (Code; IRC) or the full regulatory burdens applicable to non-top-hat deferred compensation plans under ERISA, such plans are extremely flexible, are largely contractual in nature, and may be designed to serve a wide range of organizational objectives.

Before selecting a particular kind of nonqualified plan, an employer should examine its organizational objectives with respect to the plan to determine the design features that would best achieve those objectives (see Q 13:3).

Q 13:2   What advisors should an employer consult to help draft a nonqualifed plan?

Appropriate advisors should be involved from the beginning of the plan design process. The advisors should include the employer's senior management and Human Resources Managers who have the information and the authority to make and implement decisions regarding the plan. Outside advisors should include an attorney who is experienced in the nonqualifed plan area, an investment advisor who is knowledgeable about investment alternatives available for funding nonqualified plan benefits, and an accountant who is familiar with the employer's finances and the impact of a nonqualified plan on the employer's financial status.

Designing a Nonqualified Plan

Q 13:3   What kinds of organizational objectives might affect a plan's establishment or design?

Following are some typical objectives that are important to many organizations in setting up nonqualified plans.

Attracting and retaining qualified executives. This is generally a basis of all nonqualified plans and, indeed, of all employee benefit plans. For a nonqualified plan, this objective would be maximized by competitive plan benefit levels, deferred vesting of substantial benefits, and similar incentives to encourage executives to remain in the sponsor's employ.

Maximizing income tax deferral and tax deferred savings possibilities. If the employer merely desires to permit its executives to maximize the tax efficiency of their savings dollars, the employer could select a salary-reduction-only vehicle that provides for the investment of the deferred dollars, thus increasing total return relative to after-tax savings. The employer may thus choose a compensation deferral plan under which the employer contributes the amount of the reduced compensation, on a pretax basis, to a rabbi trust that invests those dollars for the benefit of the executive (see chapter 4).

Achieving parity with regard to the percentages of allowed deferred compensation by executives and nonexecutive employees. Code Section 401(a)(17) limits the amount of compensation that can be recognized under a tax-qualified plan to $150,000 annually. Thus, a highly compensated executive earning in excess of that amount would receive a smaller percentage of his or her compensation in the employer's tax-qualified plan than a nonexecutive employee. These rules also force the employer to pay less in terms of funding benefits for executive employees, resulting in an unwanted reduction of the agreed-upon compensation package due from the employer to the executive. These dynamics frequently justify the establishment of a nonqualified plan that levels the deferred compensation playing field for executives and rank-and-file employees.

Preventing competition by executives after termination. Unfunded nonqualified plans are not subject to the vesting rules of ERISA. Thus, notwithstanding the length of an executive's service with the employer, nonqualified plan benefit payments may be made contingent upon the executive's continued satisfaction of conditions set forth in the plan, including a condition that the executive refrain from employment with a competitor of the employer.

Q 13:4 Should nonqualified plan contributions be elective, nonelective, or both?

If the contributions are nonelective, they may be:

1. *Vested or nonvested.* Employers frequently subject amounts of nonelective employer contributions to a deferred vesting schedule, creating a "golden handcuff" effect (see chapter 1).

2. *Mandatory or discretionary.* Employers may make nonelective contributions each year either on a mandatory basis or based on a discretionary amount determined by the employer. Mandatory contributions offer a more attractive benefit to the

executive but may lead to hardship if the employer encounters cash-flow problems in a future year. However, a properly drafted and expansive amendment section in a nonqualified plan has the effect of making any mandatory-contribution language discretionary in fact, permitting the employer to amend such a provision if the need arises.

3. *Uniform or discriminatory.* Because no nondiscrimination rules apply to nonqualified plans (other than the *requirement* that the plan discriminate by including only members of the "select group"), the employer has the discretion to make different levels of contributions for different employees, may set different defined contributions for different named employees, or may make contributions uniform for all participants.

If the contributions are elective, the timing of an employee's recognition of income with respect to elective salary reduction contributions to a nonqualified plan could be affected by the constructive receipt and economic benefit doctrines. For example, the employee can effectively defer taxation on the deferred compensation only if the election to defer the compensation is made prior to the executive's acquiring the right to receive the compensation. Accordingly, care should be taken in the drafting of elective deferral-type nonqualified plans to avoid constructive receipt and to ensure that the election to defer is made prior to the availability of the compensation to the executive.

Q 13:5   Should the nonqualified plan be structured as a defined contribution plan or a defined benefit plan?

Defined benefit plan. A defined benefit nonqualified plan expresses the benefit either as a set amount payable at a specific date in the future (presumably at retirement) or as an amount determined with respect to a formula (such as a percentage of compensation multiplied by the years of service at the payment date). Although nonqualified plans structured as defined benefit plans do not carry with them the typical burdens of tax-qualified defined benefit plans, if the employer wishes the funding of the defined benefit plan to be substantially precise, the services of an actuary, at an additional cost to the employer, might be needed. Defined benefit plans often are used where no side fund or other arrangement is established for "funding" the nonqualified plan promise. In contrast, defined contribution nonqualified plans generally have identifiable funds set aside for payment of benefits.

Defined contribution plan. Defined contribution nonqualified plans are generally easier to understand than defined benefit nonqualified plans and thus are more appreciated by executives because of the identifiable account balance from year to year. Employers also favor these plans because they shift the risk of the investment performance of underlying assets to participating executives.

Q 13:6 Who should participate in the nonqualified plan?

When using a generic participant definition, considerable care should be taken to ensure that all persons in the class of eligible participants satisfy the "select group of management or highly compensated employees" standard, particularly in light of the narrow construction the DOL currently gives those terms. When defining the participants group, consider these possibilities:

1. *Certain named individuals.* Participants might be certain named individuals who qualify as members of a select group of management or highly compensated employees of the sponsoring employer.

2. *Certain office holders.* Participants might be individuals holding certain offices within the organization (such as president or vice president).

3. *Certain highly compensated individuals.* Participants might be individuals earning greater than a certain level of compensation (such as $150,000 annually). If the established dollar amount is sufficiently high relative to the compensation of all of the members of the employer's workforce, such a definition may be a workable way of establishing an eligible top-hat class of executives, particularly because participants need only be management *or* highly compensated to ensure that the plan is a top-hat plan.

Q 13:7 Who should direct investments of deferred amounts?

Because the fiduciary responsibility provisions of ERISA do not apply to nonqualified plans, the liability considerations motivating a plan sponsor to select one person or another to direct the investment of plan assets generally do not apply to nonqualified plans. The design choice in this area generally is motivated by considerations of fairness (giving the investment discretion to the party who will suffer or gain the most from good or bad asset performance), expertise (giving the investment discretion to the party most likely to maximize asset appreciation), and similar, nonliability-based factors. Some possible choices for the position of investment manager are:

1. *The participant.* In a defined contribution nonqualified plan, participants frequently are given the power to direct investment of assets deferred through the plan.

2. *The employer.* In a defined benefit nonqualified plan (where the employer bears the risk of disappointing investment perform-ance) and in some defined contribution plans, the employer directs the investments of deferred amounts.

3. *An outside investment manager.* Investment direction fre-quently is vested in an outside investment manager, particu-larly where professional asset management is desired.

4. *No one.* Often, no specific assets are set aside to fund the employer's obligations under a nonqualified plan, as is the case in many defined benefit nonqualified plans and defined contri-bution nonqualified plans that merely impute interest on de-ferred amounts.

Q 13:8   What events trigger a distribution of benefits from a nonqualified plan?

The following are common distribution events under nonqualified plans:

- Death;
- Disability;
- Involuntary termination of employment;
- Hardship;
- Constructive termination;
- Change in control of plan sponsor;
- Voluntary termination of employment at any time; and

- Voluntary termination after a certain period of years of service or age.

As long as the plan does not become "funded" (see Q 1:6) so as to cause income tax inclusion at the vesting date, income tax inclusion should not occur until the occurence of a distribution event.

Care must be taken when in establishing a hardship distribution entitlement to ensure that the preconditions to distribution are sufficient to prevent the participant's constructive receipt of benefits.

A change in control over benefits entitlement in a nonqualified plan may affect the ability of the sponsor's shareholders to sell control over the sponsor. Further, negative tax consequences may attend payment upon a change in control under the golden parachute rules (see chapter 9).

If substantial limitation exists as to the participant's current receipt of nonqualified plan benefits, income tax inclusion should not occur merely because the plan includes a voluntary termination of employment distribution event, as long as a voluntary termination of employment has not occured.

While the inclusion of a voluntary termination of employment benefit entitlement diminishes a nonqualified plan's golden handcuff effect (see chapter 1), it increases the attractiveness of the arrangement from the perspective of the participating executives.

Q 13:9   Who should pay administration fees and/or taxes attributable to the nonqualified plan?

The sponsor frequently pays the cost of administration of the plan and, less frequently, pays taxes that are attributable to appreciation of the assets intended to satisfy the employer's obligation under the plan (for example, in the case of a nonqualified plan funded by a rabbi trust, where the assets of the trust are taxed to the employer, as grantor, at the employer's tax rate).

Administration fees and/or taxes also often are "netted out" of assets used to fund the nonqualified plan or out of any eventual distribution. This adversely affects the value of nonqualified plan benefits to the participant.

Q 13:10   What distribution options may be available?

Unlike participants in nonqualified, ineligible deferred compensation plans maintained by tax-exempt entities and governmental employers (see chapter 10), participants in nonqualified plans sponsored by for-profit employers can continue to defer taxation on nonqualified deferred compensation amounts beyond the date of the participant's vesting in the benefits and until receipt of the benefits by the participant, provided the participant does not constructively receive the benefits before actually receiving them.

Common nonqualified plan distribution options are:

- Cash lump sum;
- Installments; and
- Annuity distributions (because Title I of ERISA does not apply to nonqualified plans, the spousal-right rules do not apply those plans).

Q 13:11   How should the nonqualified plan be funded?

The issue of funding a nonqualified plan goes to the very essence of it's nonqualified status, because a nonqualified plan is required to be "unfunded" for purposes of Title I of ERISA. The plan's funded/unfunded status also affects the taxation of vested plan benefits to participating executives. The following may be approaches used to satisfy the employer's obligations under a nonqualified plan.

Completely unfunded. Under this approach, the employer does not set aside any funds internally or otherwise for purposes of satisfying its obligations under the nonqualified plan. Although this approach ensures unfunded status under ERISA and the Internal Revenue Code, it provides very little security to participants against the sponsor's change of financial condition, change of control, change of heart, or poor planning (see Qs 2:5–2:7).

Rabbi trust. A rabbi trust is a fund for setting aside deferred compensation assets. The rabbi trust's assets are at all times (until paid to the nonqualified plan participant) subject to the claims of the nonqualified plan sponsor's bankruptcy or insolvency creditors. The rabbi trustee who holds the assets has a state law fiduciary responsibility to dispose of trust assets (that is, to pay benefits) in accordance with the terms of the trust, except in the case of the employer's bankruptcy or insolvency. Although this approach does not protect the participant in the event of the employer's insolvency or bankruptcy, it does provide certain security against nonbankruptcy-related failures to pay, such as failure of change of control or change of heart (see chapter 4).

Secular trust. The insulation of assets from the employer's creditors in such a way that the assets may not be used other than for the payment of nonqualified plan benefits would disqualify the arrangement as a top-hat plan because it would be considered funded for purposes of both ERISA and the Code (see chapter 5).

Third-party guaranty. A third-party guaranty, such as from the plan sponsor's corporate parent, can add additional solvency-related security for participants and, as long as the guarantor's promise to pay is unsecured and unfunded, would not cause the arrangement to be funded for ERISA or Internal Revenue Code purposes (see Q 2:7).

Surety bond or insurance protection. A plan participant can purchase insurance or other surety protection against the sponsor's non-payment under the nonqualified plan (see Q 2:3).

Corporate-owned life insurance. This method of funding nonqualified plan benefits can provide a variety of tax benefits to the sponsoring employer and the executive (for example, tax-deductible policy loan payments, tax-deferred build-up of cash value within the insurance policy, and tax-free death benefits) and, if properly structured, will not cause the plan to be funded for ERISA and Internal Revenue Code purposes (see chapter 7).

Planning Pointer. If the plan sponsor provides a bonus to the executive for the overt purpose of covering the cost of any surety bond or insurance, such an action might cause the IRS or the DOL to argue that the plan is funded for ERISA and/or Internal Revenue Code purposes.

Implementing, Operating, and Terminating a Nonqualified Plan

Q 13:12 What are the typical steps in the adoption of a nonqualified plan?

Adopting a nonqualified plan typically requires action by the board of directors as well as execution by appropriate officer(s) of the organization. The board's responsibilities include:

1. Preparing and executing resolutions approving the plan and funding methodology, if applicable, and directing the appropriate officers of the sponsoring employer to execute the governing documentation;

2. Appraising the board of any tax or other liability risks associated with plan design or the selected funding methodology; and

3. Specifying the eligible participants in the plan (if the board is empowered to select eligible participants under the plan documentation). After the board has reached final agreement, an appropriate officer of the sponsoring employer should execute the plan document and any other plan-related documents that call for employer signatures.

Q 13:13 What are the typical steps in implementing a nonqualified plan?

Election forms. Each participant should sign and fill out the following initial elections, as applicable:

- Beneficiary designation form;
- Salary reduction election form;
- Form of payment election form; and
- Deemed investment election form.

Planning Pointer. The timing of execution of salary reduction election forms and form of payment election forms could have important tax consequences under the constructive receipt doctrine.

Notification of payroll department. The employer's payroll department should be notified of elections for purposes of salary payment adjustments, federal/state income tax reporting, tax-qualified retirement plan contributions, FICA/FUTA tax reporting, and so forth.

Recordkeeping. Proper controls should be established to track and reflect accrued benefits, deferred compensation earnings, and other plan accounting and recordkeeping matters.

Compliance filing. A top-hat alternative method of compliance filing should be made with the Department of Labor, if required.

Q 13:14   How is the investment strategy selected for a nonqualified plan?

The investment strategy for a nonqualified plan is determined by several factors, including how the plan will be funded and who will be permitted to direct investments of deferred amounts. If the employer determines that assets should be set aside to fund the benefit obligation, the employer should develop an investment strategy that meets the employer's organizational objectives. If the plan benefit will be the participant's plan account balance held in a rabbi trust, the employer may decide to give the participant the right to direct investments.

Q 13:15   What are the typical steps in the operation of a nonqualifed plan?

The following steps generally need to be taken annually in the operation of a nonqualified plan:

1. Collect salary reduction/bonus deferral election forms, if applicable;

2. Ensure that all participants continue to be members of a select group of management or highly compensated employees;

3. Select new employees for participation;

4. Determine and have the board authorize the annual contribution amount; and

5. Determine whether any amounts were made available (that is, paid to or constructively received by any participant) during the year and withhold/report tax accordingly.

Q 13:16 What steps typically need to be taken to terminate a nonqualified plan?

A nonqualified plan can terminate in two ways: by operation of law or by action of the sponsoring employer's board of directors.

Termination of the plan by operation of law occurs when all participants have been paid their full plan benefits and no further benefit obligations exist under the plan. If, following the payment of all plan benefits, assets remain which were set aside to fund the benefit obligations, the employer should take the necessary action to recover those assets. If assets are held in a trust, the employer must notify the trustee that no further benefit obligations exist. The trustee should then terminate the trust, distribute all remaining assets to the employer, and prepare any final accounting required under the trust agreement.

Termination of the plan by action of the board of directors is necessary if the employer decides to terminate the plan before it otherwise would terminate by operation of law. Typically, termination of a plan by board action requires the following steps:

1. Determine how benefits will be paid to plan participants upon plan termination. Alternatives include payment as otherwise provided under the plan and participants' distribution elections, immediate cash-out of benefits (the plan and the participant distribution elections should be drafted to permit this option), and the purchase of annuities that provide for the payment of benefits identical to the payments otherwise provided under the plan and any distribution elections.

2. Apprise the board of any tax or other liability risks associated with the termination of the plan and the distribution of benefits.

3. Prepare and execute board resolutions terminating the plan, approving the distribution methodology, and directing the appropriate officers of the employer to take the actions necessary to terminate the plan and distribute benefits.

4. Notify participants of the termination of the plan and the methodology for the distribution of benefits that have accrued.

5. Notify the trustee of any related trust of the plan's termination and direct the trustee to pay benefits pursuant to the methodology adopted by the board.

6. Distribute benefits pursuant to the methodology adopted by the board.

Following the distribution of all benefits, the steps necessary for a termination by operation of law should occur:

- Removal of restrictions on remaining assets set aside to fund the benefit obligations;
- Notification of the trustee of any related trust of the termination of the plan;
- Termination of any related trust; and
- Preparation by the trustee of any final accounting required under the trust agreement.

Appendix A

Model Grantor Trust Document (Revenue Procedures 92-64 and 92-65)

Part III. Administrative Procedural, and Miscellaneous

26 CFR 601.201: Rulings and determination letters.

(Also Part I, Sections 61, 83, 402, 451, 671, and 677; 1.83-1, 1.83-3, 1.451-2, 1.671-1, 1.671-3, and 1.677(a)-1.)

Rev. Proc. 92-64

SECTION 1. PURPOSE

This revenue procedure contains a model grantor trust for use in executive compensation arrangements that are popularly referred to as "rabbi trust" arrangements. This revenue procedure also provides guidance for requesting rulings on nonqualified deferred compensation plans that use such trusts.

SEC. 2. BACKGROUND

The Internal Revenue Service receives and responds to many requests for rulings on the federal income tax consequences of trusts established in connection with unfunded deferred compensation arrangements. In many of these requests, the trust instruments are very similar. Consequently, in order to aid taxpayers and to expedite the processing of ruling requests on these arrangements, this revenue procedure provides a model trust instrument that plan sponsors may use.

SEC. 3. SCOPE AND OBJECTIVE

The model trust provided in this revenue procedure is intended to serve as a safe harbor for taxpayers that adopt and maintain grantor trusts in connection with unfunded deferred compensation arrangements. If the model trust is used in accordance with this revenue procedure, an employee will not be in constructive receipt of income or incur an economic benefit solely on account of the adoption or maintenance of the trust. However, the desired tax effect will be achieved only if the nonqualified deferred compensation arrangement effectively defers compensation. Thus, no inference may be drawn by reason of adoption of the model trust concerning constructive receipt of economic benefit issues that may be present in the underlying nonqualified deferred compensation plan. In addition, the use of the model trust does not change the rules generally applicable under section 6321 of the Code with respect to the attachment of a federal tax lien to a taxpayer's property and rights to property.

The Service will continue to rule on unfunded deferred compensation plans that do not use a trust, on unfunded deferred compensation plans that use the model trust, and, where the model trust is used, generally, on the issue of whether a trust constitutes a grantor trust within the meaning of subpart E, part I, subchapter J, chapter 1, subtitle A of the Internal Revenue Code of 1986. However, rulings will not be issued on unfunded deferred compensation arrangements that use a trust other than the model trust, except in rare and unusual circumstances.

Taxpayers that adopt the model trust and wish to obtain a ruling on the underlying nonqualified deferred compensation plan must include a representation that the plan, as amended, is not inconsistent with the terms of the trust and must follow the guidelines outlined in Section 4 of this revenue procedure and Revenue Procedure 92-65 [Internal reference: page 16, this Bulletin]. Rulings issued on such deferred compensation arrangements will continue to provide that the Service expresses no opinion as to the consequences of the arrangement under Title I of the Employee Retirement Income Security Act of 1974 ("ERISA"). The Department of Labor has advised that whether a "top hat" or excess benefit plan is funded or unfunded depends upon all of the facts and circumstances. However, it is the DOL's view that such plans will not fail to be "unfunded" for purposes of sections 4(b)(5), 201(2), 301(a)(3) and 401(a)(1) of ERISA solely because there is maintained in connection with such a plan a trust which conforms to the model trust described in Section 5 of this revenue procedure.

In addition, rulings issued on deferred compensation arrangements using the model trust will provide that the Service expresses no opinion on the consequences under subchapter C of chapter 1 of subtitle A of the Code or under sections 1501 through 1504 on the trust's acquisition, holding, sale or disposition of stock of the grantor.

SEC. 4. GUIDANCE REGARDING TRUSTS

01. A private letter ruling on a nonqualified deferred compensation arrangement using a grantor trust subject to the claims of the employer's creditors will be issued only if the trust conforms to the model language contained in Section 5 of this revenue procedure. The model language must be adopted verbatim, except where substitute language is expressly permitted.

The request for a ruling must be accompanied by a representation that the trust conforms to the model trust language contained in this revenue procedure, including the order in which sections of the model trust language appear, and that the trust adopted does not contain any inconsistent language, in substituted portions or elsewhere, that conflicts with the model trust language. Of course, provisions may be renumbered if appropriate, language in brackets may be omitted, and blanks may be completed. In addition, the taxpayer may add sections to the model language provided that such additions are not inconsistent with the model language. Finally, the submission must also include a copy of the trust on which all substituted or additional language is either underlined or otherwise clearly marked and on which the location of the required investment authority language is indicated.

02. The request for a ruling must contain a representation that the trust is a valid trust under state law and that all of the material terms and provisions of the trust, including the creditors' rights clause, are enforceable under the appropriate state laws.

03. The trustee of the trust must be an independent third party that may be granted corporate trustee powers under state law, such as a bank trust department or other similar party.

SEC. 5. MODEL PROVISIONS

01. The model trust language in this section contains all provisions necessary for operation of the trust except for provisions describing the trustee's investment powers. Provisions agreed to by the parties should be used to describe investment powers. The trustee must be given some investment discretion, such as the authority to invest within broad guidelines established by the parties (e.g., invest in government securities, bonds with specific ratings, or stocks of Fortune 500 companies).

The model trust language contains a number of optional provisions, which are printed in italics and marked as *"OPTIONAL."* The taxpayer may substitute language of its choice for any optional provision, provided that the substituted language is not inconsistent with the language of the model trust. The model trust language also contains several alternative provisions, which are printed in italics and marked as *"ALTERNATIVE."* The taxpayer must choose one of these alternatives. Items in brackets are explanatory.

02. The text of the model trust follows.

TRUST UNDER _____ PLAN

OPTIONAL

(a) This Agreement made this __ day of _____, by and between _____ (Company) and _____ (Trustee);

OPTIONAL

(b) WHEREAS, Company has adopted the nonqualified deferred compensation Plan(s) as listed in Appendix __.

OPTIONAL

(c) WHEREAS, Company has incurred or expects to incur liability under the terms of such Plan(s) with respect to the individuals participating in such Plan(s);

(d) WHEREAS, Company wishes to establish a trust (hereinafter called "Trust") and to contribute to the Trust assets that shall be held therein, subject to the claims of Company's creditors in the event of Company's Insolvency, as herein defined, until paid to Plan participants and their beneficiaries in such manner and at such times as specified in the Plan(s);

(e) WHEREAS, it is the intention of the parties that this Trust shall constitute an unfunded arrangement and shall not affect the status of the Plan(s) as an unfunded plan maintained for the purpose of providing deferred compensation for a select group of management or highly compensated employees for purposes of Title I of the Employee Retirement Income Security Act of 1974;

(f) WHEREAS, it is the intention of Company to make contributions to the Trust to provide itself with a source of funds to assist it in the meeting of its liabilities under the Plan(s);

NOW, THEREFORE, the parties do hereby establish the Trust and agree that the Trust shall be comprised, held and disposed of as follows:

Section 1. *Establishment of Trust.*

(a) Company hereby deposits with Trustee in trust ____ [insert amount deposited], which shall become the principal of the Trust to be held, administered and disposed of by Trustee as provided in this Trust Agreement.

ALTERNATIVES—Select one provision.

(b) The Trust hereby established shall be revocable by Company.

(b) The Trust hereby established shall be irrevocable.

(b) The Trust hereby established is revocable by Company; it shall become irrevocable upon a Change of Control, as defined herein.

(b) The Trust shall become irrevocable __ [insert number] days following the issuance of a favorable private letter ruling regarding the Trust from the Internal Revenue Service.

(b) The Trust shall become irrevocable upon approval by the Board of Directors.

(c) The Trust is intended to be a grantor trust, of which Company is the grantor, within the meaning of subpart E, part I, subchapter J, chapter 1, subtitle A of the Internal Revenue Code of 1986, as amended, and shall be construed accordingly.

(d) The principal of the Trust, and any earnings thereon, shall be held separate and apart from other funds of Company and shall be used exclusively for the uses and purposes of Plan participants and general creditors as herein set forth. Plan participants and their beneficiaries shall have no preferred claim on, or any beneficial ownership interest in, any assets of the Trust. Any rights created under the Plan(s) and this Trust Agreement shall be mere unsecured contractual rights of Plan participants and their beneficiaries against Company. Any assets held by the Trust will be subject to the claims of Company's general creditors under federal and state law in the event of Insolvency, as defined in Section 3(a) herein.

ALTERNATIVES—Select one or more provisions, as appropriate.

(e) Company, in its sole discretion, may at any time, or from time to time, make additional deposits of cash or other property in trust with Trustee to augment the principal to be held, administered and disposed of by Trustee as provided in this Trust Agreement. Neither Trustee nor any Plan participant or beneficiary shall have any right to compel such additional deposits.

(e) Upon a Change of Control, Company shall, as soon as possible, but in no event longer than __ [fill in blank] days following the Change of Control, as defined herein, make an irrevocable contribution to the Trust in an amount that is sufficient to pay each Plan participant or beneficiary the benefits to which Plan participants or their beneficiaries would be entitled pursuant to the terms of the Plan(s) as of the date on which the Change of Control occurred.

(e) Within __ [fill in blank] days following the end of the Plan year(s), ending after the Trust has become irrevocable pursuant to Section 1(b) hereof, Company shall be required to irrevocably deposit additional cash or other property to the Trust in an amount sufficient to pay each Plan participant or beneficiary the benefits payable pursuant to the terms of the Plan(s) as of the close of the Plan year(s).

Section 2. *Payments to Plan Participants and Their Beneficiaries.*

(a) Company shall deliver to Trustee a schedule (the "Payment Schedule") that indicates the amounts payable in respect of each Plan participant (and his or her beneficiaries), that provides a formula or other instructions acceptable to Trustee for determining the amount so payable, the form in which such amount is to be paid (as provided for or available under the Plan(s)), and the time of commencement for payment of such amounts. Except as otherwise provided herein, Trustee shall make payments to the Plan participants and their beneficiaries in accordance with such Payment Schedule. The Trustee shall make provision for the reporting and withholding of any federal, state or local taxes that may be required to be withheld with respect to the payment of benefits pursuant to the terms of the Plan(s) and shall pay amounts withheld to the appropriate taxing authorities or determine that such amounts have been reported, withheld and paid by Company.

(b) The entitlement of a Plan participant or his or her beneficiaries to benefits under the Plan(s) shall be determined by Company or such party as it shall designate under the Plan(s), and any claim for such benefits shall be considered and reviewed under the procedures set out in the Plan(s).

(c) Company may make payment of benefits directly to Plan participants or their beneficiaries as they become due under the terms of the Plan(s). Company shall notify Trustee of its decision to make payment of benefits directly prior to the time amounts are payable to participants or their beneficiaries. In addition, if the principal of the Trust, and any earnings thereon, are not sufficient to make payments of benefits in accordance with the terms of the Plan(s), Company shall make the balance of each such payment as it falls due. Trustee shall notify Company where principal and earnings are not sufficient.

Section 3. *Trustee Responsibility Regarding Payments to Trust Beneficiary When Company Is Insolvent.*

(a) Trustee shall cease payment of benefits to Plan participants and their beneficiaries if the Company is Insolvent. Company shall be considered "Insolvent" for purposes of this Trust Agreement if (i) Company is unable to pay its debts as they become due, or (ii) Company is subject to a pending proceeding as a debtor under the United States Bankruptcy Code.

OPTIONAL

, or (iii) Company is determined to be insolvent by ____ [insert name of applicable federal and/or state regulatory agency].

(b) At all times during the continuance of this Trust, as provided in Section 1(d) hereof, the principal and income of the Trust shall be subject to claims of general creditors of Company under federal and state law as set forth below.

(1) The Board of Directors and the Chief Executive Officer [or substitute the title of the highest ranking officer of the Company] of Company shall have the duty to inform Trustee in writing of Company's Insolvency. If a person claiming to be a creditor of Company alleges in writing to Trustee that Company has become Insolvent, Trustee shall determine whether Company is Insolvent and, pending such determination, Trustee shall discontinue payment of benefits to Plan participants or their beneficiaries.

(2) Unless Trustee has actual knowledge of Company's Insolvency or has received notice from Company or a person claiming to be a creditor alleging that Company is Insolvent, Trustee shall have no duty to inquire whether Company is Insolvent. Trustee may in all events rely on such evidence concerning Company's solvency as may be furnished to Trustee and that provides Trustee with a reasonable basis for making a determination concerning Company's solvency.

(3) If at any time Trustee has determined that Company is Insolvent, Trustee shall discontinue payments to Plan participants or their beneficiaries and shall hold the assets of the Trust for the benefit of Company's general creditors. Nothing in this Trust Agreement shall in any way diminish any rights of Plan participants or their beneficiaries to pursue their right as general creditors of Company with respect to benefits due under the Plan(s) or otherwise.

(4) Trustee shall resume the payment of benefits to Plan participants or their beneficiaries in accordance with Section 2 of this trust Agreement only after Trustee has determined that Company is not Insolvent (or is no longer Insolvent).

(c) Provided that there are sufficient assets, if Trustee discontinues the payment of benefits from the Trust pursuant to Section 3(b) hereof and subsequently resumes such payments, the first payment following such discontinuance shall include the aggregate amount of all payments due to Plan participants or their beneficiaries under the terms of the Plan(s) for the period of such discontinuance, less the aggregate amount of any payments made to Plan participants or their beneficiaries by Company in lieu of the payments provided for hereunder during any such period of discontinuance.

Section 4. *Payments to Company.*

[The following need not be included if the first alternative under 1(b) is selected.]

Except as provided in Section 3 hereof, after the Trust has become irrevocable, Company shall have no right or power to direct Trustee to return to Company or to divert to others any of the Trust assets before all payment of benefits have been made to Plan participants and their beneficiaries pursuant to the terms of the Plan(s).

Section 5. *Investment Authority.*

ALTERNATIVES—Select one provision, as appropriate.

(a) *In no event may Trustee invest in securities (including stock or rights to acquire stock) or obligations issued by Company, other than a de minimis amount held in common investment vehicles in which Trustee invests. All rights associated with assets of the Trust shall be exercised by Trustee, and shall in no event be exercisable by or rest with Plan participants.*

(a) *Trustee may invest in securities (including stock or rights to acquire stock) or obligations issued by Company. All rights associated with assets of the Trust shall be exercised by Trustee or the person designated by Trustee, and shall in no event be exercisable by or rest with Plan participants.*

OPTIONAL

, except that voting rights with respect to Trust assets will be exercised by Company.

OPTIONAL

, except that dividend rights with respect to Trust assets will rest with Company.

OPTIONAL

Company shall have the right, at any time, and from time to time in its sole discretion, to substitute assets of equal fair market value for any asset held by the Trust.

[If the second Alternative 5(a) is selected, the trust must provide either (1) that the trust is revocable under Alternative 1(b), or (2) the following provision must be included in the Trust]:

"Company shall have the right at any time, and from time to time in its sole discretion, to substitute assets of equal fair market value for any asset held by the Trust. This right is exercisable by Company in a nonfiduciary capacity without the approval or consent of any person in a fiduciary capacity."

Section 6. *Disposition of Income.*

ALTERNATIVES—Select one provision.

(a) During the term of this Trust, all income received by the Trust, net of expenses and taxes, shall be accumulated and reinvested.

(a) During the term of this Trust, all, or ____ [insert amount] part of the income received by the Trust, net of expenses and taxes, shall be returned to Company.

Section 7. *Accounting by Trustee.*

OPTIONAL

Trustee shall keep accurate and detailed records of all investments, receipts, disbursements, and all other transactions required to be made, including such specific records as shall be agreed upon in writing between Company and Trustee. Within __ [insert number] days following the close of each calendar year and within __ [insert number] days after the removal or resignation of Trustee, Trustee shall deliver to Company a written account of its administration of the Trust during such year or during the period from the close of the last preceding year to the date of such removal or resignation, setting forth all investments, receipts, disbursements and other transactions effected by it, including a description of all securities and investments purchased and sold with the cost or net proceeds of such purchases or sales (accrued interest paid or receivable being shown separately), and showing all cash, securities and other property held in the Trust at the end of such year or as of the date of such removal or resignation, as the case may be.

Section 8. *Responsibility of Trustee*

OPTIONAL

(a) Trustee shall act with the care, skill, prudence and diligence under the circumstances then prevailing that a prudent person acting in like capacity and familiar with such matters would use in the conduct of an enterprise of a like character and with like aims, provided, however, that Trustee shall incur no liability to any person for any action taken pursuant to a direction, request or approval given by Company which is contemplated by, and in conformity with, the terms of the Plan(s) or this Trust and is given in writing by Company. In the event of a dispute between Company and a party, Trustee may apply to a court of competent jurisdiction to resolve the dispute.

OPTIONAL

(b) If Trustee undertakes or defends any litigation arising in connection with this Trust, Company agrees to indemnify Trustee against Trustee's costs, expenses and liabilities (including, without limitation, attorneys' fees and expenses) relating thereto and to be primarily liable for such payments. If Company does not pay such costs, expenses and liabilities in a reasonably timely manner, Trustee may obtain payment from the Trust.

OPTIONAL

(c) Trustee may consult with legal counsel (who may also be counsel for Company generally) with respect to any of its duties or obligations hereunder.

OPTIONAL

(d) Trustee may hire agents, accountants, actuaries, investment advisors, financial consultants or other professionals to assist it in performing any of its duties or obligations hereunder.

(e) Trustee shall have, without exclusion, all powers conferred on Trustees by applicable law, unless expressly provided otherwise herein, provided, however, that if an insurance policy is held as an asset of the Trust, Trustee shall have no power to name a beneficiary of the policy other than the Trust, to assign the policy (as distinct from conversion of the policy to a different form) other than to a successor Trustee, or to loan to any person the proceeds of any borrowing against such policy.

OPTIONAL

(f) However, notwithstanding the provisions of Section 8(e) above, Trustee may loan to Company the proceeds of any borrowing against an insurance policy held as an asset of the Trust.

(g) Notwithstanding any powers granted to Trustee pursuant to this Trust Agreement or to applicable law, Trustee shall not have any power that could give this Trust the objective of carrying on a business and dividing the gains therefrom, within the meaning of section 301.7701-2 of the Procedure and Administrative Regulations promulgated pursuant to the Internal Revenue Code.

Section 9. *Compensation and Expenses of Trustee.*

OPTIONAL

Company shall pay all administrative and Trustee's fees and expenses. If not so paid, the fees and expenses shall be paid from the Trust.

Section 10. *Resignation and Removal of Trustee.*

(a) Trustee may resign at any time by written notice to Company, which shall be effective __ [insert number] days after receipt of such notice unless Company and Trustee agree otherwise.

OPTIONAL

(b) Trustee may be removed by Company on __ [insert number] days' notice or upon shorter notice accepted by Trustee.

OPTIONAL

(c) Upon a Change of Control, as defined herein, Trustee may not be removed by Company for __ [insert number] year(s).

OPTIONAL

(d) If Trustee resigns within __ [insert number] year(s) after a Change of Control, as defined herein, Company shall apply to a court of competent jurisdiction for the appointment of a successor Trustee or for instructions.

OPTIONAL

(e) If Trustee resigns or is removed within __ [insert number] year(s) of a Change of Control, as defined herein, Trustee shall select a successor Trustee in accordance with the provisions of Section 11(b) hereof prior to the effective date of Trustee's resignation or removal.

(f) Upon resignation or removal of Trustee and appointment of a successor Trustee, all assets shall subsequently be transferred to the successor Trustee. The transfer shall be completed within __ [insert number] days after receipt of notice of resignation, removal or transfer, unless Company extends the time limit.

(g) If Trustee resigns or is removed, a successor shall be appointed, in accordance with Section 11 hereof, by the effective date of resignation or removal under paragraph(s) (a) [or (b)] of this section. If no such appointment has been made, Trustee may apply to a court of competent jurisdiction for appointment of a successor or for instructions. All expenses of Trustee in connection with the proceeding shall be allowed as administrative expenses of the Trust.

Section 11. *Appointment of Successor.*

OPTIONAL

(a) If Trustee resigns [or is removed] in accordance with Section 10(a) [or (b)] hereof, Company may appoint any third party, such as a bank trust department or other party that may be granted corporate trustee powers under state law, as a successor to replace Trustee upon resignation or removal. The appointment shall be effective when accepted in writing by the new Trustee, who shall have all of the rights and powers of the former Trustee, including ownership rights in the Trust assets. The former Trustee shall execute any instrument necessary or reasonably requested by Company or the successor Trustee to evidence the transfer.

OPTIONAL

(b) If Trustee resigns or is removed pursuant to the provisions of Section 10(e) hereof and selects a successor Trustee, Trustee may appoint any third party such as a bank trust department or other party that may be granted corporate trustee powers under state law. The appointment of a successor Trustee shall be effective when accepted in writing by the new Trustee. The new Trustee shall have all the rights and powers of the former Trustee, including ownership rights in Trust assets. The former Trustee shall execute any instrument necessary or reasonably requested by the successor Trustee to evidence the transfer.

OPTIONAL

(c) The successor Trustee need not examine the records and acts of any prior Trustee and may retain or dispose of existing Trust assets, subject to Sections 7 and 8 hereof. The successor Trustee shall not be responsible for and Company shall indemnify and defend the successor Trustee from any claim or liability resulting from any action or inaction of any prior Trustee or from any other past event, or any condition existing at the time it becomes successor Trustee.

Section 12. *Amendment or Termination.*

(a) This Trust Agreement may be amended by a written instrument executed by Trustee and Company. [Unless the first alternative under 1(b) is selected, the following sentence must be included.] Notwithstanding the foregoing, no such amendment shall conflict with the terms of the Plan(s) or shall make the Trust revocable after it has become irrevocable in accordance with Section 1(b) hereof.

(b) The Trust shall not terminate until the date on which Plan participants and their beneficiaries are no longer entitled to benefits pursuant to the terms of the Plan(s) [unless the second alternative under 1(b) is selected, the following must be included:], "unless sooner revoked in accordance with Section 1(b) hereof." Upon termination of the Trust any assets remaining in the Trust shall be returned to Company.

OPTIONAL

(c) Upon written approval of participants or beneficiaries entitled to payment of benefits pursuant to the terms of the Plan(s), Company may terminate this Trust prior to the time all benefit payments under the Plan(s) have been made. All assets in the Trust at termination shall be returned to Company.

OPTIONAL

(d) Section(s) _____ [insert number(s)] of this Trust Agreement may not be amended by Company for __ [insert number] year(s) following a Change of Control, as defined herein.

Section 13. *Miscellaneous.*

(a) Any provision of this Trust Agreement prohibited by law shall be ineffective to the extent of any such prohibition, without invalidating the remaining provisions hereof.

(b) Benefits payable to Plan participants and their beneficiaries under this Trust Agreement may not be anticipated, assigned (either at law or in equity), alienated, pledged, encumbered or subjected to attachment, garnishment, levy, execution or other legal or equitable process.

(c) This Trust Agreement shall be governed by and construed in accordance with the laws of _____.

OPTIONAL

(d) For purposes of this Trust, Change of Control shall mean: [insert objective definition such as: "the purchase or other acquisition by any person, entity or group of persons, within the meaning of section 13(d) or 14(d) of the Securities Exchange Act of 1934 ("Act"), or any comparable successor provisions, of beneficial ownership (within the meaning of Rule 13d-3 promulgated under the Act) of 30 percent or more of either the outstanding shares of common stock or the combined voting power of Company's then outstanding voting securities entitled to vote generally, or the approval by the stockholders of Company of a reorganization, merger or consolidation, in each case, with respect to which persons who were stockholders of Company immediately prior to such reorganization, merger or consolidation do not, immediately thereafter, own more than 50 percent of the combined voting power entitled to vote generally in the election of directors of the reorganized, merged or consolidated Company's then outstanding securities, or a liquidation or dissolution of Company or of the sale of all or substantially all of Company's assets"].

Section 14. *Effective Date.*

The effective date of this Trust Agreement shall be _____, 19 .

SEC. 6. EFFECTIVE DATE

01. This revenue procedure is effective on July 28, 1992.

02. Ruling requests with respect to grantor trusts used in executive compensation arrangements and subject to the claims of the employer's creditors that are submitted to the Service subsequent to the effective date of this revenue procedure must comply with the terms of this revenue procedure.

03. This revenue procedure does not affect any private letter rulings that were issued prior to the effective date. If a plan or trust that was the subject of such a ruling is amended, and such amendments affect the rights of participants or other creditors, such ruling will generally not remain in effect.

SEC. 7. PUBLIC COMMENT

Written comments, including suggested language, concerning the model trust provision contained in this revenue procedure may be sent to the Internal Revenue Service, Office of the Associate Chief Counsel, (Employee Benefits and Exempt Organizations), Attention: CC:EE:1:1, Room 5201, P.O. 7604, Ben Franklin Station, Washington, D.C. 20044.

DRAFTING INFORMATION

The principal author of this revenue procedure is Catherine Livingston Fernandez of the Office of the Associate Chief Counsel, (Employee Benefits and Exempt Organizations). For further information regarding this revenue procedure contact Ms. Fernandez at (202) 622-6030 (not a toll-free call).

---

26 CFR 601.201: Rulings and determination letters.

(Also Part I, Sections 404, 451: 1.404(a)-12, 1.451-1)

Rev. Proc. 92-65

SECTION 1. PURPOSE

01. The purpose of the Revenue Procedure is to set forth the conditions, or circumstances, under which the Internal Revenue Service will issue advance rulings concerning the application of the doctrine of constructive receipt to unfunded deferred compensation arrangements and to amplify Rev. Proc. 71-19, 1971-1 C.B. 698.

SEC. 2. BACKGROUND

In 1960, the Service issued Rev. Rul. 60-31, 1960-1 C.B. 174, concerning the application of the doctrine of constructive receipt to certain deferred compensation arrangements. Rev. Rul. 60-31 was modified by Rev. Rul. 64-279, 1964-2 C.B. 121, and Rev. Rul. 70-435, 1970-2 C.B. 100. The conditions under which the Service would issue advance rulings on unfunded deferred compensation arrangements were originally published in Rev. Proc. 71-19, 1971-1 C.B. 698.

SEC. 3. SCOPE AND OBJECTIVE

01. In each request for a ruling involving the deferral of compensation, the Service will determine whether the doctrine of constructive receipt is applicable on a case by case basis. The Service will ordinarily issue rulings regarding unfunded deferred compensation arrangements only if the requirements of Rev. Proc. 71-19 are met and, in addition, the arrangement meets the following guidelines.

(a) Section 3.01 of Rev. Proc. 71-19 states that, if the plan provides for an election to defer payment of compensation, such election must be made before the beginning of the period of service for which the compensation is payable, regardless of the existence in the plan of forfeiture provisions. The period of service for purposes of this requirement generally has been regarded by the Service as the employee's taxable year for cash basis, calendar year taxpayers. Rev. Rul. 68-86, 1968-1 C.B. 184; Rev. Rul. 69-650, 1969-2 C.B. 106; Rev. Rul. 71-419, 1971-2 C.B. 220. The Service will issue advance rulings under two exceptions to this general requirement, as follows:

(1) In the year in which the plan is first implemented, the eligible participant may make an election to defer compensation for services to be performed subsequent to the election within 30 days after the date the plan is effective for eligible employees.

(2) In the first year in which a participant becomes eligible to participate in the plan, the newly eligible participant may make an election to defer compensation for service to be performed subsequent to the election within 30 days after the date the employee becomes eligible.

(b) The plan must define the time and method for payment of deferred compensation for each event (such as termination of employment, regular retirement, disability retirement or death) that entitles a participant to receive benefits. The plan may specify the date of payment or provide that payments will begin within 30 days after the occurrence of a stated event.

(c) The plan may provide for payment of benefits in the case of "unforeseeable emergency." "Unforeseeable emergency" must be defined in the plan as an unanticipated emergency that is caused by an event beyond the control of the participant or beneficiary and that would result in severe financial hardship to the individual if early withdrawal were not permitted. The plan must further provide that any early withdrawal approved by the employer is limited to the amount necessary to meet the emergency. Language similar to that described in section 1.457-2(h)(4) and (5) of the Income Tax Regulations may be used.

(d) The plan must provide that participants have the status of general unsecured creditors of the employer and that the plan constitutes a mere promise by the employer to make benefit payments in the future. If the plan refers to a trust, the plan must also provide that any trust created by the employer and any assets held by the trust to assist it in meeting its obligations under the plan will conform to the terms of the model trust, as described in Rev. Proc. 92-64 [Internal reference: page 11, this Bulletin]. Finally, the plan must state that it is the intention of the parties that the arrangements be unfunded for tax purposes and for purposes of Title I of ERISA.

(e) The plan must provide that a participant's rights to benefit payments under the plan are not subject in any manner to anticipation, alienation, sale, transfer, assignment, pledge, encumbrance, attachment, or garnishment by creditors of the participant or the participant's beneficiary.

SEC. 4. PROCEDURE

The general procedures of Rev. Proc. 92-1, 1992-1 I.R.B. 9, relating to the issuance of ruling and determination letters, and Rev. Proc. 71-19, 1971-1 C.B. 698, apply to requests relating to unfunded deferred compensation arrangements to the extent they are not covered by this revenue procedure.

SEC. 5. EFFECT ON OTHER REVENUE PROCEDURES

Rev. Proc. 71-19, 1971-C.B. 698, is hereby amplified to set forth the conditions under which the Service will issue advance rulings on unfunded deferred compensation plans.

SEC. 6. EFFECTIVE DATE

The revenue procedure is effective on July 28, 1992.

DRAFTING INFORMATION

The principal author of this revenue procedure is Catherine Livingston Fernandez of the Office of the Assistant Chief Counsel, (Employee Benefits and Exempt Organizations). For further information regarding this revenue procedure contact Ms. Fernandez at (202) 622-6030 (not a toll-free call).

Appendix B

Uniform Premiums for $1,000 of Group–Term Life Insurance Protection

5-year age bracket	Cost per $1,000 of protection for 1-month period
Under 30	$0.08
30 to 34	.09
35 to 39	.11
40 to 44	.17
45 to 49	.29
50 to 54	.48
55 to 59	.75
60 to 64	1.17
65 to 69	2.10
70 and above	3.76

[Amended November 17, 1989 by T.D. 8273, and July 29, 1992 by T.D. 8424.]

Appendix C

Proposed Rules Regarding Golden Parachutes

FEDERAL DEPOSIT INSURANCE CORPORATION

12 CFR Part 359

RIN 3064–AB11

Regulation of Golden Parachutes and Other Benefits Which Are Subject to Misuse

Agency: Federal Deposit Insurance Corporation ("FDIC" or "Corporation").

Action: Notice of proposed rulemaking.

Summary: The FDIC is proposing a rule limiting golden parachute and indemnification payments to institution-affiliated parties by insured depository institutions, depository institution holding companies and their subsidiaries and affiliates. The purpose of this proposed rule is to prevent the improper disposition of institution assets and to protect the financial soundness of insured depository institutions, depository institution holding companies, their subsidiaries and affiliates, and the federal deposit insurance funds.

Dates: Comments must be received by December 6, 1991.

Addresses: Send comments to Hoyle L. Robinson, Executive Secretary, Federal Deposit Insurance Corporation, 550 17th Street N.W., Washington, DC 20429. Comments may be hand-delivered to room 400, 1776 F Street N.W., Washington, DC 20429, on business days between 8:30 a.m. and 5 p.m. (FAX number: (202) 898–3838.)

For Further Information Contact: Michael D. Jenkins, Examination Specialist, Division of Supervision, (202) 898–6896; Jeffrey M. Kopchik, Counsel, Legal Division, (202) 896–3872; Federal Deposit Insurance Corporation, 550 17th Street NW., Washington, DC 20429.

Supplementary Information

Paperwork Reduction Act

No collections of information pursuant to section 3504(h) of the Paperwork Reduction Act (44 U.S.C. 3501 et seq.) are contained in the proposed rule. Consequently, no information has been submitted to the Office of Management and Budget for review.

Regulatory Flexibility Act

Pursuant to section 605(b) of the Regulatory Flexibility Act (Pub. L. 96–354, 5 U.S.C. 601 et seq.), it is certified that the proposed rule would not have a significant impact on a substantial number of small entities.

Discussion

Section 2523 of the Comprehensive Thrift and Bank Fraud Prosecution and Taxpayer Recovery Act of 1990[1] ("Fraud Act") amended the Federal Deposit Insurance Act ("FDI Act") by adding a new section 18(k). Public Law No. 101–647, section 2523 (1990). This new section 18(k)(1) provides that "[t]he Corporation may prohibit or limit, by regulation or order, any golden parachute payment or indemnification payment." 12 U.S.C. 1828(k)(1). The terms "golden parachute payment" and "indemnification payment" are defined in sections 18(k)(4) and (5)(A) of the FDI Act, respectively. *Id.* at 1828(k)(4) and (5)(A).

The FDIC has decided to commence a rulemaking proceeding because it is of the opinion that the intent of section 18(k) is best administered by regulation. A regulation will enable insured depository institutions, depository institution holding companies, their subsidiaries and affiliates, and institution-affiliated parties ("IAP's") to enter into lawful compensation and indemnification agreements without inadvertently violating the intent of section 18(k). The Corporation is extremely interested in receiving comments concerning this important regulation. It is especially interested in comments concerning the "*bona fide* deferred compensation plan or arrangement" exception which is contained in section 18(k) (12 U.S.C. 1828(k)(4)(C)(ii)) and defined in § 359.1(d) of the proposed regulation.

Background

Although a golden parachute payment can take a variety of forms, generally it is a substantial cash payment which is made to an executive officer of a corporation at the termination of his/her employment. Golden parachute payments originally were used by non-financial services companies to protect executive officers involved in hostile takeovers. However, over the course of the past several years, their use has expanded. Golden parachute payments and arrangements have become much more common in the financial services industry than ever before and their use is no longer limited to circumstances involving hostile takeovers. The majority of golden parachute agreements which the FDIC has encountered over the course of the past several years provide for payments upon termination of employment for any reason, except dishonesty or breach of fiduciary duty. The FDIC's concern with regard to such payments is that they may be inappropriate, and represent unsafe and unsound practices in the case of an institution which is experiencing financial difficulties. In the case of an institution which is close to insolvency, a significant golden parachute payment could "push the institution over the edge." Moreover, when an insured institution fails, amounts paid prior to failure pursuant to golden parachute agreements ultimately increase the cost of the failure to the deposit insurance funds.

Indemnification payments are payments which either reimburse officers, directors and employees for legal and other professional expenses incurred in defending themselves in legal proceedings growing out of their affiliation with the institution or pay such expenses "up front." Such payments can be made by the institution directly or pursuant to some form of commercial insurance policy. Although indemnification agreements may represent accepted business practice, the FDIC is concerned that, in certain circumstances, such agreements may undermine the ability of the various financial institution regulatory agencies to enforce federal banking laws and regulations. The deterrent effect of a penalty levied or judgment obtained against an IAP is negated if that penalty or judgment is paid or reimbursed by the institution or its holding company pursuant to an indemnification agreement.

With regard to golden parachute payments, the following are examples of abuses which the FDIC has encountered in actual situations:

(1) A bank was rated a composite "4," had equity capital significantly below the established regulatory minimum and experienced significant losses during its last year of operation with no immediate prospects for improvement. The institution's chief executive officer had held his position with the institution for a significant period of time and was responsible for the policies and practices which led to the institution's financial difficulties. The CEO elected to retire two and one-half years prior to the termination of his existing employment agreement and requested payment of 100 percent of salary, approximately $1,250,000, plus retirement benefits equal to $300,000 per year. He received a portion of the requested payments. These payments caused a significant dissipation of assets and adversely affected the earnings of the bank.

(2) A savings association was in a "troubled" condition. As part of its plan for correction with the regulator, the institution's board of directors agreed to look for a buyer. The institution's president and cashier requested and received agreements that each of them would be paid $500,000 if the institution were sold.

(3) As a result of an examination, the FDIC concluded that a small, local bank was insolvent and informed the bank's president and board of directors of the finding.

The board initially agreed to cooperate with the regulators and allow on-site review of loan files by prospective bidders until the FDIC could arrange for the institution's sale within the next couple of months. Approximately one month after the FDIC informed the institution that it was insolvent, the institution's president informed the board that he had decided to resign prior to the bank's closure and requested that he be paid for the remainder of the term of his employment agreement in a lump sum. The institution's board of directors agreed, and paid the resigning president approximately $62,000.

These examples are representative of some of the types of abuses which the FDIC has encountered involving golden parachute payments. In each of these cases, institutions which were experiencing severe financial difficulties paid or agreed to pay substantial sums to institution-affiliated parties. These payments were not in the best interests of the institution and, therefore, not in the best interest of the FDIC. They demonstrate the need for limitations on such payments in order to prevent the dissipation of an institution's assets and to protect the deposit insurance funds.

With regard to indemnification payments, the following are examples of abuses which the FDIC has encountered in actual situations:

(1) An institution was rated a composite "5" and scheduled to be placed in conservatorship. Two months prior to commencement of the conservatorship, the institution's board of directors transferred $100,000 of the institution's funds to its holding company which deposited those funds in another institution in order to pay anticipated legal expenses of the institution's senior officers and directors. In addition, the board authorized a $100,000 prepayment to the institution's outside law firm for the same purpose. These payments were made to protect directors from possible lawsuits if the institution closed, and for the defense of actions taken by regulators.

(2) As a result of an FDIC examination, a bank was determined to be insolvent. The FDIC informed the bank's board of directors that the institution would likely be closed within the next several months. Approximately one week after the FDIC's notice, the board made a $100,000 prepayment to cover anticipated legal expenses to the bank's outside law firm. Several weeks later, the bank's president utilized bank funds to purchase a $100,000 certificate of deposit at another financial institution to be used as a "self insurance indemnity trust account." These payments were made to protect directors from possible lawsuits if the bank closed, and for the defense of actions taken by regulators.

These examples are representative of the types of abuses which the FDIC has encountered involving indemnification payments. They demonstrate that limitations on indemnification payments are necessary in order to protect the financial integrity of insured institutions and to preserve the deterrent effect of administrative or civil enforcement actions which result in judgments against institution-affiliated parties.

Prior to the passage of the Fraud Act, the Chairman of the FDIC testified in support of a statutory provision restricting golden parachute payments on four separate occasions.[2] On one such occasion, the Chairman stated that:

> The FDIC thinks it unconscionable that directors, officers and others responsible for an insured institution's failure—or near failure—should be able to line their pockets with an insured institution's money at the expense of the Federal deposit insurance funds. Paying golden parachute money to a director, officer, or other responsible party in the case of a failed or failing insured institution amounts essentially to paying that person with a check drawn on the Federal deposit insurance funds.

Testimony of L. William Seidman, Chairman, Federal Deposit Insurance Corporation, Committee on the Judiciary, United States Senate, July 24, 1990.

The legislative history of the Fraud Act indicates that the authority to prohibit or limit golden parachute and indemnification payments was conferred on the FDIC by Congress as part of its effort to provide the Corporation with "additional tools to combat fraud and abuse affecting financial institutions." 136 Cong. Rec. E3684 (daily ed. November 2, 1990) (statement of Rep. Schumer). More specifically, subtitle B of the Fraud Act, where section 2523 appears, "is aimed at protecting assets from wrongful disposition * * *." *Id.* In supporting this new authority, the FDIC was aware of several recent examples (in addition to those described above) of insured depository institutions which had paid institution-affiliated parties substantial sums upon the termination of their employment despite the fact that each institution was in an unsound condition when the payment was made and that the individual who received the payment was a longstanding member of senior management who caused, was responsible for, or had been in a position to have been able to influence the institution's activities and policies which resulted in its unsatisfactory financial condition.

Thus, it is the FDIC's opinion that golden parachute and indemnification payments, as defined in the Fraud Act, are not appropriate or justified except in the clearly-defined circumstances discussed below.

Enforcement

It is the FDIC's view that enforcement of this proposed regulation will be a matter for the appropriate federal banking agency, although the regulation requires the FDIC's written concurrence in the event that an institution or its holding company requests permission to make a golden parachute payment. In the event that an institution or holding company chooses to make such a request, the FDIC expects that the institution would make simultaneous and identical submissions to its primary regulator and the FDIC so that each agency could properly and promptly evaluate the institution's request. Also, the legislative history of section 18(k) makes clear that this section of the Fraud Act is not intended to limit or restrict the appropriate federal banking agencies from exercising their existing authority to restrict such payments or other unsafe and unsound practices. *Id.*

Generally, the proposed regulation prohibits institutions which are insolvent, in conservatorship or receivership, rated "4" or "5," in a troubled condition as defined in the regulations of the appropriate federal banking agency, or which are subject to a proceeding to terminate deposit insurance from making any payment to an institution-affiliated party which is contingent on the termination of that person's affiliation with the institution, except payments of death or disability payments, payments pursuant to qualified retirement plans and two other exceptions which are described in more detail below. The proposed regulation also prohibits institutions from paying or reimbursing an institution-affiliated party's legal and other professional expenses incurred in administrative or civil proceedings instituted by an appropriate federal banking agency unless certain criteria are satisfied. Under no circumstances does the regulation allow the reimbursement or payment of fines or penalties assessed or judgments or settlements obtained against an institution-affiliated party as a result of such a proceeding.

Exceptions to Golden Parachute Payment Prohibition

The FDIC is proposing three "exceptions" to the prohibition against golden parachute payments.[3] First, § 359.4 of the proposed regulation allows an insured depository institution, depository institution holding company and any subsidiary or affiliate thereof to make a golden parachute payment to an institution-affiliated party who is hired by an institution or holding company with the written consent of the appropriate federal banking agency at a time when the institution or holding company satisfies any of the criteria set forth in § 359.1(g)(1)(ii) of the proposed regulation,[4] and whose golden parachute agreement is approved by the FDIC. These criteria are taken from section 18(k). (12 U.S.C. 1828(k)(4)(A)(II)).

The purpose of this exception is to permit a troubled institution or depository institution holding company to attempt to reverse its slide toward economic failure by attracting competent, new management which enjoys the confidence of that institution's primary federal regulator and the FDIC. However, the FDIC is aware that individuals who possess the experience and expertise which qualify them for such a position are highly sought after business persons who, in most circumstances, already have established successful careers with other financial institutions. In order to induce such an individual to leave an established, stable career for a job in a troubled institution which may not survive regardless of that individual's efforts, it is generally necessary to agree to pay that individual some sort of severance payment in the event that the efforts of the individual for the institution are not successful. It is the FDIC's view that, as long as the individual is not guilty of improper conduct while in the troubled institution's employ (as delineated in § 359.2(b) of the proposed regulation), such agreements reflect good business judgment, recognize the realities of the marketplace and may benefit both the institution and the deposit insurance funds.

The second "exception" is contained in § 359.1(g) of the proposed regulation, which defines a "golden parachute payment." The FDIC recognizes that one important tool in restoring an institution to financial health may be institutional downsizing through personnel reductions in force. In such situations, institutions may choose to employ an existing severance pay plan or adopt a new plan to assist employees whose employment is terminated. In addition, many corporations (in various industries) maintain severance pay plans which pay benefits to employees who lose their jobs through no fault of their own, for reasons such as an overall reduction in force.

It is the FDIC's view that section 18(k) is not intended to discourage financial institutions from making the difficult, but sometimes necessary, decision to reduce expenses by reducing staff and from providing some sort of reasonable and responsible financial assistance to affected employees. The FDIC is also of the opinion that section 18(k) is not intended to invalidate traditional severance benefits for employees who lose their jobs (through no fault of their own) for other reasons. Thus, § 359.1(g)(2)(iv) of the proposed regulation provides that the term "golden parachute payment" does not include any payment made pursuant to a nondiscriminatory severance plan or arrangement which provides for the payment of severance benefits to all eligible employees upon involuntary termination for other than cause. However, the proposal limits the maximum severance benefit that any employee may receive pursuant to such a plan to six months' base salary because in the view of the FDIC, absent such a limitation, the intent of the Fraud Act could be circumvented. In the event that any senior executive officer, as defined in § 303.14(a)(3) of these regulations, is eligible for such severance benefits, the depository institution or holding company must provide 30 days prior written notice to its primary regulator and the FDIC before making such a payment to those individuals.

The third "exception" to the golden parachute payment prohibition is contained in § 359.1(d) of the proposed regulation which defines "*bona fide* deferred compensation plan or arrangement." Section 18(k) of the FDI Act explicitly authorizes the FDIC to define, by regulation or order, permissible "*bona fide* deferred compensation plan(s) or arrangements(s)." (12 U.S.C. 1828(k)(4)(C)(ii)). The FDIC is aware that many corporations, including financial institutions, supplement an employee's retirement benefits through the use of deferred compensation plans. Generally, these plans (which are not qualified under section 401 of the Internal Revenue Code of 1986) are intended to supplement traditional tax qualified defined benefit or defined contribution retirement plans. Such deferred compensation plans are utilized almost exclusively for the benefit of senior executive officers. Although such plans can be structured in numerous ways, they are primarily categorized as "elective," "excess," or "supplemental."

In an elective plan, an institution-affiliated party voluntarily elects to defer compensation which he/she could receive when it is earned. These deferred funds are maintained in a trust account which the institution-affiliated party can access when he/she leaves the institution. In view of the fact that the institution-affiliated party earns these funds at the time the work is performed, has the option of receiving payment at that time and pays income taxes on such earnings at that time, the FDIC is of the opinion that the receipt of such funds at a later time (when the institution otherwise is subject to any of the criteria of § 359.1(g)(1)(ii) of the proposed regulation) would not be a prohibited golden parachute payment.

Excess plans are maintained by an employer solely for the purpose of providing benefits for certain employees in excess of the limitations on contributions and benefits imposed by section 415 of the Internal Revenue Code of 1986. (Thus, they are often referred to as "piggyback" plans.) In an excess plan, the institution-affiliated party does not have the option of taking the deferred compensation while still employed by the institution. The deferred compensation is received only when the institution-affiliated party leaves the institution or retires. Such plans generally are unfunded and, thus, exempt from the requirements imposed by the Employee Retirement Income Security Act of 1974 ("ERISA"). If such a plan is funded, a trust generally is used and the plan would not be exempt from ERISA's reporting, disclosure and fiduciary rules. The use of such plans to attract and retain qualified executives is common in the financial services industry and other businesses. The FDIC is aware that undue restrictions on these plans could be disadvantageous to the financial services industry and contrary to the intent of Congress in enacting the Fraud Act. However, the Corporation is also concerned that such plans could be utilized to circumvent the intent of section 18(k) of the FDI Act. Thus, the proposed regulation permits payments pursuant to these excess plans as long as the plan is funded, was in effect at least one year prior to the occurrence of any of the events described in § 359.1(g)(1)(ii) of the proposed regulation and the institution-affiliated party is vested under the terms of such a plan. The FDIC is of the opinion that application of these factors is the best way to distinguish between a permissible *bona fide* deferred compensation plan as intended by Congress and an impermissible attempt to circumvent the restriction on golden parachute payments.

Supplemental (or "top hat") plans are maintained by an employer primarily for the purpose of providing deferred compensation for a select group of management or highly compensated employees. It is the FDIC's understanding that supplemental plans are not funded because funding would render them subject to all the requirements imposed by title I of ERISA. Instead, benefits are paid from the general assets of the corporation. As such, these assets are also available to the corporation's creditors in the event that the corporation becomes insolvent. Because these plans are not funded, they are essentially a promise to pay a sum of money at some time in the future when the IAP leaves the institution. As such, supplemental plans are indistinguishable from a prohibited golden parachute payment, and thus do not fall within the exception for *bona fide* deferred compensation plans or arrangements.

The proposed regulation does not permit institutions, holding companies and institution-affiliated parties to continue to contribute to such excess and supplemental plans upon the occurrence of any of the events delineated in § 359.1(g)(ii) of the proposed regulation. At that point in time, further contributions would be prohibited.

However, the institution-affiliated party would have the right to receive funds which were lawfully contributed prior to the institution's troubled condition.

Additional Exceptions and Factors Considered

Section 18(k)(2) of the FDI Act provides that the FDIC "shall prescribe, by regulation, the factors to be considered by the Corporation in taking any action pursuant to paragraph (1) [its authority to prohibit or limit golden parachute payments and indemnification payments]." The section also set forth a number of illustrative factors that should be considered. The Corporation has carefully considered these factors in arriving at the conclusion that golden parachute payments generally should be prohibited, except in the narrow circumstances delineated in § 359.4 of the proposed regulation. However, § 359.2(b) of the proposed regulation also sets forth a procedure to allow an institution which desires to make a payment or enter into an agreement which it determines should not be prohibited, but which is not clearly covered by any of the express "exceptions" to the prohibition, to solicit appropriate regulatory approvals. In so doing, the institution will be required to address certain of the factors enumerated in section 18(k), and the appropriate federal banking agency and the Corporation may consider the remaining factors and any other circumstances which bear on the issue of whether the proposed payment would be contrary to the intent of the prohibition. It is the Corporation's expectation that such approvals would be granted infrequently.

Indemnification Payments

Section 18(k) also authorizes the FDIC to prohibit or limit indemnification payments. An "indemnification payment" is defined as payment by an insured depository institution or depository institution holding company for the benefit of an IAP in order to pay or reimburse such person for any liability or legal expense sustained with regard to an administrative or civil enforcement action which results in a final order against the IAP. (12 U.S.C. 1828(k)(5)). The legislative history of the Fraud Act makes it clear that this section is intended (i) to preserve the deterrent effects of administrative enforcement or civil actions by insuring that institution-affiliated parties who are found to have violated the law, engaged in unsafe or unsound banking practices or breached any fiduciary duty to the institution, pay any civil money penalties and associated legal expenses out of their own pockets without reimbursement from the institution or its holding company and (ii) to safeguard the assets of financial institutions by prohibiting the expenditure of funds to defend, pay penalties imposed on or reimburse institution-affiliated parties who have been found to have violated the law. 136 Cong. Rec. E3687 (daily ed. November 2, 1990) (statement of Rep. Schumer).

The difficulty in enforcing such a prohibition, however, is that the parties involved do not know whether the proceeding will result in a final order against the institution-affiliated party until the proceeding has been concluded. Pending such conclusion, legal and other professional costs incurred in defending such an action can be substantial and impose significant hardships upon institution-affiliated parties who do not possess the financial resources to absorb such expenses. In recognition of this concern, the Office of the Comptroller of the Currency has issued a staff opinion which describes guidelines that permit national banks under certain circumstances to pay or reimburse an officer, director or employee for legal expense incurred in defending against a civil action instituted by the Comptroller prior to the entry of a final order in the IAP's favor. OCC Investment Securities Letter No. 43 (July 1990). Section 8.53 of the Model Business Corporation Act also contains suggested provisions which address director and officer indemnification similar to the OCC's guidelines.

The FDIC is of the opinion that it would be inconsistent with the intent of the Fraud Act categorically to prohibit insured depository institutions and holding companies from advancing funds to pay or reimburse IAP's for reasonable legal or other professional expenses incurred in defending against an administrative or civil action brought by the appropriate federal banking agency prior to the entry of a final order. Therefore, § 359.5 of the proposed regulation sets forth the circumstances under which such indemnification payments may be made. The FDIC is of the opinion that six criteria must be satisfied in order to permit an institution to make or agree to make any indemnification payment to or for the benefit of any IAP prior to the entry of a final order in the IAP's favor. First, the institution's board of directors, in good faith, must certify in writing that the IAP has a substantial likelihood of prevailing on the merits in the proceeding. In the FDIC's view, it would be inconsistent with the intent of section 18(k) to allow an institution's board of directors to authorize indemnification of an institution-affiliated party if, after examining the relevant facts and information, the directors conclude that the IAP does not have a substantial likelihood of prevailing on the merits. Second, the board must determine in writing that the indemnification payments will not adversely affect the institution's safety and soundness. It is well-established that a board of directors' primary duty is to the financial institution itself and that its financial soundness cannot be jeopardized to benefit any director, officer or employee. Third, the board of directors is obligated to cease making or authorizing indemnification payments in the event that it believes, or reasonably should believe, that the first two conditions discussed above are no longer being met. This condition imposes a duty on the institution's board actively to monitor the situation. If, for example, the board becomes aware of facts (previously unknown to it) which establish that the IAP knowingly and unambiguously violated an applicable statute or regulation, it could no longer reasonably believe that the IAP has a substantial likelihood of prevailing on the merits, and should terminate indemnification payments. To fail to do so would be a violation of the regulation. The FDIC believes that the imposition of such an obligation is reasonable and consistent with the intent of the Fraud Act and a board's responsibility to the institution it serves. The fourth condition makes clear that any indemnification payment authorized by the institution's board of directors is limited to the payment or reimbursement of legal or other professional expenses incurred in connection with an IAP's involvement in any administrative proceeding or civil action instituted by the appropriate federal banking agency and shall not include payment or reimbursement for the amount of, or any cost incurred in connection with, any settlement of the proceeding or any judgment or penalty imposed with respect to any proceeding. This condition is intended to clarify that under no circumstances may indemnification payments be used to pay, directly or indirectly, the amount of any settlement of a proceeding or any penalty or judgment imposed on or obtained against the IAP. Fifth, the IAP must agree in writing to reimburse the institution for an indemnification if he/she does not prevail on the merits. In the Corporation's view, such a commitment represents an equitable arrangement. The IAP obtains the benefits of indemnification made in advance, but the institution can recover payments made pursuant to such indemnification agreements if it is ultimately determined that the IAP acted improperly. Sixth, the insured depository institution or depository institution holding company must provide the appropriate federal banking agency and the FDIC with prior written notice of its board's authorization of such indemnification.

The definition of "indemnification payment" in section 359.1(h) of the proposed regulation includes (i) payments made by an institution to an institution-affiliated party to reimburse him/her for expenses already incurred and paid, (ii) payments made on behalf of an institution-affiliated party by the institution directly to a law firm or other professional organization which is providing professional services to the IAP in connection with the defense of an administrative or civil action and (iii) payments made by the institution to purchase commercial insurance or fidelity bond coverage which will pay or reimburse the IAP for such expenses.[5] It also should be noted that the definition of indemnification payment does not include, and therefore the regulation does not prohibit, payments made pursuant to insurance coverage purchased directly by the IAP at his/her own expense.

Other Issues

The FDIC also would like to clarify several other points concerning the scope of the proposed regulation. First, the proposed regulation will affect existing agreements between institutions and institution-affiliated parties to pay golden parachute and indemnification payments in the future. For example, a healthy institution which enters into a permissible golden parachute agreement and subsequently meets any of the criteria of § 359.1(g)(1)(ii) of the proposed regulation would no longer be permitted to make a golden parachute payment pursuant to that agreement so long as it continues to meet any of these criteria. Second, the FDIC will consider any payment of unearned wages pursuant to an employment contract which is terminated prior to its stated termination date (e.g., payment of an institution-affiliated party's salary for the final year of an employment contract which is terminated with one year remaining) to be a prohibited golden parachute payment, if the circumstances in § 359.1(g)(1)(ii) of the proposed regulation are present when the payment is made. Third, the FDIC and the other federal banking agencies will examine very closely any attempt by an institution or holding company to circumvent the proposed regulation by continuing to employ the IAP in some other capacity (e.g., as a "consultant") subsequent to the payment of what otherwise would clearly be a prohibited golden parachute payment.

Request for Public Comment

The FDIC hereby requests comment on all aspects of the proposed rule, including both legal and policy considerations. In particular, with respect to both the golden parachute and indemnification limitations, we request comments on whether the regulation appropriately balances the protection of the insurance funds with the needs of insured depository institutions and depository institution holding companies to attract and retain qualified directors and management. Further, we request comments on the overall public benefit and cost-effectiveness of the proposed restrictions concerning indemnification and the permissible scope of directors' and officers' liability insurance, taking into account the cost and availability of such insurance to insured depository institutions and their holding companies. Interested persons are invited to submit comments during a 60-day comment period.

List of Subjects in 12 CFR Part 359

Banks, banking; Golden parachute payments; Indemnification payments.

For the reasons set out in the preamble, the FDIC hereby proposes to add part 359 to title 12, chapter III, subchapter B, of the Code of Federal Regulations to read as follows:

PART 359—GOLDEN PARACHUTE AND INDEMNIFICATION PAYMENTS

Sec.

359.1   Definitions

359.2   Golden parachute payments prohibited

359.3   Indemnification payments prohibited

359.4   Permissible golden parachute payments

359.5   Permissible indemnification payments

Authority: 12 U.S.C. 1828(k)

§ 359.1   Definitions.

(a) *Act* means the Federal Deposit Insurance Act, as amended (12 U.S.C. 1811, et seq.).

(b) *Appropriate federal banking agency* means:

(1) The Comptroller of the Currency, in the case of any national banking association, any District bank, or any Federal branch or agency of a foreign bank and its subsidiaries;

(2) The Board of Governors of the Federal Reserve System, in the case of —

(i) Any State member insured bank (except a District bank) and its subsidiaries; and

(ii) Any bank holding company and any subsidiary of a bank holding company (other than a bank or a subsidiary of a bank);

(3) The Federal Deposit Insurance Corporation in the case of a State nonmember insured bank (except a District bank), or a foreign bank having an insured branch and its subsidiaries; and

(4) The Director of the Office of Thrift Supervision in the case of any savings association or any savings and loan holding company.

(c) *Bank holding company* has the meaning given to such term in section 2 of the Bank Holding Company Act of 1956 (12 U.S.C. 1841 et seq.).

(d) *Bona fide deferred compensation plan or arrangement* means any plan, contract, agreement or other arrangement whereby:

(1) An institution-affiliated party voluntarily elects to defer (by reducing wages paid) until the termination of such party's employment, a portion of the reasonable compensation for services rendered which otherwise would have been paid to such party at the time the services were rendered; or

(2) An insured depository institution or depository institution holding company establishes a nonqualified deferred compensation plan:

(i) Solely for the purpose of providing benefits for certain employees in excess of the limitations on contributions and benefits imposed by section 415 of the Internal Revenue Code of 1986 (26 U.S.C. 415); or

(ii) Primarily for the purpose of providing deferred compensation for a select group of management or highly compensated employees;

Provided, however, that such plan was in effect at least one year prior to any of the events described in paragraph (g)(1)(ii) of this section, the institution-affiliated party is vested in such plan at the time of termination of employment and such plan is funded by the institution or holding company. For purposes of this paragraph (d)(2), a plan is funded if specific assets are segregated or otherwise set aside so that such assets are not available to the institution or holding company for any purpose other than distribution to the participating employee(s) and are not available to satisfy claims of the institution's or holding company's creditors.

(e) *Corporation* means the Federal Deposit Insurance Corporation.

(f) *Depository institution holding company* means a bank holding company or a savings and loan holding company, or any direct or indirect subsidiary thereof, other than an insured depository institution.

(g) *Golden parachute payment.* (1) The term *golden parachute payment* means any payment (or any agreement to make any payment) by any insured depository institution or depository institution holding company for the benefit of any person who is or was an institution-affiliated party pursuant to an obligation of such institution or holding company that:

(i) Is contingent on or payable on or after the termination of such party's primary employment or affiliation with the institution or holding company; and

(ii) Is received on or after, or is made in contemplation of, any of the following events:

(A) The insolvency of the insured depository institution or depository institution holding company, or any insured depository institution subsidiary of such holding company; or

(B) The appointment of any conservator or receiver for such insured depository institution; or

(C) A determination by the insured depository institution's or depository institution holding company's appropriate federal banking agency, respectively, that the insured depository institution or depository institution holding company is in a troubled condition, as defined in the applicable regulations of the appropriate federal banking agency (§ 303.14(a)(4) of this chapter); or

(D) The insured depository institution is assigned a composite rating of 4 or 5 by the appropriate federal banking agency or informed in writing by the Corporation that it is rated a 4 or 5 under the Uniform Financial Institutions Rating System of the Federal Financial Institutions Examination Council; or

(E) The Corporation initiates a proceeding against the insured depository institution to terminate or suspend deposit insurance for such institution.

(2) *Exceptions.* The term *golden parachute payment* shall not include:

(i) Any payment made pursuant to a retirement plan which is qualified (or is intended within a reasonable period of time to be qualified) under section 401 of the Internal Revenue Code of 1986 (26 U.S.C. 401) or other nondiscriminatory benefit plan; or

(ii) Any payment made pursuant to a *bona fide* deferred compensation plan or arrangement as defined in paragraph (d) of this section or which the Corporation determines by order to be permissible; or

(iii) Any payment made by reason of the death or disability of an institution-affiliated party; or

(iv) Any payment made pursuant to a nondiscriminatory severance pay plan or arrangement which provides for payment of severance benefits to all eligible employees upon involuntary termination other than for cause; *provided, however,* that no employee shall receive any such payment which exceeds the base compensation paid to such employee during the six months immediately preceding termination of employment, the institution may prescribe reasonable eligibility requirements applicable to all employees such as a minimum length of service requirement, and such severance pay plan or arrangement shall not have been modified to increase the amount or scope of severance benefits at a time when the insured depository institution or depository institution holding company was in a condition specified in paragraph (g)(1)(ii) of this section or in contemplation of such a condition; *provided further, however,* that no such payment shall be made to any senior executive officer (as defined in § 303.14(a)(3) of this chapter) of any insured depository institution or depository institution holding company without providing 30 days prior written notice to the appropriate federal banking agency and the FDIC.

(h) *Indemnification payment.* (1) The term *indemnification payment* means any payment (or any agreement or arrangement, pursuant to any charter or bylaw provision, to make any payment) by any insured depository institution or depository institution holding company for the benefit of any person who is or was an institution-affiliated party, to pay or reimburse such person for any liability or legal expense with regard to any administrative proceeding or civil action instituted by any federal or state banking agency which results in a final order pursuant to which such person:

(i) Is assessed a civil money penalty;

(ii) Is removed from office or prohibited from participating in the conduct of the affairs of the insured depository institution; or

(iii) Is required to cease and desist from or take any affirmative action described in section 8(b) of the Act with respect to such institution.

(2) *Exception.* The term *indemnification payment* shall not include any payment by an insured depository institution or depository institution holding company which is used to purchase any commercial insurance policy or fidelity bond, except that such insurance policy or bond shall not be used to make any prohibited indemnification payment other than reimbursement to the insured depository institution or depository institution holding company as required under a formal order described in paragraph (h)(1)(iii) of this section.

(i) *Insured depository institution* means any bank or savings association the deposits of which are insured by the Corporation pursuant to the Act, or any subsidiary thereof.

(j) *Institution-affiliated party* means:

(1) Any director, officer, employee, or controlling stockholder (other than a depository institution holding company) of, or agent for, an insured depository institution or depository institution holding company;

(2) Any other person who has filed or is required to file a change-in-control notice with the appropriate federal banking agency under section 7(j) of the Act (12 U.S.C. 1817(j)) in respect of an insured depository institution or depository institution holding company;

(3) Any shareholder (other than a depository institution holding company), consultant, joint venture partner, and any other person as determined by the appropriate federal banking agency (by regulation or case-by-case) who participates in the conduct of the affairs of an insured depository institution or depository institution holding company; and

(4) Any independent contractor (including any attorney, appraiser, or accountant) who knowingly or recklessly participates in: Any violation of any law or regulation, any breach of fiduciary duty, or any unsafe or unsound practice, which caused or is likely to cause more than a minimal financial loss to, or a significant adverse effect on, the insured depository institution or depository institution holding company.

(k) *Liability or legal expense* means:

(1) Any legal or other professional fees and expenses incurred in connection with any claim, proceeding, or action;

(2) The amount of, and any cost incurred in connection with, any settlement of any claim, proceeding, or action; and

(3) The amount of, and any cost incurred in connection with, any judgment or penalty imposed with respect to any claim, proceeding, or action.

(l) *Payment* means:

(1) Any direct or indirect transfer of any funds or any asset;

(2) Any forgiveness of any debt or other obligation; and

(3) Any segregation of any funds or assets, the establishment or funding of any trust or the purchase of or arrangement for any letter of credit or other instrument, for the purpose of making, or pursuant to any agreement to make, any payment on or after the date on which such funds or assets are segregated, or at the time of or after such trust is established or letter of credit or other instrument is made available, without regard to whether the obligation to make such payment is contingent on:

(i) The determination, after such date, of the liability for the payment of such amount; or

(ii) The liquidation, after such date, of the amount of such payment.

(m) *Savings and loan holding company* has the meaning given to such term in section 10 of the Home Owners' Loan Act (12 U.S.C. 1461 et seq.)

§ 359.2 Golden parachute payments prohibited.

(a) No insured depository institution or depository institution holding company shall make or agree to make any golden parachute payment, except as provided in paragraphs (b) and (d) of this section and § 359.4 of this part.

(b) Notwithstanding paragraph (a) of this section, an insured depository institution or depository institution holding company may make or agree to make a golden parachute payment if, and to the extent that, the appropriate federal banking agency, with the written concurrence of the Corporation, determines that such a payment or agreement is permissible. An insured depository institution or depository institution holding company seeking such a determination shall demonstrate that:

(1) There is no reasonable basis to believe, at the time such payment is proposed to be made, that the institution-affiliated party has committed any fraudulent act or omission, breach of trust or fiduciary duty, or insider abuse with regard to the depository institution or depository institution holding company that has had or is likely to have a material adverse effect on the institution or holding company;

(2) There is no reasonable basis to believe, at the time such payment is proposed to be made, that the institution-affiliated party is substantially responsible for the insolvency of the insured depository institution, depository institution holding company or any insured depository institution subsidiary of such holding company, the appointment of a conservator or receiver for the depository institution or any insured depository institution subsidiary of the insured depository institution holding company, or the troubled condition of the insured depository institution, insured depository institution holding company or any insured depository institution subsidiary of such holding company, as defined in the applicable regulations of the appropriate federal banking agency;

(3) There is no reasonable basis to believe, at the time such payment is proposed to be made, that the institution-affiliated party has materially violated any applicable Federal or State banking law or regulation that has had or is likely to have a material effect on the insured depository institution or depository institution holding company; and

(4) There is no reasonable basis to believe, at the time such payment is proposed to be made, that the institution-affiliated party has violated or conspired to violate section 215, 656, 657, 1005, 1006, 1007, 1014, 1032, or 1344 of title 18 of the United States Code, or section 1341 or 1343 of such title affecting a federally insured financial institution as defined in title 18 of the United States Code.

(c) In making a determination under paragraph (b) of this section, the appropriate federal banking agency and the Corporation may consider:

(1) Whether, and to what degree, the institution-affiliated party was in a position of managerial or fiduciary responsibility;

(2) The length of time the institution-affiliated party was affiliated with the insured depository institution or depository institution holding company, and the degree to which the proposed payment represents a reasonable payment for services rendered over the period of employment; and

(3) Any other factors or circumstances which would indicate that the proposed payment would be contrary to the intent of section 18(k) of the Act or this part.

(d) Notwithstanding paragraphs (a) and (b) of this section, a depository institution holding company that is a diversified holding company as defined in section 10(a)(1)(F) of the Home Owner's Loan Act (12 U.S.C. 1461 et seq.) may make a golden parachute payment if, and to the extent that, such depository institution holding company determines and can demonstrate that:

(1) The conditions delineated in paragraphs (b)(1), (2), (3) and (4) of this section have been satisfied; and

(2) The institution-affiliated party falls within the definition of "institution-affiliated party" solely because such person is a director, officer, employee or controlling stockholder of a diversified holding company.

§ 359.3   Indemnification payments prohibited.

No insured depository institution or depository institution holding company shall make or agree to make any indemnification payment, except as provided in § 359.5 of this part.

§ 359.4   Permissible golden parachute payments.

An insured depository institution or depository institution holding company may agree to make a golden parachute payment if:

(a) Such an agreement is made with respect to an institution-affiliated party who was hired by an insured depository institution or depository institution holding company at a time when that institution or holding company satisfied any of the criteria set forth in § 359.1(g)(1)(ii) of this part and the institution's appropriate federal banking agency and the Corporation consented in writing to the amount and terms of the golden parachute payment; and

(b) At the time the payment is made, the factors delineated in § 359.2(b)(1), (2), (3), or (4) of this part have been satisfied, and the factors delineated in § 359.2(c)(3) of this part are not present.

§ 359.5 Permissible indemnification payments.

(a) An insured depository institution or depository institution holding company may make or agree to make reasonable indemnification payments to an institution-affiliated party if:

(1) The institution's or holding company's board of directors, in good faith, determines in writing that the institution-affiliated party has a substantial likelihood of prevailing on the merits;

(2) The institution's or holding company's board of directors, in good faith, determines in writing that the payment of such expenses will not adversely affect the institution's safety and soundness;

(3) At any time the institution's or holding company's board of directors believes, or should reasonably believe, that the conditions of paragraphs (a)(1) and (2) of this section are no longer being met, it ceases making or authorizing such payments;

(4) The indemnification payments are limited to the payment or reimbursement of reasonable legal or other professional expenses incurred in connection with an institution-affiliated party's involvement in an administrative proceeding or civil action instituted by the appropriate federal banking agency; but in no event shall such indemnification pay or reimburse an institution-affiliated party for the amount of, or any cost incurred in connection with, any settlement of any such claim, proceeding or action or any judgment or penalty imposed with respect to any such claim, proceeding or action;

(5) The institution-affiliated party agrees in writing to reimburse the institution for such indemnification payments in the event that the proceeding results in a final order under which the institution-affiliated party:

(i) Is assessed a civil money penalty;

(ii) Is removed from office or prohibited from participating in the conduct of the affairs of the insured depository institution; or

(iii) Is required to cease and desist from or take any affirmative action described in section 8(b) of the Act with respect to such institution; and

(6) The institution or holding company provides the appropriate federal banking agency and the FDIC with prior written notice of its board of directors' authorization of such indemnification.

(b) An institution-affiliated party requesting indemnification payments shall not participate in any way in the board's discussion and approval of such payments; *provided, however,* that such institution-affiliated party may present his/her request to the board and respond to any inquiries from the board concerning his/her involvement in the circumstances giving rise to the administrative proceeding or civil action.

By order of the Board of Directors, dated at Washington, DC, this 24th day of September, 1991.

Federal Deposit Insurance Corporation.

Robert E. Feldman,

Deputy Executive Secretary.

[FR Doc. 91–23747 Filed 10–4–91; 8:45 am]

Billing Code 6714–91–M

---

[1] The Comprehensive Thrift and Bank Fraud Prosecution and Taxpayer Recovery Act of 1990 is title XXV of the Crime Control Act of 1990, S. 3266, which was passed by Congress on October 27, 1990 and signed by the President on November 28, 1990.

[2] *See* Testimony of L. William Seidman, Chairman, Federal Deposit Insurance Corporation, before the Banking and Financial Institutions Subcommittee, Committee on Banking, United States House of Representatives, March 14, 1990; Testimony of L. William Seidman, Chairman, Federal Deposit Insurance Corporation, on the Prosecution of Financial Crimes before the Subcommittee on Criminal Justice, Committee on the Judiciary, United States House of Representatives, July 11, 1990; Testimony of L. William Seidman, Chairman, Federal Deposit Insurance Corporation, on the Prosecution of Financial Crimes before the Committee on the Judiciary, United States Senate, July 24, 1990; Testimony of L. William Seidman, Chairman, Federal Deposit Insurance Corporation, on the Prosecution of Financial Crimes before the Committee on Banking, Housing and Urban Affairs, United States Senate, August 2, 1990.

[3] More precisely, only one of these is an actual exception in that it permits a payment or agreement which is covered by the statutory language. The other two are definitions of statutory terms which have been developed or refined by the Corporation.

[4] These criteria are that the institution or holding company is insolvent, in conservatorship of receivership, troubled, rated "4" or "5," or subject to a proceeding to terminate deposit insurance.

[5] In the event that the IAP is required to provide reimbursement and his/her legal expenses have been paid pursuant to a commercial insurance policy or fidelity bond purchased by the institution or its holding company, the IAP shall reimburse the institution or its holding company for that portion of the cost of the policy or bond attributable to the IAP's defense in the administrative or civil action. The FDIC anticipates that this information should be available to the institution from the insurer.

Appendix D

IRS Notices

Notice 94-96

I. Background

Section 3121(v)(2) of the Internal Revenue Code determines when amounts deferred under nonqualified deferred compensation plans are taken into account as wages for purposes of the Federal Insurance Contributions Act (FICA). Section 3121(v)(2)(A) provides that any amount deferred under a nonqualified deferred compensation plan shall be taken into account as of the later of (i) when the services are performed, or (ii) when there is no substantial risk of forfeiture of the rights to the amount. Section 3121(v)(2)(B) provides that an amount taken into account as wages by reason of subparagraph (A) (and the income attributable to that amount) will not thereafter be treated as wages. Section 3121(v)(2)(C) defines the term "nonqualified deferred compensation plan." Section 3306(r)(2) provides parallel rules for purposes of determining when amounts deferred under nonqualified deferred compensation plans are wages for purposes of the Federal Unemployment Tax Act (FUTA).

Section 13207 of the Omnibus Budget Reconciliation Act of 1993 (Pub. L. 103-66) repealed the dollar limit on wages subject to hospital insurance (HI) tax under sections 3101(b) and 3111(b) of the Code, effective for 1994 and later years. This change increases the number of taxpayers who incur FICA tax liability on amounts deferred under nonqualified deferred compensation plans.

II. Reasonable, Good Faith Interpretation

The Service and Treasury intend to publish guidance under sections 3121(v)(2) and 3306(r)(2) in a forthcoming notice of proposed rulemaking. The effective date of the proposed regulations will not be earlier than January 1, 1995. Thus, the Service will not challenge an employer's determination of FICA or FUTA tax liability with respect to a nonqualified deferred compensation plan for periods preceding the effective date, if the employer's determination is based on a reasonable, good faith interpretation of sections 3121(v)(2) and 3306(r)(2). See Example 1 and Example 3, paragraphs (a) and (b).

Whether an employer has made a reasonable, good faith interpretation of sections 3121(v)(2) and 3306(r)(2) will be determined based on all of the relevant facts and circumstances, including consistency of treatment by the employer. For example, one relevant circumstance could be an employer's effort to achieve more favorable FICA and FUTA tax treatment by using different methods to value the benefits of two participants who are subject to the same plan provisions. However, in no event will an employer's treatment of amounts deferred under a nonqualified deferred compensation plan be considered to be in accordance with a reasonable, good faith interpretation of sections 3121(v)(2) and 3306(r)(2) if the employer treats these amounts, for FICA and FUTA tax purposes, as deferred compensation for services performed prior to the adoption of the plan (or the amendment to the plan) providing for the deferred compensation, i.e., if the employer includes these amounts in FICA and FUTA wages for periods prior to the adoption or amendment. See Example 2.

An employer's reasonable, good faith treatment of an amount as deferred compensation taken into account under sections 3121(v)(2)(A) and 3306(r)(2)(A) for periods preceding the effective date of the forthcoming regulations may not necessarily be determinative for purposes of applying sections 3121(v)(2)(B) and 3306(r)(2)(B) under the regulations for periods after their effective date. Thus, the regulations could provide that sections 3121(v)(2) and 3306(r)(2) will be applied to determine the amount to be taken into account as FICA and FUTA wages for periods after the regulations' effective date independent of the amount (if any) that the employer took into account as FICA or FUTA wages for periods preceding the effective date under its reasonable, good faith interpretation. See Example 3. However, in that event, it is anticipated that provision would be made so that any such application of the regulations would not require a taxpayer to pay more tax than would have been payable had the regulations been in effect since the effective dates of sections 3121(v)(2) and 3306(r)(2).

Example 1. (a) An employer establishes a nonqualified deferred compensation plan in 1985 for the benefit of an executive. Under a reasonable, good faith interpretation of sections 3121(v)(2) and 3306(r)(2), the employer determines that the amount deferred under the plan (and hence includible in FICA and FUTA wages) for each year from 1985 through 1994 is $50,000. However, since the executive's total wages (without regard to the amount deferred) are above the FICA and FUTA wage bases in 1985 through 1993, no FICA or FUTA taxes are paid on those amounts in those years. In 1994, the amount deferred is subject to the HI portion of FICA tax. Regulations are issued with an effective date of January 1, 1995. In accordance with the valuation rules provided for under the regulations, the amount deferred (and hence includible in FICA and FUTA wages) for each year beginning in 1985 would have been $60,000.

(b) Because the employer applied a reasonable, good faith interpretation of sections 3121(v)(2) and 3306(r)(2), the Service will not challenge the employer's determination of the FICA and FUTA tax liability for 1985 through 1994. Accordingly, no FICA or FUTA taxes will be owed for 1985 through 1993, and no additional FICA or FUTA taxes will be owed for 1994.

Example 2. (a) An employer establishes a severance pay plan on January 1, 1994. The plan covers an executive who has ten years of service as of that date. The plan provides that, in consideration of the executive's outstanding services over the past ten years, the executive will be paid a $500,000 lump sum upon termination of employment at any time. On January 15, 1994, the executive's employment with the employer terminates. The employer treats the $500,000 as deferred compensation for services performed in 1993 and earlier years (i.e., treats the amount as having been included in FICA and FUTA wages for those years).

(b) Because 1993 and earlier years are prior to the adoption of the plan, the employer's treatment is not in accordance with a reasonable, good faith interpretation of sections 3121(v)(2) and 3306(r)(2).

Example 3. (a) In 1985, an employer establishes a nonqualified deferred compensation plan for participants A and B. Prior to the effective date of the regulations, and in accordance with a reasonable, good faith interpretation of sections 3121(v)(2) and 3306(r)(2), the employer treats the plan as a nonqualified deferred compensation plan under sections 3121(v)(2) and 3306(r)(2). Each year, consistent with this treatment, the employer determines the amount that it will treat as deferred in that year and accordingly includes that amount in FICA and FUTA wages for that year. The employer also determines that each participant's total wages (without regard to the amount deferred) exceed the applicable FICA and FUTA wage bases for each of those years. Consequently, neither the employer nor either participant pays any FICA or FUTA taxes on the amounts that are determined to be deferred. Participant A ceases performing services for the employer in 1988, while participant B continues performing services beyond the effective date of the regulations. Plan payments to participant A begin in 1989 and are expected to continue after the effective date of the regulation. In accordance with its treatment of the plan as a nonqualified deferred compensation plan, the employer does not treat the payments in 1989 through 1994 as FICA or FUTA wages for those years.

(b) *Pre-effective date periods.* Because the employer's determination of its FICA and FUTA tax liability for 1985 through 1994 was made in accordance with a reasonable, good faith interpretation, neither the employer nor either participant will be subject to FICA or FUTA tax for those years.

(c) *Post-effective date periods—classification of plan.* If, under the regulations, the plan did not constitute a nonqualified deferred compensation plan within the meaning of sections 3121(v)(2) and 3306(r)(2), the regulations could provide that, even though the employer treated amounts under the plan as having been deferred in pre-effective date periods (and hence, in the case of participant A, as includible in FICA and FUTA wages in 1985-1988), those amounts would not be treated as having been included in wages for those periods for purposes of applying sections 3121(v)(2) and 3306(r)(2) to periods after the effective date. Under this approach, any payments made after the effective date would be includible in FICA and FUTA wages under sections 3121(a) and 3306(b) when they are paid. (If instead of continuing after the effective date, all payments to participant A were completed prior to the effective date, the regulations would have no effect on FICA or FUTA tax liability with respect to participant A under the plan because the employer followed a reasonable, good faith interpretation.)

(d) *Post-effective date periods—valuation of amounts deferred.* Alternatively, if, under the regulations, the plan did constitute a nonqualified deferred compensation plan within the meaning of sections 3121(v)(2) and 3306(r)(2), but the employer's valuation of amounts deferred prior to the effective date (though based on a reasonable good faith interpretation) differed from the valuation that would have resulted if the regulations were applied, the regulations could provide that the amounts includible in FICA and FUTA wages for participant B for post-effective date periods would be determined without regard to the valuation the employer used for pre-effective date periods.

III. Withholding

An employer must withhold the applicable FICA and FUTA taxes with respect to nonqualified deferred compensation treated as wages under sections 3121(v)(2) and 3306(r)(2) on the date or dates it treats such amounts as paid. For this purpose, the employer may choose to treat amounts deferred under a nonqualified deferred compensation plan as wages paid on a pay period, quarterly, semiannual, annual, or other basis, provided that the amounts are treated as paid no less frequently than annually. The employer must deposit the withheld taxes under the regular rules for tax deposits.

The principal author of this notice is David Pardys of the Office of Associate Chief Counsel (Employee Benefits and Exempt Organizations). For further information regarding this notice, contact David Pardys on (202) 622-4606 (not a toll-free call).

Notice 95-34

Section 419—Funded Welfare Benefit Plans

Taxpayers and their representatives have inquired as to whether certain trust arrangements qualify as multiple employer welfare benefit funds exempt from the limits of section 419 and section 419A of the Internal Revenue Code. The Service is issuing this Notice to alert taxpayers and their representatives to some of the significant tax problems that may be raised by these arrangements.

In general, contributions to a welfare benefit fund are deductible when paid, but only if they qualify as ordinary and necessary business expenses of the taxpayer and only to the extent allowable under section 419 and section 419A of the Code. Those sections impose strict limits on the amount of tax-deductible prefunding permitted for contributions to a welfare benefit fund.

Section 419A(f)(6) provides an exemption from section 419 and section 419A for certain welfare benefit funds. In general, for this exemption to apply, an employer normally cannot contribute more than 10 percent of the total contributions, and the plan must not be experience rated with respect to individual employers. The legislative history states that the exemption under section 419A(f)(6) is provided because "the relationship of a participating employer to [such a] plan often is similar to the relationship of an insured to an insurer." Even if the 10 percent contribution limit is satisfied, the exemption does not apply to a plan that is experience rated with respect to individual employers, because the "employer's interest with respect to such a plan is more similar to the relationship of an employer to a fund than an insured to an insurer." [H.R. Rep. No. 98-861, 98th Cong., 2d Sess., 1159 (1984-3 C.B. (Vol. 2) 1, 413].

In recent years a number of promoters have offered trust arrangements that they claim satisfy the requirements for the ten-or-more-employer plan exemption and that are used to provide benefits such as life insurance, disability, and severance pay benefits. Promoters of these arrangements claim that all employer contributions are tax-deductible when paid, relying on the ten-or-more-employer exemption from the section 419 limits and on the fact that they have enrolled at least ten employers in their multiple employer trusts.

These arrangements typically are invested in variable life or universal life insurance contracts on the lives of the covered employees, but require large employer contributions relative to the cost of the amount of term insurance that would be required to provide the death benefits under the arrangement. The trust owns the insurance contracts. The trust administrator may obtain the cash to pay benefits, other than death benefits, by such means as cashing in or withdrawing the cash value of the insurance policies. Although, in some plans, benefits may appear to be contingent on the occurrence of unanticipated future events, in reality, most participants and their beneficiaries will receive their benefits.

The trusts often maintain separate accounting of the assets attributable to the contributions made by each subscribing employer. Benefits are sometimes related to the amounts allocated to the employees of the participant's employer. For example, severance and disability benefits may be subject to reduction if the assets derived from an employer's contributions are insufficient to fund all benefits promised to that employer's employees. In other cases, an employer's contributions are related to the claims experience of its employees. Thus, pursuant to formal or informal arrangements or practices, a particular employer's contributions or its employees' benefits may be determined in a way that insulates the employer to a significant extent from the experience of other subscribing employers.

In general, these arrangements and other similar arrangements do not satisfy the requirements of the section 419A(f)(6) exemption and do not provide the tax deductions claimed by their promoters for any one of several reasons, including the following:

1. The arrangements may actually be providing deferred compensation. This is an especially important consideration in arrangements similar to that in *Wellons v. Commissioner* [31 F.3d 569 (7th Cir 1994), aff'g, 64 T.C.M. (CCH) 1498 (1992)], where the courts held that an arrangement purporting to be a severance pay plan was actually deferred compensation. If the plan is a nonqualified plan of deferred compensation, deductions for contributions will be governed by section 404(a)(5), and contributions to the trust may, in some cases, be includible in employees' income under section 402(b). Section 404(a)(5) provides that contributions to a nonqualified plan of deferred compensation are deductible when amounts attributable to the contributions are includible in the employees' income, and that deductions are allowed only if separate accounts are maintained for each employee.

2. The arrangements may be, in fact, separate plans maintained for each employer. As separate plans, they do not qualify for the ten-or-more-employer plan exemption in section 419A(f)(6).

3. The arrangements may be experience rated with respect to individual employers in form or operation. This is because, among other things, the trust maintains, formally or informally, separate accounting for each employer and the employers have reason to expect that, at least for the most part, their contributions will benefit only their own employees. Arrangements that are experience rated with respect to individual employers do not qualify for the exemption in section 419A(f)(6).

4. Even if the arrangements qualify for the exemption in section 419A(f)(6), employer contributions to the arrangements may represent prepaid expenses that are nondeductible under other sections of the Internal Revenue Code.

Taxpayers and their representative should be aware that the Service has disallowed deductions for contributions to these arrangements and is asserting the positions discussed above in litigation.

Finally, in response to questions raised by taxpayers and their representatives, we note that the Service has never issued a letter ruling approving the deductibility of contributions to a welfare benefit fund under section 419A(f)(6). Although a trust used to provide benefits under an arrangement of the type discussed in this Notice may have received a determination letter stating that the trust is exempt under section 501(c)(9), a letter of this type does not address the tax deductibility of contributions to such a trust.

Appendix E

Private Letter Rulings

Letter Ruling 9235006

This is in response to your request for a ruling on behalf of X, concerning the federal income tax consequences of the establishment of a trust to assist X in providing nonqualified deferred compensation benefits under a plan (the "plan") for certain X employees and employees of X's participating affiliates (the "employers") that participate in the plan, as determined under the plan.

X is the parent of an affiliated group of corporations, within the meaning of Section 1504(a) of the Internal Revenue Code, that files a consolidated income tax return.

The plan is a nonqualified deferred compensation plan that provides retirement benefits for certain X executives and executives of the employers (the "participants"). The plan is composed of three parts. Two parts are excess benefit plans, within the meaning of Section 3(36) of the Employee Retirement Income Security Act of 1974 as amended ("ERISA"). The third part is a "top-hat" plan, within the meaning of Title I of ERISA. The plan neither requires nor permits participants to make elective salary deferrals, and accruals are made solely by X and the employers.

The plan provides for the payment of retirement benefits to participants and their beneficiaries upon attainment of normal retirement age, as defined in the plan. Benefits are paid in equal monthly installments under a formula described in the plan and will commence as of the last day of the month following a participant's retirement date. In the event of a participant's death either before or after benefit payments have commenced, benefit payments will be made to a participant's beneficiary in the same manner that they would have been made to the participant. Upon the change of control of X, as defined in the plan, all benefits under the terms of the plan that have become due and payable will be paid to a participant who separates from service.

The plan provides that it is unfunded and all payments thereunder will be made out of X's and the employers' general assets and no special or separate fund is to be established nor other segregation of assets made to create plan assets or cause the plan to be a funded plan. The plan provides that X may, in its sole discretion, place assets in a trust that may be used to meet X and the employer's obligations under the plan, and any right of a participant to any benefit payment under the plan is reduced by any payment from either X, the employers, or the trustee of any such trust. The plan further provides that the assets of any trust that may be established shall be available to the general creditors of X and the employers in the event of the insolvency or bankruptcy of X or the employers. The plan also states that no interest under the plan shall be subject in any manner to alienation by anticipation, sale, transfer, assignment, bankruptcy, pledge, attachment, charge, or encumbrance of any kind.

By a proposed agreement with an unrelated third party (the "trustee"), X proposes to establish an irrevocable trust (the "trust") in order to pay X and the employer's benefit obligations to participants. Under the terms of the trust, X or the employers may, in their discretion, contribute funds to provide the deferred compensation benefits due pursuant to the plan. The trust provides that neither X nor the employers are relieved of the liability of providing benefits under the plan except to the extent that the liability is satisfied through application of trust assets or payments made by X. Under the terms of the trust, the trust will terminate upon X's certification to the trustee that all liabilities for plan benefits have been satisfied with respect to all participants and their beneficiaries. The trustee has the duty to invest trust assets as set forth in the trust agreement but may not take any actions that will constitute "carrying on of a business" within the meaning of Section 301.7701-2 of the Procedure and Administration Regulations. The trust provides that the rights of any participant under the plan and trust are the rights of a general, unsecured creditor of X or the employers, as applicable, and that no right or interest of a participant may be transferred, assigned, or subject to alienation, anticipation, assignment, attachment, garnishment, execution, or encumbrance.

The trust provides that if at any time while it is still in existence, X becomes insolvent, as defined in the trust, the trustee must, upon receiving notice of the insolvency, suspend all payments from the trust and hold trust assets until the trustee receives a court order directing the disposition of the trust. If one of the employers becomes insolvent, as defined in the trust, the trustee must, upon receiving notice of the insolvency, suspend all payments from the trust to or on behalf of participants who are employees of that employer and must hold the assets of the trust attributable to that employer's participants in suspense until the trustee receives a court order directing the disposition of these assets. The trust provides that X's chief executive officer and its board of directors have the duty and responsibility of giving the trustee prompt written notice of X's insolvency or of the insolvency of any of the employers, as defined in the trust.

The trust provides that X desires that the assets of the trust be principally or exclusively stock issued by X, purchased by the trustee on the open market, and expressly waives any diversification of investments that might otherwise be necessary, appropriate, or required under applicable state law. Nevertheless, the trustee will have the full range of investment powers traditionally available to a trustee, including the power to dispose of X stock by distribution to participants or by sale or exchange to unrelated parties. The trust provides that the trustee will exercise the voting and other rights of ownership with respect to the shares held in the trust and that dividends paid on X stock held by the trust will be reinvested in X stock. X is entitled at any time, and from time to time in its sole discretion, subject to certain restrictions, to substitute assets of equal fair market value for any asset held by the trust. X has received an opinion of counsel that under local law the trust constitutes a valid trust, and that the stock held by the trustee as an asset of the trust will be issued and outstanding. X represents that the trust will not hold in excess of 1 percent of the stock that is outstanding under local law.

The trust provides that, in connection with any substitution of assets, X stock may not revert to X in kind at any time following a voting record date for any meeting of X stockholders and before such meeting, but such reversion may occur immediately following the stockholders' meeting to which such record date relates. Any such substitution may be made only out of funds available for the purchase of shares of stock under applicable state law. X represents that under applicable law, it would not be acting in a fiduciary capacity on behalf of trust beneficiaries if it were to exercise its power to substitute other assets of equal value for X stock held by the trust pursuant to the terms of the trust.

Section 83(a) of the Code provides that the excess (if any) of the fair market value of property transferred in connection with the performance of services over the amount paid (if any) for the property is includible in the gross income of the person who performed the services for the first taxable year in which the property becomes transferable or is not subject to a substantial risk of forfeiture.

Section 1.83-3(e) of the Income Tax Regulations provides that for purposes of Section 83 the term "property" includes real and personal property other than money or an unfunded and unsecured promise to pay money or property in the future. Property also includes a beneficial interest in assets (including money) transferred or set aside from claims of the transferor's creditors, for example, in a trust or escrow account.

Section 404(a)(5) of the Code provides the general deduction timing rules applicable to any plan or arrangement for the deferral of compensation, regardless of the Code section under which the amounts might otherwise be deductible. Pursuant to Section 404(a)(5) of the Code and Section 1.404(a)-12(b)(2) of the regulations, and provided that they otherwise meet the requirements for deductibility, contributions or compensation deferred under a nonqualified plan or arrangement are deductible in the taxable year in which they are paid or made available, whichever is earlier.

Section 451(a) of the Code and Section 1.451-1(a) of the regulations provide that an item of gross income is includible in gross income for the taxable year in which actually or constructively received by a taxpayer using the cash receipts and disbursements method of accounting. Under Section 1.451-2(a) of the regulations, income is constructively received in the taxable year during which it is credited to a taxpayer's account or set apart or otherwise made available so that the taxpayer may draw on it at any time. However, income is not constructively received if the taxpayer's control of its receipt is subject to substantial limitations or restrictions.

Various revenue rulings have considered the tax consequences of nonqualified deferred compensation arrangements. Revenue Ruling 60-31, Situations 1-3, 1960-1 C.B. 174, holds that a mere promise to pay, not represented by notes or secured in any way, does not constitute receipt of income within the meaning of the cash receipts and disbursements method of accounting. See also Revenue Ruling 69-650, 1969-2 C.B. 106, Revenue Ruling 69-649, 1969-2 C.B. 106.

Under the economic benefit doctrine, an employee has currently includible income from an economic or financial benefit received as compensation, though not in cash form. Economic benefit applies when assets are unconditionally and irrevocably paid into a fund or trust to be used for the employee's sole benefit. [Sproull v Commissioner, 16 T.C. 244 (1951), *aff'd per curiam,* 194 F2d 541 (6th Cir 1952), Rev Rul 60-31, Situation 4] In Revenue Ruling 72-25, 1972-1 C.B. 127, and Revenue Ruling 68-99, 1968-1 C.B. 193, an employee does not receive income as a result of the employer's purchase of an insurance contract to provide a source of funds for deferred compensation because the insurance contract is the employer's asset, subject to claims of the employer's creditors.

Under the terms of the trust, assets have been placed in trust to provide deferred compensation benefits to participants. However, the trustee has the obligation to hold the trust assets and income for the benefit of X's and the employers' general creditors in the event of X's or the employers' insolvency. The trust agreement further provides that a participant receives no beneficial ownership in or preferred claim on the trust assets. Therefore, although the assets are held in trust, in the event of X's or the employers' insolvency, they are fully within reach of X's or the employers' general creditors, as are any other assets of X or the employers.

Section 671 of the Code provides that where a grantor shall be treated as the owner of any portion of a trust under subpart E, part I, subchapter J, chapter 1 of the Code, there shall then be included in computing the taxable income and credits of the grantor those items of income, deductions, and credits against tax of the trust which are attributable to that portion of the trust to the extent that such items would be taken into account under chapter 1 in computing taxable income or credits against tax of an individual.

Letter Ruling 9317037

This is in response to a ruling request, dated June 16, 1992, as amended by letters dated October 1, November 9, and December 11, 1992, submitted on your behalf as Employee Z, by your authorized representative, concerning certain matters relating to the tax treatment of elective deferrals proposed to be made under Plan A. The following facts and representations were submitted in support of the rulings requested.

Employee Z is a highly compensated employee employed by Employer X. Employer X maintains Plan A and Plan B. Plan A is a qualified profit-sharing plan under Section 401(a) of the Internal Revenue Code (the "Code") containing a qualified cash-or-deferred arrangement as described in Code Section 401(k). Plan B is a nonqualified deferred compensation plan that is treated for tax purposes as a grantor trust under Code Sections 671 through 677. Employer X intends to implement Plan B upon receipt of this ruling.

Employee Z is a participant who is eligible to make pre-tax elective deferrals under Plan A, subject to the annual dollar limitation of Code Section 402(g) and the actual deferral percentage limitation of Code Section 401(k)(3). Employer X will also make matching contributions to Plan A with respect to Employee Z's elective deferrals up to the lesser of 100 percent of the participant's elective deferrals or 3 percent of the participant's annual earnings. Plan A operates with a calendar year plan year.

Employee Z is also a member of the select group of management or highly compensated employees that will be eligible to participate in Plan B. Prior to each January 1 or to the implementation of Plan B, Employee Z may elect to enter into a salary reduction agreement with Employer X pursuant to which Employee Z will specify the percentage of his compensation otherwise payable to Employee Z for the ensuing calendar year that will be deferred and credited to an individual account that is maintained in Employee Z's name under Plan B. Employer X will also make matching contributions to Plan B with respect to Employee Z's elective deferrals up to the lesser of 100 percent of such elective deferrals or 3 percent of Employee Z's annual earnings.

Immediately following each current plan year (i.e., calendar year) of Plan A, and not later than January 31 of the next ensuing year, Employer X will perform preliminary actual deferral percentage and actual contribution percentage testing to determine the maximum amount of additional elective contributions that could be made for such current plan year, consistent with Section 402(g) and the limitations of Section 401(k)(3), on behalf of Employee Z as a participant in Plan B. The lesser of that amount or Employee Z's salary deferral amount under Plan B for that year will be distributed to Employee Z between March 1 and March 15 of the year such determination is made, unless Employee Z previously elects to have such amount contributed to Plan A as an elective contribution. Employee Z's election to have such amount contributed to Plan A must be made not later than January 31 of the year the determination is made and, once made, the election is irrevocable. If Employee Z so elects, Employer X shall cause that amount to be contributed directly to Plan A.

In addition, to the extent that Employer X is required to make matching contributions under Plan A with respect to such elective contributions, Employer X will make such contributions out of matching amounts previously credited to Employee Z's account under Plan B. All such Plan A contributions will be debited from Employee Z's account under Plan B.

No earnings credited under Plan B will be contributed to Plan A. Thus, the elective deferrals under Plan A that result from salary deferred under Plan B will consist solely of amounts that were otherwise payable to Employee Z as current compensation for the plan year involved and for which deferral elections have been made. Any matching contributions associated with such elective contributions shall be in the same amounts as would be made if the elective deferrals were directly made, subject to the actual contribution percentage test of Code Section 401(m).

All elective deferrals and matching contributions under Plan A will be treated similarly. Employee Z will be fully vested in his elective deferrals and will not be entitled to a distribution thereof except upon separation from service, attainment of age 59½, death, disability, or hardship.

With respect to the foregoing, the following rulings are requested:

1. Assuming that Plan A otherwise satisfies the requirements for a qualified cash or deferred arrangement and that the elective deferral and actual deferral percentage limitations of Code Sections 402(g) and 401(k)(3) are not exceeded, elective deferrals made by Employee Z under Plan A that are initially held by Employer X pursuant to the terms of Plan B will be excluded from gross income under Code Section 402(a)(8).

2. For purposes of satisfying the Section 402(g) limit, elective deferrals under Plan A made by Employee Z for a given plan and calendar year that are initially held by Employer X pursuant to the terms of Plan B will be treated as having been made in the calendar year in which they would have been otherwise received as wages by Employee Z.

Code Section 402(a)(8) provides, in pertinent part, that contributions made by an employer on behalf of an employee to a trust which is a part of a qualified cash or deferred arrangement (as defined in Section 401(k)(2)) shall not be treated as distributed or made available to the employee nor as contributions made to a trust by the employee merely because the arrangement includes provisions under which the employee has an election whether the contribution will be made to the trust or received by the employee in cash.

Code Section 401(k)(2) provides, in pertinent part, that a qualified cash or deferred arrangement is any arrangement which is part of a profit-sharing or stock bonus plan, a pre-ERISA money purchase plan, or a rural cooperative plan which meets the requirements of Section 401(a), and under which a covered employee may elect to have the employer make payments as contributions to a trust under the plan on behalf of the employee, or to the employee directly in cash.

Section 1.401(k)-1(a)(3)(i) of the Income Tax Regulations provides that a cash or deferred election is any election (or modification of an earlier election) by an employee to have the employer either (a) provide an amount to the employee in the form of cash or some other taxable benefit that is not currently available, or (b) contribute an amount to a trust or provide an accrual or other benefit, under a plan deferring the receipt of compensation. A cash or deferred election includes a salary reduction agreement between an employee and employer under which a contribution is made under a plan only if the employee elects to reduce cash compensation or to forgo an increase in cash compensation.

Under Section 1.401(k)-1(a)(3)(ii) of the regulations, a cash or deferred election can only be made with respect to an amount that is not currently available to the employee on the date of the election. Under Section 1.401(k)-1(a)(3)(iii) of the regulations, cash or another taxable amount is currently available to the employee if it has been paid to the employee or if the employee is able currently to receive the cash or other taxable amount at the employee's discretion.

Under Section 1.401(k)-1(b)(4)(i) of the regulations, an elective contribution is taken into account for purposes of the actual deferral percentage test for a plan year only if (a) the elective contribution is allocated to the employee's account under the plan as of a date within that plan year, and (b) the elective contribution relates to compensation that either (1) would have been received by the employee in the plan year but for the employee's election to defer under the arrangement, or (2) is attributable to services performed by the employee in the plan year and, but for the employee's election to defer, would have been received by the employee within two and one-half months after the close of the plan year. An elective contribution is considered allocated as of a date within the plan year only if (i) the allocation is not contingent upon the employee's participation in the plan or performance of services on any date subsequent to that date, and (ii) the elective contribution is actually paid to the trust no later than the end of the 12-month period immediately following the plan year to which the contribution relates.

Under Code Section 401(g)(1), the elective deferrals of any individual for any taxable year are included in such individual's gross income to the extent the amount of such deferrals for the taxable year exceeds $7,000 (as adjusted under Code Section

402(g)(5)), notwithstanding Code Section 402(a)(8) regarding elective deferrals under a qualified cash or deferred arrangement.

With respect to issue one, Employee Z may make an irrevocable election to defer compensation under Plan A on or before January 31 of the next-following plan year. The amount subject to such election will be equal to the lesser of (i) the maximum amount of elective contributions that could be made for the current plan year on behalf of Employee Z under the actual deferral percentage and actual contribution percentage tests, and subject to the limitation on elective deferrals under Code Section 402(g), or (ii) Employee Z's salary deferral amount under Plan B for that current year. Such amount will be distributed in cash to Employee Z between March 1 and March 15 of the year such determination is made, unless Employee Z previously elects to have such amount contributed to Plan A as an elective contribution. If Employee Z so elects, Employer X shall cause that amount to be contributed directly to Plan A.

Accordingly, we conclude that, assuming Plan A otherwise satisfies the requirements for a qualified cash or deferred arrangement and that the elective deferral and actual deferral percentage limitations of Code Sections 402(g) and 401(k)(3) are not exceeded, elective deferrals made by Employee Z under Plan A that are initially held by Employer X pursuant to the terms of Plan B will be excluded from gross income under Code Section 402(a)(8).

With respect to issue two, we also conclude that, for purposes of satisfying the Code Section 402(g) limit, elective deferrals under Plan A made by Employer Z for a given plan and calendar year that are initially held by Employer X pursuant to the terms of Plan B will be treated as having been made in the calendar year in which they would have been otherwise received as wages by Employee Z, provided that elective deferrals are allocated to Employee Z's account by the end of the current plan year and the elective deferrals continue to relate to compensation that either would have been received by Employee Z in the plan year but for his election, or is attributable to services performed by Employee Z in the plan year and would have been received by Employee Z within two and one-half months after the plan year but for his election. This conclusion is consistent with the treatment of elective deferrals under Section 1.401(k)-1(b)(4)(i) of the regulations for purposes of the actual deferral percentage test under Code Section 401(k)(3).

The above rulings are based on the assumption that at all times relevant to these rulings, Plan A is qualified under Section 401(a) of the Code, its related trust is tax-exempt under Code Section 501(a), and its cash or deferred arrangement is qualified under Code Section 401(k)(2).

Letter Ruling 9405009

This is in reply to a letter dated April 8, 1993, and later correspondence, submitted on your behalf by your authorized representative, requesting rulings concerning the federal income tax consequences of a nonqualified deferred compensation plan (the "plan") established by X to provide certain benefits to key employees.

The plan provides for the payment of benefits to employees or their beneficiaries in amounts and at times determined in accordance with the plan following termination of employment. An eligible employee (a "participant") is an employee who is selected by the board of directors of X. Under the plan, a participant may elect deferred compensation in lieu of a fixed percentage or dollar amount of cash compensation. X contributes the maximum permissible amount of elective deferrals to a qualified plan (the "thrift plan") under a qualified cash or deferred arrangement on the participant's behalf. X credits the remainder of the participant's elected deferred compensation to the participant's separate account in the plan. X may also credit to the participant's account the amount of matching contributions that it would have made for the participant under the thrift plan, but for certain limitations under the Internal Revenue Code of 1986 ("Code"). X may also credit to the participant's account supplemental amounts determined by X's board of directors in its discretion. Certain amounts forfeited by participants are reallocated to the accounts of the remaining participants. X periodically adjusts the account balances in the plan to reflect income or losses.

Benefits are paid to the participant in a lump sum within 30 days after termination of service. If a participant dies, benefits are paid in a lump sum to his or her designated beneficiary.

The plan provides that a committee appointed by X may, in its discretion, establish a trust. X may, in its discretion, make contributions to the trust to provide for all or any part of its benefit obligations under the plan. The plan provides that any trust agreement must conform in all respects to the model trust contained in Revenue Procedure 92-64.

The plan provides that a participant or beneficiary has only an unsecured right to benefits under the Plan, and no right or claim against X's assets or the assets of any trust established under the plan. Benefits under the plan may not be alienated, assigned, or anticipated, and are not subject to attachment, garnishment, levy, execution, or other legal or equitable process.

Section 83(a) of the Internal Revenue Code provides that the excess (if any) of the fair market value of property transferred in connection with the performance of services over the amount (if any) paid for the property is includible in the gross income of the person who performed the services for the first taxable year in which the property becomes transferable or is not subject to a substantial risk of forfeiture.

Section 1.83-3(e) of the Income Tax Regulations provides that for purposes of Section 83 the term "property" does not include an unfunded and unsecured promise to pay money or property in the future. However, the term "property" does include a beneficial interest in assets (including money) transferred or set aside from claims of the transferor's creditors, for example, in a trust or escrow account.

Section 451(a) of the Code and Section 1.451-1(a) of the regulations provide that under the cash receipts and disbursements method of accounting, an item of gross income is included in gross income for the taxable year in which the taxpayer actually or constructively receives it. Section 1.451-2(a) of the regulations provides that income is constructively received in the taxable year during which it is credited to the taxpayer's account, set apart for him, or otherwise made available so that he may draw upon it at any time. However, income is not constructively received if the taxpayer's control of his receipt is subject to substantial limitations or restrictions.

Various revenue rulings have considered the tax consequences of nonqualified deferred compensation arrangements. Revenue Ruling 60-31, Situations 1-3, 1960-1 C.B. 174, holds that a mere promise to pay, not represented by notes or secured in any way, does not constitute receipt of income within the meaning of the cash receipts and disbursements method of accounting. See also Revenue Ruling 69-650, 1969-2 C.B. 106, and Revenue Ruling 69-649, 1969-2 C.B. 106.

Under the economic benefit doctrine, an employee has currently includible income from an economic or financial benefit received as compensation, though not in cash form. The economic benefit doctrine applies when assets are unconditionally and irrevocably paid into a fund or trust to be used for the employee's sole benefit. [Sproull v Commissioner, 16 T.C. 244 (1951), *aff'd per curiam*, 194 F2d 541 (6th Cir 1952); Rev Rul 60-31, Situation 4] In Revenue Ruling 72-25, 1972-1 C.B. 127, and Revenue Ruling 68-99, 1968-1 C.B. 193, it was held that an employee does not receive income as a result of the employer's purchase of an insurance contract to provide a source of funds for deferred compensation, because the insurance contract is the employer's asset, subject to claims of the employer's creditors.

Section 404(a) of the Code provides the general deduction timing rules applicable to any plan or arrangement for the deferral of compensation, regardless of the Code section under which the amounts might otherwise be deductible. Pursuant to Section 404(a)(5) of the Code and Section 1.404(a)-12(b)(2) of the regulations, amounts of contributions or compensation deferred under a nonqualified plan or arrangement are deductible in the taxable year in which they are paid or made available to the employee, whichever is earlier, provided that they otherwise meet the requirements for deductibility.

Based on the information submitted and representations made, we conclude that:

1. Neither the creation of the plan nor the crediting of earnings to a participant's account under the plan will constitute the transfer of property to a participant for purposes of Section 83 of the Code or Section 1.83-3(e) of the regulations.

2. Neither the creation of the plan nor the crediting of earnings to a participant's account under the plan will cause any amount to be included in the gross income of a participant or beneficiary under the cash receipts and disbursements method of accounting, pursuant to either Code Section 451, constructive receipt, or the economic benefit doctrine.

3. Amounts distributed under the plan will be included in the gross income of the recipient under the cash receipts and disbursements method of accounting in the taxable year in which actually paid or otherwise made available to the recipient, whichever is earlier.

4. X is entitled to deduct the amounts payable under the plan under Section 404(a)(5) of the Code only in the taxable year in which such amounts are includible in the gross income of the recipient, to the extent such payments are otherwise deductible under Section 162 of the Code.

Rulings 1 through 3 are based on the assumption that the participants' rights under the plan did not result in constructive receipt or economic benefit before the date of this ruling. No opinion is expressed as to whether benefits were actually or constructively received in prior years.

This ruling is contingent on the adoption of the amended plan that your authorized representative submitted on August 4, 1993. This ruling is directed only to the taxpayer who requested it. Section 6110(j) of the Code provides that this ruling may not be used or cited as precedent. Except as specifically stated above, no opinion is expressed on the federal tax consequences of the transaction described above under any other provision of the Code. Specifically no opinion is expressed on the consequences of the plan under Title I of the Employee Retirement Income Security Act of 1974 ("ERISA"). Moreover, if the plan is significantly amended, this ruling may no longer apply.

In accordance with the Power of Attorney on file, a copy of this ruling is being sent to your authorized representative.

Letter Ruling 9431021

This is in reply to the ruling request dated December 22, 1993, and subsequent correspondence that your authorized representative submitted concerning the consequences of the transactions described below under federal income tax law.

Based on the information submitted, we understand the relevant facts to be as follows. The employee is an officer of the company. On three occasions the company transferred restricted shares of common stock in the company (the "restricted stock") to the employee at no cost to him. The terms governing the transfer of the restricted stock were substantially similar in all three grants. Under those terms, the restricted stock vests in increments of one third of the total number of shares granted on the anniversary date in each of the fifth, sixth, and seventh years after grant; the restricted stock cannot be sold, assigned, transferred, pledged, hypothecated, or otherwise disposed of before it becomes vested; if the employee's employment with the company is terminated for reasons other than death or disability, then nonvested shares of the restricted stock are forfeited, and a committee of the company may, but is not required to, waive the forfeiture provisions if the employee's employment is terminated because of normal or early retirement.

Some of the shares of restricted stock have vested and some remain nonvested. The company and the employee propose to postpone the vesting dates for the nonvested shares of restricted stock. The term of postponement ranges from approximately 17 months to approximately 33 months. The company and the employee wish to know the tax consequences, if any, of postponing the vesting date of the restricted stock.

Section 83 of the Code provides that if, in connection with the performance of services, property is transferred to any person other than the person for whom the services are performed, the excess of the fair market value of the property (determined without regard to any restriction other than a restriction that by its terms will never lapse) at the first time the rights of the person having the beneficial interest in the property are transferable or not subject to a substantial risk of forfeiture, whichever occurs earlier, over the amount paid for the property is included in the gross income of the person who performed the services in the first taxable year in which the rights of the person having the beneficial interest are transferable or not subject to a substantial risk of forfeiture.

Under Section 83(c)(1) of the Code, the rights of a person in property are subject to a substantial risk of forfeiture if the person's rights to full enjoyment of the property are conditioned upon the future performance of substantial services by any individual.

Under Section 1.83-3(c) of the regulations, whether a risk of forfeiture is substantial or not depends on the facts and circumstances. A substantial risk of forfeiture exists where rights in property that are transferred are conditioned, directly or indirectly, upon the future performance of substantial services by any person. The regularity of the performance of services and the time spent in performing such services tend to indicate whether services required by a condition are substantial.

Under Section 1.83-3(d) of the regulations, the rights of a person in property are transferable if the person can transfer any interest in the property to any person other than the transferor of the property, but only if the transferee's rights in the property are not subject to a substantial risk of forfeiture. Property is considered transferable under the regulations if the person performing the services or receiving the property can sell, assign, or pledge (as collateral for a loan, or as security for the performance of an obligation, or for any other purpose) her or his interest in the property to any person other than the transferor and if the transferee is not required to give up the property or its value in the event the substantial risk of forfeiture materializes.

In this case the employee has received restricted stock. Nonvested shares are subject to restrictions against transfer that render the shares not transferable for purposes of Section 83 of the Code. See Section 1.83-3(d) of the regulations. The employee will definitely forfeit the nonvested shares upon termination of his employment with the company for reasons other than death or disability, although forfeiture may, but is not required to, be waived in the event of retirement. For a risk of forfeiture to be substantial, the regulations require that the employee's rights in the property be conditioned on the future performance of substantial services. In this case the employee's rights in the nonvested shares of restricted stock are conditioned on the performance of future services. If the future services required of the employee are substantial, then the employee is not required to include the value of the nonvested shares of restricted stock in gross income until they become transferable or are no longer subject to a substantial risk of forfeiture.

The postponement of the vesting dates for the nonvested shares of restricted stock does not cause them to become transferable. Neither does the postponement of the vesting dates free the employee from the obligation to provide future services to retain his rights in the nonvested shares of restricted stock. As long as the future services required of the employee were and continue to be substantial, the postponement of the vesting date of the nonvested shares of restricted stock will not in itself require the employee to include in gross income the value of those shares.

Accordingly, subject to the condition that the future services required of the employee to avoid forfeiting the nonvested shares of restricted stock have been and continue to be substantial, we rule that the postponement of the lapsing of restrictions on the transferability of the restricted stock and the prolongation of the period during which the restricted stock is subject to a risk of forfeiture will not cause the value of the restricted stock to be included in the gross income of the employee under Section 83(a) of the Code.

Except as ruled in the preceding paragraph, we express no opinion about the federal tax consequences of the transactions described in this letter.

This ruling is directed only to the taxpayer who requested it. Section 6110(j)(3) of the Code prohibits the use or citation of it as precedent.

Letter Ruling 9444028

This is in response to your letter dated March 31, 1994, and later correspondence requesting a ruling on behalf of X on the federal income tax consequences of a nonqualified deferred compensation plan benefiting certain employees of X, and a related trust. X is a tax-exempt organization under Section 501(c)(3) of the Internal Revenue Code of 1986 (the "Code"). The plan is intended to be an ineligible deferred compensation plan to which Section 457(f) applies.

X has adopted the X Nonqualified Deferred Compensation Plan (the "plan") to provide deferred compensation to X's employees who are members of a category defined in the plan (the "participants"). X has represented that the participants are a "select group of management or highly compensated employees" of X, within the meaning of Sections 201(2), 301(a)(3), and 401(a)(1) of the Employee Retirement Income Security Act, as amended ("ERISA").

Under the plan, X maintains a bookkeeping account for the deferred compensation of each participant. X may from time to time credit the accounts of some or all participants with amounts of deferred compensation. The amounts and their allocation among the participants are determined by X in its discretion. X is not required to credit any deferred compensation. Each participant's account is deemed to be invested in one or more investment options selected by the participant from a group of options offered by X. The participant's account is increased or decreased by the net amount of investment earnings or losses that it would have achieved had it actually been invested in the deemed investments. X is not required to purchase or hold any of the deemed investments; instead the deemed investments serve only as a determinant of the participant's benefits.

When X credits an amount of deferred compensation to a participant's account, X designates the plan year in which the participant will become vested in that amount. The participant becomes vested if he or she is still employed by X on January 1 of the designated plan year, which may be no earlier than the third plan year beginning after the plan year in which the amount is credited. The participant also becomes vested in his or her entire account when he or she becomes disabled, as defined in the plan, and his or her beneficiary becomes vested if the participant dies while employed by X. A participant is fully vested in any deemed earnings when they are added to his or her account. If the participant's employment is terminated (other than because of death or disability), and the participant is not reemployed by X within 90 days, the participant forfeits all amounts in which he or she is not yet vested. Each year X determines in its discretion whether (1) to reallocate the forfeitures among the remaining participants in a manner determined by X, or (2) to hold the forfeitures in a suspense account to be applied as X directs in the future.

A participant is entitled to a distribution of the deferred compensation amount (and the related deemed earnings) in his or her account when he or she becomes vested in it. A participant's designated beneficiary is entitled to a distribution of the entire account balance when the participant dies. A participant who forfeits any amount is entitled to a distribution of the deemed earnings related to that amount within 30 days after the end of the first calendar quarter beginning after the forfeiture occurs. Before each plan year, a participant must elect whether amounts credited to his or her account for that plan year will be distributed as a lump sum or in annual installments over a period of ten years or less. A lump sum distribution or the first installment is paid within 30 days after the end of the calendar quarter in which the participant or beneficiary becomes entitled to it.

The plan provides that any person entitled to any amount under the plan will be a general unsecured creditor of X with respect to that amount. A participant's rights to benefits under the plan are not subject in any manner to anticipation, alienation, sale, transfer, assignment, pledge, encumbrance, attachment, or garnishment by creditors of the participant or the participant's beneficiary.

The plan provides that X may establish a trust to pay the benefits that X is obligated to pay under the plan. By agreement (the "trust agreement") with an unrelated third party (the "trustee"), X has established an irrevocable trust (the "trust") for this purpose. X has represented that the trust agreement conforms to the model trust agreement contained in Revenue Proceeding 92-64, 1992-2 C.B. 422, including the order in which sections of the model trust language appear. X has also represented that the trust agreement does not contain any language that is inconsistent with or conflicts with the language of the model trust agreement, and that the trust is a valid trust under state law. Under the plan and the trust, the interests of the participants and beneficiaries in the trust estate are no greater than those of any other general unsecured creditor of X.

Section 83(a) of the Code provides that the excess (if any) of the fair market value of property transferred in connection with the performance of services over the amount paid (if any) for the property is includible in the gross income of the person who performed the services for the first taxable year in which the property becomes transferable or is not subject to a substantial risk of forfeiture.

Section 1.83-3(e) of the Income Tax Regulations provides that for purposes of Section 83 the term "property" includes real and personal property other than money or an unfunded and unsecured promise to pay money or property in the future. Property also includes a beneficial interest in assets (including money) transferred or set aside from claims of the transferor's creditors, for example, in a trust or escrow account.

Section 451(a) of the Code and Section 1.451-1(a) of the regulations provide that under the cash receipts and disbursements method of accounting, an item of gross income is included in gross income for the taxable year in which the taxpayer actually or constructively receives it. Section 1.451-2(a) of the regulations provides that income is constructively received in the taxable year during which it is credited to the taxpayer's account, set apart for him, or otherwise made available so that he may draw upon it at any time. However, income is not constructively received if the taxpayer's control of his receipt is subject to substantial limitations or restrictions.

Various revenue rulings have considered the tax consequences of nonqualified deferred compensation arrangements. Revenue Ruling 60-31, Situations 1-3, 1960-1 C.B. 174, holds that a mere promise to pay, not represented by notes or secured in any way, does not constitute receipt of income within the meaning of the cash receipts and disbursements method of accounting. See also Revenue Ruling 69-650, 1969-2 C.B. 106, and Revenue Ruling 69-649, 1969-2 C.B. 106.

Under the economic benefit doctrine, an employee has currently includible income from an economic or financial benefit received as compensation, though not in cash form. The economic benefit doctrine applies when assets are unconditionally and irrevocably paid into a fund or trust to be used for the employee's sole benefit. [Sproull v Commissioner, 16, T.C. 244 (1951), aff'd per curiam, 194 F2d 541 (6th Cir 1952); Rev Rul 60-31, Situation 4] In Revenue Ruling 72-25, 1972-1 C.B. 127, and Revenue Ruling 68-99, 1968-1 C.B. 193, an employee does not receive income as a result of the employer's purchase of an insurance contract to provide a source of funds for deferred compensation because the insurance contract is the employer's asset, subject to the claims of the employer's creditors.

Under the terms of the trust agreement, assets will be placed in trust to be used to provide benefits to participants under the plan. However, the trustee has the obligation to hold the trust assets and income for the benefit of X's general creditors in the event of X's insolvency. The trust agreement further provides that a participant receives no beneficial ownership in or preferred claim on the trust assets. Therefore, although the assets are held in trust, in the event of X's insolvency they are fully within the reach of X's general creditors, as are any other assets of X.

Section 301.7701-4(a) of the Procedure and Administration Regulations provides that, generally, an arrangement will be treated as a trust if it can be shown that the purpose of the arrangement is to vest in trustees responsibility for the protection and conservation of property for beneficiaries who cannot share in the discharge of this responsibility and, therefore, are not associates in a joint enterprise for the conduct of business for profit.

Section 671 of the Code provides that where a grantor is treated as owner of any portion of trust under subpart E, part I, subchapter J, chapter 1 of the Code, there shall then be included in computing the taxable income and credits of the grantor those items of income, deductions, and credits against tax of the trust that are attributable to that portion of the trust to the extent that such items would be taken into account under chapter 1 in computing taxable income or credits against tax of an individual.

Section 677(a)(2) of the Code provides that the grantor shall be treated as the owner of any portion of a trust whose income without the approval or consent of any adverse party is, or, in the discretion of the grantor or a nonadverse party, or both, may be held or accumulated for future distribution to the grantor.

Section 1.677(a)-1(d) of the regulations provides that under Section 677 of the Code, a grantor is, in general, treated as the owner of a portion of a trust whose income is, or in the discretion of the grantor or a nonadverse party, or both, may be, applied in discharge of a legal obligation of the grantor.

Section 457 of the Code provides rules governing the deferral of compensation by an individual participating in a deferred compensation plan of an eligible employer. Under Section 457(e)(1)(B), a tax-exempt organization is an eligible employer covered by Section 457. Since X is a tax-exempt organization under Section 501(c)(3), X is an eligible employer within the meaning of Section 457(e)(1).

Section 457(a) of the Code provides that in the case of a participant in an eligible deferred compensation plan, any amount of compensation deferred under the plan and any income attributable to the amounts so deferred are includible in gross income only for the taxable year in which the compensation or other income is paid or otherwise made available to the participant or beneficiary.

Section 457(b) of the Code and Section 1.457-2 of the Income Tax Regulations define the term "eligible deferred compensation plan." The plan is not an eligible deferred compensation plan within the meaning of these provisions.

Under Section 457(f)(1)(A) of the Code, if an eligible employer's plan deferring compensation is not an eligible deferred compensation plan, the compensation is included in gross income for the first year in which the participant's right to the compensation is not subject to a substantial risk of forfeiture. Section 457(f)(1)(B) provides that the tax treatment of any amount made available under the ineligible plan to a participant is determined under Code Section 72 (relating to annuities, etc.). Section 457(f)(3)(B) provides that the rights of a person to compensation are subject to a substantial risk of forfeiture if the person's rights to the compensation are conditioned upon the future performance of substantial services by any individual.

Section 83(c)(1) of the Code, concerning compensatory transfers of property, includes the same definition of substantial risk of forfeiture as Section 457(e)(3). Section 1.83-3(c)(1) of the regulations states that whether a risk of forfeiture is substantial or not depends upon the facts and circumstances. Section 1.83-3(c)(2) provides that requirements that property be returned to the employer if the employee is discharged for cause or for committing a crime do not result in a substantial risk of forfeiture of the employee's rights to the property. Example 1 of Section 1.83-3(c)(4) involves stock transferred to an employee, who must resell the stock to the employer if the employee leaves the employ of the employer for any reason within two years after the transfer. The regulations state that the stock is subject to a substantial risk of forfeiture during the two-year period.

Provided (i) that the creation of the trust does not cause the plan to be other than "unfunded" for purposes of Title I of ERISA, (ii) that the participants are a "select group of management or highly compensated employees" of X, within the meaning of Sections 201(2), 301(a)(3), and 401(a)(1) of ERISA, and (iii) that the provision in the trust requiring use of the trust assets to satisfy the claims of X's general creditors in the event of X's insolvency is enforceable by the general creditors of X under federal and state law, and based on the information submitted and representations made, we conclude that:

1. Neither the adoption of the plan, the creation of the trust, nor the contribution of assets by X to the trust will result in a transfer of property for purposes of Section 83 of the Code or Section 1.83-3(e) of the regulations.

2. Neither the adoption of the plan, the creation of the trust, nor the contribution of assets by X to the trust will cause any amount to be included in the gross income of a participant or beneficiary under the cash receipts and disbursements method of accounting, pursuant to either Code Section 451, constructive receipt, the economic benefit doctrine, or Section 457(f).

3. No amount will be made available to a participant merely because the participant has a right to designate the "deemed investment" of the deferred compensation amounts credited to his or her account in the plan.

4. The trust will be classified as a trust under Section 301.7701-4(a) of the Procedure and Administration Regulations. X will be treated as the owner of the trust under Section 677(a) of the Code and Section 1.677(a)-1(d) of the regulations. Under Code Section 671, X must include all of the income, deductions, and credits of the trust in computing its own taxable income and credits.

5. Under Code Section 457(f), the amounts of deferred compensation credited to a participant's account under the plan are includible in the gross income of the participant (or, in the case of the participant's death, the gross income of his or her beneficiary) for the first taxable year for which the participant's or beneficiary's rights to these amounts are not subject to a substantial risk of forfeiture. This will be the taxable year of the participant or beneficiary in which the participant becomes disabled, dies, or becomes vested in the amounts of deferred compensation. The entire amount of deferred compensation is includible in gross income for that taxable year even if the participant elected to receive installment distributions.

6. Amounts made available to a participant or beneficiary under the plan are includible in the gross income of the participant or beneficiary in accordance with the rules of Code Section 72. Amounts are made available when the participant or beneficiary becomes entitled to receive them under the plan. Therefore, no portion of the deemed earnings credited to a participant's account under the plan will be includible in gross income until the taxable year in which the participant or beneficiary becomes entitled to receive them. The portion of any installment distribution includible in gross income will be determined under Section 72.

This ruling is contingent upon the adoption of the modifications to the plan and trust that you submitted with your letters of July 27 and 29, and August 3, 1994. If the plan or trust agreement is otherwise modified significantly, this ruling may no longer apply.

This ruling is directed only to the taxpayer who requested it. Section 6110(j)(3) of the Code provides that it may not be used or cited as precedent. Except as specifically ruled on above, no opinion is expressed as to the federal tax consequences of the transaction described above under any other provision of the Code. Furthermore, no opinion is expressed as to the effect of any other statute. Specifically, no opinion is expressed on the consequences of the plan or trust under Title I of ERISA.

Temporary or final regulations pertaining to one or more of the issues addressed in this ruling have not yet been adopted. Therefore, this ruling may be modified or revoked if temporary or final regulations are issued that are inconsistent with any conclusion in the ruling. See Section 11.04 of Revenue Procedure 94-1, 1994-1 I.R.B. 3, 32-33. However, when the criteria in Section 11.05 of Revenue Procedure 94-1 are satisfied, a ruling is not revoked or modified retroactively except in rare or unusual circumstances.

Letter Ruling 9511046

This is in response to your letter dated December 22, 1994, and prior submissions in which you request rulings concerning the estate tax consequences with respect to a split-dollar second-to-die insurance policy owned by an irrevocable trust.

You represent that an irrevocable life insurance trust created in January 1990 owns a second-to-die life insurance policy on the taxpayer and his spouse. The beneficiaries of the trust are the children and grandchildren of the taxpayer and his spouse. The trustee of the trust is a third party, and the successor trustees are the taxpayer's children and a corporate bank. Neither the taxpayer nor his spouse may act as trustee of the trust and neither have any powers with respect to the trust that would be considered incidents of ownership for purposes of Section 2042 of the Internal Revenue Code.

The taxpayer, as trustee of his inter vivos revocable trust, owns 50 percent of the outstanding shares of a closely held corporation. The taxpayer's spouse, as trustee of her inter vivos revocable trust, owns the other 50 percent of the outstanding shares of the corporation. The corporation has made an election to be treated as a subchapter S corporation.

The taxpayer's inter vivos revocable trust will become irrevocable upon the taxpayer's death. At that time, all capital stock of the corporation held by the taxpayer's trust is to be allocated to an irrevocable trust that will be eligible for treatment as a qualified terminable interest property (QTIP) trust upon election by the executor. The trust will also be a qualified subchapter S trust. At the death of the taxpayer's spouse, the principal of the QTIP trust is to continue to be held in trust for the benefit of the taxpayer's children and grandchildren. The terms of the spouse's inter vivos revocable trust are similar to those of the taxpayer's revocable trust with the only difference being that the taxpayer is the primary beneficiary of the QTIP trust.

The corporation and the trustee of the irrevocable life insurance trust propose to enter into a split-dollar life insurance agreement. The agreement is to provide that the corporation, through the taxpayer and his spouse, is required to pay the entire premium on the second-to-die policy held by the trust, less any amount paid by the trustee. The corporation is required to make these payments for the duration of the agreement.

The agreement further provides that only the trustee of the insurance trust may obtain loans against the policy or pledge the policy for a loan. The corporation is prohibited from borrowing any portion of the net cash value of the policy. Dividends on the policy must be applied as determined by the trustee. The trustee as owner of the policy is entitled to all benefits, rights, and privileges granted by the policy. The agreement will terminate on the earlier of the surrender of the policy or the delivery of a notice of termination of the agreement. Only the trustee can surrender the policy or terminate the agreement. If the policy is surrendered, the corporation has a security interest in the net cash value of the policy in an amount equal to the lesser of the amount of the premiums paid by the corporation or the net cash value of the policy. If the agreement is terminated, the trustee must pay the corporation the lesser of these two amounts. If the agreement does not terminate before the death of the second to die of the taxpayer and his spouse, then the corporation has a security interest in the proceeds of the policy in the amount of the premiums paid by the corporation. In order to secure payment to the corporation under the agreement, the agreement provides for a collateral assignment of the policy to the corporation. The corporation is prohibited from assigning its interest to anyone other than the trustee or the trustee's nominee.

You request that we rule that the corporation will hold no incidents of ownership in the second-to-die life insurance policy or its proceeds that are paid to the trustee under Section 2042, and that the proceeds of the policy that are paid to the trustee will not be included in the gross estate of the second to die of the taxpayer or his spouse.

Section 2042(2) provides that the value of the gross estate of the decedent shall include the proceeds of all life insurance policies on the decedent's life receivable by beneficiaries, other than the executor of the decedent's estate, to the extent that the decedent possessed at his death any incidents of ownership exercisable either alone or in conjunction with any other person. An incident of ownership includes a reversionary interest arising by the express terms of the instrument or by operation of law only if the value of such reversionary interest exceeds 5 percent of the value of the policy immediately before the death of the decedent.

Section 20.2042-1(c)(2) of the Estate Tax Regulations provides that "incidents of ownership" is not limited in its meaning to ownership of a policy in the technical legal sense. Generally speaking, the term has reference to the right of the insured or his estate to the economic benefits of the policy. Thus, it includes the power to change the beneficiary, to surrender or cancel the policy, to assign the policy, to revoke an assignment, to pledge the policy for a loan, or to obtain from the insurer a loan against the surrender value of the policy.

Section 20.2042-1(c)(4) provides that a decedent is considered to have an incident of ownership an insurance policy on his life held in trust if, under the terms of the policy, the decedent, either alone or in conjunction with another person or persons, has the power, as trustee or otherwise, to change the beneficial ownership of the policy or its proceeds or the time or manner of enjoyment thereof, even though the decedent has no beneficial interest in the trust.

Section 20.2042-1(c)(6) provides that, where the decedent is the sole or controlling stockholder of a corporation, the corporation's incidents of ownership will not be attributed to the decedent through his stock ownership to the extent that the proceeds of the policy are payable to the corporation. However, if the proceeds of the policy are payable to a third party for a nonbusiness purpose and not to or for the benefit of the corporation and, thus, are not taken into account in valuing the decedent's stock holdings, the proceeds will be includible in the gross estate of the decedent under Section 2042(2). The decedent will not be deemed to be the controlling stockholder of a corporation unless, at the time of his death, he owns stock possessing more than 50 percent of the total combined voting power of the corporation. Solely for purposes of the preceding sentence, a decedent shall be considered to be the owner of only the stock with respect to which legal title was held, at the time of his death, by, (1) the decedent or his agent, (2) the decedent and another person jointly, and (3) by a trustee of a voting trust to the extent of the decedent's beneficial interest therein or any other trust with respect to which the decedent was treated as an owner under subpart E, part I, subchapter J, chapter 1 of the Code immediately prior to his death.

Section 1361(d)(1) provides that, in the case of a subchapter S trust with respect to which a beneficiary has made the appropriate election, such trust will be treated as a trust (under subpart E of part I of subchapter J) as owned by an individual who is a citizen or resident of the United States, and for purposes of Section 678(a), the beneficiary of the trust shall be treated as the owner of that portion of the trust which consists of stock in an S corporation with respect to which the appropriate election is made.

Revenue Ruling 76-274, 1976-2 C.B. 278, holds that where a third party obtains an insurance policy on a decedent's life and enters into a split-dollar agreement with a corporation controlled by the decedent, and the rights of the corporation with respect to the policy are restricted, incidents of ownership will not be attributed to the corporation and, thus, policy proceeds that pass at the decedent's death to beneficiaries other than the corporation will not be included in the gross estate of the decedent. Under the facts presented, the corporation could borrow against the policy only to the extent of the cash surrender value but not in excess of its loan of premium monies. The terms of the agreement and the terms of the policy clearly prohibited the corporation from taking any action that would endanger the interest of the decedent. The corporation was specifically prohibited in any way from surrendering the policy for cancellation and from assigning its rights to anyone other than the third party/owner of the policy.

In the present case, after the first to die of either the taxpayer or his spouse, the shares of the corporation previously held by the decedent will pass into a QTIP trust for the benefit of the surviving spouse. This trust is intended to qualify under Section 1361(d) as a qualified subchapter S trust, and if the trust so qualifies, the surviving spouse will be considered the owner under subpart E, part I, subchapter J of the Code. Accordingly, the surviving spouse will be considered the owner of the stock in the QTIP trust for purposes of determining control under Section 20.2042-1(c)(6). Combining the 50 percent of the stock owned by the surviving spouse through the QTIP trust with the 50 percent of the stock owned outright by the surviving spouse, the surviving spouse will control the corporation for purposes of Section 20.2042-1(c)(6). Thus, if the corporation holds incidents of ownership in the policy, the corporation's incidents of ownership will not be attributed to the decedent through his stock ownership to the extent that the proceeds of the policy are payable to the corporation. However, if the proceeds of the policy are payable to a third party for a nonbusiness purpose and not to or for the benefit of the corporation, the proceeds will be includible in the gross estate of the decedent under Section 2042(2).

Under the split-dollar agreement in the present case, the corporation will, however, hold no incidents of ownership. The corporation will have no de facto ability to force the trustee to borrow against the policy because the corporation is required to make the necessary premium payments for the duration of the trust. The power to change the beneficiary, the power to surrender or cancel the policy, the power to assign the policy or to revoke an assignment, and the power to pledge the policy for a loan or to obtain from the insurer a loan against the surrender value of the policy are vested in the third party trustee of the irrevocable trust and are not attributable to the corporation. Accordingly, although the surviving spouse will hold control of the corporation for purposes of Section 20.2042-1(c)(6), the corporation will hold no incidents of ownership in the second-to-die life insurance policy, and, thus, no incidents of ownership in the policy will be attributable to the surviving spouse.

We conclude that the corporation will hold no incidents of ownership in the second-to-die life insurance policy or its proceeds that are paid to the trustee under Section 2042, and that the proceeds of the policy that are paid to the trustee will not be included in the gross estate of the second to die of the taxpayer or his spouse.

Except as we have specifically ruled herein, we express no opinion under the cited provisions or under any other provision of the Code.

This ruling is based on the facts and applicable law in effect on the date of this letter. If there is a change in material fact or law (local or federal) before the transactions considered in the ruling take effect, the ruling will have no force or effect. If the taxpayer is in doubt whether there has been a change in material fact or law, a request for reconsideration of this ruling should be submitted to this office.

This ruling is directed only to the taxpayer who requested it. Section 6110(j)(3) provides that it may not be used or cited as precedent.

Letter Ruling 9530038

This is in response to your ruling request, dated June 16, 1992, amended by letters dated October 1, November 9, and December 11, 1992, and February 3, March 17, and July 21, 1994, submitted on your behalf as Employee Z, by your authorized representative, concerning certain matters relating to the tax treatment of elective deferrals proposed to be made under Plan A. The following facts and representations were submitted in support of the rulings requested.

Employee Z is a highly compensated employee employed by Employer X. Employer X maintains Plan A and proposes to implement Plan B. Plan A is a qualified profit-sharing plan under section 401(a) of the Internal Revenue Code (the "Code") which Employer X represents contains a qualified cash-or-deferred arrangement as described in Code Section 401(k). Plan B provides that it is intended to be an unfunded nonqualified deferred compensation plan. Deferrals under Plan B are held as part of the general assets of Employer X. The terms of the arrangement provide that assets are subject to the claims of Employer X's general creditors. Employer X intends to implement Plan B upon receipt of this ruling although rulings on Plan B have not been requested or provided.

Employee Z is a participant who is eligible to make pre-tax elective deferrals under Plan A, subject to the annual dollar limitation of Code Section 402(g) and the actual deferral percentage limitation of Code Section 401(k)(3). Employer X will also make matching contributions to Plan A with respect to Employee Z's elective deferrals up to the lesser of 100 percent of the participant's elective deferrals or 3 percent of the participant's annual earnings. Plan A operates with a calendar year plan year.

Employer X represents that Employee Z is a member of the select group of management or highly compensated employees and will be eligible to participate in Plan B. Prior to each January 1 or to the implementation of Plan B, Employee Z may elect to enter into a salary reduction agreement with Employer X, no later than December 31 of the calendar year preceding the year in which the compensation to which the salary deferral election relates is earned. Pursuant to the election, Employee Z will specify the percentage of his compensation otherwise payable to Employee Z for the ensuing calendar year that will be deferred under Plan B. Employer X will also make matching credits to Plan B with respect to Employee Z's salary deferrals up to the lesser of 100 percent of such salary deferrals or 3 percent of Employee Z's annual earnings. Plan B provides that amounts deferred by Employee Z remain an asset of Employer X and available to Employer X's general creditors.

As soon as practicable each plan year (i.e., calendar year) of Plan A, and not later than January 31 of the next ensuing year, Employer X will perform preliminary actual deferral percentage and actual contribution percentage testing to determine the maximum amount of additional elective contributions that could be made for such current plan year, consistent with Section 402(g) and the limitations of Section 401(k)(3), on behalf of Employee Z as a participant in Plan A. The lesser of those amounts, or Employee Z's salary deferral under Plan B for that year, will be paid to Employee Z as soon as practicable, but in no event later than March 15 of the plan year following the plan year for which such determination is made, unless Employee Z previously elected to have such amount contributed to Plan A as an elective contribution. Employee Z's election to have such amount contributed to Plan A must be made at the same time as Employee Z's election to enter into a salary reduction agreement with Employer X under Plan B which must be no later than December 31 of the calendar year preceding the year in which the compensation to which the salary deferral relates is earned and, once made, the election is irrevocable. If Employee Z so elects, Employer X shall cause that amount to be contributed directly to Plan A.

Amounts paid to Employee Z, because Employee Z does not elect to have such amounts contributed to Plan A as an elective contribution, will be includible in Employee Z's gross income in the year in which the compensation to which the salary deferral under Plan B relates was earned, and Employer X will include this amount in Employee Z's W-2 compensation for that year.

In addition, to the extent that Employer X is required to make matching contributions under Plan A with respect to such elective contributions, Employer X will make such contributions out of matching amounts previously credited under Plan B. All such Plan A contributions will be debited under Plan B.

No earnings credited under Plan B will be contributed to Plan A. Thus, the elective deferrals under Plan A that result from salary deferred under Plan B will consist solely of amounts that were otherwise payable to Employee Z as current compensation for the plan year involved and for which deferral elections have been made. Any matching contributions associated with such elective contributions shall be in the same amounts as would be made if the elective deferrals were directly made, subject to the actual contribution percentage test Code Section 401(m).

All elective deferrals and matching contributions under Plan A will be treated similarly. Employee Z will be fully vested in his elective deferrals and will not be entitled to a distribution thereof except upon separation from service, attainment of age 59½, death, disability, or hardship.

With respect to the foregoing, the following rulings are requested:

1. Assuming that Plan A otherwise satisfies the requirement for a qualified cash or deferred arrangement and that the elective deferral and actual deferral percentage limitations of Code Sections 402(g) and 401(k)(3) are not exceeded, elective deferrals made by Employee Z under Plan A that are initially held by Employer X pursuant to the terms of Plan B will be excluded from gross income under Code Section 402(e)(3).

2. For purposes of satisfying the Section 402(g) limit, elective deferrals under Plan A made by Employee Z for a given plan and calendar year that are initially held by Employer X pursuant to the terms of Plan B will be treated as having been made in the calendar year in which they would have been otherwise received as wages by Employee Z.

Code Section 402(e)(3) provides, in pertinent part, that contributions made by an employer on behalf of an employee to a trust which is a part of a qualified cash or deferred arrangement (as defined in Section 401(k)(2)) shall not be treated as distributed or made available to the employee nor as contributions made to a trust by the employee merely because the arrangement includes provisions under which the employee has an election whether the contribution will be made to the trust or received by the employee in cash.

Code Section 401(k)(2) provides, in pertinent part, that a qualified cash or deferred arrangement is any arrangement which is part of a profit-sharing or stock bonus plan, a pre-ERISA money purchase plan, or a rural cooperative plan which meets the requirements of Section 401(a), and under which a covered employee may elect to have the employer make payments as contributions to a trust under the plan on behalf of the employee, or to the employee directly in cash.

Section 1.401(k)-1(a)(3)(i) of the Income Tax Regulations provides that a cash or deferred election is any election (or modification of an earlier election) by an employee to have the employer either (A) provide an amount to the employee in the form of cash or some other taxable benefit that is not currently available, or (B) contribute an amount to a trust, or provide an accrual or other benefit, under a plan deferring the receipt of compensation. A cash or deferred election includes a salary reduction agreement between an employee and employer under which a contribution is made under a plan only if the employee elects to reduce cash compensation or to forgo an increase in cash compensation.

Under Section 1.401(k)-1(a)(3)(ii) of the regulations, a cash or deferred election can only be made with respect to an amount that is not currently available to the employees on the date of the election. Under Section 1.401(k)-1(a)(3)(iii) of the regulations, cash or another taxable amount is currently available to the employee if it has been paid to the employee or if the employee is able currently to receive the cash or other taxable amount at the employee's discretion.

Under Section 1.401(k)-1(b)(4)(i) of the regulations, an elective contribution is taken into account for purposes of the actual deferral percentage test for a plan year only if (A) the elective contribution is allocated to the employee's account under the plan as of a date within that plan year, and (B) the elective contribution relates to compensation that either (1) would have been received by the employee in the plan year but for the employee's election to defer under the arrangement, or (2) is attributable to services performed by the employee in the plan year and, but for the employee's election to defer, would have been received by the employee within two and one-half months after the close of the plan year. An elective contribution is considered allocated as of a date within the plan year only if (i) the allocation is not contingent upon the employee's participation in the plan or performance of services on any date subsequent to that date, and (ii) the elective contribution is actually paid to the trust no later than the end of the 12-month period immediately following the plan year to which the contribution relates.

Under Code Section 402(g)(1), the elective deferrals of any individual for any taxable year are included in such individual's gross income to the extent the amount of such deferrals for the taxable year exceeds $7,000 (as adjusted under Code Section 402(g)(5), notwithstanding Code Section 402(e)(3) regarding elective deferrals under a qualified cash or deferred arrangement.

With respect to issue one, Employee Z may make an irrevocable election to defer compensation under Plan A no later than December 31 of the calendar year preceding the year the compensation to which the salary deferral relates is earned. The amount subject to such election will be equal to the lesser of (i) the maximum amount of elective contributions that could be made for the current plan year on behalf of Employee Z under the actual deferral percentage and actual contribution percentage tests, and subject to the limitation on elective deferrals under Code Section 402(g), or (ii) Employee Z's salary deferral amount under Plan B for that current year. Such amount will be distributed in cash to Employee Z as soon as practicable, but in no event later than March 15 of the year next following the plan year with respect to which such determination is made, unless Employee Z has previously elected to have such amount contributed to Plan A as an elective contribution. If Employee Z so elects, Employer X shall cause that amount to be contributed directly to Plan A. Any amount distributed to Employee Z shall be includible in Employee Z's gross income in the year in which the compensation to which the salary deferral under Plan B relates was earned.

Accordingly, we conclude that, assuming Plan A otherwise satisfies the requirements for a qualified cash or deferred arrangement and that the elective deferral and actual deferral percentage limitations of Code Sections 402(g) and 401(k)(3) are not exceeded, elective deferrals made by Employee Z under Plan A that are initially held by Employer X pursuant to the terms of Plan B will be excluded from gross income under Code Section 402(e)(3).

However, no opinion is expressed as to the income tax consequences to Employee Z resulting from the establishment of and participation in Plan B, except as expressly stated herein.

With respect to issue two, we also conclude that, for purposes of satisfying the Code Section 402(g) limit, elective deferrals under Plan A made by Employer Z for a given plan and calendar year that are initially held by Employer X pursuant to the terms of Plan B will be treated as having been made in the calendar year in which they would have been otherwise received as wages by Employee Z, provided that elective deferrals are allocated to Employee Z's account by the end of that current plan year and the elective deferrals continue to relate to compensation that either would have been received by Employee Z in the plan year but for his election, or is attributable to services performed by Employee Z in the plan year and would have been received by Employee Z within two and one-half months after the plan year but for his election. This conclusion is consistent with the treatment of elective deferrals under Section 1.401(k)-1(b)(4)(i) of the regulations for purposes of the actual deferral percentage test under Code Section 401(k)(3).

The above rulings are based on the assumption that at all times relevant to these rulings, Plan A is qualified under Section 401(a) of the Code, its related trust is tax-exempt under Code Section 501(a), and its cash or deferred arrangement is qualified under Code Section 401(k)(2).

This ruling is directed only to the taxpayer that requested it and applies only with respect to Plan A, as amended. If the plan is amended, this ruling may not remain in effect. Section 6110(j)(3) of the Code provides that this private letter ruling may not be used or cited as precedent. Title I of the Employee Retirement Income Security Act of 1974 (ERISA) is within the jurisdiction of the Department of Labor. Accordingly, we express no opinion as to whether the subject transactions comply with Title I of ERISA.

Tables

Internal Revenue Code Sections

[References are to question numbers.]

[References are to question numbers.]

Tables

[References are to question numbers.]

IRC Section

1:19, 1:22, 2:30, 2:31, 3:21,
3:22, 3:23, 4:17, 4:35, 4:36, 4:37,
5:18, 5:25, 5:27, 5:28, 5:29, 5:30,
5:38, 7:16, 8:20

404(b)(2)(A)	12:18
404(b)(2)(B)	12:18
404(d)	5:28
408(a)	10:37
408(a)(8)	11:17
408(k)(6)	11:17
410(b)	1:3, 5:36, 12:7
414	1:31
414(q)	2:12, 2:13, 5:36
414(q)(8)(B)	9:13
414(q)(8)(C)	9:13
414(s)	2:33
415	1:3, 1:4, 1:5, 1:15, 1:31, 2:29, 3:1, 3:2, 3:4, 3:5, 3:6, 3:9, 3:28, 3:29, 4:10, 5:12
415(b)	2:3, 3:4
415(c)	2:3, 3:4
419	12:1, 12:4, 12:17, 12:18, 12:20
419(e)	12:18, 12:20
419A	12:4, 12:17, 12:18
419A(f)(6)	12:1, 12:4, 12:6, 12:11, 12:12, 12:15, 12:17, 12:18, 12:22
421	11:10, 11:16
421(a)	8:7, 8:27
421(b)	8:7
422	1:5, 8:3,

IRC Section

8:4, 8:5, 8:6, 8:8, 8:9, 8:11, 8:25,
9:6, 9:7

422(a)	8:5
422(b)	8:5, 8:6
422(b)(1)	8:5
422(b)(2)	8:5
422(b)(3)	8:5
422(b)(4)	8:5
422(b)(5)	8:5
422(c)(4)	8:6
422(c)(5)	8:5
422(c)(7)	8:5
422(d)	8:5
423	8:25, 8:26, 11:7, 11:10, 11:16
423(a)	8:27
423(a)(1)	11:7
423(a)(2)	8:27
423(b)(1)	8:26
423(b)(2)	8:26
423(b)(3)	8:26
423(b)(4)	8:26
423(b)(5)	8:26
423(b)(6)	8:26
423(b)(7)	8:26
423(b)(8)	8:26
423(b)(9)	8:26
424(h)	8:5
446	12:18
451	1:18, 1:20, 2:32, 3:25, 4:17, 5:25, 5:35, 8:20, 10:8, 10:45
451(a)	1:21, 4:39, 5:33, 8:23
457	1:38, 4:28,

Tables

Treasury Regulations

[References are to question numbers.]

Tables

ERISA Sections

[References are to question numbers.]

Revenue Rulings and Procedures

[References are to question numbers.]

Rev Rul

54-122, 1954-1 CB 223 . . . . . 11:1

55-713, 1955-2 CB 23 . . . 6:22, 6:23

56-249, 1956-1 CB 488 . . . . . 11:3

58-128, 1958-1 CB 89 . . . . . . 11:3

60-31, 1960-1 CB 174 . . . 1:13, 1:18, 1:21, 3:25, 4:39

60-330, 1960-2 CB 46 . . . . . . 11:3

64-279, 1964-2 CB 121 . . 1:13, 1:18, 1:21, 3:25, 4:39

64-328, 1964-2 CB 11 . . . . 6:1, 6:2, 6:5, 6:11, 6:14, 6:20, 6:22, 6:23

66-110, 1966-1 CB 12 . . . 6:11, 6:18

68-99, 1968-1 CB 193 . . . . 7:3, 7:4

69-300, 1969-1 CB 167 . . . . . 4:26

69-649, 1969-2 CB 106 . . . . . 4:39

69-650, 1969-2 CB 106 . . . . . 4:39

70-148, 1970-1 CB 60 . . . . 6:11, 7:8

70-435, 1970-2 CB 100 . . 1:13, 1:18, 1:21, 3:25, 4:39

71-52, 1971-1 CB 278 . . 11:7, 11:10, 11:16

71-361, 1971-2 CB 90 . . . . . 11:21

71-419, 1971-2 CB 220 . . . . . 4:39

72-25, 1972-1 CB 127 . . . . 7:3, 7:4

Rev Rul

76-265, 1976-2 CB 448 . . . . 4:26

77-347, 1977-2 CB 362 . . . . 11:3

79-50, 1979-1 CB 138 . . . . . . 6:3

79-305, 1979-2 CB 350 . . . . 11:3

80-300, 1980-2 CB 165 . . . . 1:21

81-26, 1981-1 CB 200 . . . . . 10:22

82-46, 1982-1 CB 158 . . . . . 11:1

82-145, 1982-2 CB 213 . . . . 6:21

86-103, 1986-2 CB 62 . . . . . 10:32

86-109, 1986-2 CB 196 . . . . 11:8

90-109, 1990-2 CB 191 . . 6:22, 7:18

Rev Proc

71-19, 1971-1 CB 698 . . 4:15, 4:16, 4:27

71-419, 1971-2 CB 220 . . . . . 1:21

90-17, 1990-1 CB 479 . . . . . 4:32

92-64, 1992-33 IRB 11 . . . 4:5, 4:11, 4:14, 4:15, 4:16, 4:18, 4:19, 4:24, 4:25, 4:26, 4:30, 4:32

92-65, 1992-33 IRB 16 . . 4:14, 4:15, 4:16, 4:27, 4:28

94-1, 1994-1 IRB 10 . . . 4:32, 5:24

95-1, 1995-2 IRB 59 . . . . . . 4:32

Private Letter Rulings

[References are to question numbers.]

Tables

Ltr	Rul		Ltr	Rul
9043036	9:17		9212011	10:8, 10:39
9050014	4:17, 4:18		9212019	5:2, 5:25, 5:38, 5:41
9103018	4:16			
9104040	9:6, 9:7, 9:8, 9:10, 9:14, 9:16, 9:22		9212024	5:2, 5:25, 5:38, 5:41
9105011	10:5		9212025	9:14, 9:16
9119051	9:5, 9:6, 9:7		9215019	10:41
			9235006	4:15
9145010	10:32, 10:38		9317037	1:32
9149032	10:12		9329010	10:40
9152026	10:17		9337016	5:41
9202016	9:3, 9:8		9344038	4:43
9206009	5:2, 5:25, 5:38		9405009	1:32
9207010	5:2, 5:25, 5:38		9431021	10:43
			9444028	10:40, 10:42
9211037	10:8, 10:41		9511046	6:25
9212006	10:39		9530038	1:32

Other Citations

[References are to question numbers.]

Code of Federal Regulations

17 CFR Section

230.144	8:40
230.144(d)	8:41
230.147	8:32
230.501-230.508	8:33
230.701	8:36
230.701(b)	8:36
230.701(b)(3)	8:36
230.701(b)(5)	8:36
230.701(c)(3)	8:42
230.702(T)(a)	8:36
230.703(T)	8:36
231.1459	8:32
239.16b	8:37
240.10b-5	8:30
240.16(a)-1(3)(i)	8:44
240.16a-1(c)	8:44
240.16b-3	8:44
240.16b-3(e)	8:44
240.16b-3(f)	8:44
240.16b-6(b)	8:44

General Counsel Memoranda

GCM

32941, Nov 20, 1964	6:1
33373, Nov 21, 1966 . .	1:12, 1:13, 2:14, 3:14, 5:7
35196, Jan 16, 1973 . . .	1:12, 1:13, 2:14, 3:14, 5:7
35326, May 3, 1973 . . .	1:12, 1:13, 2:14, 3:14, 5:7
37256, Sept 15, 1977 . . .	1:13, 5:7
39230, Jan 20, 1984 . . .	1:12, 1:13, 2:14, 3:12, 3:13, 4:22, 4:38, 4:40

United States Code

11 USC Section

541(c)(2)	1:35

15 USC Section

77c(a)(11)	8:31
77d(2)	8:31
77e(a)	8:30
77e(c)	8:30
77q	8:39
78j	8:30
78p(a)	8:43
78p(b)	8:43
77l	8:39

Cases

[References are to question numbers.]

A

Albertson's v Comm'r, CA9, No
91-70380, 12/30/93 . . 1:30, 5:28

American Medical International, Inc,
v Valliant, US Dt Ct ND Cal N Cr
94-2107-5C (Nov 11, 1994) . . 9:25

Anderson, United States v, 132 F 2d
98 (6th Cir 1942) 4:26

B

Bagley v United States, 348 F Supp
418 (D Minn 1972) 6:23

Balch v Comm'r, 100 TC 331 (1993),
aff'd 34 F 3d 480 (7th Cir 1994) 9:19

Barrowclough v Kidder, Peabody &
Co, Inc, 752 F 2d 923
(3d Cir 1985) 2:20, 2:24

Belka v Rowe Furniture Corp, 571 F
Supp 1249 (D Md
1983) 2:12, 3:12, 7:17

Belsky v First National Life Insurance
Co, 653 F Supp 80, aff'd, 818 F 2d
661 (8th Cir 1987) 2:14

C

Carr v First Nationwide Bank, ND Cal
1993 . . . . 2:28

Carson v Local 1588, International
Longshoremen's Association, 769 F
Supp 141 (SD NY 1991) . . . 2:21

Citric Orthopedic Medical Group Inc v
Comm'r, 72 TC 461 (1979) . . 12:20

City Nat Bank & Trust Co v United
States, 109 F 2d 191
(7th Cir 1940) 4:26

Cline v Comm'r, 34 F 3d 480, CA-7,
1994 . . . . 9:25

Cohen, Theodore H, In re, 39 TC
1055 (1963), acq 1964-1 (Part 1)
CB 4 . . . . 7:10

Cowden v Comm'r, 32 TC 853 (1959,
rev'd and remanded 289 F 2d 20
(5th Cir 1961, opinion on remand,
20 TCM 1 134 (1961), TC Memo
1961-229) 1:23, 3:25

D

Darden v Nationwide Mutual
Insurance Co, 717 F Supp 388 (ED
NC 1989), 922 F 2d 303, 208 n3
(4th Cir 1991) 2:12, 2:14

De Bonchamps, United States v, 278 F
2d 127 (9th Cir 1960) 4:26

Dependahl v Falstaff Brewing Corp,
653 F 2d 1208 (8th Cir 1981), cert
den, 454 US 968, 102 S Ct 512
(1981) 2:14, 3:12,
3:13, 3:14

E

Edwards v Comm'r, TC Memo
1989-409, 57 TCM 1217 (1989) 10:22

[References are to question numbers.]

Tables

[References are to question numbers.]

Index

[References are to question numbers.]

A

Administration
Code Section 457 eligible plans, 10:34
costs, plan design, 13:9
excess benefit plan, 3:19
top-hat plan, 2:2, 2:24

Adoption
nonqualified plan, 13:12

ADP violations
mirror 401(k) plan correction, 1:33

Agency account
deferred compensation funding, 1:10
rabbi trust, 4:26

Annuity
secular, 5:5

Assignment of assets. *See also* Bankruptcy or insolvency; Creditors
split-dollar life insurance, 6:22

Attachment of assets. *See* Bankruptcy or insolvency; Creditors

B

Bankruptcy or insolvency
claims, taxation of property transferred for services, 1:25

creditors
rights against plan assets, 1:35
rights against plan interest, 1:35
ERISA considerations, secular trust, 5:15, 5:16
parachute payments, 9:14
rabbi trust considerations, 4:15-4:22

Beneficiary
nonqualified plan, 1:4

Benefit
death benefit
Code Section 457 rules, 10:7
multiple employer death benefit trust, 12:9-12:12
split-dollar life insurance, 6:14, 6:20, 6:21
withholding exclusion, 11:21
deferred compensation, and top-hat plan, 2:4
denial
excess benefit plan, 3:31
top-hat plan, 2:25
distribution
rabbi trust, 4:27, 4:28
triggers, 13:8
FICA taxes, 11:8
funding sources, 1:6
nonqualified plan, 1:4

[References are to question numbers.]

Index

[References are to question numbers.]

Index

[*References are to question numbers.*]

Index

third-party guarantee, 2:7, 13:11
top-hat plan, 2:5-2:7, 2:16, 2:17, 2:22
withholding taxes, 11:3
FUTA, withholding, 11:14-11:18

G

Golden parachute. *See* Parachute payments
Governmental entities. *See* Code Section 457 rules

H

Heavenly trust, defined, 5:6
Highly compensated individual
multiple employer welfare benefit trust, 12:20
parachute payments, 9:13
plan participation, 13:6
top-hat plan rules, 2:12, 2:13

I

Implementation
nonqualified plan, 13:13
Incentive stock options. *See* Stock plan
Income
inclusion
employee gross income, 1:20
top-hat plan contributions, 2:32
Independent contractor
golden parachute, 9:3
separation from service, Code Section 457 rules, 10:23
Individual retirement account (IRA)
rollover to, Code Section 457 rules, 10:32

Insurance. *See also* Corporate-owned life insurance; Split-dollar life insurance
plan termination
excess benefits plan, 3:30
top-hat plan, 2:26
tax consequences, rabbi trust, 4:43
Interest
creditors' rights, 1:35
deductions
impact on nonqualified plans, 1:30
secular trust, 5:28
FICA withholding, 11:9
FUTA withholding, 11:14, 11:15
withholding tax, 11:4
Investment
employer considerations, 1:39
management, plan design, 13:7
participant-directed, rabbi trust, 4:24, 4:25
participant direction, IRS concerns, 1:34
securities, nonqualified plan interests as, 1:38
strategy, nonqualified plan, 13:14
Irrevocable trust. *See* Secular trust

K

Key employee
termination of employment, COLI change of insured, 7:18

L

Letter of credit
as deferred compensation source, 1:11
top-hat plan funding, 2:7

[References are to question numbers.]

[References are to question numbers.]

Index

[References are to question numbers.]

[References are to question numbers.]

[References are to question numbers.]

[References are to question numbers.]